THE KING AND THE CEMETERIES

SUPPLEMENTS

TO

VETUS TESTAMENTUM

EDITED BY
THE BOARD OF THE QUARTERLY

H.M. BARSTAD – PHYLLIS A. BIRD – R.P. GORDON
A. HURVITZ – A. van der KOOIJ – A. LEMAIRE
R. SMEND – J. TREBOLLE BARRERA
J.C. VANDERKAM – H.G.M. WILLIAMSON

VOLUME LXXXVIII

THE KING
AND
THE CEMETERIES

Toward a New Understanding of Josiah's Reform

BY

W. BOYD BARRICK

BRILL
LEIDEN · BOSTON · KÖLN
2002

This book is printed on acid-free paper.

Library of Congress Cataloging-in-Publication Data

Barrick, W. Boyd, 1946-
   The king and the cemeteries : toward a new understanding of Josiah's reform
/by W. Boyd Barrick.
      p.   cm. — (Supplements to Vetus Testamentum, ISSN 0083-5889 ;
      v. 88)
   Includes bibliographical references (p.) and index.
   ISBN 9004121714 (alk. paper)
      1. Bible. O.T. Kings, 2nd, XXIII, 4-20—Criticism, interpretation, etc. 2.
Josiah, King of Judah. 3. Jews—History—To 586 B.C. I. Title. II. Series.

BS410 .V452 vol. 88
[BS1335.52]
221s—dc21
[222'.5406

10026521 15

                                                                  2001043307

Die Deutsche Bibliothek – CIP-Einheitsaufnahme

Barrick, W. Boyd:
The king and the cemeteries ; toward a new understanding of Josiah's
reform / by W. Boyd Barrick. – Leiden ; Boston ; Köln : Brill, 2002
   (Supplements to Vetus testamentum ; Vol. 88)
   ISBN 90-04-12171-4

⊤   ISSN   0083-5889
          ISBN   90 04 12171 4

PRINTED IN THE NETHERLANDS

CONTENTS

FOREWORD

There are times I almost think
I am not sure of what I absolutely know.
Very often find confusion
In conclusion I concluded long ago.
In my head are many facts
That as a student, I have studied to procure,
In my head are many facts
Of which I wish I was more certain I was sure!

Is a puzzlement!

King Mongkut (Rama IV) of Siam
—*apud* O. Hammerstein II

This study grew out of a protracted investigation of the Hebrew word *BMH*, conventionally (but erroneously) "high place," which began under the tutelage of my Doktor-Vater, the late Gösta W. Ahlström, at the University of Chicago. From his example I learned—and continue to learn—to question the conventional and to value the imaginative in scholarly inquiry; he too attempted to move a cemetery or two, and left us much too early. I also learned—and continue to learn—these lessons in different ways, and much else, from my father, William H. Barrick, a mover of cemeteries of a different sort, to whom this small contribution is dedicated in appreciation and with respect, admiration, and love (Prov. 4:3–15, 20–27; Eccl. 2:24–25).

ACKNOWLEDGEMENTS

In addition to the individuals acknowledged in the citations, I would be remiss if I did not recognize and thank:

Ms. Cheryl Hoover and her Interlibrary Loan staff at Montana State University-Billings, and the staff of the Interlibrary Loan Department of the Parmly Billings Library, for giving me access to material not native to Montana;

Prof. Andre Lemaire for accepting this work for the Vetus Testamentum Supplements series, and Ms. Mattie Kuiper and Ms. Hanneke Teunissen of Brill Academic Publishers for shepherding the project with skill and good cheer;

Prof. Robert D. Haak of Augustana College (Rock Island, Ill.) for his long ago "matchmaking" which initiated the whole affair; and

those many scholars whose work on the matters dealt with here have taught me much.

ABBREVIATIONS

AASOR	Annual of the American Schools of Oriental Research
AB	Anchor Bible
ABD	*Anchor Bible Dictionary*, 6 vols. (ed. by D. N. Freedman *et al.*; New York/London/Toronto/Sydney/Auckland: Doubleday, 1992)
ABRL	Anchor Bible Reference Library
ACLS	American Council of Learned Societies
AfO	*Archiv für Orientforschung*
AJA	*American Journal of Archaeology*
ANET	*Ancient Near Eastern Texts Relating to the Old Testament*, 3rd edn. (ed. by J. B. Pritchard; Princeton: Princeton University, 1969)
AOAT	Alter Orient und Altes Testament
ASOR	American Schools of Oriental Research
ATANT	Abhandlingen zur Theologie des Alten und Neuen Testaments
AUSS	*Andrews University Seminary Studies*
BA	*Biblical Archaeologist*
BARev	*Biblical Archaeology Review*
BASOR	*Bulletin of the American Oriental Society*
BBB	Bonner biblische Beiträge
BETL	Bibliotheca Ephemeridum Theologicarum Lovaniensium
BFCT	Beiträge zur Förderung christlicher Theologie
Bib	*Biblica*
BiOr	*Bibliotheca Orientalis*
BIOSCS	*Bulletin of the International Organization of Septuagint and Cognate Studies*
BJRL	*Bulletin of the John Rylands Library*
BKAT	Biblischer Kommentar: Altes Testament
BN	*Biblische Notizen*
BRev	*Bible Review*
BT	*Bible Translator*
BZ	*Biblische Zeitschrift*
BZAW	Beihefte zur Zeitschrift für die alttestamentliche Wissenschaft
CBOT	Coniectanea Biblica: Old Testament
CBC	Cambridge Bible Commentaries
CBQ	*Catholic Biblical Quarterly*
CBQM	Catholic Biblical Quarterly Monograph Series
CC	Continental Commentary
CR:BS	*Currents in Research: Biblical Studies*
DDD	*Dictionary of Deities and Demons in the Bible* (ed. by K. van der Toorn *et al.*; Leiden: Brill, 1998)
EHAT	Exegetisches Handbuch zum Alten Testament
E-I	*Eretz-Israel*
ErF	Erträge der Forschung

ETL	*Ephemerides Theologicae Lovanienses*
EvT	*Evangelische Theologie*
FOTL	Forms of Old Testament Literature
FRLANT	Forschungen zur Religion und Literatur des Alten und Neuen Testaments
GKC	*Gesenius' Hebrew Grammar* (2nd edn.; ed. by E. Kautzsch; trans. by A. E. Cowley; Oxford: Clarendon, 1910)
HAR	*Hebrew Annual Review*
HAT	Handbuch zum Alten Testament
HSAT	Die Heilige Schrift des Alten Testaments
HSM	Harvard Semitic Monograph Series
HTR	*Harvard Theological Review*
HUCA	*Hebrew Union College Annual*
IB	*Interpreter's Bible*, 12 vols. (ed. by G. A. Buttrick; Nashville: Abingdon, 1952–1955)
IDB	*Interpreter's Dictionary of the Bible*, 4 vols. (ed. by G. A Buttrick; Nashville: Abingdon, 1962)
IDBSup	*Interpreter's Dictionary of the Bible Supplement* (ed. by K. Crim; Nashville: Abingdon, 1976)
IBS	*Irish Biblical Studies*
ICC	International Critical Commentary
IEJ	*Israel Exploration Journal*
JANES	*Journal of the Near Eastern Society of Columbia University*
JAOS	*Journal of the American Oriental Society*
JB	Jerusalem Bible
JBL	*Journal of Biblical Literature*
JNES	*Journal of Near Eastern Studies*
JNSL	*Journal of Northwest Semitic Languages and Literatures*
JPSTC	Jewish Publication Society Torah Commentary
JSOT	*Journal for the Study of the Old Testament*
JSOTSup	Journal for the Study of the Old Testament Supplement Series
JSS	*Journal of Semitic Studies*
JTS	*Journal of Theological Studies*
KAI	*Kanaanäische und Aramäische Inschriften*, 3 vols. (ed. by H. Donner and W. Röllig; Wiesbaden: Harrassowitz, 1964)
KAT	Kommentar zum Alten Testament
KHCAT	Kurzer Hand-Commentar zum Alten Testament
LXX	Septuagint
MT	Masoretic Text
NAB	New American Bible
NCB	New Century Bible
NCBC	New Century Bible Commentary
NEB	New English Bible
NIBC	New International Biblical Commentary
NICOT	New International Commentary on the Old Testament
NIV	New International Version
NJPSV	New Jewish Publication Society Version

OBO   Orbis Biblicus et Orientalis
OED   *Oxford English Dictionary*, 12 vols. (Oxford: Clarendon, 1970)
OIP   Oriental Institute Publications
OLA   Orientalia Louvaniensia Analecta
Or   *Orientalia*
OTL   Old Testament Library
OTS   *Oudtestamentische Studien*
PEFQSt   *Palestine Exploration Fund Quarterly Statement*
PEGLMWBS   *Proceedings of the Eastern Great Lakes and Midwest Biblical Society*
PEQ   *Palestine Exploration Quarterly*
RB   *Revue Biblique*
RelStRev   *Religious Studies Review*
RivB   *Rivista Biblica*
RSO   *Rivista degli Studi Orientali*
RSV   Revised Standard Version
SAA   State Archives of Assyria
SBL   Society of Biblical Literature
SBLDS   Society of Biblical Literature Dissertation Series
SBLM   Society of Biblical Literature Monograph Series
SBLSP   Society of Biblical Literature Seminar Papers
SBOT   Sacred books of the Old Testament
SBT   Studies in Biblical Theology
ScrHier   Scripta Hierosolymitana
SEÅ   *Svensk Exegetisk Årsbok*
SHANE   Studies in the History of the Ancient Near East
SHCANE   Studies in the History and Culture of the Ancient Near East
SJOT   *Scandinavian Journal for the Study of the Old Testament*
SJT   *Scottish Journal of Theology*
SOTSM   Society for Old Testament Studies Monograph Series
SPCK   Society for the Promotion of Christian Knowledge
TA   *Tel Aviv*
TBü   Theologische Bücherei
TDOT   *Theological Dictionary of the Old Testament* (ed. by G. J. Botterweck, H. Ringgren, and H. J. Fabry; trans. by J. T. Willis, G. W. Bromiley, and D. E. Green; Grand Rapids: Eerdmans, 1974–)
TOTC   Tyndale Old Testament Commentaries
TR   *Theologische Rundschau*
TWAT   *Theologisches Wörterbuch zum Alten Testament* (ed. by G. J. Botterweck, H. Ringgren, and H. J. Fabry; Stuttgart: Kohlhammer, 1970–)
TynBul   *Tyndale Bulletin*
TZ   *Theologische Zeitschrift*
UBL   Ugaritisch-Biblische Literatur
UF   *Ugarit Forschungen*

VT	*Vetus Testamentum*
VTSup	Vetus Testamentum Supplement Series
WBC	Word Bible Commentary
WTJ	Westminster Theological Journal
ZAH	*Zeitschrift für Althebräistik*
ZAW	*Zeitschrift für die alttestamentliche Wissenschaft*
ZDPV	*Zeitschrift der Deutschen Palästinavereins*
ZTK	*Zeitschrift für Theologie und Kirche*

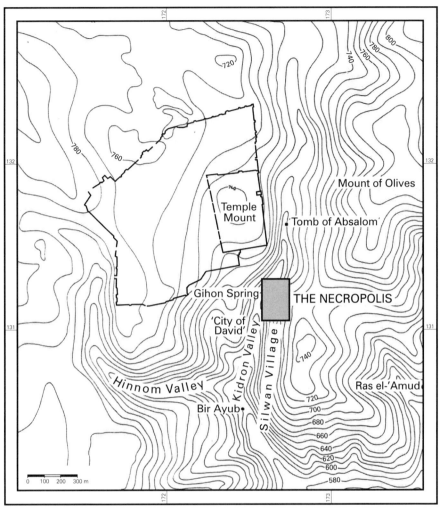

Drawn by F.E.Derksen-Janssens after D. Ussishkin, *The Village of Silwan: The Necropolis from the Period of the Judean Kingdom* (Jerusalem: Israel Exploration Society/Yad Izhak Ben-Zvi,1993) 23, used here by permission

CHAPTER ONE

PRELIMINARY MATTERS

According to the Book of Kings, the apogee of Israel's religious history is an extensive change in the religious life of the kingdom of
Judah executed by Josiah. The report of this endeavor (2 Kgs. 23:4–20
+ 24) is replete with intertextual reverberations spanning the entire
history of the monarchy.[1] The compositional integrity and historical
credibility of the report are very much in doubt, however. While
few today would agree with M. Noth's contention that the report is
"an extract, in chronological order, from the Royal Annals,"[2] there
is very little critical consensus concerning what (if anything) of this
material comes from its original author-compiler, what comes from
his[3] sources (if any), what may come from later hand(s), and what
(if anything) reflects the historical realities of the reign of Josiah b.
Amon of Judah.[4]

---

[1] See in particular the analysis by H.-D. Hoffmann, *Reform und Reformen: Unter-
suchungen zu einem Grundthema der deuteronomistischen Geschichtsschreibung* (ATANT 66;
Zurich: Theologische, 1980) 169–270, and cf. the critique by G. N. Knoppers, *Two
Nations Under God, The Deuteronomistic History of Solomon and the Dual Monarchies 2: The
Reign of Jeroboam, the Fall of Israel, and the Reign of Josiah* (HSM 53; Atlanta: Schol-
ars, 1994) especially 181–91.

[2] M. Noth, *The History of Israel* (2nd edn.; trans. by P. R. Ackroyd; New York:
Harper & Row, 1960) 272; also *idem, The Deuteronomistic History* (trans. by J. Doull
et al.; JSOTSup 15; Sheffield: JSOT, 1981) 66, 73, 80–1. Cf. also, e.g., C. F. Burney, *Notes on the Hebrew Text of the Books of Kings* (Oxford: Clarendon, 1903) 355.

[3] Although the seals inscribed with women's names (for examples see R. Deutsch
and M. Heltzer, *Forty New Ancient West Semitic Inscriptions* [Tel Aviv/Jaffa; Archaeological Center, 1994] 58–9 and the literature cited there) indicate the presence of
literate, educated women in late monarchic (and later) Judah, it is unlikely that the
author-compilers of the Kings History or of its subsequent revisions were women.

[4] In addition to comprehensive surveys (e.g., E. Jenni, "Zwei Jahrzehnte Forschung
über Josua bis Könige," *TR* 27 [1961] 1–32, 97–140; N. Lohfink, "Recent Discussion on 2 Kings 22–23: The State of the Question," *A Song of Power and the Power
of Song: Essays on the Book of Deuteronomy* [trans. by L. M. Maloney; ed. by D. L.
Christensen; Sources for Biblical and Theological Study 3; Winona Lake: Eisen-
brauns, 1993] 36–61 [= *Das Deuteronomium: Entstehung, Gestalt und Botschaft* (ed. by N.
Lohfink; BETL 68; Leuven: Leuven University, 1985) 24–48]; G. N. Knoppers,
*Two Nations Under God, The Deuteronomistic History of Solomon and the Dual Monarchies 1:
The Reign of Solomon and the Rise of Jeroboam* [HSM 52; Atlanta: Scholars, 1993] 17–56;
P. S. F. van Keulen, *Manasseh through the Eyes of the Deuteronomists: The Manasseh Account*

N. Lohfink has discerned the chiastic structure of the Kings account of Josiah's reign:[5]

A. Introductory Formula (22:1)
   B. Evaluation (22:2)
      C.1. "King Josiah sent" (22:3): Temple, book, repentance
         C.2. "The king commanded" (22:12): prophetic inquiry
            C.3. "The king sent" (23:1): covenant-making
         C.2'. "The king commanded" (23:4): cult reform
      C.1'. "The king commanded" (23:21): Passover in Jerusalem
   B'. Evaluation (23:25–27)
A'. Concluding formula (23:28–30)

That this structure is an artificial literary construct which does not reflect historical reality seems clear enough: the covenant between Yahweh and the people, based upon "the book of the covenant" (23:2b; cf. v. 3b) is the centerpiece, literally and figuratively, of Josiah's reign; the reform measures are ancillary (C.2'), and secular matters practically nonexistent (vv. 29–30). But this structure applies only to the final form of the narrative which may incorporate earlier version(s) of the story which could have been structured differently. This probably explains the imperfect symmetry: "King Josiah," rather than "the king," in 22:3a (also 23:23, 29), and the interrupted "sent"/"commanded" alternation at 23:4 or 23:21. The primary concern of the present study is the catalogue of reform measures (23:4–20) in the midst of this narrative.

[2 Kings 2:1:1–18] and the Final Chapters of the Deuteronomistic History [OTS 38; Leiden/New York/Köln: Brill, 1996] 4–52) see R. H. Lowery, The Reforming Kings: Cults and Society in First Temple Judah (JSOTSup 120; Sheffield: JSOT, 1991) 11–38; B. Gieselmann, "Die sogenannten josianische Reform in der gegenwärtigen Forschung," ZAW 106 (1994) 223–42; E. Eynikel, The Reform of King Josiah & the Composition of the Deuteronomistic History (OTS 33; Leiden/New York/Köln: Brill, 1996) ch. 1.

[5] Adapted from N. Lohfink, "The Cult Reform of Josiah of Judah: 2 Kings 23:22–23 as a Source for the History of Israelite Religion," Ancient Israelite Religion: Essays in Honor of Frank Moore Cross (ed. by P. D. Miller et al.; Philadelphia: Fortress, 1987) 461. For different views of the structure of this material cf., e.g., Hoffmann, Reform und Reformen, 219, and Eynikel, Reform of King Josiah, ch. 3 (especially pp. 149–55); L. Eslinger, "Josiah and the Torah Book: Comparison of 2 Kgs. 22:1–23:28 and 2 Chr. 34:1–35:19," HAR 10 (1985) 37–62 (especially pp. 39–47; B. O. Long, 2 Kings (FOTL 10; Grand Rapids: Eerdmans, 1991) 272–7; D. J. Wiseman, 1–2 Kings: Introduction and Commentary (TOTC 9; Downers Grove/Leicester: Inter-Varsity, 1993) 293–305.

2 Kgs. 23:4–20 is a literary unit demarked by *wayĕṣaw hammelek* in v. 4a and v. 21a. It reports various measures undertaken by Josiah under the influence of the "book" (*sēper*) found in the Temple and the covenant resulting from it. It divides naturally into two unequal parts: activities in Jerusalem and Judah (vv. 4–14); and activities in Samaria, the territory of the defunct northern kingdom to the north (vv. 15–20). The inventory of activities in the south is deliberately structured to focus on the concentration of Yahweh worship exclusively at the Jerusalem Temple:[6]

    1. Equipage in Temple (v. 4)
      2. Priests at bamoth in "the cities of Judah" (v. 5)
        3. Asherah in Temple (v. 6)
          4. Houses of cult functionaries in Temple (v. 7)
            5. Bamoth and bamoth-priests in "the cities of Judah" (v. 8a)
            6. "Bamoth of the gates" (v. 8b) Narrative: Bamoth-priests
               (v. 9)
          7. Tophet in Ben-Hinnom Valley (v. 10)
        8. Horses and chariot(s)[7] of the sun at entrance to Temple (v. 11)
      9. Rooftop and courtyard altars in Temple/palace (v. 12)
    10. Solomon's bamoth on Mount of Olives (vv. 13–14)

The artificiality of this arrangement is obvious: the activities in "the cities of Judah" in v. 5 and the "bamoth of the gates" in v. 8b seem to fit this structure uncomfortably, and their excision would leave it intact;[8] the activities in the north seem like an appendix; and the list of miscellaneous measures in Judah and Jerusalem in v. 24a violates this structure entirely and is commonly considered secondary to it.[9]

---

[6] Adapted from Lohfink, "Cult Reform of Josiah of Judah," 465. There are other possibilities (cf. the references cited in the preceding note), and according to S. L. McKenzie, "the material in this section, especially vv. 4–14, does not follow any clear structure or organizational thread" (*The Trouble with Kings: The Composition of the Book of Kings in the Deuteronomistic History* [VTSup 42; Leiden: Brill, 1991] 113).

[7] LXX reads singular, adopted by some commentators (e.g., J. A. Montgomery, *A Critical and Exegetical Commentary on the Books of Kings* [ed. by H. S. Gehman; ICC; Edinburgh: Clark, 1951] 532; J. Gray, *II Kings: A Commentary* [2nd ed.; OTL; Philadelphia: Westminster, 1970] 731 and n. f).

[8] For the *waw*-copulative + Perfect issue see Chapter 5 below.

[9] So, e.g., R. D. Nelson, *The Double Redaction of the Deuteronomistic History* (JSOT-Sup 18; Sheffield: JSOT, 1981) 83–4 ("sounding like an afterthought," "probably

How do we get behind this story to its earlier version(s), if any, to its component parts, and finally to the historical events themselves? It is possible, of course, that some, most, or all of it is fiction, as some of today's "minimalists" assert[10] and some practitioners of the "new literary criticism" pretend.[11] As R. P. Carroll puts it, "history and the Bible are hardly the best of bedfellows."[12] The ascen-

---

the supplementary work of the exilic editor [his Dtr²]); G. H. Jones, *1–2 Kings* (NCB; Grand Rapids/London: Eerdmans/Marshall, Morgan & Scott, 1984) 628 (it "is best considered an appendix to vv. 21–23 rather than a continuation of vv. 4–20"). S. L. McKenzie vacillates on the matter, first considering vv. 24–25 "an addition to Dtr 1's ['Josianic'] edition by a hand other than [exilic] Dtr 2" (*The Chronicler's Use of the Deuteronomistic History* [HSM 33; Atlanta: Scholars 1984] 191, cf. 160), but later attributing the verses to Dtr 1 (*Trouble with Kings*, 114–5, 151). This change seems to have two bases (*ibid.*, 114): that v. 24a "show[s] that Josiah also did away with the heterodox practices introduced by Manasseh (21:6)"; and that v. 24b, with the "patently Deuteronomistic" expression *hāqîm 'et-dibrê hattôrâ* and reference to Hilkiah's finding of the book, functions "almost as a fulfillment remark showing that Josiah carried out all the prescriptions of the law book to their fullest extent" and as part of an *inclusio* framing the reform report. Cf. also Hoffmann, *Reform und Reformen*, 260; T. J. Lewis, *Cults of the Dead in Ancient Israel and Ugarit* (HSM 39; Atlanta: Scholars, 1989) 125–6; Long, *2 Kings*, 279–80. This judgment minimizes the differences between 23:24a and 21:6 (and Deut. 18:11), and ignores the *wayĕṣaw hammelek inclusio* (v. 4a and v. 21a). For *'et-dibrê hattôrâ* see Chapter 6.B below.

[10] For the term and a critique see B. Halpern, "Erasing History: The Minimalist Assault on Ancient Israel," *BRev* 10/6 (1995) 26–35, 47, and H. Shanks, "The Biblical Minimalists," *BRev* 13/3 (1997) 32–9, 50–2. For an extreme example see L. K. Handy, "Historical Probability and the Narrative of Josiah's Reform in 2 Kings," *The Pitcher Was Broken: Memorial Essays for Gösta W. Ahlström* (ed. by S. W. Holloway and L. K. Handy; JSOTSup 190; Sheffield: Sheffield Academic, 1995) 252–75. Similarly, e.g., E. Würthwein, "Die josianische Reform und das Deuteronomium" *ZTK* 73 (1976) 395–423, and Hoffmann, *Reform und Reformen*, especially 251, 264–70. Cf. the critique by A. Laato, *Josiah and David Redivivus: The Historical Josiah and the Messianic Expectations of Exilic and Postexilic Times* (CBOT 33; Stockholm: Almqvist & Wiksell, 1992) 37–52.

[11] See, e.g., the rather nihilistic observations of B. O. Long, *1 Kings, with an Introduction to Historical Literature* (FOTL 9; Grand Rapids: Eerdmans, 1984) 14–21. A similar spirit imbues the "literary objection" to the "quest for the historical King Arthur" (as summarized by G. Ashe, *The Discovery of King Arthur* [Garden City: Doubleday, 1985] 185): "'We have the Arthurian stories, which are immortal literature. Looking for historical facts behind them is a mistake. At best it is sterile and irrelevant, at worst it spoils the stories by contrasting them with a smaller and meaner reality'."

[12] R. P. Carroll, "Razed Temple and Shattered Vessels: Continuities and Discontinuities in the Discourses of Exile in the Hebrew Bible. An Appreciation of the Work of Peter R. Ackroyd on the Occasion of his Eightieth Birthday," *JSOT* 75 (1997) 104.

dancy of synchronic analysis,[13] however, has not obviated the validity of or need for diachronic study of this material.[14] But a diachronic, or compositional, analysis of this material, perhaps moreso than a synchronic analysis,[15] ought not proceed from historical presuppositions concerning an actual religious reform during Josiah's reign: whatever historical, or compositional, realities that underlie the report must be teased from the text and not superimposed upon it. This

---

[13] For an overview see D. J. A. Clines and J. C. Exum, "The New Literary Criticism," *The New Literary Criticism and the Hebrew Bible* (ed. by J. C. Exum and D. J. A. Clines; JSOTSup 143; Sheffield/Valley Forge: JSOT/Trinity, 1993) 11–25; cf. A. Berlin, "A Search for a New Biblical Hermeneutics: Preliminary Observations," *The Study of the Ancient Near East in the Twenty-First Century: The William Foxwell Albright Centennial Conference* (ed. by J. S. Cooper and G. N. Schwartz; Winona Lake: Eisenbrauns, 1996) 195–207. Large-scale literary analyses of the Kings History include Long, *1 Kings*, and *idem, 2 Kings*; T. R. Hobbs, *2 Kings* (WBC 13; Waco: Word, 1985); G. Savran, "1 and 2 Kings," *The Literary Guide to the Bible* (ed. by R. Alter and F. Kermode; Cambridge: Belknap/Harvard University, 1987) 146–64; I. W. Provan, *1–2 Kings* (NIBC; Peabody, MA/Carlisle, Cumb.: Hendrickson/Paternoster, 1995). Literary analyses of individual narrative units are more numerous: for the unit under consideration in the present study see now F. Smyth, "Quand Josias fait son oeuvre ou le Roi bien enterré: Une Lecture synchronique de 2 R 22,1–23,28," *Israël Construit son Histoire: L'historiographie deutéronomiste à la lumière des recherches récentes* (ed. by A. de Pury, T. Römer, and J.-D. Macchi; Le Monde de la Bible 34; Geneva: Labor et Fides, 1996) 325–39.

[14] See the essays in *Synchronic or Diachronic? A Debate on Method in Old Testament Exegesis* (ed. by J. C. de Moor; OTS 34; Leiden: Brill, 1995), especially R. P. Carroll, "Synchronistic Deconstructions of Jeremiah: Diachrony to the Rescue?" 39–51, and J. Hoftijzer, "Holistic or Compositional Approach? Linguistic Remarks to the Problem," 98–114. Other valuable discussions of this issue include R. Alter, "A Literary Approach to the Bible," *Commentary* (December, 1975) 70–7, and *idem*, "Introduction to the Old Testament," *The Literary Guide to the Bible* (ed. by R. Alter and F. Kermode; Cambridge: Belknap/Harvard University, 1987) 11–35; C. Conroy, "Reflections on the Exegetical Task: Apropos of Recent Studies on 2 Kgs. 22–23," *Pentateuchal and Deuteronomistic Studies* (ed. by C. Brekelmans and J. Lust; BETL 94; Leuven: University, 1990) 255–68; D. V. Edelman, *King Saul and the Historiography of Judah* (JSOTSup 121; Sheffield: JSOT, 1991) ch. 1.

[15] In this connection note Lohfink's observation ("Recent Discussion," 43 [= *Deuteronomium*, 30–1]): "We know quite a bit more [since the 1920s] about the context in which the events in these two chapters took place. The factual events, the material culture, the major political events, the social and ideological shifts—all these are much more clearly delineated. Nevertheless, 2 Kings 22–23 is a text. These new insights into its historical context may prevent our freely-wandering fantasy from pursuing certain directions of interpretation. But in the final analysis the text must first be understood and classified as a text. And besides, it remains our principal source for the epoch and the region of Judah, so that, again, much of our historical insight depends finally on its interpretation."

caveat is especially applicable to three hypotheses so ubiquitous in scholarly discussion of this material that they can be mistaken for established facts.

The "Assyrian Vassalship Hypothesis," by which at least some of Josiah's actions were tied in some way to a change in Judah's vassal relationship with Assyria, has long been a mainstay among commentators and modern historians of the period.[16] But however plausible this might be, it is not apparent in the Book of Kings itself. In point of fact, Assyria completely disappears from Kings following the miraculous deliverance of Jerusalem in Hezekiah's reign (19:32–37); by this "selective silence . . . the text seems to suggest that [Hezekiah's] rebellion was so successful that [it] changed the political situation in the area forever."[17] It is an historical certainty that Hezekiah's rebellion was a disastrous failure which firmly reestablished Judah's vassal status; there is no doubt that the Manasseh of history was a loyal Assyrian vassal,[18] and it may be that some of the religious innovations credited him in 21:1–18 (if factual) were the result of this relationship. But the Manasseh of Kings lives in a world without Assyria, and in that world his religious "reform," the anti-type of Josiah's, is the product solely of his own religious perversity—"he has no motivation other than to be apostate," in T. R. Hobbs' apt phrase[19]— as Josiah's is motivated only by his "book"-based piety; this Manasseh is a literary construct meant to bear the burden of the Exile, an ideological paradigm rather than a historical personality. S. Lasine puts it nicely:[20]

---

[16] Classically formulated by T. Oestreicher, *Das deuteronomische Grundsetz* (BFCT 47. 4; Gütersloh: Bertelsmann, 1923). Cf. also the influential study by F. M. Cross and D. N. Freedman, "Josiah's Revolt against Assyria," *JNES* 12 (1953) 56–8. For a sample of adherents see n. 21 below. Eynikel's assertion that "[t]oday nearly all of Josiah's reform is explained as an internal religious-dtr matter" (*Reform of King Josiah*, 8) is a great overstatement; contrast, e.g., Lohfink, "Cult Reform of Josiah," 466–8.

[17] E. Ben Zvi, "The Account of the Reign of Manasseh in II Reg 21,1–18 and the Redactional History of the Book of Kings," *ZAW* 103 (1991) 364 n. 28.

[18] This is the picture presented in the Assyrian evidence: see now R. Gane, "The Role of Assyria in the Ancient Near East during the Reign of Manasseh," *AUSS* 35 (1997) 21–32. 2 Chron. 33:11 implies that Manasseh was brought to Babylon as a prisoner because he had rebelled, but this nuance may be the Chronicler's artistic license to dramatize Manasseh's "distress" (v. 12) and "deliverance" (v. 13) rather than an historical recollection.

[19] Hobbs, *2 Kings*, 311.

[20] S. Lasine, "Manasseh as Villain and Scapegoat," *The New Literary Criticism and*

While the narrator of 2 Kings 21 leaves no doubt about the extent
and variety of Manasseh's idolatrous actions, his portrait of the king
does not include the person who performed these actions. Moreover,
this faceless portrait is set against a blank background.

It may be that Josiah attempted to change Judah's political relationship with Assyria and its religious ramifications (if any) in the
course of his reign, and most modern reconstructions of Josiah's reign
adopt some form of this "Assyrian Vassalship Hypothesis."[21] But this
political dimension must be read into the text. It is not at all the
case, as Noth asserts, that removal of "the elements of the Assyrian
state religion from the royal sanctuary" is "clearly implied" in 23:4[22]—
or anywhere else in the reform report in Kings (or, for that matter,
in Chronicles). As an exegetical guide to 2 Kgs. 23:4–20 the "Assyrian Vassalship Hypothesis" may well mislead.

Similar caution should be exercised with the "Deuteronomic Book
Hypothesis" concerning the relationship of the "book" said to have
been found in the Temple (22:3–23:3) with the reform and with the

---

the Hebrew Bible (ed. by J. C. Exum and D. J. A. Clines; JSOTSup 143; Sheffield/Val-
ley Forge: JSOT/Trinity, 1993) 163–83 (quotation from (p. 164). Cf. also Long,
2 Kings, 248–9; K. A. D. Smelik, "The Portrayal of King Manasseh: A Literary
Analysis of II Kings xxi and II Chronicles xiii," Converting the Past: Studies in Ancient
Israelite and Moabite Historiography (OTS 28; Leiden: Brill, 1992) 129–89; W. M.
Schniedewind, "History and Interpretation: The Religion of Ahab and Manasseh
in the Book of Kings," CBQ 55 (1993) 649–61; E. Ben Zvi, "Prelude to a Reconstruction of the Historical Manassic Judah," BN 81 (1996) 31–44; van Keulen, Manasseh; K. Schmid, "Manasse und der Untergang Judas: 'Golaorientierte' Theologie
in den Königsbüchern?" Bib 78 (1997) 87–99; E. Eynikel, "The Portrait of Manasseh and the Deuteronomistic History," Deuteronomy and Deuteronomic Literature: Festschrift
C. H. W. Brekelmans (ed. by M. Vervenne and J. Lust; BETL 133; Leuven: University, 1997) 233–61. A similar ideological agenda prompts the narrator of 2 Kings
18–20 (and Isaiah 36–39) to represent Isaiah as a loyal supporter of the god-fear-
ing Hezekiah and his anti-Assyrian foreign policy, while the historical Isaiah seems
to have belonged to the pro-Assyrian faction at court: see further Chapter 7 below.
[21] It is present to one degree or another in the standard historical reconstructions: e.g., J. Bright, A History of Israel (3rd edn.; Philadelphia: Westminster, 1981)
316–25 , little changed from the original 1959 edn. (pp. 294–304); Noth, History of
Israel, 272–9; S. Hermann, A History of Israel in Old Testament Times (2nd edn.; trans.
by J. Bowden; Philadelphia: Fortress, 1981) 263–73; J. A. Soggin, A History of Ancient
Israel (trans. by J. Bowden; Philadelphia: Westminster, 1984) 240–7; J. M. Miller
and J. H. Hayes, A History of Ancient Judah and Israel (Philadelphia: Westminster,
1986) 397–401; G. W. Ahlström, The History of Ancient Palestine from the Palaeolithic
Period to Alexander's Conquest (ed. by D. V. Edelman; JSOTSup 146; Sheffield: JSOT,
1993) ch. 18. Cf. also, e.g., M. Cogan and H. Tadmor, II Kings (AB 11; Garden
City: Doubleday, 1988) 291–304; Laato, Josiah and David Redivivus, 45–6, 75–80.
[22] Noth, History of Israel, 272.

Book of Deuteronomy. Biblical scholarship in general has assumed
that the story of the "book" is essentially credible,[23] that the document in question was some form of Deuteronomy, and that it supplied the ideological motivation for at least some of Josiah's actions.
Some scholars, feeling the accidental discovery of the "book" too
good to be true, even imagine that the Temple had to have been
"salted" by advocates of reform.[24] Suspiciously convenient coincidences of this sort do occur, occasionally, in history without human
chicanery or discernible superhuman intervention,[25] but the (re)dis-
covery of a "lost" document to justify a royal initiative is so much
a literary convention in the ancient Near East that the historicity of
the episode cannot be taken for granted.[26]

---

[23] Some scholars do take the story of the "book" to be the invention of a
"deuteronomistic historian" to link Josiah's reforms artificially to the "book" of
Deuteronomy: see further Chapter 6.B below.

[24] E.g., A. T. Olmstead, *History of Palestine and Syria to the Macedonian Conquest* (New
York/London: Scribner's Sons, 1939) 495 ("in reality [the book] had been composed not long before, and it is difficult not to suspect that Hilkiah himself was
perfectly aware of its origins"); Ahlström, *History of Ancient Palestine*, 777 (if the story
is historical, the book was "a product of Josiah's own chancellery, written in order
to give divine support for the king's actions"). For earlier exponents of this view
see M. J. Paul, "Hilkiah and the Law (2 Kings 22) in the 17th and 18th Centuries:
Some Influences on W. M. L. de Wette," *Das Deuteronomium: Entstehung, Gestalt und
Botschaft* (ed. by N. Lohfink; BETL 68; Leuven: Leuven University, 1985) 9–12. See
further n. 26 below.

[25] E.g., the convenient discovery of the purported remains of King Arthur by
the monks of Glastonbury in 1191, a few years after a fire virtually destroyed the
abbey, proves not to have been a trumped up publicity stunt to aid the building
fund: see Ashe, *Discovery of King Arthur*, 174–6, and especially *idem, Avalonian Quest*
(London: Methuen, 1982) 58–75. M. Weinfeld cites an excellent Hittite parallel
concerning Muwatalli (*Deuteronomy 1–11* [AB 5; New York: Doubleday, 1991] 18–9;
idem, in *ABD* [1992] 2.175); for Egyptian and Mesopotamian examples see Cogan-
Tadmor, *II Kings*, 294 and n. 11. For a comparable incident in Roman history see
E. M. Hooker, "The Significance of Numa's Religious Reform," *Numen* 10 (1963)
87–132. Despite these parallels, see the following note.

[26] See most recently T. C. Römer, "Transformations in Deuteronomistic and
Biblical Historiography: On 'Book-Finding' and other Literary Strategies," *ZAW* 109
(1997) 1–11 (especially 5–10), drawing on W. Speyer, "Bücherfunde in der Glaubenswerbung der Antike. Mit einem Ausblick auf Mittelalter und Neuzeit," *Hypomnemata* 24 (1970) 125–8; cf. also B. Diebner and C. Nauerth, "Die Inventio des
spr htwrh in 2 Kön 22: Struktur, Intention und Funktion von Auffindungslegenden," *Dielheimer Blätter zum Alten Testament* 18 (1984) 95–118 (with earlier literature). See further M. Smith, "Pseudepigraphy in the Israelite Literary Tradition,"
Studies in the Cult of Yahweh (ed. by S. J. D. Cohen; Religions in the Greco-Roman
World 130/1; Leiden/New York/Köln, 1996) 1.55–72 (= *Entretiens sur l'Antiquité classique, XVIII: Pseudepigrapha I*,18 [1972] 191–215). S. L. McKenzie tries to have it
both ways ("Postscript: The Laws of Physics and Pan-Deuteronomism," *Those Elusive Deuteronomists: The Phenomenon of Pan-Deuteronomism* [ed. by L. S. Schearing and

This "deuteronomic" connection (whether in fact or in the narrator's imagination) implies that some of Josiah's actions, and especially those concerning installations the narrators call "bamoth," were related in some fashion to the proscriptions in Deuteronomy 12; those proscriptions do not mention "bamoth," however, and the variety and specificity of the installations called "bamoth" in the reform report (contrast 2 Chron. 34:3–8a, 33) seem discordant with the stereotypical language of the deuteronomic provision which, if taken literally, would appear to have a different type of installation in mind.[27] Similarly, the provisions of Deut. 18:6–8 concerning the status of Yahweh priests in the hinterland vis-à-vis the Jerusalem Temple is at odds with the status of the displaced bamoth-priests reported in 2 Kgs. 23:8a + 9.[28] Furthermore, neither Josiah's emotional response upon hearing the content of the "book" (2 Kgs. 22:11; cf. 2 Chron. 34:19) nor Huldah's oracle "concerning the words of this book [which] our fathers have not obeyed" (2 Kgs. 22:13–20; cf. 2 Chron. 34:21–28), undoubtedly ghostwritten (in whole or in part)[29] by the

---

S. L. McKenzie; JSOTSup 268; Sheffield: Sheffield Academic, 1999] 262–3 n. 3): acknowledging that book-finding was "a literary and historical motif in the ancient world for justifying social and religious change," he opines that "the 'law book' may have been written to legitimate Josiah's reforms[,] ... more likely than the possibility that the reformers just happened upon a book that exactly suited their needs.... Nonetheless, the connection [of *Ur*-Deuteronomy] with Josiah's reign is probably not entirely fictional. It seems unlikely that Dtr would invent the story that a document as important as he makes out the law to be—the fundamental guide for Israel and the grounds upon which its kings are evaluated—existed in a single copy that disappeared for an undetermined length of time and was therefore not available for consultation until it suddenly resurfaced under Josiah." See further Chapter 6 below.

[27] As G. N. Knoppers observes ("Solomon's Fall and Deuteronomy," *The Age of Solomon: Scholarship at the Turn of the Millennium* [ed. by L. K. Handy; SHCANE 11; Leiden/New York/Köln: Brill, 1997] 402–3, and see also 403 n. 49): "Given the consistent concern with high places in the Deuteronomistic History, especially in the history of the Judahite monarchy, the discrepancy between Deuteronomy and the Deuteronomistic History is striking. Even though the Deuteronomist applied the law of centralization to cover *bmwt*, the very fact that Deuteronomy does not mention them suggests some distance between this work and the Deuteronomistic History." For the "bamoth" in 2 Kgs 23:4–20 see Chapter 5.D–E and Chapter 9 below.

[28] This alone invalidates the assertion that "Josiah followed the religious philosophy of the book of Deuteronomy to the letter" (S. Japhet, "From the King's Sanctuary to the Chosen City," *Jerusalem: Its Sanctity and Centrality to Judaism, Christianity, and Islam* [ed. by L. I. Levine; New York: Continuum, 1999] 9 [= *Judaism*, 46 (1997) 135]).

[29] From the use of the non-"deuteronomic" term *'SP* in 22:20 J. Priest proposes that "the Deuteronomistic historian preserved this authentic oracle [from

author-compiler(s) of the story, is readily explicable in terms of the
stipulations in Deuteronomy.[30] The dissidence at these crucial points
of contact is sufficient to refrain from accepting the "Deuteronomic
Book Hypothesis" as a certainty in analyzing the biblical accounts
of Josiah's reform.

Finally, there is the "Deuteronomistic History Hypothesis" which
has dominated the compositional analysis of biblical historiographical literature since the appearance (in 1943) and postwar dissemi-
nation of M. Noth's watershed *Überlieferungsgeschichtliche Studien*.[31] Three
generations of scholarly investigations have moved the discussion of
the literary prehistory of 1–2 Kings well beyond Noth to gravitate
around three basic models:[32] (1) Noth saw 1–2 Kings as the concluding portion of a massive work of theological historiography encom-
passing Deuteronomy and the Former Prophets; although containing

---

Huldah] and retained the technical term which was contrary to his own usage"
("Huldah's Oracle," *VT* 30 [1980] 366–8 [quotation from p. 367]); cf. now P. S. F.
van Keulen, "The Meaning of the Phrase *wn'spt 'l-qbrtyk bšlwm* in 2 Kings xxii 20,"
VT 46 (1996) 256–60. The fact that the other occurrences of the term in the
phrase "to be gathered to one's fathers/peoples" (see Priest, "Huldah's Oracle," 368
n. 6) are usually attributed to "P" might suggest a rather different conclusion; cf.
D. Edelman, "Huldah the Prophet—of Yahweh or Asherah?" *A Feminist Companion
to Samuel and Kings* (ed. by A. Brenner; Feminist Companion to the Bible 5; Sheffield:
Sheffield Academic 1994) 231–50. See further Chapter 6.B below.

[30] Eight issues are identified by Ahlström, *History of Ancient Palestine*, 775–7. J. H.
Tigay (among others) connects Josiah's response (and Huldah's oracle) to the curses
of Deuteronomy 28 (*Deuteronomy* [JPSTC 5; Philadelphia/Jerusalem: Jewish Publication Society, 1996] xx); noting both the similarities and differences between the
biblical book and the reform report, he concludes that "while Josiah's reform was
inspired by Deuteronomy, the book itself was not composed by those who carried
it out" but nonetheless sometime in the course of the 8th–7th centuries (pp. xx–xxi).
As L. K. Handy points out ("The Role of Huldah in Josiah's Cult Reform," *ZAW*
106 [1994] 49–50 n. 23), "clearly the devastation of the religion of the land cannot be read as the fulfillment of any portion of Deuteronomy without carefully cut-
ting out the majority of the legislation contained in the current legal section of that
book."

[31] M. Noth, *Überlieferungsgeschtliche Studien*, 1 (Tübingen: Niemeyer, 1943; 2nd edn.,
1957; 3rd edn., 1967), later translated into English as *The Deuteronomistic History*
(1981) and *The Chronicler's History* (trans. by H. G. M. Williamson; JSOTSup 50;
Sheffield: JSOT, 1987).

[32] Most recent commentaries include discussion of the interpretational history of
this material, and some are quite extensive and perceptive. Additionally, see, e.g.,
I. W. Provan, *Hezekiah and the Books of Kings: A Contribution to the Debate about the Composition of the Deuteronomistic History* (BZAW 72; Berlin/New York: de Gruyter, 1988)
ch. 1; H. Weippert, "Das deuteronomistische Geschichtswerk: Sein Zeil und Ende
in der neueren Forschung," *TR* 50 (1988) 213–49; McKenzie, *Trouble with Kings*,
1–19, *idem*, in *ABD* (1992) 2.160–8, and *idem*, "The Book of Kings in the Deuteron-

materials from diverse older sources and subsequent augmentations, this work is a compositional unity produced by a single author-compiler during the Exile. This model is most compatible with the modes of inquiry of the "new literary criticism," contributing to its continuing popularity.[33] (2) Many Continental scholars (the "Göttingen School") accept Noth's original Exilic author-compiler, but postulate a series of identifiable redactors who continued to shape the work into the post-Exilic period.[34] (3) Other commentators (including the American "Cross School") maintain that the original work was composed earlier, during the reign of Josiah, and was revised subsequently at least once after the fall of Jerusalem.[35] It is implicit in all

---

omistic History," *History of Israel's Tradition: The Heritage of Martin Noth* (ed. by S. L. McKenzie and M. P. Graham; JSOTSup 182; Sheffield: Sheffield Academic, 1994) 281–307; S. W. Holloway, in *ABD* (1992) 4.70–3; Eynikel, *Reform of King Josiah*, ch. 1; W. Schniedewind, "The Problem with Kings: Recent Study of the Deuteronomistic History," *RelStRev* 22 (1996) 22–7; T. Römer and A. de Pury, "L'historiographie deutéronomiste (HD): Histoire de la recherche et enjeux du débat," *Israël Construit son Histoire: L'historiographie deutéronomiste à la lumière des recherches récentes* (ed. by A. de Pury, T. Römer, and J.-D. Macchi; Le Monde de la Bible 34; Geneva: Labor et Fides, 1996) 9–120.

[33] This is the basic position championed by Hoffmann, *Reform und Reformen*, especially 315–8 *et passim*. Cf. also, e.g., J. Van Seters, *In Search of History* (New Haven: Yale, 1983) especially 316 n. 84 *et passim*; J. G. McConville, "Narrative and Meaning in the Books of Kings," *Bib* 70 (1989) especially 31–2; and now by McKenzie, "Postscript: The Laws of Physics and Pan-Deuteronomism," 263–4.

[34] Exponents of this model include R. Smend, "Das Gesetz und die Völker: Ein Beitrag zur deuteronomistischen Redaktionsgeschichte," *Probleme biblischer Theologie: Gerhard von Rad zum 70. Geburtstag* (ed. by H. W. Wolff; Munich: Kaiser, 1971) 494–509, and idem, *Die Entstehung des Alten Testaments* (Theologische Wissenschaft 1; Stuttgart: Kohlhammer, 1978) 111–25; W. Dietrich, *Prophetie und Geschichte: Eine redaktionsgeschichtliche Untersuchung zum deuteronomistischen Geschichtswerk* (FRLANT 108; Göttingen: Vandenhoeck & Ruprecht, 1972), and idem, "Josia und das Gesetzbuch (2 Reg xxii)," *VT* 27 (1977) 13–35. One of the few commentators writing in English to have adopted this model is Jones, *1–2 Kings*, especially 44 *et passim*.

[35] Popular before Noth, this is arguably the dominant model among commentators writing in English since being advanced anew by F. M. Cross, *Canaanite Myth and Hebrew Epic: Essays in the History of the Religion of Israel* (Cambridge: Harvard University, 1973) 74–89 (= "The Structure of the Deuteronomistic History," *Perspectives on Jewish Learning* [ed. by J. M. Rosenthal; Chicago: Spertus College of Judaica, 1967] 3.9–24). A measure of the elegance and appeal of Cross's presentation was his concentration on the themes producing the "big picture"; subsequent work has tended to deal less impressionistically with smaller narrative units: see, e.g., Nelson, *Double Redaction*; R. E. Friedman, "From Egypt to Egypt: Dtr[1] and Dtr[2]," *Traditions in Transformation: Turning Points in Biblical Faith* (ed. by B. Halpern and J. D. Levenson; Winona Lake: Eisenbrauns, 1981) 167–92; Z. Zevit, "Deuteronomistic Historiography in 1 Kings 12–2 Kings 17 and the Reinvestiture of the Israelian Cult," *JSOT* 32 (1985) 57–73; McKenzie, *Trouble with Kings*.

three models that the basic principles informing the work as a whole, and 1–2 Kings in particular, are enunciated in the Book of Deuteronomy and tied historically, directly or indirectly, to the reformulation of Judahite religious life initiated by Josiah. Each of these models allows for source materials of various sorts[36] from which these "Deuteronomistic Historians" extracted information which they adapted or incorporated more-or-less intact into their own historiographical work. A growing number of commentators believe they have found traces of one such source: an earlier historiographical work which views the history of the kingdoms of Israel and Judah from the vantage-point, most would argue, of the profoundly altered circumstances created by the Assyrian crisis of the late 8th century.[37]

If the mainstream of compositional analysis of biblical historiography since Noth has flowed in the channels mapped out above, there is little agreement as to details. Moreover, some of the foundational assumptions of the "Deuteronomistic History Hypothesis" have been seriously challenged, and a half-century after Noth a number of leading commentators now doubt its existence.[38] Recently, R. E. Friedman has shown that it is possible, theoretically, to explain

---

[36] On the general topic of putative sources see Van Seters, *In Search of History*, 292–302, and B. Halpern, *The First Historians: The Hebrew Bible and History* (San Francisco: Harper & Row, 1988) 207–18.

[37] Cf., e.g., A. D. H. Mayes, *The Story of Israel between Settlement and Exile: A Redactional Study of the Deuteronomistic History* (London: SCM, 1983); A. F. Campbell, *Of Prophets and Kings: A Late Ninth-Century Document (1 Samuel 1–2 Kings 10)* (CBQM 17; Washington, DC: Catholic Biblical Association of America, 1986); A. Lemaire, "Vers l'Histoire de la Redaction des Livres des Rois," *ZAW* 98 (1986) 221–36; Halpern, *First Historians, passim*; A. Moenikes, "Zur Redaktionsgeschichte des sogenannten Deuteronomistischen Geschichtswerk," *ZAW* 104 (1992) 333–48; Schniedewind, "Problem with Kings," 26. I too have come to believe that the preponderance of evidence favors this conclusion: see initially W. B. Barrick, "On the 'Removal of the "High-Places"' in 1–2 Kings," *Bib* 55 (1974) 57–9, and further developed by Provan, *Hezekiah*, chs. 2–3 and pp. 84–5, B. Halpern and D. S. Vanderhooft, "The Editions of Kings in the 7th–6th Centuries BCE," *HUCA* 62 (1991) especially 199–212, and Eynikel, *Reform of King Josiah*, ch. 2.

[38] Cf., e.g., C. Westermann, *Die Geschichtsbücher des Alten Testaments: Gab es ein deuteronomistisches Geschichtswerk?* (TBü 87; Gütershoh: Kaiser, 1994); E. A. Knauf, "L''Historiographie deutéronomiste' (DtrG) Existe-t-elle?" *Israël Construit son Histoire: L'historiographie deutéronomiste à la lumière des recherches récentes* (ed. by A. de Pury, T. Römer, and J.-D. Macchi; Le Monde de la Bible 34; Geneva: Labor et Fides, 1996) 409–18; A. G. Auld, "The Deuteronomists and the Former Prophets, or What Makes the Former Prophets Deuteronomistic?" *Those Elusive Deuteronomists: The Phenomenon of Pan-Deuteronomism* (ed. by L. S. Schearing and S. L. McKenzie; JSOT-Sup 268; Sheffield: Sheffield Academic, 1999) 116–26.

the "Deuteronomistic History" and the "deuteronomistic" prose of
the Book of Jeremiah as the work of a single author-compiler, inspired
by the "Song of Moses" (Deuteronomy 32) and the deuteronomic
law code (chs. 12–26), whose career stretched from the reign of
Josiah (before 609) into the Exile (after 587), thus eliminating the
need to posit an extensive "deuteronomistic" school, movement, or
whatever;[39] this possibility cautions against assuming that earlier religious reforms in Judah (notably the one attributed to Hezekiah) and
the literature generated by them need have had anything "deuteronomistic" about them. Moving in the opposite direction, other scholars have had no difficulty finding "deuteronomistic" rhetoric and
ideas in post-Exilic and post-biblical literature[40] and in other ancient
Near Eastern literatures spanning the entire biblical period;[41] so
sweeping a chronological horizon undermines their diagnostic value
regarding authorship and date of composition.[42] Indeed, "deuteronomistic" has become something of a portmanteau word so
semantically overloaded in itself, and further befogged by differing
understandings of the compositional development of the Book of
Kings, that if "deuteronomism" ever existed in biblical Israel as a

---

[39] R. E. Friedman, "The Deuteronomistic School," *Fortunate the Eyes that See: Essays
in Honor of David Noel Freedman in Celebration of his Seventieth Birthday* (ed. by A. B.
Beck *et al.*; Grand Rapids/Cambridge, UK: Eerdmans, 1995) 70–80.

[40] For discussion see R. F. Person, "II Kings 24.18–25, 30 and Jeremiah 52: A
Text-Critical Case Study in the Redaction History of the Deuteronomistic History,"
ZAW 105 (1993) 174–205, and *idem, Second Zechariah and the Deuteronomic School* (JSOT-
Sup 167; Sheffield: JSOT, 1993) chs. 1–2, 7; Holloway, in *ABD*, 4.71. Of the rel-
evant essays in *Those Elusive Deuteronomists: The Phenomenon of Pan-Deuteronomism* (ed.
by L. S. Schearing and S. L. McKenzie; JSOTSup 268; Sheffield: Sheffield Acad-
emic, 1999), see especially R. R. Wilson, "Who Was the Deuteronomist? (Who
Was Not the Deuteronomist?): Reflections on Pan-Deuteronomism" (pp. 67–82).

[41] See, e.g., K. A. Kitchen, "Ancient Orient, 'Deuteronomism,' and the Old Testament," *New Perspectives on the Old Testament* (ed. by J. B. Payne; Evangelical Theological Society Supplementary Volume 3; Waco/London: Word, 1970) 1–24, and
lately A. Laato, "Second Samuel 7 and Ancient Near Eastern Royal Ideology,"
CBQ 59 (1997) 244–69, and *idem*, "The Royal Covenant Theology in Judah," *"Lasset uns Brücken bauen . . .": Collected Communications to the XVth Congress of the International
Organization for the Study of the Old Testament, Cambridge 1995* (ed. by K.-D. Schunck
and M. Augustin; Beiträge zur Erforschung des Alten Testaments und des Antiken
Judentums 42; Frankfort am Main/Berlin/New York/Wien: Peter Lang, 1998)
93–100.

[42] Cf. Kitchen's conclusions ("Ancient Orient," 19): "Much that is called Deuteronomic is common ground conceptually in the religions and society of the Biblical
Near East at large, and not even specifically Israelite, let alone specially Deuteronomic within Israel."

distinct point of view expressed in a distinct literary style, its characteristic features must be defined with greater precision for it to be a useful exegetical category.[43] Even the fulcrum of all this speculation—*Ur*-Deuteronomy—has become increasingly difficult both to differentiate from later "deuteronomistic" accretions and to date relative to pivotal material in the Former Prophets.[44] These factors caution against taking the "Deuteronomistic History Hypothesis," in any of its permutations, as a secure premise for a compositional analysis of what for purposes of neutral identification can be called the "Kings History" (KH).

Noth's *Überlieferungsgeschichtliche Studien* also has stimulated a renaissance of interest in 1–2 Chronicles.[45] It has long been recognized that the Kings History was a source used selectively by the Chronicler: material in Kings which did not "fit" his conception of Israel's past (e.g., the depiction of Solomon as a womanizing idolater, synchronisms with the northern kingdom, etc.) he simply omitted or, less frequently, transformed into something completely different.

---

[43] Wilson puts it well ("Who Was the Deuteronomist?" 78): "This lack of commonly accepted criteria [for identifying a passage as 'deuteronomistic'] gives the impression that a number of scholars are playing the same game, but without a commonly agreed upon set of rules. It should come as no surprise, then, that there are often disputes among the players." See further R. Coggins, "What Does 'Deuteronomistic' Mean?" *Those Elusive Deuteronomists: The Phenomenon of Pan-Deuteronomism* (ed. by L. S. Schearing and S. L. McKenzie; JSOTSup 268; Sheffield: Sheffield Academic, 1999) 22–35 (= *Words Remembered, Texts Renewed: Essays in Honour of John F. A. Sawyer* [ed. by J. Davies *et al.*; JSOTSup 195; Sheffield: Sheffield Academic, 1995] 135–48), and N. Lohfink, "Was there a Deuteronomistic Movement?" *Those Elusive Deuteronomists: The Phenomenon of Pan-Deuteronomism* (ed. by L. S. Schearing and S. L. McKenzie; JSOTSup 268; Sheffield: Sheffield Academic, 1999) 36–66 (= *Jeremia und die "deuteronomistische Bewegung"* [ed. by W. Gross; BBB 98; Weinheim: Beltz Athenäum, 1995] 313–382).

[44] Cf., e.g., N. Lohfink, "Deutéronome et Pentateuque: État de la Recherche," *Le Pentateuque: Débats et Recherches—XIVᵉ Congrès de l'ACFEB, Angers (1991)* (ed. by P. Haudebert; Lectio Divina 151; Paris: Cerf, 1992) 35–64; Weinfeld, in *ABD*, 2.168–83; T. Römer, "The Book of Deuteronomy," *The History of Israel's Tradition: The Heritage of Martin Noth* (ed. by S. L. McKenzie and M. P. Graham; JSOTSup 182; Sheffield: Sheffield Academic, 1994) 178–212; M. A. O'Brien, "The Book of Deuteronomy," *CR:BS* 3 (1995) 95–128; Auld, "Deuteronomists and the Former Prophets," 121–2, 125. See further Chapter 6.A below.

[45] In addition to the surveys of recent discussion of the compositional history of the Chronicles History in the latest commentaries, see, e.g., R. W. Klein, in *ABD* (1992) 1.992–1002; R. L. Braun, "Martin Noth and the Chronicler's History," *History of Israel's Tradition: The Heritage of Martin Noth* (ed. by S. L. McKenzie and M. P. Graham; JSOTSup 182; Sheffield: Sheffield Academic, 1994) 63–80; J. W. Kleinig, "Recent Research in Chronicles," *CR:BS* 2 (1994) 43–76.

Viewed against the ongoing discussion about the composition of the Kings History, a more complex literary relationship between the two historiographical works seems more likely. It is very possible, for example, that the "edition" of Kings used by the Chronicler was not the "edition" preserved in the MT and that some of the supposedly "suppressed" material was not in his *Vorlage* in the first place. According to S. L. McKenzie, the Chronicler's *Vorlage* was the unrevised "Josianic" version of Kings (commonly Dtr[j]),[46] an intriguing but neither the only nor necessarily the most persuasive possibility; thus, e.g., B. Halpern and A. G. Auld contend, in different ways, that an independent source concerning at least the reign of Solomon (cf. "the Book of the Acts of Solomon" [1 Kgs. 11:41b]) may have been used in different measure by both the Kings Historian and the Chronicler.[47]

The following nine chapters present new examinations of the reports of Josiah's reform in 2 Kgs. 23:4–20 (+ 24) and 2 Chron. 34:3–7 and related biblical passages (especially 1 Kgs. 12:33–13:32), concentrating on the likely compositional history of this material and its usefulness as a source for reconstructing the likely history of Josiah's reign. They are, by design, neither exhaustive nor definitive.

---

[46] McKenzie, *Chronicler's Use*, especially chs. 6–7; cf. the critique by H. G. M. Williamson, in *VT* 37 (1987) 112–4. For Williamson's alternative hypothesis see his "The Death of Josiah and the Continuing Development of the Deuteronomistic History," *VT* 32 (1982) 242–7; *idem, 1–2 Chronicles* (NCBC; Grand Rapids/London: Eerdmans/Marshall, Morgan & Scott, 1982) 408–11; *idem*, "Reliving the Death of Josiah: A Reply to C. T. Begg," *VT* 37 (1987) 9–15.

[47] B. Halpern, "Sacred History and Ideology: Chronicles' Thematic Structure— Indications of an Earlier Source," *The Creation of Sacred Literature: Composition and Redaction of the Biblical Text* (ed. by R. E. Friedman; University of California Publications, Near Eastern Studies 22; Berkeley/Los Angeles/London: University of California, 1981) 35–54; A. G. Auld, "Prophets through the Looking Glass: Between Writings and Moses," *JSOT* 27 (1983) 3–23, *idem*, "Salomo und die Deuteronomisten: Eine Zukunftvision?" *TZ* 48 (1992) 343–55, *idem*, "Solomon at Gibeon: History Glimpsed," *E-I* 24 (1993) 1*–7*, *idem, Kings without Privilege: David and Moses in the Story of the Bible's Kings* (Edinburgh: Clark, 1994), and *idem*, "Reading Joshua after Kings," *Words Remembered, Texts Renewed: Essays in Honour of John F. A. Sawyer* (ed. by J. Davies *et al.*; JSOTSup195; Sheffield: Sheffield Academic, 1995) 167–81. Of the several germane essays in *The Chronicler as Author: Studies in Text and Texture* (ed. by M. P. Graham and S. L. McKenzie; JSOTSup 263; Sheffield: Sheffield Academic, 1999) see the critique of Auld's proposal by S. L. McKenzie ("The Chronicler as Redactor," especially 80–7) and Auld's rebuttal ("What Was the Main Source of the Books of Chronicles?" 91–9). See also, e.g., W. F. Lemke, "The Synoptic Problem in the Chronicler's History," *HTR* 58 (1968) 349–63; R. W. Klein, *Textual Criticism of the Old Testament: The Septuagint after Qumran* (Guides to Biblical Scholarship; Philadelphia: Fortress, 1974) 42–50, and *idem, ABD,* 1.996–7.

Conscious of the perils of the undertaking (cf. Eccl. 12:12), particularly in the wake of the massive analysis by E. Eynikel of *The Reform
of King Josiah and the Composition of the Deuteronomistic History* (1996),
and the nihilistic "minimalism" of L. K. Handy's "Historical Probability and the Narrative of Josiah's Reform in 2 Kings" (in *The
Pitcher Was Broken: Memorial Essays for Gösta W. Ahlström* [1995] 252–75),[48]
I yet believe that this collection of coordinated exploratory probings
into this well-dug tell may prove useful in the ongoing scholarly discussion of these matters. Chapters 2–6 are devoted to issues of composition and redaction, Chapters 7–10 to issues of historical context
and circumstance.

---

[48] M. A. Sweeney's *King Josiah of Judah: The Lost Messiah of Israel* (Oxford: Oxford
University, 2001) has only just appeared and could not be consulted in the preparation of the present work.

CHAPTER TWO

JOSIAH'S REFORM AS REPORTED IN CHRONICLES (I):
THE CHRONICLER'S ACCOUNT

While the Chronicler's account of the reign of Josiah differs substantially from that in the KH, there is no doubt that it is essentially a revision of the earlier narrative, although not necessarily in
the form that we know it today:[1]

1. Introduction (34:1–2) || cf. 2 Kgs. 22:1–2
2. Purging the land (34:3–7) || cf. 2 Kgs. 23:4–20, 24
   Josiah's "conversion" (v. 3a): 8th regnal year/16th biological year
   Judah and Jerusalem (vv. 3b–5): 12th regnal year/20th biological year
   Elsewhere (vv. 6–7)
3. The covenant (34:8–33) || cf. 2 Kgs. 22:3–23:3
   Repair of the Temple (vv. 8–13): 18th regnal year/26th biological year
   Finding the book (vv. 14–21)
   Huldah's prophecy (vv. 22–28)
   Making the covenant and its consequences (vv. 29–33)
4. The Passover (35:1–19) || cf. 2 Kgs. 23:21–23
5. Conclusion (35:20–36:1) || cf. 2 Kgs. 23:28–30

---

[1] Adapted from S. Japhet, *I–II Chronicles: A Commentary* (OTL; Louisville: Westminster John Knox, 1993) 1001; cf. also Eslinger, "Josiah and the Torah Book,"
48–51. By contrast, the layout of this material by the editors of *Chronicles and its
Synoptic Parallels in Samuel, Kings, and Related Biblical Texts* ([ed. by J. C. Endres *et al.*;
Collegeville, MN: Liturgical, 1998] 327–36) suggests that 2 Chron. 34:3–7 is compositionally unrelated to 2 Kgs. 23:4–20 + 24. Auld's thesis that Kings and Chronicles are elaborations of a common *Urtext* (see Chapter 1 n. 47 above) seems
better suited for the material from Solomon to Hezekiah. For Josiah, Auld accepts
the basic sequence of events in Kings with a short version of the Passover episode
as in Kings and a short version of the reform episode as in Chronicles (*Kings without Privilege*, 95–8, 123–6); of his representation of the latter, essentially the account
in Chronicles, he notes (p. 125 n. 1): "Since Chronicles regularly makes at least
small changes to the source reports of cultic modifications, this paragraph will only
give an impression of the original wording. But it can hardly be doubted that the
long report in 2 Kgs. 23:4–20 has been substantially expanded, and in more than
one stage."

Unlike the Kings account which implies that Josiah's entire reform program was carried out in the course of his 18th regnal year (22:3; 23:23), the Chronicler posits a reform in three stages and spanning a decade. This chronology, although accepted by many,[2] is suspicious in light of the Chronicler's theological agenda and other factors,[3] with but one exception. His choice of Josiah's 12th regnal year for the start of the reform can be explained on the basis of its coincidence with the young king's biological/legal majority status.[4] The choice of his 8th regnal year for his "conversion" would seem arbitrary[5] were it not for its coincidence with the birth of his son Jehoahaz (by Hamutal of Libnah in the Shephelah) who would be chosen by the "people of the land" to succeed him in preference to his elder brother Jehoiakim (born by Zebidah of Rumah, probably in the Galilee); the significance of this date is not biological or sociological, but political.[6] Whether the Chronicler actually knew of this or deduced

---

[2] E.g., A. Jepsen, "Die Reform des Josia," *Festschrift Friedrich Baumgärtel zum 70. Geburtstag 14. Januar 1958* (ed. by L. Rost; EF A/10; Erlangen: Universitatsbibliothek Erlangen, 1959) 97–108; J. M. Myers, *II Chronicles* (AB 13; Garden City: Doubleday, 1965) 205–8; R. J. Coggins, *The First and Second Books of the Chronicles* (CBC; Cambridge: Cambridge University, 1976) 291–2; Bright, *History*, 317–8; Herrmann, *History of Israel*, 266, 272 n. 4; Laato, *Josiah and David Redivivus*, 44–6; J. R. Lundbom, *Jeremiah 1–20* (AB 21A; New York: Doubleday, 1999) 106. For a convenient review of the arguments for the priority of one version over the other see D. A. Glatt-Gilad, "The Role of Huldah's Prophecy in the Chronicler's Portrayal of Josiah's Reform," *Bib* 77 (1996) 16–8.

[3] In addition to the commentaries, see especially M. Cogan, "The Chronicler's Use of Chronology as Illuminated by Neo-Assyrian Royal Inscriptions," *Empirical Models for Biblical Criticism* [ed. by J. H. Tigay; Philadelphia: University of Pennsylvania, 1985] especially 203–5, and the comprehensive study by W. H. Barnes, "Non-Synoptic Chronological References in the Books of Chronicles," *The Chronicler as Historian* (ed. by M. P. Graham *et al.*; JSOTSup 238; Sheffield: Sheffield Academic, 1997) 106–31.

[4] Cf. Num. 1:3; 26:2; 1 Chron. 27:23; 25:5; for general discussion of this change in status see L. E. Stager, "The Archaeology of the Family in Ancient Israel," *BASOR* 260 (1985) 25–8.

[5] According to Williamson, "no particular significance appears to attach to the age of sixteen, unless it was considered the age of responsibility in the Chronicler's community" (*1–2 Chronicles*, 398), but this is doubtful. J. Fleishman's study of the relevant data finds that "the onset of legal maturity, *legitima aetas*, began in the first years of the second decade of a child's life with the appearance of signs of sexual maturity," with the age of twenty considered "the age of full legal maturity, *plene pubertas*" ("The Age of Legal Maturity in Biblical Law," *JANES* 21 [1992] 35–48 [quotation from p. 48]). That Josiah was not a physiological "late bloomer" is evident from his age at the births of his sons Jehoiakim (14) and Jehoahaz (16).

[6] For discussion see J. A. Wilcoxen, "The Political Background of Jeremiah's

it from his Kings source and inferred a religious implication, this date may well be a reliable benchmark for reconstructing Josiah's reign and the role played by his reform activities in the geo-politics of the period, and indicative that neither the King's nor the Chronicler's chronology should be accepted at face value as true to history.

2 Chron. 34:3b–7 is the Chronicler's reform report. As in the Kings version, it contains activities in "Judah and Jerusalem" (vv. 3b–5), followed by activities elsewhere (vv. 6–7). Commentators agree that the pericope is a condensation of 2 Kgs. 23:4–20 + 24 consistent with the Chronicler's attempt "to provide the period with more solid theological cohesiveness."[7] This begins with the representation of Manasseh (2 Chron. 33:1–20) which differs substantially from that in Kings (21:1–18): 2 Chron. 33:1–10 + 18–20 and 2 Kgs. 21:1–10a + 17–18 are virtually identical,[8] but in place of the middle section of the Kings account (vv. 11–16, a thoroughgoing "deuteronomistic" condemnation of Manasseh) is a unique report (vv. 11–17): while a prisoner in Babylon Manasseh "entreated the favor of Yahweh his god and humbled himself greatly before the god of his fathers," and when restored to his kingdom he proceeded to undo many of his cultic innovations in "the House of Yahweh." This report, whatever its historicity,[9] obviates the need for Josiah to purge the Temple,

---

Temple Sermon," *Scripture in History and Theology: Essays in Honor of J. C. Rylaarsdam* (ed. by A. L. Merrill and T. W. Overholt; Pittsburgh Theological Monograph 17; Pittsburgh: Pickwick, 1977) 151–66, and W. B. Barrick, "Dynastic Politics, Priestly Succession, and Josiah's Eighth Year," *ZAW* 112 (2000) 564–82. See further Chapter 7 below.

[7] Japhet, *I–II Chronicles*, 1019.

[8] 33:10 is a terse summary of 21:10–15 ("its first part is cited almost verbatim, its middle part epitomized, and its conclusion rephrased" [*ibid.*, 1001, cf. also 1008–9]), but there is no echo of the supplemental v. 16 ("innocent blood") which, conceivably, may not have been part of the Chronicler's *Vorlage*.

[9] Whether this report has some historical basis or is entirely the Chronicler's homiletical invention is much debated (see the commentaries). The recent discussion by A. F. Rainey ("Manasseh, King of Judah, in the Whirlpool of the Seventh Century BCE," *"kinatlùtu ša dārâti": Raphael Kutscher Memorial Volume* [ed. by A. F. Rainey; Tel Aviv Occasional Publications 1; Tel Aviv: Tel Aviv University, 1993] 147–64) takes its essential historicity for granted and provides circumstantial extra-biblical evidence in support; similarly, e.g., G. W. Ahlström, *Royal Administration and National Religion in Ancient Palestine* (SHANE 1; Leiden: Brill, 1982) ch. 5 ("cannot be a complete invention" [p. 76]), and *idem, History of Ancient Palestine*, 730–9 ("may not be a complete invention" [p. 733]). Against this view cf., e.g., Ben Zvi, "Prelude to a Reconstruction," 38–42. B. Oded thinks the story is "an historical

and this accounts for the Chronicler's omission of 2 Kgs. 23:4, 6–7, 9, 11–12.[10]

2.A. THE BEGINNING OF THE PURGE IN JUDAH AND JERUSALEM (v. 3b)

ûbištêm ʿeśrēh šānâ hēḥēl lĕṭahēr ʾet-yĕhûdâ wîrûšālaim min-habbāmôt wĕhāʾăšērîm wĕhappĕsîlîm wĕhammassēkôt;

And in the twelfth year [of his reign, Josiah] began to purge Jerusalem of the bamoth, the asherim, and the pesel-images and massekah-images.

In terms of narrative continuity, the "bamoth" in question must be those which Manasseh rebuilt (33:3a) and at which "the people continued to sacrifice, only to Yahweh their god" (33:17); this passing mention is the Chronicler's equivalent of 2 Kgs. 23:8a (where the priests are presumed to be Yahwistic [cf. v. 9]). The "bamoth" are not mentioned again, consistent with diminished ideological importance of the bamoth issue in Chronicles generally.[11]

2.B. THE ALTARS AND THE HAMMANIM (v. 4a)

wayĕnatĕṣû lĕpānāyw ʾēt mizbĕḥôt habbĕʿālîm wĕhaḥammānîm ʾăšer-lĕmaʿlâ mēʿălêhem giddēaʿ;

And they broke down the altars of the Baals before him, and the hammanim which stood above them he hewed down.

---

midrash" based on Isaiah's words in 2 Kgs. 20:18, but feels that "it is difficult to assume that the author of Chronicles created a totally imaginary episode with no historical kernel" ("Judah and the Exile," *Israelite and Judaean History* [ed. by J. H. Hayes and J. M. Miller; OTL; Philadelphia: Westminster, 1977] 454–5). This seems to me to be special pleading, for it is not at all difficult to overestimate the Chronicler's historiographical imagination (cf. the abundant creativity of the screenwriters of many "history-based" motion pictures, not least Cecil B. DeMille's 1956 spectacular *The Ten Commandments*: for this and other examples see M. C. Carnes, ed., *Past Imperfect: History according to the Movies* [New York: Holt, 1995]). The real difficulty is finding more than circumstantial evidence for giving the Chronicler the benefit of the doubt in this matter: the reference to Josiah's 8th year is one possibility; for another see W. M. Schniedewind, "The Source Citations of Manasseh: King Manasseh in History and Homily," *VT* 41 (1991) 450–61.

[10] For 34:8 (*lĕṭahēr hāʾāreṣ wĕhabbāyit*) see Eslinger "Josiah and the Torah Book," 48–50 n. 23.

[11] For the Chronicler's interest in the bamoth issue see S. Japhet, *The Ideology of*

For a "summary of the Kings' account, using generalizing expressions whose origin in the earlier text is nonetheless clear,"[12] the passage is oddly specific—the altars were demolished in Josiah's presence, and the hammanim were located somewhere "above" them—and the origin of this specificity has not been satisfactorily explained. The chiastic grammatical structure suggests that the author regarded the disposition of the altars and the hammanim as "two sides of a single event,"[13] but it is not self-evident what actions in the reform report in Kings would lend themselves to being represented in this fashion. Only the cemetery episode in 23:16–18 has Josiah actually on the scene, but in the final form of Kings that episode occurs north of the border at Benjaminite Bethel.

2.C. The Idols and their Devotees (v. 4b)

wĕhā'ăšērîm wĕhappĕsîlîm wĕhammassēkôt šibbar wĕhēdaq wayyizrōq 'al-pĕnê haqqĕbārîm hazzōbĕḥîm lāhem;

and the asherim and the pesel-images and the massekah-images he broke in pieces and crushed, and he scattered before the graves [the remains of] those who had sacrificed to them.

Although v. 4bβ is usually translated along the lines of the RSV—"and he made dust of them and strewed it over the graves of those who had sacrificed to them" (similarly, e.g., NJPSV)—this understanding of the passage is problematic. The definite article and absolute ending of *haqqĕbārîm* makes taking *haqqĕbārîm hazzōbĕḥîm* as a construct chain ("the graves of the sacrificers") grammatically dubious;[14] to achieve the same idea by supposing that the two words are in synonymous apposition ("strewed over the graves, [that is,] the sacrificers") is forced. As a transitive verb *ZRQ* takes a direct object, and while *hā'ăšērîm wĕhappĕsîlîm wĕhammassēkôt* could serve as a collective object, grammatical and stylistic clarity argue otherwise. Taking

---

the Book of Chronicles and its Place in Biblical Thought (2nd edn.; trans. by A. Barber; Beiträge zur Erforschung des Alten Testaments und des Antiken Judentums 9; New York/Frankfurt am Main/Berlin/Bern/Paris/Wein: Lang, 1997) especially 217–21.

[12] Williamson, *1–2 Chronicles*, 399.

[13] D. L. Washburn, "Perspective and Purpose: Understanding the Josiah Story," *Trinity Journal* 12 (1991) 62–3 (quotation from p. 63); also S. J. DeVries, *1 and 2 Chronicles* (FOTL 11; Grand Rapids, Eerdmans, 1989) 403.

[14] Cf. GKC, 247, 414–5, and B. K. Waltke and M. O'Connor, *An Introduction to*

hazzōbĕḥîm lahem as the direct object of both *ZRQ* and *DQQ* (cf.
2 Sam. 22:43 and Mic. 4:13) yields "and he crushed and scattered
those who sacrificed to them over the graves."[15] *DQQ* is more commonly used of the "crushing/grinding" of objects (cf. 2 Kgs. 23:6,
15), however,[16] and it is unambiguously used in this way in 15:16b
(*wayyikrōt ʾāsāʾ ʾet-mipĕlaṣtāh wayyādeq wayyiśrōp bĕnahal qidrôn*) and 34:7
(see below). Furthermore, it is reasonable to suppose that *ʿal-penê* has
a meaning comparable to *lĕpānāyw* in v. 4a.[17] The translation given
above is preferable for these reasons.

While the "crushing" of the idols may echo 2 Kgs. 23:6, the
Chronicler has generalized the practice (15:16, following 1 Kgs. 15:13)
and has already purified the Temple in the course of Manasseh's
reign, making it unlikely that v. 4bα is his equivalent of that verse.[18]
The interpretation just proposed for v. 4bβ further distances the two;
it is reminiscent of the treatment of the bones taken from tombs
described in Jer. 8:1–3, but is difficult to explain on the basis of
anything in the final form of the Kings reform report.

2.D. The Burning of the Bones of Priests (v. 5)

*wĕʿaṣmôt kōhănîm śārap ʿal-mizbĕḥôtaym, wayĕṭahēr ʾet-yĕ-hûdâ wĕʾet-yerû-
šālāim;*

And bones of priests he burned on their altars, and purged Judah and
Jerusalem.

It is striking that the Chronicler imagines that Josiah's burning of
priests' bones occurred during his purge of "Judah and Jerusalem," and
not in the North as is the case in Kings. The common explanation,
that he is simply consolidating his Kings *Vorlage*,[19] does not account
for the relocation unless his *Vorlage* too contained something of this

---

Biblical Hebrew Syntax (Winona Lake: Eisenbrauns, 1990) 138–40. An enclitic *mem*
in *haqqebarîm* is posited by, most recently, the translators for *Chronicles and its Synoptic Parallels*, 327.

[15] Washburn, "Perspective and Purpose," 65.

[16] See Eynikel, *Reform of King Josiah*, 222–3.

[17] So, e.g., Myers, *II Chronicles*, 201 ("before the graves").

[18] Cf., e.g., P. R. Ackroyd, *I–II Chronicles, Ezra, Nehemiah* (London: SCM, 1973)
200–1; Williamson, *1–2 Chronicles*, 399; Japhet, *I–II Chronicles*, 1021–3.

[19] It is not the case that the Chronicler is "making one issue out of two" (23:16
and 23:20) as Japhet claims (*I–II Chronicles*, 1023).

sort. Three passages in Kings could underlie the Chronicler's paraphrase (v. 5a):

2 K 23:16aβ: *wayyiqqaḥ ʾet-hāʿăṣāmôt min-haqqĕbārîm wayyiśrōp ʿal-hammizbēaḥ wayĕṭammĕʾēhû*

2 K 23:20aα: *wayyizbaḥ ʾet-kol-kōhănê habbāmôt ʾăšer šām ʿal-hammizbĕḥôt*

2 K 23:20aβ: *wayyiśrōp ʾet-ʿaṣmôt ʾādām ʿălêhem*

Despite the mention of "priests" in 23:20aα, the use of *ŚRP* favors 23:16aβ or 23:20aβ. 23:20aβ is inextricably tied to the North, the antecedent of *ʿălêhem* being "the altars" (v. 20aα) of the bamoth-houses in the "cities of Samaria" (v. 19), but 23:16aβ is tied to the North only contextually—it follows v. 15 which deals with the North (Bethel) and has no equivalent in Chronicles. Furthermore, 2 Chron. 34:5a does *not* say that the bones burned were those of priests slain in the course of Josiah's pogrom as in 23:20;[20] v. 4b suggests, on the contrary, that they are either identical with, or a sub-group of, the deceased "sacrificers" (*hazzōbĕḥîm*) whose remains (bones) are spread out before the tombs, again reminiscent of Jer. 8:1–3. The reason for the bone-burning is not given.

2.E. JOSIAH AND THE NORTH (vv. 6–7)

ûbĕʿārê mĕnaššeh wĕʾeprayim wĕšimeʿôn wĕʿad-naptālî, bhr btyhm sābîb; wayĕnatēṣ ʾet-hammizbĕḥôt wĕʾet-hāʾăšērîm wĕhappĕsîlîm kittat lĕhēdaq wĕkol-hahammānîm giddaʿ bĕkol-ʾereṣ yiśrāʾēl, wayyāšāb lîrûšālāim;

And in the cities of Manasseh, Ephraim, and Simeon and as far as Naphtali, *bhr btyhm* round about, and he broke down the altars, and beat the asherim and the pesel-images into powder, and hewed down all the hammanim throughout all the land of Israel. And then he returned to Jerusalem.

---

[20] According to R. P. Dillard (*2 Chronicles* [WBC 15; Waco: Word, 1987] 278): "the Chronicler implies that Josiah executed the priests of Baal . . ., following the precedent set by Jehu (2 Kgs. 10) and Jehoiada (23:17 || 2 Kgs. 11:18). Josiah suits the punishment to the crime: the priests who burned sacrifices to Baal have their own bones burned on the same altars; some are even disinterred for this purpose (2 Kgs. 23:16)." But the altars (for the Baal*s*) have already been destroyed in v. 4a (the same incongruity created when 23:15a was inserted before v. 16 [see Chapter 3.D below]), and the other episodes are not really comparable: 2 Kgs. 11:18 (2 Chron. 23:17) reports only that "they slew Mattan the priest before the altars [*lipnê hammizbĕḥôt*]," already demolished, and nobody's bones are burned, while 2 Kgs. 10:18–27 reports the slaughter of Baalists in general ("the prophets of Baal, all his worshipers and all his priests" [v. 19a]) and the burning of the massebah from the House of Baal (v. 26).

This appears to be the Chronicler's version of 23:19–20, the geographical horizon of which has been enlarged to include the extreme
south (Simeon; cf. 15:9) and the extreme north (Naphtali).[21] By using
the same terminology the Chronicler implies that Josiah's pogrom
outside Judah replicated what he did in "Judah and Jerusalem"—
with the single exception of the grave-robbing and bone-burning (vv.
4bβ–5a), both very specific and unique actions which 23:16–18 locates
in the North (Bethel). Even if the Chronicler thought of Benjaminite Bethel as somehow affiliated with Judah[22] (which was the case
in, at least, the early post-Exilic period: see, e.g., Ezra 4:1–3, 6–23;
Neh. 2:20),[23] it is difficult to see why he would have moved the
scene south, even to the Jerusalem vicinity, while eliminating mention of the priestly slaughter and bone-burning in "the cities of
Samaria" (v. 20). The vocalization of *lhdq* is problematic: the LXX
suggests a nominal form (*lĕhaddāq?*) which seems preferable to MT.[24]
bhr btyhm is more difficult (cf. already LXX): commentators generally reject both the Ketib (*bāhar bāttēhem*, "their houses in the mountain[s]") and the Qere (*bĕharbōtêhem*, "with their sword") in favor of
emendation. Context and *bātê-habbāmôt* in 23:19 (an expression which
the Chronicler has not dealt with elsewhere, having no verbal equivalent to 1 Kgs. 12:26–13:34 and 2 Kgs. 17:29, 32) make *biʿēr bātêhem*,
"he destroyed their sanctuaries," an attractive alternative.[25] If so, this
would indicate that the Chronicler had before him a version of the
Kings History which contained 23:19 and presumably v. 20 as well,
a datum germane to ascertaining the compositional history of that work,
but without supportive text-critical evidence this reading (like the oth-

---

[21] For discussion see Japhet, *I–II Chronicles*, 1023–4; cf. H. G. M. Williamson,
Israel in the Books of Chronicles (Cambridge: Cambridge University, 1977) 104 n. 2.

[22] Cf. v. 9 which links Benjamin to Judah and distinct from "Manasseh and
Ephraim."

[23] For further discussion of post-monarchic Bethel see Chapter 3.B and Chapter
6.A below, and, e.g., Hermann, *History of Israel*, 315–6 (but cf. pp. 326–7); P. R.
Ackroyd, "A Subject People: Judah under Persian Rule," *The Chronicler and his Age*
(JSOTSup 101; Sheffield: JSOT, 1991) 232–3; Ahlström, *History of Ancient Palestine*,
848–9.

[24] Washburn, "Perspective and Purpose," 66, citing the non-elided *lhnq[b]*, "to
the tunnel," in the Siloam Tunnel inscription (KAI 189.2), on which cf. J. C. L.
Gibson's reading "to be (cut through)" (*Textbook of Syrian Semitic Inscriptions 1: Hebrew
and Moabite Inscriptions* [Oxford: Clarendon, 1971] 22; similarly *ANET*, 321).

[25] With, e.g., E. L. Curtis and A. A. Madsen, *A Critical and Exegetical Commentary
on the Books of Chronicles* (ICC; New York/Edinburgh: Scribner's/Edinburgh, 1910)
504–5; Williamson, *1–2 Chronicles*, 399, and Dillard, *2 Chronicles*, 273, 275; cf.
I. Seeligmann, "Indications of Editorial Alteration," *VT* 11 (1961) 202 n. 1.

ers which have been advanced)[26] is at best an educated guess; indeed, the failure to mention the priestly slaughter and bone-burning in "the cities of Samaria" (v. 20) could as well indicate that 23:19–20 were not in his *Vorlage*, the Chronicler's geographic enlargement of Josiah's actions being his own invention consistent with his *Tendenz*.

2.F. SUMMARY (v. 33a)

Finally, after the finding of "the book of the torah of Yahweh given through Moses" (34:14) in the course of "repairing and restoring the Temple" (v. 10b: a project financed by contributions from "Manasseh and Ephraim and from all Judah and Benjamin and from the inhabitants of Jerusalem" [v. 9]), its reading by Josiah to "all the men of Judah and the inhabitants of Jerusalem" (v. 30), and the covenant he makes with Yahweh to which "all who were present in Jerusalem and in Benjamin" attest (v. 32a), the Chronicler reports (v. 33a): "Josiah took away all the abominations from all the territory that belonged to the people of Israel, and made all who were in Israel serve Yahweh their god." This notice, necessitated by the Chronicler's sequencing of Josiah's reign,[27] is a summary statement which forms an *inclusio* with vv. 6–7.[28]

Several questions arise from this examination of the Chronicler's version of Josiah's reform:

(1) Why did the Chronicler locate the burning of the bones of priests in "Judah and Jerusalem" (v. 5) and not in the North (vv. 6–7)?
(2) What is the physical relationship between the altars and the hammanim which Josiah destroys in "Judah and Jerusalem," and what is the basis of this notice (v. 4a)?
(3) What is the basis for the notice that "the [remains of] sacrificers" were scattered before (their) tombs, also "in Judah and Jerusalem" (v. 4bβ)?

---

[26] Other commentators favor emendations producing "their plazas" (e.g., Myers, *II Chronicles*, 204), "their cities" (e.g., DeVries, *1–2 Chronicles*, 403), or "their ruins" (e.g., Japhet, *I–II Chronicles*, 1015, 1016, 1025).

[27] See Williamson, *1–2 Chronicles*, 403: "It represents in effect an allusion to the reforms of 2 Kgs. 23:4–20, and the tension which results with vv. 3–7 above is a further pointer to the fact that the Chronicler had no other source than Kings for this whole chapter."

[28] Cf. Dillard, *2 Chronicles*, 282, and Eslinger, "Josiah and the Torah Book," 50.

(4) Why are priests whose bones were burned apparently included among them (vv. 4bβ–5a)?

Making due allowance for the creative imagination of an author (whether ancient or modern), answering these questions requires a consideration of the sources from which the Chronicler drew his basic information about Josiah's reform. Although access to a lost independent historiographical document(s) cannot be ruled out of consideration, the answers must be sought in the account of Josiah's reform in the Kings History which certainly served as the Chronicler's primary source.

CHAPTER THREE

JOSIAH'S REFORM AS REPORTED IN KINGS (I):
BETHEL AND/OR JERUSALEM?

2 Kgs. 23:4a, 6–7, 9, and 11–12 (all actions pertaining to the Temple), and perhaps vv. 19–20 (extending the reform to the North), appear to be accounted for, one way or another, in the Chronicler's version of Josiah's reform. The portions of the reform report in Kings which appear not to be accounted for in Chronicles may prove instructive for this inquiry, much as the "curious incident of the dog in the night time"—the dog did not bark as expected—provided Sherlock Holmes the essential clue leading to the solution of a puzzling mystery.[1] Missing are:

23:4bβ:	bringing "ashes" to Bethel
23:5:	disposition of priestly personnel at the bamoth in "the cities of Judah and around Jerusalem" and of persons burning incense to Baal and various astral deities
23:8a:	removal to Jerusalem of priestly personnel from "the cities of Judah" and the defilement of the bamoth at which they had served
23:8b:	destroying the bamoth at the Gate of Joshua
23:10:	defiling the tophet in the Ben-Hinnom Valley
23:13–14:	defiling the Solomonic bamoth on the Mount of Olives
23:15:	destroying the altar at Bethel
23:16–18:	the "cemetery scene" at Bethel (and its corollary, 1 Kings 13)
23:19–20:	slaughtering priests and burning their bones in "the cities of Samaria"
23:24:	eliminating miscellaneous cultic practices in Judah

The omission of vv. 4b (the "ashes" of the Temple equipage) and 8a (the priests who are reassigned to the Temple) might be due to the fact that they both deal with matters pertaining to the Temple, but an explanation for the other omissions is not self-evident from the Chronicler's account itself or from his historiographical methodology generally. Much of the missing material deals with the same themes as the exegetical questions arising from the study of 2 Chron. 34:4–5 in the preceding chapter: Bethel; cemeteries and other locales

---

[1] From A. C. Doyle's "Silver Blaze," in *The Memoirs of Sherlock Holmes.*

with chthonic associations, and the desecrating of tombs; slaughtering priests; and bone-burning. These curiosities may prove akin to
Holmes's suspiciously silent dog.[2]

3.A. THE CEMETERIES OF BETHEL AND JERUSALEM

2 Kgs. 23:15–18 give the impression that the tombs at Bethel ran-
sacked by Josiah's agents were close to the sanctuary with the altar
upon which their osteal contents were burned.[3] This is problematic:
in view of the cultic contamination associated with human remains
in Israelite thought, IA tombs typically were outside the city walls
and at a distance from sanctuaries to prevent contamination of the
sacred realm.[4] No IA tombs have been found at Bethel (mod. Beitin),
but "numerous" rock-cut tombs, "mostly" of Hellenistic-Roman date,
were found in the valley south and southwest of the site.[5]

---

[2] Previous studies generally have found Chronicles unhelpful in this regard: cf.,
e.g., Hoffmann, *Reformen*, 254–9; H. Spieckermann, *Juda unter Assur in der Sargonidenzeit*
(FRLANT 129; Göttingen: Vandenhoeck & Ruprecht, 1982) 30–41; Eynikel, *Reform
of King Josiah*, 339–41.

[3] Thus, e.g., P. H. Vaughan's observation (*The Meaning of "bāmâ" in the Old Testament: A Study of Etymological, Textual, and Archaeological Evidence* [SOTSM 3; Cambridge: Cambridge University, 1974] 68 n. 4) that although the location of the
tombs is not stated, "the most natural interpretation" is that they were "in the
immediate vicinity" of the sanctuary.

[4] See D. P. Wright, *The Disposal of Impurity: Elimination Rites in the Bible and in Hittite and Mesopotamian Literatures* (SBLDS 101; Atlanta: Scholars, 1987) ch. 5, pp. 196–9,
and pp. 279–89, and *idem*, in *ABD* (1992) 6.729–41 (especially pp. 730–1); cf. also
idem, "The Spectrum of Priestly Impurity," *Priesthood and Cult in Ancient Israel* (ed. by
G. A. Anderson and S. M. Olyan; JSOTSup 125; Sheffield: JSOT, 1991) 150–81.
For a wider, anthropological perspective see, e.g., M. Douglas, *Purity and Danger: An
Analysis of Concepts of Population and Taboo* (2nd edn.; London: Routledge & Kegan
Paul, 1969) 29–40; V. Turner, "Dead and the Dead in the Pilgrimage Process,"
Religious Encounters with Death (ed. by F. Reynolds and E. Waugh; University Park:
Pennsylvania State University, 1977) 24–39. That Judahite kings evidently were
buried in the City of David and (later) elsewhere "within the bounds of the city"
is an exception to this rule, probably due to local political rather than strictly religious considerations: for references and discussion see Wright, *Disposal*, 117–22 (quotation from p. 119); cf. S. Yeivin, "The Sepulchres of the Kings of the House of
David," *JNES* 7 (1948) 30–45, and the works cited in n. 21 below. It is probably
irrelevant to the question of the Bethel tombs since Bethel, unlike Jerusalem, was
not the political capital of the state; furthermore, it is inconceivable that the defilement of *royal* tombs and burning deceased northern *kings* would be mentioned so
anonymously, given the general animus of the KH for (North-)Israel.

[5] See W. F. Albright, in J. L. Kelso *et al.*, *The Excavation of Bethel (1934–1960)*

Virtually nothing is known about the Bethel sanctuary, including its location. Some commentators, guided by Gen. 12:8, believe that it was on Burj Beitin, a hill less than a mile southeast of the site.[6] While this possibility cannot be ruled out, the matter is not so easily resolved. Biblically-preserved traditions (cf. Gen. 12:8–9; Gen. 28:19 and Josh. 16:1–3; Josh. 18:12–13 and Judg. 1:22, and Gen. 35:6–7) seem to identify (perhaps sequentially) *two* sacred places at Bethel:[7] one somewhere between Bethel and Ai (presumably et-Tell, 2 miles east of Beitin) and one inside the city of Bethel itself. The man-of-god pericope and its larger literary context presume that the sanctuary was "in" (*B*) Bethel (1 Kgs. 12:29, 33; 13:4, 11, 32), as was the old prophet's residence (13:11, 25). Amos's eye-witness testimony (9:1) mentions an altar, and also "capitals" (*kaptorîm*) and "thresholds" (*sippîm*), suggestive of a sanctuary complex of some architectural substance; its proximity to Jerusalem and the circumstances which reportedly prompted its establishment (1 Kgs. 12:26–32) make it reasonable to suppose that it would have resembled Solomon's Temple to some extent.

The existing archaeological record at Bethel (excavation was done at various loci inside the ancient city area) contains nothing relevant to this question, and the principal excavator cautions what "until the temple is found it is not wise for a serious historian to speculate about it."[8] This advice can be tempered now by the discovery of a major IA sanctuary at Dan (Area T): a large stepped stone platform (originally c. 7 m. × 18 m., later enlarged to c. 18 m. × 19 m.) in a paved courtyard and flanked by various buildings, one of which contained objects (including two iron shovels and a jar filled with ashes) indicative of some sort of cultic function; the platform may

---

(AASOR 39; Cambridge, MA; ASOR, 1968) 2–3; cf. W. G. Dever, in *ABD* (1992) 1.651–2.

[6] E.g., Gray, *I–II Kings*, 316); cf. N. Naaman, "Beth-aven, Bethel and Early Israelite Sanctuaries," *ZDPV* 103 (1987) 13–21.

[7] For Genesis 35 being younger than Gen. 28:10–22 see J. A. Soggin, "Jacob in Shechem and in Bethel (Genesis 35:1–7)," *"Shaʿarei Talmon": Studies in the Bible, Qumran, and the Ancient Near East Presented to Shemaryahu Talmon* (ed. by M. Fishbane and E. Tov; Winona Lake: Eisenbrauns, 1992) 195–7 ("predominantly Deuteronomic or Deuteronomistic" [p. 197]). Cf. also J. Van Seters, "Divine Encounter at Bethel (Gen 28,10–22) in Recent Literay-Critical Study of Genesis," *ZAW* 110 (1998) 503–513.

[8] Kelso in Kelso *et al.*, *Excavation of Bethel*, 51.

have supported an open-air altar or a building of some sort.[9] The
earlier building phase of the platform and precinct very likely is the
sanctuary established by Jeroboam b. Nebat; his companion sanctuary at Bethel may well have resembled this complex locationally—
the Dan *temenos* is inside the city wall—if not also architecturally. Be
this as it may, the apparent proximity of the tombs and the sanctuary in 2 Kgs. 23:16–18 is suspicious.[10]

---

[9] The Dan platform was initially thought (following the preliminary reports by
A. Biran, the principal excavator of the site) to be a bamah *qua* platform: for the
archaeological data see now A. Biran, *Biblical Dan* (Jerusalem: Israel Exploration
Society, 1994) ch. 10, with earlier literature. The possibility that it supported a cult
building of some sort (cf. the Judahite palace at Lachish) is favored by, e.g.,
Y. Shiloh, "Iron Age Sanctuaries and Cult Elements in Palestine," *Symposia Celebrating
the Seventy-Fifth Anniversary of the Founding of the American Schools of Oriental Research* (ed.
by F. M. Cross; Cambridge: ASOR, 1979) 152–3; L. E. Stager and S. R. Wolff,
"Production and Commerce in Temple Courtyards: An Olive Press in the Sacred
Precinct at Tel Dan," *BASOR* 243 (1981) 98–9; J. S. Holladay, "Religion in Israel
and Judah under the Monarchy: An Explicitly Archaeological Approach," *Ancient
Israelite Religion: Essays in Honor of Frank Moore Cross* (ed. by P. D. Miller *et al.*; Philadelphia: Fortress, 1987) 284 n. 23; A. Mazar, *Archaeology of the Land of the Bible 10,000–586
BCE* (ABRL; New York: Doubleday, 1990) 492–4, and *idem*, "Temples of the Mid-
dle and Late Bronze Ages and the Iron Age," *The Architecture of Ancient Israel from
the Prehistoric to the Persian Periods* (ed. by A. Kempinski and R. Reich; Jerusalem:
Israel Exploration Society, 1992) 184–6. Mazar reports that Biran is now of this
opinion, but this is not apparent in his latest discussions (in *ABD* [1992] 2.12–7;
Biblical Dan, passim; "Tel Dan: Biblical Texts and Archaeological Data," *Scripture and
Other Artifacts: Essays on the Bible and Archaeology in Honor of Philip J. King* [ed. by
M. D. Coogan *et al.*; Louisville: Westminster John Knox, 1994] 1–17 [but note fig.
1–13 (p. 14): an isometric drawing of the 8th-century sanctuary which depicts the
walls of a "broad-room" building atop the platform and the walls of a four-cham-
bered building abutting its rear]; "Sacred Spaces: Of Standing Stones, High Places
and Cult Objects at Tel Dan," *BARev* 24/5 [1998] especially 38–40). B. A. Nakhai
writes that the platform "may originally have supported a sanctuary," but the cap-
tion to the photograph of the structure states that it "exemplifies the traditional
understanding of a *bamah* as a raised platform where religious rites were performed"
("What's a Bamah? How Sacred Space Functioned in Ancient Israel," *BARev* 20/3
[1994] 27, 18). W. G. Dever allows for both possibilities (*Recent Archaeological Discoveries and Biblical Research* [Seattle/London: University of Washington, 1990] 133–4),
but more recently speaks of it as "no doubt a large outdoor altar" ("The Silence
of the Text: An Archaeological Commentary on 2 Kings 23," *Scripture and Other
Artifacts: Essays on the Bible and Archaeology in Honor of Philip J. King* [ed. by M. D.
Coogan *et al.*; Louisville: Westminster John Knox, 1994] 148). Finally, G. Barkay
agrees that the platform supported a building, but thinks that it was secular in
nature (probably a palace) because of its location near the edge of the mound (like
the Megiddo palaces) and because bamoth were not building-centered cult places
("The Iron Age II–III," *The Archaeology of Ancient Israel* (ed. by A. Ben-Tor; trans.
by R. Greenberg; New Haven/London: Yale University/Open University of Israel,
1992) 312).

[10] E. Bloch-Smith accepts the pericope at face-value as evidence that "kings and

A very different situation obtains with the representation of the Jerusalem cemeteries. The Wadi Kidron plays a prominent role in the reform report as the place where the cultic paraphernalia removed from the Temple complex were destroyed. 2 Kgs. 23:4a–bα reports that Josiah's agents removed from the "Temple[-room?]" (*hêkāl*) "all the equipage made for Baal and for Asherah and for all the Host of Heaven, and he burned them outside Jerusalem *běšaděmôt* of the Kidron." V. 6 adds that "he took out the asherah from the "Temple of Yahweh" [*mibbêt yhwh*] to the Wadi Kidron outside Jerusalem and he burned it at/in the Wadi Kidron and he pulverized (it) to dust; and he cast its dust upon the graves/tombs of the *běnê hāʿām*." And according to v. 12, "the altars which (were) on the roof of Ahaz's upper story[11] which the kings of Judah had made and the altars which Manasseh had made in the two courts of the House of Yahweh the king broke down, *wayyārāṣ miššām*[12] and he cast their dust (in)to the Wadi Kidron." *šaděmôt qidrôn* (cf. also Jer. 31:40) is usually understood as the "fields" of the Wadi Kidron (so, e.g., RSV and NJPSV; cf. NEB's "open country").[13] Alternatively, the reference may be to the "terraces" of the Kidron—i.e., "artificially flattened surfaces or 'fields'," suitable for agricultural (especially vineyards and orchards) or architectural uses, built onto the natural slope leading

---

prophets ... were sometimes buried near holy sites" and cites Ezek. 43:7–8 as also "pertinent" (*Judahite Burial Practices and Beliefs about the Dead* [JSOTSup 123/ASOR Monograph 7; Sheffield: JSOT, 1992] 116). Nothing is known of the burial of (North-)Israelite kings; Ezek. 43:7–8 pertains to the burial of Judahite kings (cf. n. 4 above) and illustrates that the proximity of royal tombs to the Temple were considered contaminatory in some priestly circles especially (hyperbolically?) sensitive to matters of cultic purity.

[11] For *ʿalîyâ* see Stager, "Archaeology of the Family," 16–7. The reference is probably a secondary interpolation based on 20:11 (see Chapter 5 n. 43 below).

[12] For the text-critical problem see Chapter 5 n. 35 below.

[13] See Illustration, p. xiii. "Fields" is preferred by W. H. Mare, in *ABD* (1992) 4.38. Hobbs thinks in terms of "pasture land ... suitable for grazing sheep and goats, as [the valley] is today" (*2 Kings*, 33), Wright proposes "the garden areas of the Kidron south of the Gihon spring," (*Disposal of Impurity*, 82–3 n. 9), and for J. Robinson "the place to the south of the city where the valley of Hinnom joins the Kidron may be meant" (*The Second Book of Kings* [CBC; Cambridge: Cambridge University, 1976] 219). Considering "flat plots" to be "singularly inappropriate to the ravine of the Kidron," Gray emends *šaděmôt* to *miśrěpôt*, "burning-places [lime-kilns]" (cf. LXX^L): *I–II Kings*, 730 and n. c, 732 (against M. R. Lehmann's reading *šeděmôt*, "fields of Mot/death": "A New Interpretation of the Term *šdmwt*," *VT* 3 [1953] 361–71; cf. J. S. Croatta and J. A. Soggin, "Die Bedeutung von *šdmwt* im Alten Testament," *ZAW* 64 [1962] 44–50); this possibility is viewed favorably by Burney, *Notes*, 357, and Jones, *1–2 Kings*, 618.

down from the city proper to the valley below;[14] if this is the intended meaning of the phrase, the "terraces" in question presumably did not support buildings or other such structures which would have impeded the "burning" of the cultic objects there. The issue is complicated by the newly discovered late 8th-century (presumably Hezekian) wall low on the eastern slope, a realignment of the city's defenses necessitated by its great population increase and the Assyrian threat,[15] which suggests that the intramural area (its extent north of the Gihon spring is not yet documented) probably was densely occupied by the time of Josiah's reform.

The destruction of the cultic "equipage" (*kēlîm*)[16] and the asherah described in 23:4a–bα and v. 6 recalls the destruction of the golden calf described in Ex. 32:20 and Deut. 9:21, and all are consistent with ancient Near Eastern practice known from documentary and archaeological sources (cf. 2 Kgs. 19:18a [Isa. 37:19]).[17] M. Brandes's study of the destruction of cultic and royal statuary in Mesopotamia demonstrates that as the destruction of the statue of a king symbolically represents and magically effects the destruction of the king himself and the triumph of his human adversary, destroying the statue of a deity bespeaks the elimination of that deity and its power by a stronger (and now, demonstrably, only) deity.[18] Josiah's ritual-

---

[14] Stager, "Archaeology of the Family," 5–9 (quotation from p. 5); see especially his exposition in "The Archaeology of the East Slope of Jerusalem and the Terraces of the Kidron," *JNES* 41 (1982) 111–21. Cf. Cogan-Tadmor, *II Kings*, 285. On Jer. 31:40 see W. L. Holladay, *Jeremiah 2* (Hermeneia; Minneapolis: Fortress Augsburg, 1989) 155, 200.

[15] H. Shanks, "Everything You Ever Knew about Jerusalem Is Wrong (Well, Almost)," *BARev* 25/6 (1999) 20–9. See further Chapter 7.A below.

[16] Although "vessels" is conventional (and, for all we know, may be historically correct), "equipage" better suits the semantic range of *kēlîm* in the Kings History (1 Kgs. 7:45, 48. 51; 8:4; 15:15; 2 Kgs. 12:14; 14:14; 24:13; 25:14–15), cf. Eynikel, *Reform of King Josiah*, 195. Note the desecration of a 7th–6th-century Edomite shrine at En Hatzeva, whereby 75 pottery jars, presumably used in the cultus there, were thrown into a pit and deliberately crushed by ashlars (R. Cohen and Y. Yisrael, "Smashing the Idols: Piecing together an Edomite Shrine in Judah," *BARev* 22/4 [1996] 41–51, 65).

[17] See C. T. Begg, "The Destruction of the Calf (Ex. 32,20/Deut. 9,21)," *Das Deuteronomium: Entstehung, Gestalt und Botschaft* (ed. by N. Lohfink; BETL 68; Leuven: University, 1985) 208–51 (especially pp. 211–29) and literature cited there, and subsequently *idem*, "The Destruction of the Golden Calf Revisited (Exod. 32,20/Deut 9,21)," *Deuteronomy and Deuteronomic Literature: Festschrift C. H. W. Brekelmans* (ed. by M. Vervenne and J. Lust; BETL 133; Leuven: University, 1997) 469–79.

[18] M. Brandes, "Destruction et Mutilation de Statues en Mésopotamie," *Akkadica*

istic destruction of the equipage and the asherah has the same implications. The special role of the Wadi Kidron in the elimination of
cultic objects (including Maacah's Asherah-image removed by Asa
[1 Kgs. 15:13], and the "uncleanness" in the Temple removed by
Hezekiah [2 Chron. 29:16])[19] is taken for granted—it even informs
the deuteronomic retelling of the calf's destruction[20]—but is nowhere
explained. A significant factor, perhaps more than the convenience
of proximity, surely was the presence of burials and other chthonic
associations which would have rendered it ritualistically marginal.

The archaeological record reveals that ancient Jerusalem was encircled by burial grounds. The best known are the late-monarchic Silwan tombs in the Wadi Kidron, cut into the vertical cliffs of the
steep slope of the Mount of Olives, opposite the City of David south
of the Temple Mount (see Illustration, p. xiii), and belonging to the
elite of Jerusalem.[21] The Kidron, according to 2 Kgs. 23:6, also was the

---

16 (1980) 28–41; for a Sargonic example, found in a pit in a wall surrounding an
IA vaulted tomb, see A. Rooaert, "A Neo-Assyrian Statue from Til Barsib," *Iraq*
58 (1996) 79–87. For the "vivification" of the statue see A. Berlejung, "Washing
the Mouth: The Consecration of Divine Images in Mesopotamia," *The Image and
the Book: Iconic Cults, Aniconism, and the Rise of Book Religion in Israel and the Ancient Near
East* (ed. by K. van der Toorn; CBET 21; Leuven: Peeters, 1997) 45–72, and
C. Walker and M. B. Dick, "The Induction of the Cult Image in Ancient Mesopotamia:
The Mesopotamian *mīs pî* Ritual," *Born in Heaven, Make on Earth: The Making of the
Cult Image in the Ancient Near East* (ed. by M. B. Dick; Winona Lake: Eisenbrauns,
1999) 55–121; on the relationship between deity and deity-image see also T. Jacob-
sen, "The Graven Image," *Ancient Israelite Religion: Essays in Honor of Frank Moore Cross*
(ed. by P. D. Miller *et al.*; Philadelphia: Fortress, 1987) 15–32.

[19] Both accounts probably are, to some extent, literary reflexes of the Josianic
episode.

[20] "And I threw its dust (in)to the wadi that descends out of the mountain"; the
Ex. 32:20 equivalent is "he scattered it(s dust) on the face of the water." See Begg,
"Destruction of the Calf," especially 239–40, and *idem*, "Destruction of the Golden
Calf Revisited," 474–9.

[21] See D. Ussishkin, "The Necropolis from the Time of the Kingdom of Judah
at Silwan, Jerusalem," *BA* 33 (1970) 34–46, *idem*, "A Recently Discovered Tomb
in Siloam," *Jerusalem Revealed: Archaeology in the Holy City 1968–1974* (ed. by Y. Yadin,
Jerusalem: Israel Exploration Society, 1975) 62–65, and especially *idem*, *The Village
of Silwan: The Necropolis from the Period of the Judean Kingdom* (trans. by I. Pommerantz;
Jerusalem: Israel Exploration Society/Yad Izhak Ben-Zvi, 1993); E. Y. Rahmani,
"Ancient Jerusalem's Funerary Customs and Tombs: Part Two," *BA* 44 (1981)
229–35; Mazar, *Archaeology of the Land of the Bible*, 521–6; D. Tarler and J. M. Cahill,
in *ABD* (1992) 2.64–5; W. G. Dever, "Social Structure in Palestine in the Iron II
Period on the Eve of Destruction," *The Archaeology of Society in the Holy Land* (ed. by
T. E. Levy; New York: Facts on File, 1995) 421–3. For other tombs on the Jerusalem

location of "graves/tombs of the *bĕnê hā'ām*," presumably the same
burial ground where the corpse of the prophet Uriah was con-
temptuously thrown (Jer. 26:22–23); this is usually understood as
"the burial place of the common people" (e.g., RSV, NJPSV; cf.
2 Chron. 35:5, 12, 13),[22] but the reference in Jer. 17:19 to "the Gate
of the *bĕnê hā'ām*, by which the kings of Judah enter and depart [the
Temple?]" (otherwise unknown) suggests a higher socio-economic status, perhaps "the offspring of the landed gentry," more akin to their
Silwan neighbors.[23] Since it is unlikely that any burials would have

---

perimeter cf. also A. Mazar, "Iron Age Burial Caves North of the Damascus Gate,"
IEJ 26 (1976) 1–8; G. Barkay and A. Kloner, "Jerusalem Tombs from the Days
of the First Temple," *BARev* 12/2 (1986) 22–39; and several essays in *Ancient Jerusalem
Revealed* (ed. by H. Geva; Jerusalem/Washington DC: Israel Exploration Soci-
ety/Biblical Archaeological Society, 1994): G. Barkay, "Excavations at Ketef Hinnom in Jerusalem," 85–106; *idem*, A. Kloner, and A. Mazar, "The Northern Necropolis
of Jerusalem during the First Temple Period," 119–27; A. Kloner and D. Davis,
"A Burial Cave of the Late First Temple Period on the Slope of Mount Zion,"
107–10; R. Reich, "The Ancient Burial Ground in the Mamilla Neighborhood,
Jerusalem," 119–27; M. Broshi and S. Gibson, "Excavations along the Western and
Southern Walls of the Old City of Jerusalem," especially 147–50. For further discussion see E. Bloch-Smith, "Cult of the Dead in Judah: Interpreting the Material Remains," *JBL* 111 (1992) 213–24, and especially *idem, Judahite Burial Practices*;
cf. also now I. Yezerski, "Burial-Cave Distribution and the Borders of the Kingdom of Judah toward the End of the Iron Age," *TA* 26 (1999) 253–270.

[22] Archaeological examples of field burials (most from the Second Temple era)
measuring about 1 foot deep (some in natural niches or depressions in the rock)
have been discovered at five sites around Jerusalem (in Mamilla; on the western
slope of Mt. Zion; at Ketef Hinnom; in Ramot; and near the Damascus Gate): see,
e.g., Reich, "Ancient Burial Ground in the Mamilla Neighborhood, Jerusalem,"
117; R. Reich and E. Shukron, "Jerusalem, Mamilla," *Excavations and Surveys in Israel*
14 (1994) 93–94; B. Bagatti and J. T. Milik, *Gli Scavi del "Dominus Flevit"* (Jerusalem:
Franciscan, 1958) 1.18, no. 425; Barkay, "Excavations at Ketef Hinnom in Jerusalem,"
92; J. B. Hennessy, "Preliminary Report on the Excavations at the Damascus Gate,
1961–1964," *Levant* 2 (1960) 22–27.

[23] P. J. King, *Jeremiah: An Archaeological Companion* (Louisville: Westminster/John
Knox, 1993) 128. Note the group of rock-cut tombs west of the Old City wall and
the Jaffa Gate which, on the basis of their inferior workmanship and the nature of
grave-goods, appear to have been used "by the lower classes of society" in the 8th–
6th centuries (Reich, "Ancient Burial Ground in the Mamilla Neighborhood," 113).
Dating Jer. 17:19 to the 5th century, W. L. Holladay sees *bĕnê-[h]ā'ām* as "laity" (citing 2 Chron. 35:5, 12, 13), but then is forced to understand the "kings" as "laity"
also (*Jeremiah 1* [Hermeneia; Philadelphia: Fortress, 1986] 510). The MT's *bĕnê-
[h]ā'ām* is sometimes emended to *binyāmîn*, "the Benjamin Gate" (a well-known city-
gate [37:13; 38:7] probably in the north wall: cf. E. W. Cohn, "The History of
Jerusalem's Benjaminite Gate: A Case of Interrupted Continuity?" *PEQ* 118 [1986]
138–43), but there is no text-critical evidence for doing so; R. P. Carroll accepts
the emendation, but thinks the reference is to a different gate (*Jeremiah: A Commentary* [OTL; Philadelphia: Westminster, 1986] 366). More locationally suitable would
be "the Upper Benjamin Gate in the House of Yahweh" (Jer. 20:2: *ša'ar binymin*

been made in the floor of the Kidron (especially if water flowed through it during the rainy season),[24] this cemetery must have been located further up the slopes; it is not inconceivable that it was part of—or identical with—the Silwan cemetery as L.-H. Vincent once supposed.[25] The Ben-Hinnom Valley also has sepulchral associations: it is the site of the ritual burning of children at the "tophet" which Josiah is said to have attacked (23:10: see Chapter 6.A below), and has given its name to the traditional gateway to the nether-world ("Gehenna").[26] It is usually identified with the Wadi er-Rababeh to the south and west of Jerusalem, consistent with Josh. 15:8 and 18:16 which envision the Ben-Hinnom stretching westward from En-Rogel (mod. Bir Ayyub) at the southern end of the Kidron Valley east of the city (again, see Frontispiece).[27] Post-biblical Jewish, Christian, and Moslem writers often identified it with the Kidron, and some late biblical passages (e.g., Isa. 66:24; Jer. 31:40 [5th century?];[28] Zech. 14:4–5) suggest that the two were not always sharply differentiated.[29] It may well be that the various topographical features of the immediate vicinity of Jerusalem were thought of as a single complex closely associated with the nether-world.[30]

---

hāʿelyôn ʾăšer bêbêt yhwh), but this is even more text-critically distant. Cf. the latest discussion by Lundbom, *Jeremiah 1–20*, 805.

[24] Ussishkin, *Village of Silwan*, 22, 320.

[25] *Apud ibid.*, 323.

[26] Cf. J. A. Montgomery, "The Holy City and Gehenna," *JBL* 27 (1908) 24–47; L. R. Bailey, "Gehenna: The Topography of Hell," *BA* 49 (1986) 187–91; D. F. Watson, in *ABD* (1992) 2.926–8.

[27] See D. F. Watson, in *ABD* (1992) 3.202–3.

[28] On the date see Holladay, *Jeremiah 2*, 155, 200.

[29] Older discussions of the issue are especially instructive in this regard: e.g., S. Bestwick, "Valley of Hinnom," *PEFQSt* (1881) 102–4; W. F. Birch, "The Valley of Hinnom and Zion," *PEFQSt* (1882) 55–8; P. Haupt, "Hinnom and Kidron," *JBL* 38 (1919) 45–8. Cf. the itinerary of Mark Twain's 1867 visit, described in *The Innocents Abroad* (in *The Complete Travel Books of Mark Twain* [ed. by C. Neider; Garden City: Doubleday, 1966 (originally published in 1869)] 387).

[30] As M. H. Pope envisions: "Notes on the Rephaim Texts from Ugarit," *Probative Pontificating in Ugaritic and Biblical Literature* (ed. by M. S. Smith; UBL 10; Münster: Ugarit, 1994) 191–2 (= *Essays on the Ancient Near East in Memory of Jacob Joel Finkelstein* [ed. by M. Ellis; Memoirs of the Connecticut Academy of Arts and Sciences 19; Hamden, CT: Archon, 1977] 174), and *Song of Songs* (AB 7C; Garden City: Doubleday, 1977) 574–82. The Mount of Olives also would have been part of this complex (see nn. 74 and 76 below).

3.B. Josiah and the North

2 Kgs. 23:15–20 reports that Josiah's reform included an attack on "Samaria," the territory of the defunct northern kingdom.[31] This brief account is supplemented by 1 Kings 13, the story of a portentous visit to Bethel by an anonymous man-of-god from Judah during the reign of Jeroboam b. Nebat, in the course of which Josiah's future attack on the sanctuary there is predicted. This is one of the most intriguing chapters in Kings; despite extensive scholarly analyses spanning the methodological spectrum,[32] no consensus has emerged concerning such fundamental issues as the origin, unity, and boundaries of the narrative, its genre, its relationship with its literary context, and its message or moral. Nonetheless, most commentators readily grant it a greater or lesser measure of historicity, a postulate seemingly justified by the corollary in the reform report (23:16–18);[33] the fact that the correspondences are not exact (see below) should signal caution, however. Similarly, Josiah's "northern crusade"[34] has no *a priori* claim to historicity and cannot be verified

---

[31] Knoppers favors the LXX which reads "Samaria" rather than the MT's "cities of Samaria" in 1 Kgs. 13:32 (*lectio brevior: Two Nations Under God 2*, 68 n. 44 and 211 n. 71; see also n. 43 below), but duplicates MT in 2 Kgs. 23:19.

[32] For a recent discussion of 1 Kings 13 and review of the extensive scholarly literature see Knoppers, *Two Nations Under God 2*, ch. 3. Add now D. W. Van Winkle, "1 Kings xii 25–xiii 34: Jeroboam's Cultic Innovations and the Man of God from Judah," *VT* 46 (1996) 101–14; B. Herr, "Der wahre bezeugt seine Botschaft mit dem Tod: Ein Versuch zu 1 Kön 13," *BZ* 41 (1997) 69–78; J. K. Mead, "Kings and Prophets, Donkeys and Lions: Dramatic shape and Deuteronomistic Rhetoric in 1 Kings xiii," *VT* 49 (1999) 191–205; J. Van Seters, "On Reading the Story of the Man of God from Judah in 1 Kings 13," *The Labour of Reading: Desire, Alienation, and Biblical Interpretation* (ed. by F. C. Black *et al.*; SBL Semeia Studies 36; Atlanta: Scholars, 1999) 225–34, and *idem*, "The Deuteronomistic History: Can It Avoid Death by Redaction?" *The Future of the "Deuteronomistic History"* (ed. by T. Römer; BETL 147; Leuven: University, 2000) 213–22.

[33] Thus, e.g., U. Simon, concludes his largely literary study ("I Kings 13: A Prophetic Sign—Denial and Persistence," *HUCA* 47 [1976] 117): "The ancient word of the Lord, obliterated except for the marker of the sepulcher of the man of god, reappeared and broke through into history in its full power [in the events reported in 2 Kgs. 23:15–20]." Among the commentaries, e.g., Cogan-Tadmor simply take it for granted that "Josiah fulfilled an ancient prophecy, which an unnamed man of God had pronounced against Jeroboam's altar" (*II Kings*, 299–300), while Gray considers 23:16–20 to be a later interpolation, "notwithstanding the historicity of the events" (*I–II Kings*, 714). Halpern regards 1 Kings 13 to be a fiction ("literally untrue"; "it details what might, not what must, have been") designed to justify Josiah's eradication of the northern priests (*First Historians*, 249–54).

[34] So characterized by Knoppers, *Two Nations Under God 2*, 71 *et passim*.

independently: the sum of the available data favors no more than an encroachment by Judah into Benjamin during this period, in the course of which some sort of interference with the Bethel cult by Josiah might have been undertaken[35]—doubtless to the consternation of those who wished for more (possibly including Zephaniah,[36] Jeremiah,[37] and even the king and the elements at court responsible for the reform program).[38] Yet it is not an absolute historical certainty

---

[35] Against the widely-held notion of an extensive Josianic "empire"—an extreme form is Cross's view that Josiah "attempted to restore the kingdom or empire of David in all detail" (*Canaanite Myth and Hebrew Epic*, 283)—see especially N. Naaman, "The Kingdom of Judah under Josiah," *TA* 18 (1991) 3–71, and now R. Kletter, "Pots and Politics: Material Remains of Late Iron Age Judah in Relation to its Political Borders," *BASOR* 314 (1999) 19–54 (especially pp. 27, 40–3), and Yezerski, "Burial-Cave Distribution," 253–270; cf. also, e.g., Lohfink, "Recent Discussion," 39 and n. 16 (= *Deuteronomium*, 26–7 and n. 16); W. B. Barrick, "On the Meaning of *bêt-hab/bāmôt* and *bātê-habbāmôt* and the Composition of the of the Kings History," *JBL* 115 (1996) 630–1 n. 42; I. Finkelstein and N. A. Silberman, *The Bible Unearthed: Archaeology's New Vision of Ancient Israel and the Origin of its Sacred Texts* (New York/London/Toronto/Sydney/Singapore: Free, 2001) Appendix F. Similarly, among recent historical reconstructions, e.g., Miller-Hayes, *History of Ancient Judah and Israel*, 401; Ahlström, *History of Ancient Palestine*, 763–6 and accompanying notes. Note the evolution of Bright's thinking on the subject in his *History* (despite his continued confidence in 2 Chron. 34:6): in the 1959 edition Josiah "moved to take possession of the provinces into which Assyria had divided the territory of the northern kingdom" (p. 295); in the 1972 edition Josiah "moved to take possession of the provinces of Samaria and Megiddo (and probably Gilead as well) into which Assyria had divided the territory of northern Israel" (p. 316); and in the 1981 edition he controlled "appreciable portions of northern Israel [but t]he extent of Josiah's annexations is, however, uncertain. . . . Some believe that he gained control of the provinces of Megiddo (Galilee) and Gilead as well [b]ut we cannot be certain" (p. 317). See further n. 39 below.

[36] Zeph. 2:4–15: see D. L. Christensen, "Zephaniah 2:4–15: A Theological Basis for Josiah's Program of Political Expansion," *CBQ* 46 (1984) 669–82, and M. A. Sweeney, "A Form Critical Reassessment of the Book of Zephaniah," *CBQ* 53 (1991) 388–408; but cf. R. Haak, "Zephaniah's Oracles against the Nations" (unpublished paper presented to the Chicago Society of Biblical Research, 2 February 1992), followed by A. Berlin, *Zephaniah* (AB 25A; New York: Doubleday, 1994) 117–24.

[37] See, e.g., N. Lohfink, "Der junge Jeremia als Propagandist und Poet: Zum Grundstock von Jer 30–31," *Le Livre du Jérémie: Le Prophète et son Milieu; Les Oracles et leurs Transmission* (ed. by P.-M. Bogaert; BETL 54; Leuven: University, 1981) 351–68; M. A. Sweeney, "Jeremiah 30–31 and King Josiah's Program of National Restoration and Religious Reform," *ZAW* 108 (1996) 569–83. For Isa. 11:11–16 from this perspective see M. A. Sweeney, "Jesse's New Shoot in Isaiah 11: A Josianic Reading of the Prophet Isaiah," *A Gift of God in Due Season: Essays on Scripture and Community in Honor of James A. Sanders* (ed. by R. D. Weis and D. M. Carr; JSOT-Sup 225; Sheffield: Sheffield Academic, 1996) 103–18 (especially pp. 110–11); but cf. H. G. M. Williamson, "Isaiah xi 11–16 and the Redaction of Isaiah i–xii," *VTSup* 61 (1995) 343–57.

[38] Wishful-thinking, even by the powerful, seldom corresponds to historical

that Bethel was not, in fact, already part of Judah by this time[39] as
it was during the Persian era.[40] Both accounts are first of all literary
phenomena, however, and the incongruities surely are due, at least
in part, to their compositional history which must be taken into
account before passing judgment on the historical content of either.

---

reality. Even if more than a modest encroachment did occur, however, v. 15 will
not bear R. E. Clements's conclusion of that "the destruction of the sanctuary at
Bethel . . . was the *primary target* of Josiah's cultic repression" ("The Deuteronomic
Law of Centralisation and the Catastrophe of 587 BCE," *After the Exile: Essays in
Honour of Rex Mason* [ed. by J. Barton and D. J. Reimer; Macon: Mercer Univer-
sity, 1996] 12 [emphasis supplied]).

[39] A geographical argument for moving the Josianic border north of Bethel (cf.
23:8a) is advanced by G. Galil, "Geba'-Ephraim and the Northern Boundary of
Judah in the Days of Josiah," *RB* 100 (1993) 358–67; cf. H. Brodsky, *ABD* (1992)
1.710–2. Noting that the 46 Judahite fortified cities reported taken by Sennacherib
during Hezekiah's reign "is a very large number for Judah alone," and the Assyrian practice of ceding neighboring territory as a "means of rewarding vassals who
had remained faithful when those around them were in revolt," T. H. Robinson
speculates that "perhaps the old territory of Benjamin, including the Bethel and
Gibeah districts, was handed over to Ahaz, and incorporated in the kingdom of
Judah" (*A History of Israel* [Oxford: Clarendon, 1932] 380; cf. 421; similarly E. W.
Todd, "The Reforms of Hezekiah and Josiah," *SJT* 9 [1965] 288–9); for a correlation of the 46 fortified cities with the archaeological record (cf. Isa. 10:28–32) see
B. Halpern, "Jerusalem and the Lineages in the Seventh Century BCE: Kinship
and the Rise of Individual Moral Liability," *Law and Ideology in Monarchic Israel* (ed.
by B. Halpern and D. W. Hobson; JSOTSup 124; Sheffield: JSOT, 1991) 34–41,
and cf. Chapter 7 n. 8 below. By Robinson's hypothesis, Benjamin would have
been lost under Hezekiah (along with his western holdings) after 701, but perhaps
could have been restored at some point during Manasseh's reign (as the western
holdings evidently were) to reward another loyal vassal. All of this is plausible, but
lacks concrete evidential support (except, perhaps, the *lmlk*-jar handle—probably
"Hezekian" horizon—found at Bethel: see H. Eshel, "A *lmlk* Stamp from Beth-El,"
IEJ 39 [1989] 60–2). A new piece of evidence now complicates matters: a collection of 7th-century bullae related to a tax-collecting system operating during Josiah's
reign includes one dated to his 10th regnal year—*before* his reform began according to either Kings or Chronicles—which originally had labeled revenues received
from "Arubboth," presumably the place of that name which reputedly headquartered one of Solomon's district provisioners south of Tanaak (1 Kgs. 4:10) and con-
siderably north of Bethel: see M. Heltzer, "Some Questions Concerning the Economic
Policy of Josiah, King of Judah," *IEJ* 50 (2000) 105–8 (especially pp. 106, 108).
Since this datum does not easily fit *any* prevailing reconstruction of Josiah's northern interests, the possibility must be considered that the reference is to an otherwise unknown location in Judah resettled by refugees from Arubboth in the north
(cf. B. Oded's suggestion that the Rumah near Hebron in Judah [reading "Rumah"
for MT's "Dumah" in Josh. 15:32 with nearly all other textual witnesses: cf.
Y. Elitzur, Rumah in Judah, *IEJ* 44 (1994) 123–8] had been settled by residents
of the Galilean Rumah displaced in the demographic disruption resulting from the
Assyrian conquest of that region of [North-]Israel: "II Kings 17: Between History
and Polemic," *Jewish History* 2/2 [1987] 42).

[40] For Bethel as part of Judah in (at least) the early post-Exilic period see Chapter 2 n. 23 above.

2 Kgs. 23:19, with the same distinctive grammatical structure as the secondary v. 24a (*wĕgam* + Object + Verb + Subject [*yōʾšiyāhû*]), reports Josiah's attack on "the bamoth-houses [*bātê-habbāmôt*] in the cities of Samaria, which the kings of (North-)Israel had made."[41] Josiah's treatment of these installations is said to have replicated what he had done at Bethel, an allusion to 23:16–18 which, in turn, makes explicit reference to the story in 1 Kgs. 13:1–32.[42] 23:20a locates the slaughter "upon the altars" of the bamoth-houses attacked in v. 19. Taken together, 23:19–20 fulfill "the word of Yahweh . . . against all the bamoth-houses in the cities of Samaria" as recapitulated by the old Bethel prophet in 13:32. But the old prophet misrepresents the actual words of the man-of-god which do not mention these installations and envision the bamoth-priests being slaughtered upon the altar at Bethel where they officiated (13:2):

> *wayyiqrāʾ ʿal-hammizbēaḥ bidbar yhwh wayyōʾmer mizbēaḥ mizbēaḥ koh ʾāmar*
> *yhwh, hinnēh-bēn nôlād lĕbêt-dāwid yōʾšiyāhû šĕmô wĕzābaḥ ʿāleykā ʾet-kōhānê*
> *habbāmôt hammaqṭirîm ʿāleykā weʿaṣmôt ʾādām yiśrĕpû ʿāleykā.*

The old prophet enlarges the scope of this prediction to no purpose within the story[43] or the inventory of Jeroboam's cultic establishment to which it is appended (12:26–32). The notice in 23:19b that Josiah did to the bamoth-houses "all that he had done at Bethel" seems a lame (secondary?) attempt to reconcile vv. 19–20 with vv. 16–18 where human bones removed from nearby tombs were burned but with no report of slaughtering priests as foretold by the man-of-god. These discrepancies in the fulfillment of a patently *vaticinium ex eventum* prediction are all the more remarkable in view of the

---

[41] This identification conflicts with 17:29 which claims that these bamoth-houses had been "made" by "the Samarians" (*šōmrōnîm*), an indication that the passages probably belong to different compositional strata: see Barrick, "On the Meaning of *bêt-hab/bāmôt*," 627–36.

[42] Underscored by the longer LXX version of v. 16 (see Section 3.F below).

[43] The synchronic explanation—that the old prophet's "ability to amplify the man of God's revelation attest[s] that he has now become God's agent in Bethel—recently advanced by P. T. Reis ("Vindicating God: Another Look at 1 Kings xiii," *VT* 44 [1994] 385) is unconvincing and does not take into account the high estimation of the man-of-god's original pronouncement in 23:16–18. Note also that *bêt bāmôt* in 12:31a is a sing. expression referring to the sanctuary at Bethel: see Barrick, "On the Meaning of *bêt-hab/bāmôt*," especially 623–6, and cf. also Provan, *1–2 Kings*, 110. It is conceivable that a secondary (mis)interpretation could have produced *batê-hab-bamôt* in 13:32, but "the cities of Samaria" cannot be similarly explained (although Knoppers rejects *bĕʿarê*, following the LXX, for "maximum differentiation" [*Two Nations Under God 2*, 50 E; see also n. 31 above]).

importance of the prophecy/fulfillment schema in the KH as a whole.[44] It is reasonable to suppose that they are due to the compositional history of this material.

The words of the man-of-god to the altar predict that Josiah "will sacrifice/slaughter upon you the bamoth-priests who burn incense[45] upon you and human bones will be burned upon you" (1 Kgs. 13:2). This overloaded statement is ambiguous: are the "human bones" (*ʿaṣmôt ʾādām*) those of the slaughtered priests (in which case why not use *ʿaṣmôtêhem* to avoid the ambiguity?) or of some other persons? The bones burnt in 2 Kgs. 23:16, seemingly the narrative fulfillment of the prediction, are those taken from the nearby tombs, and there is no mention at all of priests being slain at Bethel; the omission of this element of the prediction suggests that it may be a secondary literary embellishment rather than a factual datum (see Section B.3 below).[46] 23:20a presents the same ambiguity, but this interpretation of *ʿaṣmôt ʾādām* cannot be applied there without imagining a cemetery near each bamoth-house or the transport of bones from the Bethel tombs to each of the cities of Samaria for this purpose,[47] exegetical contrivances which are hard to take seriously. It seems much more likely that the phrase in 23:20a refers to the bones of the priests slaughtered in "the cities of Samaria," the author-compiler redactionally identifying the "human bones" in 13:2 with the

---

[44] See classically G. von Rad, "The Deuteronomic Theology of History in I and II Kings," *The Problem of the Hexateuch and Other Essays* (trans. by E. W. T. Dicken; New York: Harper & Row, 1966) 205–21 (= *Deuteronomium-Studien* [FRLANT 40; Göttingen: Vandenhoeck & Ruprecht, 1947] 52–64). Cf. N. Wyatt, "The Old Testament Historiography of the Exilic Period," *Studia Theologica* 33 (1979) especially 56–62.

[45] Although the burning of *incense* is not implied by *QṬR* in Piel, the Hiphil sometimes does have that implication: for discussion see D. Edelman, "The Meaning of *qiṭṭer*," *VT* 35 (1985) 395–404, and R. E. Clements, in *TWAT* (1990) 7.10–8.

[46] M. Noth considered the bone-burning primary in v. 2 (*Könige 1* [BKAT 9/1; Neukirchen-Vluyn: Neukirchener, 1968] 1.293–4), while Gray maintains that the slaughter of priests in 23:20 was "introduced as an afterthought ... under the influence of [13:2]," the "original tradition was reshaped in the light of later events" (*I–II Kings*, 326).

[47] M. Haran, *Temples and Temple Service in Ancient Israel* (Oxford: Oxford University, 1978) 138–9 and n. 8, followed by R. L. Cohn, "Literary Technique in the Jeroboam Narrative," *ZAW* 97 (1985) 32 n. 17. The inherent unlikelihood of such a locational coincidence is compounded by Haran's belief that a bamah was "essentially just a large altar" in an architecturally ephemeral open-air precinct (pp. 18–25). For the bamah phenomenon see Chapter 5.D–E and Chapter 9 below.

slaughtered Bethel priests and extending the slaughter to the other sanctuaries in Samaria (see further below).

The only other occurrence of the phrase *ʿaṣmôt ʾādām* in Kings (or anywhere else in the MT) is in 2 Kgs. 23:14b: *wayĕmallēʾ ʾet-meqômam ʿaṣmôt ʾādām*. Since this passage contains none of the suspiciously stereotypical rhetoric of v. 14a, nor can it be seen as a reflex of v. 16—"filling" (*MLʾ*) is an unlikely euphemism for "burning" (*ŚRP*)—it may well be an historical recollection.[48] Compositionally, the highly unusual phrase suggests that this passage may form a *Wiederaufnahme* bracket with v. 20aβ:[49]

23:14b
wayĕmallēʾ ʾet-meqômām ʿaṣmôt ʾădām

23:20aβ
wayyiśrōp ʾet-ʿaṣmôt ʾādām ʿălêhem

The antecedent of *ʿălêhem* in v. 20aβ is *hammizbĕḥôt* in v. 20aα which presupposes the bamoth-houses in v. 19, a passage which is stylistically set apart from what precedes it by *wĕgam* and probably belongs to a secondary compositional stratum. In other words, vv. 19–20a is a literary unit added secondarily to the reform report and extending Josiah's actions to "the bamoth-houses in the cities of Samaria," corresponding to the addition of the slaughtering of priests to the man-of-god's prediction in 1 Kgs. 13:2 and its geographic extension by the old prophet from Bethel in 13:32, and all undoubtedly belonging to the same edition of the KH. Paired with v. 14b, this unit

---

[48] According to Eynikel (*Reform of King Josiah*, 271–2 [quotation from p. 272]): "V. 14b is special because it has little in common with other verses in the dtr history. It probably contains an eye-witness history." See further Chapter 3.F and Chapter 8 below.

[49] On the *Wiederaufnahme* technique see C. Kuhl, "Die 'Wiederaufnahme': Eine literarkritisches Prinzip?" *ZAW* 64 (1952) 1–11; J. Trebolle-Barerra, "Redaction, Recension, and Midrash in the Books of Kings," *BIOSCS* 15 (1982) 12–35; B. O. Long, "Framing Repetitions in Biblical Historiography," *JBL* 106 (1987) 385–99; M. Anbar, "La 'Reprise'," *VT* 38 (1988) 385–98; S. Talmon, "The Presentation of Synchroneity and Simultaneity in Biblical Narrative," *Literary Studies in the Hebrew Bible: Form and Content—Collected Studies* (Leiden/Jerusalem: Brill/Magnes, 1993) 112–33 (= *Studies in Hebrew Narrative Art throughout the Ages* [ed. by J. Heinemann and S. Werses; ScrHier 27; Jerusalem: Magnes, 1978] 9–26); B. Peckham, "Writing and Editing," *Fortunate the Eyes that See: Essays in Honor of David Noel Freedman in Celebration of his Seventieth Birthday* (ed. by A. B. Beck *et al.*; Grand Rapids/Cambridge, UK: Eerdmans, 1995) especially 368–70.

encloses the "cemetery scene" (vv. 16–18) which is related in some way to an earlier version of 13:1–32 which did not include the priestly slaughter or the geographic expansion.

3.C. SLAUGHTERING PRIESTS AT BETHEL

The story of the man-of-god's visit to Bethel (1 Kgs. 12:33–13:32) is joined to the account of Jeroboam's establishment of the official Yahweh cultus of (North-)Israel (12:26–32) by means of the *Wiederaufnahme* grafting technique, the brackets being 12:30a + 31 and 13:33–34:[50]

12:30a + 31
wayĕhî haddābār hazzeh lĕḥaṭṭāʾt, . . . wayyaʿaś ʾet-bêt bāmôt wayyaʿaś kōhānîm miqṣôt hāʿām ʾăšer loʾ-hāyû mibbĕnê lêwî

13:33–34
ʾaḥar haddābār hazzeh lōʾ-šāb yārobʿām middarkô hārāʿâ, wayyāšāb wayyaʿaś miqṣôt hāʿām kōhănê bāmôt heḥāpēṣ yĕmalleʾ ʾet-yādô wîhî kōhănê bāmôt; wayĕhî baddābār hazzeh lĕḥaṭṭaʾt bêt yārobʿām, ûlĕhakḥîd ûlĕhašmîd meʿal pĕnê hāʾădāmâ

The linguistic resemblance is obvious but so too are the differences in content: the "sin" associated with cultic statuary in 12:28–30 is now associated with cultic personnel (13:33b); the "priests" of 12:31a have become "bamoth-priests in 13:33bβ; and their identification as "those who were not Levites" (12:31b) has become an explanatory note implying that their priestly status had no sacerdotal legitimacy whatever (13:33b). In each case the item in the opening bracket is repeated and reinterpreted in the closing bracket. This preoccupation with the northern priesthood to the exclusion of all other aspects of Jeroboam's cultic establishment reported in 12:26–32 (notably the calf-images) is shared by the Chronicler in his one reference to this episode (2 Chron. 11:13–17); it is even clearer in the speech which he puts in the mouth of Abijah (13:4b–12):[51]

---

[50] Cf. recently McKenzie, *Trouble with Kings*, 51–2, Knoppers, *Two Nations Under God 2*, 49–55; Van Seters, "Deuteronomistic History," 214–6.

[51] The translation essentially follows M. A. Throntveit, *When Kings Speak: Royal Speech and Royal Prayer in Chronicles* (SBLD 93; Atlanta: Scholars, 1987) 36–8 (quotation from p. 37).

... Have you not driven out the priests the sons of Aaron, (and the Levites,) and made priests for yourselves from the people of the land?[52] Whoever comes to 'fill his hand' with a young bull or seven rams becomes a priest of what are no gods. But as for us, Yahweh is our god and we have not forsaken him; and priests minister to Yahweh who are sons of Aaron (and the Levites are in their service), for they offer to Yahweh burnt offerings ... for we keep the charge of Yahweh our god, but you have forsaken it. Behold, our god is with us at our head and his priests with the signal trumpets to sound the battle call against you. ...

The closing bracket, 1 Kgs. 13:33–34, is certainly compatible with the post-Exilic realities that underlie the Chronicler's concerns, and need not be attributed to whatever pre-Exilic realities that may have informed a putative "Josianic" author-compiler of Kings. That those post-Exilic realities included claims of certain northerners for membership in the religious community of Yehud on the grounds that they had been good Yahwists since the days of Esarhaddon is clear from Ezra 4:1–3, claims which Abijah's speech in Chronicles and the devaluation of Jeroboam's bamoth-priests in 1 Kgs. 13:33–34 alike[53] effectively undermine.

The history of Bethel, although shadowy, is instructive in this regard. There is no literary evidence that Bethel was destroyed by the Assyrians, although Hos. 10:5–6, 15, might reflect the despoiling of its sanctuary (by Shalmaneser V in 725?).[54] 2 Kgs. 17:26–28

---

[52] Cf. LXX's *ek tou laou tēs gēs*; MT reads *kĕ'ammê hā'ărāṣôt*: see Throntveit, *When Kings Speak*, 37 and n. 73, and cf. the commentaries.

[53] 12:33 is the narrative transition into the story (note the use of *QTR* in Hiphil here as in 13:1b, 2b) and thus is part of the addition: see, e.g., Dietrich, *Prophetie und Geschichte*, 116, McKenzie, *Trouble with Kings*, 51–2; Knoppers, *Two Nations Under God 2*, 29; Eynikel, *Reform of King Josiah*, 274–8; and cf., somewhat differently, Provan, *Hezekiah*, 78–81, and Van Seters, "Deuteronomistic History," 214–6. As 13:33b pejoratively reinterprets Jeroboam's priests, 12:33a devalues his festival (cf. 12:32) by making it his own invention without any sacral legitimacy. Note *BD'*, generally considered "late" terminology (e.g., A. Rofé, "Classes of the Prophetical Stories: Didactic Legenda and Parable," *Studies on Prophecy* [VTSup 26; Leiden: Brill, 1974] 163; McKenzie, *Trouble with Kings*, 52 and n. 26). As a narrative transition, v. 33a transforms v. 32a into a reference to Jeroboam's ceremonial role during one occurrence of his festival; v. 33b (and 13:1b) move the reader to the exact moment in the course of the ritual when the man-of-god interrupted the proceedings. Despite this logical progression only 12:33b (with 13:1b) is needed to provide a satisfactory transition, in which case 12:33a and 12:33b would belong to different compositional strata.

[54] See J. H. Hayes and J. K. Kuan, "The Final Years of Samaria (730–720

presupposes a temporary interruption of the cultus there, but the historical basis of this story cannot be taken for granted. The archaeological record at Beitin, unfortunately too imperfectly known to bear much weight in historical speculation, is nonetheless suggestive. There is practically no physical evidence to support the excavators' claim of an 8th-century destruction.[55] The evidence does suggest that Bethel, like other sites in Benjamin, may also have escaped destruction by the Babylonians in the early 6th century[56] and, like the region generally, may have enjoyed "relative prosperity" by the end of that century;[57] there are hints (especially Zech. 7:1–7; cf. Hag. 2:10–14) that a recognized public Yahweh cultus of some sort was conducted there during this period.[58] A destruction c. 480, for reasons (international or internecine) not apparent in the available data, seems certain. Bethel revived during the Hellenistic period, and its legendary sanctity (probably reinforced by a revived Yahweh cultus) continued

---

BC)," *Bib* 72 (1991) 163–4. 176–7; cf. also M. Cogan, *Imperialism and Religion: Assyria, Judah and Israel in the Eighth and Seventh Centuries BCE* (SBLM 19; Missoula: Scholars, 1974) 104–5.

[55] See J. L. Kelso *et al.*, *The Excavation of Bethel (1934–1960)*, 37–8, 51 (reversing the position taken by Kelso in *IDB* [1962] 1.392); see the critique of this claim by Eshel, "*lmlk* Stamp from Beth-El," 61–2 n. 11.

[56] See L. A. Sinclair, in Kelso *et al.*, *Excavation of Bethel*, 70–6; E. Stern, *The Material Culture of the Land of the Bible in the Persian Period, 538–332 BC* (Jerusalem/Warminster: Israel Exploration Society/Aris & Phillips, 1982) 229, 253–4; W. G. Dever, in *ABD* (1992) 1.651; O. Lipschits, "The History of the Benjamin Region under Babylonian Rule," *TA* 26 (1999) 155–90. According to Barkey, "areas that capitulated to the Babylonians before the fall of Jerusalem were spared destruction, especially in the land of Benjamin"; he cites Gibeon, Tell en-Nasbeh/Mizpah?, and Bethel ("Iron Age II–III," 372). For a different reading of the archaeological record, however, see P. W. Lapp, "The Pottery of Palestine in the Persian Period," *Archäologie und Altes Testament: Festschrift für Kurt Galling* (ed. by A. Kuschke and E. Kutsch; Tübingen: Mohr, 1970) especially 181 n. 14, and J. S. Holladay's ceramic analysis in W. G. Dever, "Archaeological Methods and Results: A Review of Two Recent Publications," *Or* 40 (1971) 469.

[57] Stern, *Material Culture*, 229; cf. now Lipschits, "History of the Benjamin Region," 155–90.

[58] Nearby Mizpah (probably Tell en-Nasbeh), which had replaced Jerusalem as the seat of government, may also have had a Yahweh sanctuary during part of this period; cf. Jer. 40:6–41:18 (note that 41:5 does not require that the pilgrim's destination was Jerusalem). Cf. also the roles of Bethel and Mizpah in Judges 20–21. On all of this material see now J. Blenkinsopp, "The Judaean Priesthood during the Neo-Babylonian and Achaemenid Periods: A Hypothetical Reconstruction," *CBQ* 60 (1998) 25–43 (especially pp. 26–34); cf. more traditionally S. Japhet, "The Temple in the Restoration Period: Reality and Ideology," *Union Seminary Quarterly Review* 44 (1991) 195–251.

to be a political and theological factor to be reckoned with well into the Maccabean era.[59] The Chronicler's historiographical attack on the legitimacy of northern priests is consistent with this chronology, as would be an attack on the Bethel sanctuary by an Exilic or post-Exilic author-compiler of Kings. For the Jerusalemite monopolists, northern claims to a share in the cultic "franchise" of Yahwism, and in particular those of Bethel (with impeccable Patriarchal credentials, arguably more impressive than their own), clearly remained as much a canker after the Temple's destruction as it presumably was before—and with the ruined Temple to be restored (after a hiatus) on a much more modest scale, perhaps more so.

If the man-of-god's prediction in 1 Kgs. 13:2 reflects some action of Josiah, actual or otherwise, reflected however distantly in 2 Kgs. 23:16–18, it must be the burning of disinterred human bones on the altar which is the only action mentioned there. 13:2bα, however, also mentions the slaughter of priests on the altar: *wĕzābaḥ ʿāleykā ʾet-kōhănê habbāmôt hammaqṭirîm ʿāleykā*. These priests are said to perform the same ritual acts upon the Bethel altar which Jeroboam is performing when the prediction is made: *QṬR*, in Hiphil (12:33; 13:1b), common in Chronicles but rare in Kings which characteristically uses the Piel (note especially 2 Kgs. 23:8a, plainly from a "Josianic" edition of the Kings History [conventionally Dtr¹]).[60] They are the "bamoth-priests" (*kōhănê habbāmôt*) "made" by Jeroboam and stationed by him in Bethel before the episode (12:31, 32b) and "made" by him again after it (13:33). Their presence in the prediction is thus explicable entirely on the basis of the material which frames the pericope and need not be attributed to an actual action by Josiah. That v. 2bβ may be a secondary addition to the words of the man-of-god (a reflex of the destruction of the Jerusalem Temple [cf. Lam.

---

[59] See, e.g., the rewriting of Gen. 35:1–15 in Jubilees 31–32: for discussion see J. Schwartz, "Jubilees, Bethel and the Temple of Jacob," *HUCA* 56 (1985) 63–85.

[60] For the Hiphil in 1 Kgs. 11:8 see Chapter 9.C below. The remaining occurrences of *QṬR* (in Hiphil) in Kings are in the story of Ahaz's altar (2 Kgs. 16:13, 15) where its transitive use has no chronological implications. In Chronicles the Hiphil occurs in 1 Chron. 6:34; 23:13; 2 Chron. 2:3, 5; 13:11; 26:16, 18, 19; 28:3; 29:7, 11; 32:12. The Piel is conspicuously rare, and each occurrence can be plausibly attributed to an earlier source: 2 Chron. 25:14; 28:4 (= 2 Kgs. 16:4), 25; 34:25 (Q of *yqṭyrw* [= 2 Kgs. 22:17]). For discussion see Edelman, "Meaning of *qiṭṭer*," 401–2. For a putative source behind 2 Chron. 25:14 cf., e.g., Myers, *II Chronicles*, 144; McKenzie, *Chronicler's Use*, ch. 4 (especially p. 92).

2:20]?) finds additional support from the anomalous *waw*-copulative
+ Perfect (*wĕzābaḥ*).[61] 23:19–20a, in which priests are slaughtered in
"the cities of Samaria," presupposes 13:32–33, and both contradict
13:2 insofar as the man-of-god's prediction does not include any
actions at all in "the cities of Samaria." The bone-burning in 13:2bβ
lies outside this compositional and rhetorical nexus, and also cannot
be attributed to general "deuteronomistic" rhetoric or ideology; it is
clearly linked to 23:16a which likewise is both un-"deuteronomistic"
and, in terms of subject matter, unparalleled in biblical literature
(see Chapter 8 below). It follows from this analysis, therefore, that
some or all of 23:16–18 (minimally v. 16a) compositionally antedates
the slaughter of priests in both 13:2bα and 23:20aα—and, if the
original account of the man-of-god's prediction is itself a post-Josianic
addition, 13:2bβ as well.

3.D. Josiah at Bethel

2 Kgs. 23:15a has the same grammatical structure as v. 19a and
v. 24a, but does not name the Subject as "Josiah":

> *wĕgam ʾet-hammizbēaḥ ʾăšer bĕbêt-ʾēl*
>   *habbāmâ ʾăšer ʿaśâ yārobʿām ben-nĕbaṭ ʾăšer heḥĕṭîʾ*
>   *ʾet-yiśrāʾēl*
> *gam ʾet-hammizbēaḥ hahûʾ wĕʾet-habbāmâ nātāṣ*

The MT is textually and compositionally problematic.[62] The awkward redundancy of the two *gam* clauses has prompted some commentators to suppose that a shorter text has been expanded by an

---

[61] On the *waw*-conjunctive + Perfect issue in 2 Kgs. 23:4–20 see Chapter 5
below.

[62] Cf. Knoppers, *Two Nations Under God 2*, 197–207. The LXX differs substantially: *kai ge to thusiastērion to en Baithēl to hupsēlon . . . kai ge to thusiastērion ekeino to
hupsēlon katespase, kai sunetripse tous lithous autous kai eleptunen eis choun, kai katakause to
alsos.* Many commentators consider the MT defective (especially *wayyiśrōp et-habbāmâ*
in v. 15b) and emend in the direction of the LXX: e.g., Burney, *Notes*, 361; Montgomery, *Kings*, 534, 540; Gray, *I–II Kings*, 731; Jones, *1–2 Kings*, 624. The value of
the Greek version for such purposes is doubtful because of its exegetical *Tendenz*.
The translator saw the object of destruction to be "the altar in Bethel" alone, the
Hebr. *habbāmâ . . . wĕʾet-habbāmâ* becoming adjectival modifiers of *thusiastērion*; the
"bamah" having disappeared, *wyśrp ʾt hbmh* was read as *wyśbr ʾt ʾbn(y)w* to produce
a logical sequence of events in the altar's complete obliteration: it is dismantled, its
individual stones are broken up, and the pieces are pulverized so that not a trace
of it remained. Cf. also D. Barthélemy, *Critique textuelle de l'Ancien Testament 1* (OBO

interpolation from *'et-hammizbēaḥ* through *'et-hammizbēaḥ hahû'* or from *habbāmâ* through *we'et-habbāmâ*.[63] In view of the word-order, the antecedent of *'āšer 'aśâ yārob'ām ben-nebat 'ăšer heḥĕṭî' 'et-yiśrā'ēl* is probably *habbāmâ*, thus: "the bamah which Jeroboam b. Nebat made. . . ." Since this conflicts with the notice in 12:31a that "[Jeroboam] made a *bamoth-house*" (*wayyā'aś bêt-bāmôt*), a reference to his establishment of the sanctuary at Bethel housing the altar and part of the literary unit to which 13:1–32 has been appended,[64] it probably is a secondary reinterpretation of the altar (or the sanctuary, *pars pro toto*?) as a "bamah" consistent with 12:33a, the only other passage in Kings which claims that Jeroboam built the altar at Bethel and part of the *Wiederaufnahme* addition bracketing 13:1–32.[65] The original text may have read *wĕgam 'et-hammizbēaḥ 'ăšer bebêt-'ēl we'et-habbāmâ nātāṣ*, "and even the altar which (was) in Bethel and the bamah [Josiah] demolished," or simply *wĕgam 'et-hammizbēaḥ nātāṣ*, "and even the altar [Josiah] demolished"; in the latter case, and assuming that nothing has been deleted in the course of the evolution of the passage, the original text would have made no reference to Bethel as the location of the altar.[66]

50/1; Fribourg/Gottingen: Universitaires/Vandenhoeck & Ruprecht, 1982) 420, and Eynikel, *Reform of King Josiah*, 348

[63] Cf., e.g., B. Stade and F. Schwally, *The Books of Kings* (trans. by R. E. Brünnow and P. Haupt; SBOT 9; Baltimore/Leipzig: Johns Hopkins University, 1904] 295–6 (probably "various hands have taken part in expanding v. 15"); Montgomery, *Kings*, 534 ("a most conflate passage"); Gray, *I–II Kings*, 738 (an "ill-constructed sentence"). Jones is sympathetic (*1–2 Kings*, 624). Nelson makes the dubious suggestion (*Double Redaction*, 82) that most of v. 15 is annalistic, "the irregularities of the verse giv[ing] the impression that several shorter notices from the annals were strung together into v. 15."

[64] For *bêt-bāmâ* in 1 Kgs. 12:31a as a singular expression see Barrick, "On the Meaning of *bêt-hab/bāmôt*," especially 623–6, and cf. also Provan, *1–2 Kings*, 110.

[65] See n. 53 above. 1 Kgs. 12:32a is problematic. *kēn 'aśâ* usually is reconciled with *'ăšer 'aśâ* in v. 33a (see the commentaries), but RSV is closer to MT: "and he offered sacrifices upon the altar, so he did at Bethel, sacrificing to the calves." It is sometimes rejected as a gloss (e.g., Stade-Schwally, *Kings*, 17; Burney, *Notes*, 178–9; Montgomery, *Kings*, 259; Provan, *Hezekiah*, 79–80); "sacrificing to calves" is an unusual charge, reminiscent of 2 Chron. 11:14–15.

[66] V. 15b further complicates matters: *wayyiśrōp 'et-habbāmâ hēdaq lĕ'āpār wĕśārap 'ăšērâ*. While the Bethel sanctuary may well have contained an asherah-emblem (cf. 1 Kgs. 16:33a), it surely would have been referred to here with the same specificity as "the altar"—*hā'ăšērâ*, as in v. 6—but as it is, Josiah is said to have "burned *an* asherah-emblem" which could have been anywhere. *hēdaq lĕ'āpār* is syntactically isolated. *DQQ*, in Hiphil, elsewhere describes the "grinding" of small items, including asherim and other cultic objects (2 Kgs. 23:6; 2 Chron. 15:16; 34:4, 7) and, in Qal, the golden calf (Ex. 32:20; Deut. 9:21, with *la'āpār*): see Begg, "Destruction of

Be this as it may, a synchronic continuity between v. 15 and vv. 16–18[67] is illusory: while v. 16 envisions the altar as fully functional and awaiting defilement, v. 15 reports the complete demolition of the altar and using language completely different from that used for the destruction described in 1 Kgs. 13:3 + 5.[68] The sequential contradiction indicates that the juxtaposition of v. 15 and v. 16 is redactional, while the linguistic differences suggest that its relationship with 1 Kgs. 13:3 + 5 is distant or nonexistent. The vocabulary of v. 15 also is distinct from that of vv. 16–18,[69] and elsewhere in the reform report *NTṢ* is used of the treatment of bamoth only in v. 8b which is compositionally suspect (see further Chapter 6.A below). The change-of-scene from Jerusalem to Bethel (if original) in v. 15 is abrupt, borne entirely by *wĕgam* which is "a pretty obvious indication" of a redactional seam here[70] as it is in v. 19 which has the same distinctive grammatical structure (so also v. 24), raising the possibility that they may have been written by the same hand. These factors make it likely that v. 15 is a secondary addition, inserted into a narrative which already contained v. 16a. If v. 15 and vv. 19–20 were added at the same time, vv. 16a + 16b–18 would have been part of the reform report and were encircled by vv. 15 + 19–20. Alternatively, v. 15 could have been inserted after vv. 19–20 had

---

the Golden Calf," 233–4; cf. Eynikel, *Reform of King Josiah*, 222–4. It would be more appropriately used here of "the altar" or the "asherah" than of the charred remains of a dismantled building or sacred precinct ("the bamah"). The sequence *NTṢ* (from v. 15a) + *ŚRP* also seems better-suited for a smaller object (cf. *KTR* + *ŚRP* in 1 Kgs. 15:13) than for a building (cf. 2 Chron. 34:4, 6), and while "burning" a bamah is not at all impossible (if a bamah is understood as some sort of built structure, such as a building: see further Chapters 5.D–E and 9 below), it is not otherwise exampled in biblical usage. It is tempting, therefore, to take *hēdaq laʿāpār wĕśrāp ʾăšērâ* as a garbled inverted quotation of v. 6aβ: *wayyiśrōp ʾōtāh* [= *hāʾăšērâ*] . . . *wayyādeq lĕʿāpār*. If so, *wayyiśrōp ʾet-habbāmâ* would be a secondary addition necessitated, perhaps, by the addition of the *habbāmâ* references in v. 15a to an original *wĕgam ʾet-hammizbēaḥ nātaṣ*. For the stylistic device see P. C. Beentjes, "Inverted Quotations in the Bible: A Neglected Stylistic Pattern," *Bib* 63 (1982) 506–23, and cf. Peckham, "Writing and Editing," especially 366–71.

[67] So, e.g., Long, *2 Kings*, 276.

[68] 1 Kgs. 13:3 + 5 use *QRʿ* ("tear, rend") and *ŠPK* ("pour out"), while 23:15 uses *NTṢ* ("break down"), *ŚRP* ("burn"), and *DQQ* ("grind"). Cf. Amos 9:1 with *RʿŠ* ("shake") and *BṢʿ* ("shatter").

[69] According to Eynikel (*Reform of King Josiah*, 287) the vocabulary of "2 Kgs. 23:15 is closely linked with the preceding verses in particular, and more generally with dtr cult terminology in Deuteronomy and 1 and 2 Kings. The vocabulary of 23:16–18 gives a completely different picture."

[70] Van Seters, "Deuteronomistic History," 219.

been added to vv. 16a + 16b–18. In either case, v. 16a would have originally followed directly after vv. 13 + 14b.

If this compositional analysis of 2 Kgs. 23:15–20 is accepted, the insertion of v. 15 transformed a ritualistic decommissioning of the altar by the contamination of human bones into its physical destruction, at the expense of narrative continuity. But it also affected vv. 16–18 in a much more remarkable way: unless it displaced material now lost, v. 15 effectively *moved the cemetery to Bethel from Jerusalem*.[71] V. 16a envisions Josiah, personally on the scene, turning away from doing something else (*wayyipen*) and seeing tombs "there in the mountain" (*ʾăšer-šām bāhār*).[72] This topographical detail is not anticipated in 1 Kgs. 13:30–31,[73] but suits the present narrative context perfectly: without v. 15 to suggest otherwise, "the mountain" would be

---

[71] "Moving a cemetery" is an apt euphemism for an enterprise so dauntingly complicated and unappealing that only the foolhardy would deign to try. Nonetheless Dever speaks matter-of-factly ("Silence of the Text," 157–8) of "the references in 2 Kings 23:16–20 to tombs on the hills surrounding Jerusalem," adding: "the burning of the bones on the altar (v. 16) remains enigmatic, apart from the obvious intent to defile altars that were regarded as illegitimate. All we can say is that many eighth- to sixth-century BCE tombs in Jerusalem were visible, and thus vulnerable to robbing or desecration." Other examples of probable misplacement and relocation include 2 Kgs. 15:29 (originally concerning an event in Ahaz's reign: H. Tadmor and M. Cogan, "Ahaz and Tiglath-pileser in the Book of Kings: Historiographical Considerations," *Bib* 60 [1979] 508) and 24:13–14 (originally in reference to the exile of 586: M. Z. Brettler, "2 Kings 24:13–14 as History," *CBQ* 53 [1991] 547–51). Much of 2 Kings 17 reapplies to (North)-Israel opprobrium originally aimed at Judah: see M. Brettler, "Ideology, History, and Theology in 2 Kings xvii 7–23," *VT* 39 (1989) 268–82, and *idem, The Creation of History in Ancient Israel* (London/New York: Routledge, 1995) ch. 7 (especially pp. 119–28). The Rabbis were adept at relocating biblical stories (for examples see, e.g., Schwartz, "Jubilees, Bethel and the Temple of Jacob," 81–4), as were Medieval Christians (for examples see, e.g., S. Schein, "Between Mount Moriah and the Holy Sepulcher: The Changing Traditions of the Temple Mount in the Central Middle Ages," *Traditio* 40 [1984] 175–95).

[72] LXX reads *bʿr* ("in the city"), an error for *bhr*. *ʾăšer-šām* and *bāhār* are redundant, but reminiscent of the juxtaposition of *ʾăšer-šām* and *ʿal-hammizbēḥôt* in v. 20a. It could be argued that the prepositional phrase is a secondary explication of *šām* in both cases (similarly in 2 Kgs. 17:11a where *bĕkol-bāmôt* is probably a gloss of *šām*: cf., e.g., Stade-Schwally, *Kings*, 263; A. Šanda, *Die Bücher der Könige* [EHAT; Münster: Aschendorff, 1912] 2.221; Montgomery, *Kings*, 478; Jones, *1–2 Kings*, 549). If this is so, there would be no indication of the original location of the cemetery in 23:16–18, although circumstantial evidence would still favor Jerusalem: *bahar* could be a redactional seam joining two blocks of material concerning Jerusalem locales but deriving from different sources.

[73] The only topographical reference in 1 Kings 13 is the "oak" under which the man-of-god was sitting on his homeward journey when the old prophet overtook him (v. 14), probably "the oak below Bethel" (called Allon-bacuth) mentioned in

the Mount of Olives, "the mountain of the destroyer" (*har-hammašḥît*), near which v. 13 locates "the king" while "defiling" the bamoth attributed to Solomon. The Mount of Olives had definite chthonic associations in antiquity (cf. Zech. 14:3–5)[74] and numerous tombs did, in fact, exist there in the late monarchic period,[75] continuing a mortuary tradition stretching back to MB II.[76] These tombs would have supplied the "human bones" with which v. 14b says "he filled their places," probably the method used to "defile" the Solomonic bamoth in v. 13 (see further Chapter 8.C below). Without v. 15, therefore, but with no other textual changes or redactional sleight of hand (cf. Section 3.F below), vv. 16–18 tells a rather different story than the one told in the final form of the pericope:

> Josiah espies a particular funerary "monument"[77] which "the men of the city [of Jerusalem]" identify as "the tomb of the man-of-god who had come [to Jerusalem?/to Bethel?] from [the hinterlands of] Judah and predicted these things which you have done against the altar at Bethel"; he had been buried with a prophet "who had come [here] from [what was now the Assyrian province of] Samaria" (v. 18b). The tomb had been discovered while Josiah's functionaries, under his supervision, were carrying out his directive (v. 16a): he (through those whom "he sent") "took the bones from the tombs and burned [them] upon the altar and defiled it." Some of the disinterred bones presumably are the "bones of men" used in v. 14b to defile some cultic installations in the south (v. 14b: *meqômām*), including the bamoth there on the Mount of Olives (v. 13).

This reading demonstrates that while the final form of the reform report is closer to 1 Kgs. 13:11–32 than to 13:2, vv. 16–18 alone seems closer to 1 Kgs. 13:2 than to 13:11–32. The compositional history of 1 Kgs. 13:1–32 becomes central in clarifying this material.

Gen. 35:8 (cf. "the oak of Tabor" in 1 Sam. 10:3). What is independently known of the location of the cemetery and the sanctuary at Bethel has been reviewed in Section 3.A above.

[74] See J. B. Curtis, "An Investigation of the Mount of Olives in the Judaeo-Christian Tradition," *HUCA* 28 (1957) 137–77. Cf. also W. J. Heard, in *ABD* (1992) 5.13–5.

[75] For the Silwan tombs see n. 21 above.

[76] For MB II-LB II tombs on the west and east slopes of the Mount of Olives see D. Tarler and J. M. Cahill, in *ABD* (1992) 2.64 and literature cited there.

[77] *haṣṣîyûn hallāz ṣîyûn* has sepulchral associations in Ezek. 39:15; cf. also Jer. 31:21.

3.E. THE MAN-OF-GOD AND THE OLD PROPHET FROM BETHEL

In the present arrangement of the material 1 Kgs. 13:1–32 appears to be a single narrative consisting of two episodes, both featuring the same Judahite man-of-god and linked thematically by Yahweh's directive to "neither eat bread nor drink wine [while on your mission] nor return [to Judah] by the way that you came" (v. 9). Affinities between the tale *in toto* and the tale of Jonah, together with certain linguistic features, suggest a date as late as the 5th century for its composition.[78] Its treatment of the theme of obedience to Yahweh in the story-line, especially in vv. 11–32, more closely resembles the Chronicler's "theology of immediate retribution" whereby "reward and punishment are not deferred, but rather follow immediately on the heels of the precipitating events,"[79] than the prophecy/fulfillment schema in Kings. It certainly is not a pre-"deuteronomistic" composition,[80] and the case for "deuteronomistic" (i.e., "Josianic") authorship is not at all compelling.[81]

---

[78] Rofé, "Classes of the Prophetical Stories," 158–63, and *idem, The Prophetical Stories: The Narratives about the Prophets in the Hebrew Bible* (Jerusalem: Magnes, 1988) 170–182 (especially pp. 172–3, 175 n. 104); D. W. Van Winkle, "I Kings xiii: True and False Prophecy," *VT* 39 (1989) 34 n. 2; Van Seters, "Reading the Story of the Man of God," 232–3, and *idem*, "Deuteronomistic History," 217–8. A great many commentators posit a Josianic/"deuteronomistic" connection, typically that "the Deuteronomist" inserted this material: e.g., Knoppers, *Two Kingdoms Under God 2*, ch. 2 (quotation from p. 47 *et passim*; for other adherents see p. 47 n. 2); for a critique of Rofé's late date see pp. 51–2.

[79] See R. B. Dillard, "Reward and Punishment in Chronicles: The Theology of Immediate Retribution," *WTJ* 46 (1984) 164–72 (quotation from p. 165), and cf. the commentaries. For a more nuanced view cf. E. Ben Zvi, "A Sense of Proportion: An Aspect of the Theology of the Chronicler," *SJOT* 9/1 (1995) 37–51. A parade example is the leprosy resulting from Uzziah's ill-advised incense-burning (2 Chron. 26:16–23) which may be echoed in Jeroboam's leprosy attack in 1 Kgs. 13:4–6: cf. Van Seters, "Reading the Story of the Man of God," 231.

[80] Cf. S. J. De Vries, *I Kings* (WBC 12; Waco: Word, 1985) 168 ("very early perhaps before Jeroboam introduced the golden calf"). At the very least, the explicit reference to "Josiah" must be attributed to "the hand of an overenthusiastic deuteronomistic editor" (Knoppers, *Two Kingdoms Under God 2*, 58–9). That the composition draws upon "pre-'deuteronomistic'" (i.e., pre-Josianic) traditions is another matter: see further below.

[81] Against the case presented by W. E. Lemke, "The Way of Obedience: 1 Kings 13 and the Structure of the Deuteronomistic History," *Magnalia Dei/The Mighty Acts of God: Essays on the Bible and Archaeology in Memory of G. Ernest Wright* (ed. by F. M. Cross *et al.*; Garden City: Doubleday, 1976) 301–26, cf. McKenzie, *Trouble with Kings*, 53–4.

Some commentators resolve the conflict between 1 Kgs. 13:2b and
v. 32b by taking the latter as secondary to the former.[82] This would
mean that 13:32b and 2 Kgs. 23:19–20 which it anticipates probably belong to the same compositional stratum (there being no good
reason to give one chronological precedence over the other); 23:16a
+ 16b–18, however, probably does not belong to the same compositional stratum as 13:11–32a in view of the disparity between them
(detailed above). If 23:16a + 16b–18 is dependent on 13:11–32a
(which virtually all commentators take for granted), it would have
been added to the reform report after vv. 19–20, an improbable
chronological scenario. All of the factors considered thus far make
it more likely that 13:11–32 is actually dependent on 23:16a +
16b–18.

The episode involving Jeroboam b. Nebat and the altar (1 Kgs.
13:1–10) which anticipates 23:16a is not intrinsically tied to the
episode involving the old prophet from Bethel (13:11–32) which anticipates 2 Kgs. 23:17–18 (+ 19–20). Juxtaposed, Episode I serves as
the prelude to Episode II, explaining how it happened that the
Judahite found himself in Bethel so that the two men could meet.
The proclamation against the altar is of no consequence to the plot
of Episode II; it is mentioned as the prophet's motivation for having himself buried with the man-of-god (vv. 31–32a) and it is mis-
represented (v. 32b). Although tangential to the plot, vv. 31–32 link
it redactionally to the occasion for the man-of-god's presence (vv.
1–6) and v. 11b supplies a redactional link with his exchange with
the king (vv. 7–9), thereby integrating the two narratives.

1 Kgs. 13:11–32 is best understood as a parable (*māšāl*), a short
didactic tale with two or more intended levels of meaning.[83] The
surface meaning here is clear enough: the man-of-god is tricked by
the old prophet into breaking Yahweh's directive and dies as a result
of his disobedience. But as in all parables, other meanings "lie

---

[82] Cf., e.g., Noth, *Könige*, 1.294; T. B. Dozeman, "The Way of the Man of God
from Judah: True and False Prophecy in the Pre-Deuteronomic Legend of 1 Kings
13," *CBQ* 44 (1982) 381; McKenzie, *Trouble with Kings*, 52; Knoppers, *Two Nations
under God 2*, 211.

[83] Cf. Rofé, *Prophetic Stories*, 170–81 (and his earlier "Classes of the Prophetical
Stories," 143–64), and Van Winkle, "1 Kings xiii," 36–7. On the genre see J. D.
Crossan, in *ABD* (1992) 5.146–7, and, from a broader literary perspective, *idem*, *In
Parables: The Challenge of the Historical Jesus* (New York: Harper & Row, 1973) ch. 1,
especially 4–22.

hidden within the complexities of the narrative, and these challenge or provoke the recipient to interpretation";[84] the parabolic potential of the theme of obedience is amply demonstrated by the range of "basic" meanings or morals in this text divined by modern commentators.[85] Parabolic writings in the Bible range "from non-narrative proverb to narrative allegory, from fables with possible or impossible natural protagonists to stories with quite possible and plausible human protagonists, and with or without the specific title of parable being present."[86] Episode II, including the behavior of the lion, is both possible and plausible. And as the Tekoan woman's tale (2 Sam. 14:5–7) purports to be biographical, here one of the protagonists is represented as an historical personage with a public career (i.e., the man-of-god and his visit to the Bethel sanctuary and his proclamation against its altar) potentially knowable outside the boundaries of the story itself.

1 Kgs. 13:11–32 is a sophisticated piece of didactic fiction. It has no factual basis in itself—the events it relates are imaginary—but utilizes several separate pre-existent traditions in which separate historical realities may be imbedded. Five likely source traditions can be identified. The first is attested independently in 1 Kgs. 20:35–36 (cf. 2 Kgs. 2:23–25):

> And a certain man of the sons of the prophets said to his fellow *bidbar yhwh*: "Hit me." But the man refused to hit him. Then he said to him: "Because you have not obeyed the voice of Yahweh, behold, as soon as you leave me a lion will kill you." And as soon as he had left him a lion met him and killed him.

The parallels with 13:11–32 are too extraordinary to be coincidental or to reflect proximate historical realities. Both use the relatively rare (and non-"deuteronomistic") expression *bidbar yhwh*,[87] involve an exchange between two prophets, both "revolve around the theme of unquestioning obedience to the divine word," and in both the prophet who disobeys the word of Yahweh is killed by a lion in consequence

---

[84] Crossan, in *ABD*, 5.146–7.
[85] See, e.g., the excellent "readerly" analysis by Long, *I Kings*, 145–50. Cf. now also Van Winkle, "1 Kings xii 25–xiii 34" 101–14.
[86] Crossan, in *ABD*, 5.147.
[87] 1 Kgs. 13:1, 2, 5, 9, 17, 18, 32. Elsewhere: 1 Sam. 3:21; 1 Kgs. 20:35; Jer. 8:9; 2 Chron. 30:12; Ps. 33:6. Cf. 2 Sam. 16:23; 1 Chron. 25:5; 2 Chron. 29:15.

of his disobedience.[88] Secondly, endangerment by lions[89] recurs in 2 Kgs. 17:26–28 as a consequence of the failure of the new residents of "the cities of Samaria" to know "the proper practice [*mišpāṭ*] of the god of the land," a condition remedied by the repatriation of a priest of the old Yahwistic cultus at Bethel;[90] 1 Kgs. 13:32b probably derives from this pericope or the tradition behind it. Thirdly, the absolute prohibition of eating and drinking while on a divinely-directed mission may stem from folk traditions about angelic messengers such as are reflected in Judg. 6:17–27 and 13:15–20 (and Tobit 12:19).[91] The fourth tradition used in the formulation of the parable is the visit of a Judahite man-of-god to Bethel—Episode I or the tradition which it draws upon. And the fifth, I submit, is the tradition underlying 2 Kgs. 23:16a + 16b–18 which included a northern prophet buried (somewhere) with a Judahite man-of-god who had spoken against the altar at Bethel (see Section 3.F below).

While Episode II cannot stand alone, that Episode I (1 Kgs. 13:1–10) is a self-contained narrative is evident from v. 10 which marks a definite change-of-scene: *wayyēlek bĕderek ʾaḥer, wĕlōʾ-šāb badderek ʾăšer bāʾ bāh ʾel-bêt-ʾēl*. Without 13:11–32, this verse would conclude—albeit unedifyingly (cf. Matt. 2:12)[92]—the account of the man-of-god's visit to Bethel with the implication that he returned to Judah.[93] The exchange between the man-of-god and Jeroboam (vv. 7–9) probably also belongs to the expansion.[94] The prohibition of

---

[88] Lemke, "Way of Obedience," 314–5.

[89] See the biblical and ancient Near Eastern materials compiled by G. J. Botterweck, in *TDOT* (revised, 1977) 1.374–88. Cf. also M. A. Klopfenstein, "I Könige 13," *"Parresia": Karl Barth zum 80. Geburtstag* (ed. by E. Busch *et al.*; Zurich: EVZ, 1966) 661–5.

[90] See Barrick, "On the Meaning of *bêt-hab/bāmôt*," 625.

[91] See especially Rofé, *Prophetic Stories*, 174–81.

[92] *Pace*, e.g., Van Seters' view that "the first part is incomplete and meaningless without its completion in the second" ("Deuteronomistic History," 216–7).

[93] V. 10a alone is sufficient for this purpose, v. 10b being an explication of *derek ʾaḥer*; the redundancy (similar to that between 12:33a and 12:33b already noted [see n. 122 above]) was created when the narrative was expanded by the addition of vv. 11–32, with which v. 10b belongs.

[94] Cf. E. Würthwein, "Die Erzählung vom Gottesmann aus Juda in Bethel: Zur Komposition von 1 Kön 13," *Wort und Geschichte: Festschrift für Karl Elliger zum 70. Geburtstag* (ed. by H. Gese and H.-P. Rüger; AOAT 18; Neukirchen-Vluyn: Neukirchener, 1973) 181–9; E. Eynikel, "Prophecy and Fulfillment in the Deuteronomistic History: 1 Kgs. 13; 2 Kgs. 16–18," *Pentateuchal and Deuteronomistic Studies: Papers Read at the XIIIth IOSOT Congress* (ed. by C. Brekelmans and J. Lust; BETL 94; Leuven: University, 1990) 228, 230. The vocabulary (especially in v. 7) is noticeably late,

eating and drinking is integral to the plot of the parable; "(re)turn-ing by the way" ($\check{S}WB$ + B + $derek$ [vv. 9, 10, 17]) leads to the homiletical word-play in v. 26[95] and can be seen as an exegetical elaboration of the "other way" taken in v. 10a. The report by the old prophet's sons (v. 11b) serves as a narrative seam: it is an unco-ordinated doublet, the first $'et$ clause referring to the predictive "doings" of the man-of-god (vv. 1–6) and the second to his "words" with the king (vv. 7–9); the first is a redactional connective with the pre-existent story, the content of which is tangential to 13:11–32, the second a narrative transition projecting the content of the con-versation with the king into the plot of the following story, both hav-ing been composed by the same author-compiler.

Episode I, then, can be summarized as follows:

> A man-of-god from Judah interrupted the ritual proceedings at Bethel while "Jeroboam (was) standing upon the altar to make offerings" (13:1b). Upon hearing the altar's desecration predicted, "Jeroboam stretched out his hand from upon the altar" and commanded that the intruder be seized (v. 4a). His hand was mysteriously rendered immo-bile (v. 4b), prompting the king to ask the man-of-god to intervene with Yahweh, whereupon his hand was "returned" ($\check{S}WB$) to normal (v. 6) and the man-of-god was allowed to depart (v. 10a).

No cause for the disabling of the king's hand is discernible in the story—it just happens.[96] The incident serves the purely literary pur-pose of dramatizing to Jeroboam (and to the reader) the intruder's credentials and thus the authenticity of his message. Jeroboam might have responded to his miraculous cure as the woman of Zarephath does in a comparable situation (1 Kgs. 17:24): "Now I know that you are a man-of-god and that the word of Yahweh in your mouth is true." But instead he resumes "his evil way," having learned noth-ing from "this thing/word" (v. 33a). In terms of plot, the "thing" must be Jeroboam's encounter with the man-of-god in which the

---

consistent with that of vv. 11–32: see Rofé, *Prophetical Stories*, 172–3; McKenzie, *Trouble with Kings*, 52–3. Cf. Van Winkle, "I Kings xiii," 34 n. 2 (favoring a 6th-century date for this material).

[95] See n. 98 below.

[96] Cf. Simon, "I Kings 13," 86–9. Eynikel supposes that vv. 4 + 6 "describe a miracle by the man of God to protect himself ("Prophecy and Fulfillment," 231, citing 2 Kgs. 1:9–12 and 2:23–24 as parallels), but this idea must be read into the text: the order to "seize" the intruder has already been issued, preventing him from leaving the scene and thus explaining how he happened to still be present to inter-vene concerning the king's hand.

jeopardizing of his personal welfare (the immobilizing of his arm, to say nothing of the crumbling altar under his feet) might have caused him to "turn from his evil way" if the prediction about the altar's future did not. Only the reader is aware of the encounter between the man-of-god and the old prophet; Jeroboam learns the didactic lesson of 13:11–32 from Ahijah at the cost of his ailing son (14:7–18).[97] This continuity suggests that Episode I already had been grafted into the KH before it became the first scene of a homiletical tale by the addition of Episode II,[98] or that Episode II, already attached to Episode I, was included "without any integral relation to the larger Jeroboam story."[99]

Contextually, therefore, the "portent" (*môpēt*) of the crumbling altar—*hinnēh hammizbēaḥ niqrāʿ wĕnišpak haddešen ʾăšer-ʿālāyw* (v. 3b); *wĕhammizbēaḥ niqrāʿ wayyiššāpēk haddešen min-hammizbēaḥ* (v. 5a)—is both redundant and nonsensical. The altar falling apart with Jeroboam "standing upon" it (*ʿMD + ʿL* [v. 1b]), extending his hand "from upon" it (*MʿL* [v. 4b]), and oblivious to what was happening literally under his feet, is unbelievable except, perhaps, in the world of slap-stick comedies and cartoons.[100] The giving of the "portent" is tied to the giving of the prediction by the narrator's comment that they occurred "on the same day" (*bayyôm hahûʾ* [v. 3aα]), the same

---

[97] According to Knoppers, neither "the death of the Judahite seer or the sober reflection of the prophet from Bethel impress Jeroboam" (*Two Nations Under God 1*, 63), but there is nothing in the narrative to suggest that Jeroboam would have known either the first (which is plausible; cf. v. 25) or the second (which is not).

[98] Notwithstanding the *ŠWB + MN + derek* idiom in v. 26aα (*wayyišmaʿ hannābîʾ ʾăšer hĕšîbô min-hadderek*). This idiom is characteristic of late pre-Exilic or Exilic prose (predominately in Jeremiah "C" and Ezekiel); see Lemke, "Way of Obedience," 310, 322 n. 58, concluding that "conceivably, the expression originated with [Jeremiah (cf. 15:1)] and was then picked up by subsequent exilic writers"; cf. W. L. Holladay, *The Root "Subh" in the Old Testament* (Leiden: Brill, 1958) 128–39, and for Jer. 15:1 see now *idem, Jeremiah 1*, 442. In v. 33 it is used in the metaphorical sense of departing from a course of action or mode of behavior: *ʾaḥar haddābār hazzeh lōʾ-šāb yārobʿām middarkô hārāʿâ*; "after this thing, Jeroboam did not turn from his evil way," but continued making bamoth-priests. The metaphorical sense is also appropriate in v. 26, for it was the wily old prophet who 'turned him from the [right] way" of obedience to Yahweh's commands (see Lemke, "Way of Obedience," 310–1 and accompanying notes; cf. McKenzie, *Trouble with Kings*, 53–4); such a double entendre serves well the didactic point that disobedience will bring certain disaster and death. This linguistic link between the body of 13:11–32 and the closing *Wiederaufnahme* bracket might indicate that they come from the same authorial hand. Except for this idiom, however, vv. 11–32 and v. 33 have nothing in common.

[99] Cohn, "Literary Technique in the Jeroboam Narrative," 32.

[100] So, e.g., Würthwein, "Erzählung vom Gottesmann aus Juda in Bethel," 182;

device used to link 13:1–10 to 13:11–32 (*hayyôm* [v. 11bα]).[101] *wĕnā-tan* in v. 3aα is problematic: it probably refers to an action in the narrative past,[102] the man-of-god being the giver of the "portent" and v. 3aα being the words of the narrator, but use of the *waw*-copulative + Perfect construction instead of the *waw*-consecutive is compositionally suspicious.[103] These factors suggest that vv. 3 + 5 may be secondary to vv. 1–2 + 4 + 6 + 10a, probably added when the original story was expanded by the addition of vv. 7–9 + 10b + 11–32.[104] In view of the completely different vocabulary of 23:15a, 13:3 + 5 perhaps reflects an independent tradition of the destruction of the altar at the Bethel sanctuary by some extra-ordinary means—many commentators see earthquake imagery here[105]—prior to the coming of Josiah, and unrelated to 23:15a.

To summarize: Episode I, originally consisting of 1 Kgs. 13:1–2 + 4 + 6 + 10a, was appended secondarily to the account of Jeroboam's cultic establishment (12:26–32) and thus is secondary to the compositional stratum of the KH to which that account belongs (presumably the "first edition," hereinafter KH-1). It doubtless does not antedate the reign of Josiah, but the intransitive use *QṬR* in Hiphil in the man-of-god narrative (12:33; 13:1, 2b) suggests that the narrative is very likely also secondary to the "Josianic" edition of Kings:

Dozeman, "Way of the Man of God from Judah," 383. Attempts to explain away the obvious absurdity of the scene (e.g., W. Gross, "Lying Prophet and Disobedient Man of God in 1 Kings 13: Role Analysis as an Instrument of Theological Interpretation of an OT Narrative Text," *Semeia* 15 [1979] 102; cf. J. T. Walsh, "The Contexts of 1 Kings xiii," *VT* 39 [1989] 357 n. 4) are more clever than convincing. See also Simon, "I Kings 13," 88 n. 22. Eynikel's suggestion that "the king does not react to the altar's destruction beneath him because he is only interested in his own welfare" ("Prophecy and Fulfillment," 231) is nonsensical.

[101] Cf. Noth, *Könige*, 1.290, 296–7; Jones, *1–2 Kings*, 264.

[102] Some commentators take *wĕnātan* as "and he shall give" (cf. LXX), with Josiah the subject: cf. Noth, *Könige*, 1.290, 296–7; Würthwein, "Erzählung vom Gottesmann aus Juda," 166–7; Jones, *1–2 Kings*, 264. Simon notes the stylistic infelicity of having the narrator intrude at this juncture ("I Kings 13," 88 n. 22).

[103] Cf., e.g., Gray, *I–II Kings*, 326; Würthwein, "Erzählung vom Gottesmann aus Juda," 183 n. 6; Dozeman, "Way of the Man of God," 383 and n. 20; McKenzie, *Trouble with Kings*, 54–5 n. 29; Eynikel, "Prophecy and Fulfillment," 230 n. 14. On the *waw*-conjunctive + Perfect issue see Chapter 6.A below.

[104] Cf., e.g., Noth, *1 Könige*, 1.292–3; Gray, *I–II Kings*, Simon, "I Kings 13," 88 n. 22; Jones, *1–2 Kings*, 264; Dozeman, "Way of the Man of God," 383; McKenzie, *Trouble with Kings*, 54–5 n. 29. For the resulting structure of 13:10 and 13:11–32, which demonstrates that the expansion was not done haphazardly, see Walsh, "Contexts of I Kings xiii," 357–61.

[105] See, e.g., Gray, *I–II Kings*, 326.

as already noted, the intransitive use of QTR in Hiphil, characteristic of the Chronicler, is rare in Kings, and the other occurrences
(1 Kgs. 3:3b and 11:8b) appear to be post-"Josianic."[106] An ideological explanation—that the Hiphil conjugation was used instead of
the supposedly pejorative Piel because Jeroboam's ritual act was
directed to Yahweh—is not very persuasive in view of 11:8 (which
pertains to the deities of Solomon's foreign wives)[107] and a consideration of the verb's overall biblical usage.[108]

3.F. The "Cemetery Scene" (2 Kgs. 23:16a + 16b–18)

Since 2 Kgs. 23:16a + 16b–18 plainly functions as the coda of the
fully developed man-of-god story in 1 Kings 13, the dissidence between
them is noteworthy. Most conspicuous is the completely incongru-
ous statement in 23:18b that the prophet buried with the man-of-
god "had come from Samaria" (wayĕmallĕṭû ʿaṣmōtāyw ʾēt ʿaṣmôt hannābîʾ
ʾăšer-bāʾ miššōmrôn): in 1 Kgs. 13:1–32 neither the man-of-god nor
the old "prophet" leave Bethel and its immediate vicinity,[109] and
"Samaria" (whether šōmrôn refers to the city, the region, or the Assyrian province) did not exist in the reign of Jeroboam b. Nebat when
the incident supposedly occurred.[110] If the latter can be excused as
a careless anachronism, the former is inexplicable in terms of the
man-of-god story known to us[111] or any earlier version even faintly

---

[106] See n. 60 above.

[107] This verse is discussed in Chapter 9.C below.

[108] See Edelman, "Meaning of qiṭṭer," especially 402–3, and Clements, in *TWAT*,
especially 7.13–4. The verb usually is found in pejorative contexts, but the pejorative nuance is supplied by the context and not borne by the verb itself. For the
problems associated with the occurrence in 1 Sam. 2:16 cf. H. J. Stoebe, *Das erste
Buch Samuelis* (KAT 8:1; Gütersloh: Mohn, 1973) 108; P. K. McCarter, *I Samuel*
(AB 8; Garden City: Doubleday, 1980) 79; Edelman, "Meaning of qiṭṭer," 400
n. 12.

[109] It is not absolutely certain that hannābîʾ ʾăšer-bāʾmiššōmrôn must refer to the
old prophet from Bethel: e.g., Montgomery translates "and they left his bones alone,
the bones of the prophet who came from Samaria," and notes that "the final clause
is an absurd bit of carelessness, as the prophet came from Judah" (*Kings*, 535).

[110] See I. Ephal, "'The Samarian(s)' in the Assyrian Sources," *"Ah Assyria . . ."*:
*Studies in Assyrian History and Ancient Near Eastern Historiography Presented to Hayim Tad-
mor* (ed. by M. Cogan and I. Ephal; ScrHier 33; Jerusalem: Magnes, 1991) 36–45.

[111] "An absurd bit of carelessness" (Montgomery, *Kings*, 535). Gray supposes that
"bāʾ is written loosely here through the influence of the clause concerning the
prophet of Judah [ʾăšer bāʾ mîhûdâ] and ought to be omitted" (*I–II Kings*, 739). Provan
evades the issue through a homiletical explanation (*1–2 Kings*, 276): "The two

discernible behind it.[112] Secondly, in 13:32a the old prophet speaks of *haddābār ʾăšer qārāʾ bidbar yhwh ʿal-hammizbēaḥ ʾăšer bĕbêt-ʾēl*, "the word which [the man-of-god] proclaimed by the word of Yahweh against the altar which (is) in Bethel." 23:17b, echoing this statement, speaks of *haqqeber ʾîš-hāʾĕlōlîm ʾăšer-bāʾ mîhûdâ wayyiqrāʾ haddĕbārîm hāʾēlleh ʾăšer ʿaśîtā ʿal hammizbaḥ bêt-ʾēl*, "the tomb of the man-of-god who came from Judah and proclaimed these things that you have done to the altar of Bethel." The slight differences here are often overlooked:

1 K 13:32a: . . . *ʿal-hammizbēaḥ ʾăšer bĕbêt-ʾēl*
2 K 23:17b: . . . *ʿal hammizbaḥ   bêt-ʾēl*
2 K 23:15a: . . . *ʾet-hammizbēaḥ ʾăšer bĕbêt-ʾēl*

There is no obvious explanation for this difference, especially when compared to the phraseology in 23:15; the irregular construct form with the definite article twice in this verse (*haqqeber* and *hammizbaḥ*), possibly "elliptical forms of expression,"[113] is noteworthy. Although inconsequential in themselves, when coupled with the misidentification of the prophet in v. 18b these instances of stylistic and grammatical dissonance further distance 23:16b-18 from 13:1–32.

The extra-ordinary act described in 2 Kgs. 23:16aβ (*wayyišlah wayyiqqah ʾet-haʿaṣāmôt min-haqqebārîm wayyiśrōp ʿal-hammizbēaḥ*; "and he sent and took the bones out of the tombs and burned them upon the altar") is unique in the biblical record and probably has a basis in fact independent of 1 Kgs. 13:1–32. 23:16b-18 reflects a tradition of a prophet "from Samaria" who was buried with a Judahite man-of-god who had presaged Josiah's treatment of the altar at Bethel and whose tomb was undisturbed in the king's pogrom; the several factors considered in the course of this chapter suggest that the cemetery with this tomb was located in the vicinity of Jerusalem. The analyses of 13:1–32 do not point to such an alternative version of that story.[114] Rather than devolving secondarily from 13:1–32, this

---

prophets lie united in their grave. Is there just a hint that lasting union between the two kingdoms from which they have come will likewise now be found only in death?"

[112] E.g., there is no basis for supposing that the old prophet was imagined as having moved from the city of Samaria to Bethel before encountering the Judahite man-of-god.

[113] Cogan-Tadmor, *II Kings*, 290; cf. GKC, 127–8.

[114] Note, however, that the use of *yōʾšĭyāhû* in v. 16a is at odds with the edition(s)

tradition antedates it and was one constituent element in its evolution, and evolved along with it. The latter is evidenced by the tendency of the Greek translations of 23:16–18 or their *Vorlage* to perfect the correspondence to 13:1–32. The expanded LXX version of v. 16a reads:

> . . . thus fulfilling the word of the Lord announced by the man of God when Jeroboam stood by the altar at the feast. But when he caught sight of the grave of the man of God who had foretold these things, he asked. . . .

Many commentators favor the longer version (cf. also NEB): e.g., J. A. Montgomery claims that either the insertion, "itself clumsy, or the like is necessary, [the MT] showing the result of parablepsis due to the double occurrence of 'the man of God'," and imagines the original verse may have read simply "And Josiah faced about and he saw the tombs that were there in the mount, and he cast his eyes upon the tomb of the man of God who proclaimed these things";[115] his omission of the tomb-robbing and bone-burning episode in v. 16a is unexplained, and ill-advised since doing so deprives the king's order in v. 18 of its narratological rationale. In my opinion, all of v. 16b (including *wayyĕṭammĕʾēhû* at the end of v. 16a) is a secondary amplification of the action in v. 16a based on 13:1–32. The long insertion introducing the old prophet of 13:11–32 in the LXX^L of version of v. 18[116] suggests that some of vv. 17–18 also may be secondary reconciliations.

---

of the reform report which regularly use(s) *hammelek*, but consistent with v. 19a and v. 24a which are secondary to that edition.

[115] Montgomery, *Kings*, 535. The LXX version is often considered more authentic than the MT: in addition to the commentaries cf., e.g., Burney, *Notes*, 361; Barthélemy, *Critique textuelle de l'Ancien Testament 1*, 421; Knoppers, *Two Kingdoms Under God 2*, 208 and n. 70; Eynikel, *Reform of King Josiah*, 137.

[116] *Kai diesōthē ta osta tou prophētou tou presbuterou tou katoikountos en Baithēl meta tōn ostōn tou anthrōpou tou theou tou hēkontos ex Iouda kai lelalēkotos panta ta erga tauta ha epoiēsen Iōsias.*

CHAPTER FOUR

JOSIAH'S REFORM AS REPORTED IN CHRONICLES (II): ANOTHER LOOK AT 2 CHRONICLES 34:4–5

Answers to the questions which arose from the examination of the Chronicler's version of Josiah's reform in Chapter 2 above now can be attempted:

(1) Why did the Chronicler locate the burning of the bones of priests in "Judah and Jerusalem" (v. 5) and not in the North (vv. 6–7)?

Only 2 Kgs. 23:16 explicitly puts Josiah on the scene of the action, personally supervising the removal of bones from their tombs and their burning upon an altar. In the preceding chapter it was shown that the original location of this episode probably was Jerusalem, in the immediate vicinity of the Mount of Olives where the bamoth attributed to Solomon and dedicated to certain foreign deities were also defiled (v. 13). This would explain why the Chronicler located his reference to bone-burning in the south (34:5a): he had before him an unaugmented version of Kings which caused him to do so.

(2) What is the physical relationship between the altars and the hammanim which Josiah destroys in "Judah and Jerusalem," and what is the basis of this notice (v. 4a)?

Josiah's precise location is not given in Kings: he may or may not be envisioned to be actually on "the mountain" when he "turns" and sees tombs "there" (v. 16aα). If the Chronicler envisioned Josiah "in front of" (*lĕpānāyw*) "the altars of the Baals" (or "altars of the Baals") supervising their demolition at the foot of the Mount of Olives, in the Kidron or eastern Ben-Hinnom Valley (34:4), Solomon's bamoth could fairly be said to be "above" them. The chthonic associations of the Mount of Olives and the Wadi Kidron have already been noted. 23:13 locates Solomon's bamoth "on the right of the mountain of corruption," suggesting the southern part of the ridge known today as the Mount of Olives, opposite the "City of David"; Christian tradition places them atop Ras el-Amud/Batin el-Hawa, into the lower slope of which the Silwan necropolis was cut (see

Illustration)¹—a juxtaposition of no little significance if the tradition has a basis in fact.

Two additional factors support this explanation:

- In view of the Chronicler's uniformly glowing representation of Solomon, he most certainly would not have credited him with building installations for the worship of foreign deities.² Instead of omitting 23:13,³ he offered an interpretative précis utilizing the late term *ḥammānîm*, probably meaning "sanctuaries, shrines" (as Palmy. *ḥmn'*) and thus semantically closer to *bāmôt* than to *mizbēḥôt*⁴ (precluding the possibility that the hammanim were positioned "on top of" the altars), perhaps prompted in part by its phonetic resemblance to *hinnom*.

- Secondly, the Chronicler supposed that more than "passing sons/children through fire" (28:3b and 33:6aα, both adapted from Kings) took place in the Ben-Hinnom Valley, for he adds to his account

---

¹ See Ussishkin, *Village of Silwan*, 322.

² For the Chronicler's presentation of Solomon see the commentaries and, e.g., R. L. Braun, "Solomonic Apologetic in Chronicles," *JBL* 92 (1973) 503–16, and *idem*, "Solomon, the Chosen Temple Builder: The Significance of 1 Chronicles 22, 28, and 29 for the Theology of Chronicles," *JBL* 95 (1976) 581–90; R. B. Dillard, "The Chronicler's Solomon," *WTJ* 43 (1980) 289–300, and *idem*, "The Literary Structure of the Chronicler's Solomon Narrative," *JSOT* 30 (1984) 85–93; McKenzie, *Chronicler's Use*, 84–5, 88.

³ E.g., "the Chronicler's portrayal of a faultless Solomon would require omission of 2 Kgs. 23:13 as out of accord with that portrait" (Dillard, *2 Chronicles*, 278).

⁴ H. J. W. Drijvers, "Aramaic *ḤMN'* and Hebrew *ḤMN*: Their Meaning and Root," *JSS* 33 (1988) 178, followed by D. R. Hillers, "Palmyrene Aramaic Inscriptions and the Old Testament, especially Amos 2:8," *Zeitschrift für Altthebräistik* 8 (1995) 57–8. The customary interpretation (see K.-M. Beyse, in *TDOT* [1980] especially 4.475–7, and the literature cited there; cf. the discussion by B. A. Levine, "The Epilogue to the Holiness Code: A Priestly Statement on the Destiny of Israel," *Judaic Perspectives on Ancient Israel* [ed. by J. Neusner *et al.*; Philadelphia: Fortress, 1987] 16–7, who renders the term "'*ḥammon*-altar,' with the strong implication that the name of the deity, *Ḥammon*, is integral to it") has been convincingly refuted by V. Fritz, "The Meaning of the Word *ḤAMMĀN/ḤMN'*," *Folia Orientalia* 21 (1980) 103–15 (= "Die Bedeutung des Wortes *ḥamman/ḥmn'*," *Wort und Wirklichkeit* [ed. by B. Benzing *et al.*; Meisenheim am Glan: Hain, 1976] 1.41–50, slightly revised as "Die Bedeutung von *ḥammān* im Hebraischen und vom *ḥmn'* in dem palmyrenischen Inschriften," *BN* 15 [1981] 9–20), Drijvers, "Aramaic *ḤMN'* and Hebrew *ḤMN*," 165–80, and H. Cazelles, "*Ḥammānim-ḥamon/ḥumun* et l'Expansion phenicienne," "*Où demeures-tu?*" (*Jn 1,38*): La Maison depuis le Monde Biblique—En Hommage au Professeur Guy Couturier à l'Occasion de ses soixante-cinq Ans (ed. by J.-C. Petit; Quebec: Fides, 1994) 99–107. Drijvers derives *ḥammān* from the root *ḤMH*, "to protect," i.e., a sanctuary "surrounded and protected by a stone wall" (p. 174); cf. Hebr. *ḥomâ*, Arab. *ḥimâ*. For Ugar. *ḥmn* (2084.12; 86[305].5) cf. also G. del Olmo

of Ahaz (28:2b-3a): *wĕgam massēkôt ʿaśâ labĕʿālîm; wĕhûʾ hiqṭîr bĕgēʾ ben-ḥinnom*; "and he even made massekah-images for the Baals; and he burned incense in the Ben-Hinnom Valley."[5] The "massekah-images" attacked by Josiah in 34:3b and 34:4b are probably meant to be understood as those introduced by Ahaz. The juxtaposition of v. 2b and v. 3a permit the inference that the "incense-burning" also was "for the Baals," and some type of altar apparatus is implied.

(3) What is the basis for the notice that "the [remains of] sacrificers" were scattered before (their) tombs, also "in Judah and Jerusalem" (v. 4bβ), and (4) why are the priests whose bones were burned apparently included among the deceased "sacrificers" (vv. 4bα–5a)?

The Chronicler has made an intertextual exegetical connection between 2 Kgs. 23:16 and Jer. 8:1–2: having brought Jeremiah into his narrative world as a participant in Josiah's reign (2 Chron. 35:25), he may well have regarded the Jeremiah corpus known to him as a viable source of information about this period.[6]

Lete, "La 'capilla' o 'templete' (*ḥmn*) del Culto ugaritico," *Aula Orientalis* 2 (1984) 277–80.

[5] According to Curtis-Madsen 28:2b–3a was "added by the Chronicler as introductory to the mention of the sacrifice of his son" (*Chronicles*, 456), while for Japhet the addition supplies the "specific meaning" of the charge of having emulated the kings of (North-)Israel (*I–II Chronicles*, 898); an intertextual derivation for this material is suggested by Myers, the reference to images perhaps drawn from Isa. 2:8–13. 20, and the illicit worship in Ben-Hinnom "simply a conjecture" based on Mic. 6:7 and Jer. 7:31 (*II Chronicles*, 161). See further Chapter 5.E below.

[6] For other Jeremanic echoes in Chronicles see now B. Halpern, "Why Manasseh Is Blamed for the Babylonian Exile: The Evolution of a Biblical Tradition," *VT* 48 (1998) especially 510–3.

CHAPTER FIVE

JOSIAH'S REFORM IN KINGS (II):
THE *WAW*-CONJUNCTIVE PASSAGES

Despite the tendency of some critics to atomize the portion of the reform report pertaining to Josiah's actions in Judah (2 Kgs. 23:4–14),[1] little in this section is compositionally suspicious on internal linguistic, text-critical, or literary grounds alone. The principal exceptions are the seven passages featuring the *waw*-conjunctive + Perfect construction: a statement that burnt remains ("ashes") were carried to Bethel (v. 4bβ), followed by a series of actions against "komer-priests" (v. 5a), against worshippers of Baal and various astral deities (v. 5b), against bamoth-installations "at the entrance of the gate of Joshua" (v. 8b), against the tophet (v. 10), against the remains of rooftop altars (v. 12bβ), and against (at least) masseboth (v. 14aα). Five of these deal with persons and installations not actually inside the walls of Jerusalem: v. 4bβ concerns Bethel; v. 5a + 5b concern "the cities of Judah and around Jerusalem"; the tophet was somewhere in the Ben-Hinnom Valley adjacent to the city on the southwest (v. 10); and v. 12bβ concerns the Wadi Kidron adjacent to the city on the east. The rooftop altars apparently were both in the Temple and in the palace (v. 12a). The immediate context suggests that the masseboth in v. 14aα were associated with the Solomonic bamoth on the Mount of Olives (v. 13), consistent with this pattern. Not even context is much help in locating the "gate of Joshua" in v. 10. Otherwise, these passages seem to have nothing in common and are presented in no discernibly meaningful order. None has a counterpart in the Chronicler's version of the reform.

---

[1] An extreme recent example is C. Levin ("Joschija im deuteronomistischen Geschichtswerk," *ZAW* 96 [1984] 351–371, followed by H. Nieher, "Die Reform des Joschija: Methodische, historische und religionsgeschichtliche Aspekte," *Jeremia und die "deuteronomistische Bewegung"* [ed. by W. Gross; BBB 98; Weinheim: Beltz Athenäum, 1995] 33–55) who deletes everything except 23:8a. Cf. also, e.g., H. Hollenstein, "Literarkritische Erwägungen zum Bericht über die Reformmassnahmen Josias 2 Kön. xxiii 4ff.," *VT* 27 (1977) 321–36; Hoffmann, *Reform und Reformen*, 169–89, 208–53; Nelson, *Double Redaction*, 79–85; Spieckermann, *Juda unter Assur*, 79–120, 153–60; Jones, *1–2 Kings*, 615–7.

The status of these passages is perhaps the greatest compositional conundrum in the reform report as a whole. A cautious consensus has begun to emerge among scholars dealing with the *waw*-conjunctive + Perfect construction in Biblical Hebrew generally:[2] although the preponderance of examples occur in demonstrably late passages, the construction alone is not in itself a certain indication of the lateness of a given passage; other factors also should be present to justify such a dating. Since v. 5 and v. 8b appear intrusive in the present arrangement of the material (as noted in Chapter 1 above), it is quite possible that some or all of these seven passages were added secondarily to an earlier version of the reform report. This chapter will consider that possibility.

A further clue to their compositional status is found in the two notices about altars built by Manasseh:

> 2 K 21:4: *ûbānâ mizbĕḥôt bĕbêt yhwh, ʾăšer ʾāmar yhwh bîrûšālaim ʾāśîm ʾet-šĕemî*
> 2 K 21:5: *wayyiben mizbĕḥôt lĕkol-ṣĕbāʾ haššāmāyim, bištê ḥaṣrôt bêt-yhwh*

The altars of 21:5 are certainly those demolished by Josiah in 23:12aβ (*wĕʾet-hammizbĕḥôt ʾăšer-ʿāśâ mĕnaššeh bištê ḥaṣrôt bêt-yhwh nātaṣ hammelek*). While 21:4 could refer to different altars in the Temple complex, the use of *ûbānâ* (rather than *wayyiben* as in 21:5) suggests that it is actually a doublet of v. 5, as v. 7 (with *pesel hāʾăšērâ*, the word *pesel* being used only here in Kings [cf. 2 Chron. 33:3b–7]) is a likely doublet of v. 3bβ (with *ʾăšērâ* alone): both share clear "deuterono-

---

[2] See the comprehensive study by Spieckermann, *Juda unter Assur*, 120–130, and the review of the question by Van Keulen, *Manasseh*, 162–7. Earlier, noting the "vast array of often conflicting [scholarly] opinion" on the subject, J. McKay (*Religion in Judah under the Assyrians* [SBT 2nd Series 26; Naperville: Allenson, 1973] 84–5 n. 5) concluded that "it seems likely that it will be possible to explain the construction differently occurrences"; similarly Provan, *Hezekiah*, 86 n. 83. J. C. L. Gibson submits ("Coordination by Vav in Biblical Hebrew," *Words Remembered, Texts Renewed: Essays in Honour of John F. A. Sawyer* [ed. by J. Davies *et al.*; JSOTSup 195; Sheffield: Sheffield Academic, 1995] 274–5) that "the passages involved are by no means all late, so it is questionable whether they are properly put down to the influence of Aramaic; they are more likely the result of some inner Hebrew development." Cf. J. Joosten, "Biblical Hebrew *wĕqāṭāl* and Syriac *hwā qāṭel* Expressing Repetition in the Past," *ZAH* 5 (1992) 1–14, and K. Koch, "Gefüge und Herkunft des Berichts über die Kultreformen des Königs Josia: Zugleich ein beitrag zur Bestimmung hebräischer 'Tempora'," *Alttestamentlicher Glaube und B*ischer Theologie: Festschrift für Horst Dietrich Preuss zum 65. Geburtstag* (ed. by J. Hausmann and H.-J. Zobel; Stuttgart/Berlin/Köln: Kohlhammer, 1992) 80–92, with the critique by Eynikel, *Reform of Josiah*, 155–6 n. 29.

mistic" rhetoric (which makes an annalistic source doubtful),[3] and v. 7 is part of a homiletical commentary (vv. 7–9 + 10–15) generally considered secondary.[4] Some of the *waw*-conjunctive + Perfect passages in the reform report may replicate this precedent.[5]

5.A. In the Cities of Judah and around Jerusalem (v. 5)

wĕhišbît ʾet-hakkĕmārîm ʾăšer nātĕnû malkê yĕhûdâ wayĕqaṭṭēr babbāmôt bĕʿārê yĕhûdâ ûmĕsibbê yĕrûšālāim, wĕʾet-ha-mĕqaṭṭĕrîm labbaʿal laššemeš wĕlayyārēah wĕlammazzālôt ûlĕkol ṣĕbāʾ haššāmāyim;

wĕhišbît [both] the komer-priests whom the kings of Judah had made *wayĕqaṭṭēr*[6] in the bamoth in the cities of Judah and around Jerusalem, and [also] the "offerers" to Baal, to the sun and to the moon and to the *mazzālôt* and to all the host of heaven.

---

[3] For the view that the *waw*-copulative + Perfect construction is indicative of an archival extract cf., e.g., Burney, *Notes*, 353; J. A. Montgomery, "Archival Data in the Book of Kings," *JBL* 53 (1934) 50–1; R. Meyer, "Auffallender Erzählungsstil in einem angeblichen Auszug aus der 'Chronik der Könige von Juda'," *Festschrift für Friedrich Baumgartel zum 70. Geburtstag, 14 Januar 1958 Gewidmet* (ed. by L. Rost; ErF A/10; Erlangen: Universitatsbibliothek Erlangen, 1959) 119–23 (especially p. 122).

[4] The secondary status of v. 4 and some or all of v. 7 is widely conceded: cf., e.g., J. Skinner, *I–II Kings* (New-Century Bible 7; New York: Frowde, [1893]) 406; I. Benzinger, *Der Bücher der Könige* (KHCAT 9; Tübingen: Mohr, 1899) 188; Burney, *Notes*, 352–3; Stade-Schwally, *Kings*, 53; Šanda, *Könige*, 2.324–5; Montgomery, *Kings*, 519; Gray, *I–II Kings*, 705–6, 707–9; Dietrich, *Prophetie und Geschichte*, 31–4; Cross, *Canaanite Myth and Hebrew Epic*, 285–7; Spieckermann, *Juda unter Assur*, 162–4, 421; Nelson, *Double Redaction*, 58, 65–9; Jones, *1–2 Kings*, 596–9; Provan, *Hezekiah*, 87 and n. 84; Ben Zvi, "Account of the Reign of Manasseh," 365–6, 370–4; Van Keulen, *Manasseh*, 97–102, 161–7, 168–71; 195 n. 60; Schmid, "Manasse und der Untergang Judas," 90–4; Eynikel, "Portrait of Manasseh," 243–9, 254–5, 259. Long equivocates (*2 Kings*, 247); cf. Cogan-Tadmor, *II Kings*, 270–1. According to Smelik ("Portrayal of King Manasseh," 145, 146–7; cf. 153–9), these duplications are examples of "repetition with an increase in information," a purported literary device which seems to me more like a synchronic contrivance.

[5] Cf. Long's contention that 23:5 || v. 8a and v. 4 || vv. 6–7 are "reduplicated pairs" dealing with the same general topics (*2 Kings*, 264).

[6] MT's *wayĕqaṭṭer babbāmôt* is probably defective, not because the pious Josiah never would have patronized bamoth (so J. W. Wevers, "Principles of Interpretation Guiding the Fourth Translation of the Book of the Kingdoms [3 Kgs. 22:1–4 Kgs. 25:30]," *CBQ* 14 [1952] 50), but because it is mentioned incongruously in the recounting of his reform activities. Virtually all commentators follow either LXX and Targ. which point to *wayĕqaṭṭĕrû* (e.g., Benzinger, *Könige*, 192; Burney, *Notes*, 358; Stade-Schwally, *Kings*, 293; Wevers, "Principles of Interpretation," 50; Cogan-Tadmor, *II Kings*, 279 n. f; Eynikel, *Reform of King Josiah*, 137) or Pesh. and Vulg. which suggest *lĕqaṭṭēr* (e.g., Montgomery, *Kings*, 529, 539; Gray, *I–II Kings*, 730 n. d; Knoppers, *Two Nations Under God 2*, 190 and n. 38). L. C. Allen sees the MT reading as another example of a marginal annotation (cf. 2 Kgs.16:4) subsequently

The bamoth "in the cities of Judah and around Jerusalem" in v. 5a and the bamoth in "the cities of Judah . . . from Geba to Beersheba" in v. 8a must be the same installations. It is often claimed, however, that the "komer-priests" (*kĕmārîm*) attacked in v. 5a and the "kohen-priests" (*kōhănîm*) brought to Jerusalem in vv. 8a + 9 are different priesthoods—the former idolatrous[7] and the latter Yahwistic—serving at the same bamah-installation. This is problematic.[8] Nothing in the verse itself requires this understanding of the komer-priests and much argues against it. *kōmer* (etymologically "one who burns"?) is cognate to Aram. *kûmrāʾ*, the common Aramaic term for "priest" (cf. also Phoen. *kmr*), semantically equivalent to Hebr. *kōhēn*.[9] It recurs

---

mistaken for a scribal correction and displacing an original *lĕqaṭṭēr* in the text ("More Cuckoos in the Textual Nest: At 2 Kings xxiii.5; Jeremiah xvii.3, 4; Micah iii.3; vi.16 [LXX]; 2 Chronicles xx.25 [LXX]," *JTS* 24 [1973] 69–70). Note Washburn's defense of the MT on the grounds that v. 5aβ is a parenthetical explanation that "[a komer-priest] burned offerings at the bamoth" ("Perspective and Purpose," 69); Lowery seems to be thinking along these lines when he speaks, without explanation, of "the awkward gloss in the middle of the verse [which] describes the [komer-priest] as one who burns incense" (*Reforming Kings*, 207).

[7] E.g., Gray, *I–II Kings*, 732–3 ("pagan cults"); Jones, *1–2 Kings*, 618 ("the fertility cult"); Wiseman, *1–2 Kings*, 301 ("pagan deities"); J. J. M. Roberts, *Nahum, Habakkuk, and Zephaniah: A Commentary* (OTL; Louisville: Westminster John Knox, 1991) 172 ("pagan clergy"); Knoppers, *Two Nations Under God 2*, 188 ("idolatrous priests," probably of Baal [cf. 2 Kgs. 11:18]); P. A. Bird, "The End of the Male Cult Prostitute: A Literary-Historical and Sociological Analysis of Hebrew *qādēš-qĕdēšîm*," *Congress Volume, Cambridge 1995* (ed. by J. A. Emerton, VTSup 66; Leiden/New York/Köln: Brill, 1997) 65 n. 91 ("priests of foreign gods"). Cf. Eynikel, *Reform of King Josiah*, 217–8. For their identification as specifically astral priests cf., e.g., Spieckermann, *Juda unter Assur*, 83–85; B. Halpern, "The Baal (and the Asherah) in Seventh-Century Judah: Yhwh's Retainers Retired," *Konsequente Traditionsgeschichte; Festschrift für Klaus Baltzer zum 65. Geburtstag* (ed. by R. Bartelmus *et al.*; OBO 126; Freiburg/Göttingen: Universitäts/Vandenhoeck & Ruprecht, 1993) 131 *et passim*; R. Albertz, *A History of Israelite Religion in the Old Testament Period 1* (trans. by J. Bowden; OTL; Louisville: Westminster/John Knox, 1994) 190; C. Uehlinger, "Gab es eine joschijanische Kultreform? Plädoyer für ein begründetes Minimum," *Jeremia und die "deuteronomistische Bewegung"* (ed. by W. Gross; BBB 98; Weinheim: Beltz Athenäum, 1995) 77–9.

[8] But not for the marketing reason suggested by Provan (*1–2 Kings*, 276): "It is difficult to see Manasseh as an advocate of consumer choice throughout his dominion."

[9] Akk. *kumru* occurs in LB Syro-Palestinian texts (see D. Sivan, *Grammatical Analysis and Glossary of the Northwest Semitic Vocables in Akkadian Texts of the 15th–13th Century BC* [AOAT 214; Kevelaer/Neukirchen-Vluyn: Butzon & Bercker/Neukirchener, 1984] 238), but it is not used in 1st millennium Mesopotamian texts, making it unlikely that *kmrym* is an "Akkadian loan-word" (as, e.g., Hermann, *History*, 266): for recent discussion see, e.g., M. Görg, "Die Priestertitel *kmr* und *khn*," *BN* 39 (1985) 7–14; Cogan-Tadmor, *II Kings*, 285–6; E. Ben Zvi, *A Historical-Critical Study of the Book of Zephaniah* (BZAW 198; New York/Berlin: de Gruyter, 1991) 67 n. 110.

in only two other biblical passages: in parallel with "the remnant of Baal" and distinct from *kōhănîm* (Zeph. 1:4), and in reference to those who mourn the loss of "the calf of Beth-aven" (Hos. 10:5). The priests in Zeph. 1:4 could be Baalistic,[10] but those of Hos. 10:5 are plainly priests of the Yahweh cultus at Bethel of which the prophet is deeply critical: as Hosea disparages that cultus with the pejorative euphemism "Beth-aven" (also Hos. 4:15 and 5:8), he disparages its priesthood by calling them "komer-priests,"[11] but they are nonetheless priests of *Yahweh*. Thus, in biblical usage *kōmer* may be a term of disapproval, but like the neutral *kōhēn* does not in itself identify the priest so named as a servitor of Yahweh or of some other deity.[12] The "komer-priests" of 2 Kgs. 23:5a are not the "offerers" (*měqaṭṭěrîm*) of v. 5b, the two groups being clearly differentiated syntactically (*wěhišbît ʾet-hakkěmārîm . . ., wě ʾet-hamĕqaṭṭěrîm*).[13] There is, therefore, no contextual indication of the deity(s) which the "komer-priests" served or, for that matter, where the "offerers" were located.

It is often supposed that, because they were idolatrous, the komer-priests of v. 5a were treated more harshly than the kohen-priests of vv. 8a + 9 (cf. LXX).[14] If they were exterminated, as some contend, it is surprising that the verb used is *ŠBT* and not one more expressive of that result, as is done for the disposition of "the bamoth-priests in the cities of Samaria" (v. 20: *ẐBH*). The basic idea conveyed by *ŠBT* is "rest," i.e., the cessation of action.[15] *ŠBT*, in Hiphil, when

---

[10] Contextually, the reference could as well be to priests of Yahweh who engaged in syncretistic practices: see especially Ben Zvi, *Zephaniah*, 60–72, 274–7, and Berlin, *Zephaniah*, 74–5. On the probable explanatory gloss "with the priests" see Ben Zvi, *Zephaniah*, 67 n. 109, 69–70; cf. Roberts, *Nahum, Habakkuk, and Zephaniah*, 167–8 n. 4, 172, and Berlin. *Zephaniah*, 75.

[11] See, e.g., H. W. Wolff, *Hosea* (trans. by G. Stansell; ed. by P. D. Hanson; Hermeneia; Philadelphia: Fortress, 1974) 171, 175; F. I. Anderson and D. N. Freedman, *Hosea* (AB 24; Garden City: Doubleday, 1980) 547, 555–6 ("idol-priests").

[12] Thus, correctly, Ben Zvi (*Zephaniah*, 68): "The term *kmrym* only conveys the meaning of wrong worship."

[13] I see no justification for making the two phrases in apposition by omitting some/all of *ʾăšer nātěnû malkê yěhûdâ wayěqaṭṭēr babbāmôt bě ʿārê yěhûdâ ûměsibbê yěrûšālāim, wě ʾet* as secondary (so recently Uehlinger, "Gab es eine joschijanische Kultreform?" 73–4, 78 and n. 104).

[14] Cf. recently Bird, "End of the Male Cult Prostitute," 65, and G. Toloni, "Una Strage di Sacerdoti? Dalla Storiografia alla Storia in 2 Re 23,4b–5," *Estudios Biblicos* 56 (1998) 41–60.

[15] Cf. Ex. 5:5; 21:19; Jer. 36:29; Ezek. 34:10; Amos 8:4; Ruth 2:7; Ps. 127:2: see Eynikel, *Reform of King Josiah*, 216–7. For *lpny šbt* in the Mesad Hashavyahu letter (KAI 200.5–6) see, e.g., D. G. Pardee, "The Judicial Plea from Mesad Hashavyahu

used of persons means "to cause someone to stop doing something." The verb is used in 23:11 where both slaughtering (of live horses) or physical destruction (of statues) are possible, but neither is imperative—if either is the intended sense, here too it is surprising that a verb more expressive of the action is not used, as is the case elsewhere in the reform report (vv. 4b, 6, 8b, 12, 15, 20); they may have been relocated[16] or converted for other work or released. Hebrew usage would suggest that *hišbît . . . 'et-haměqaṭṭěrîm* means only that Josiah stopped the "offerers" from offering, and *hišbît 'et-hakkěmārîm* means only that he stopped the individuals in question from doing whatever caused them to be called "komer-priests." Accordingly, while Josiah may have given the komer-priests "a permanent sabbatical,"[17] this probably was not accomplished by killing them.

These same factors suggest an alternative understanding of this material: the komer-priests of v. 5a and the kohen-priests of vv. 8a + 9 are, like the bamoth mentioned in both passages, *identical*.[18] V. 5a is a doublet of vv. 8a + 9, reporting the same episode from a different perspective:

v. 5a	vv. 8a + 9
komer-priests	kohen-priests
appointed by "the kings of Judah"	——
"burn offerings" (*QTR* in Piel)	"burn offerings" (*QTR* in Piel)
at bamoth	at bamoth
	bamoth "defiled" (*TMʾ*)
in "the cities of Judah"	in "the cities of Judah"
and "around Jerusalem"	——
——	"from Geba to Beersheba"
"given rest" (*ŠBT*)	——
——	transferred to Jerusalem
——	new status in Jerusalem

(Yavneh-Yam): A New Philological Study," *MAARAV* 1 (1978) 36, 44 ("stopping work/quitting time"), and *idem, Handbook of Ancient Hebrew Letters: A Study Edition* (Sources of Biblical Literature 15; Chico: Scholars, 1982) 20, 22; S. Talmon, "The New Hebrew Letter from the Seventh Century BCE in Historical Perspective," *King, Cult and Calendar in Ancient Israel: Collected Studies* (Jerusalem: Magnes, 1986) 82 (= *BASOR* 177 [1965] 32).

[16] Washburn, "Perspective and Purpose," 71–3.

[17] Eslinger, "Josiah and the Torah Book" 41; cf. also Roberts, *Nahum, Habakkuk, and Zephaniah*, 172 ("did away with"), and Knoppers, *Two Nations Under God 2*, 190 ("put an end to").

[18] Lowrey simply asserts (*Reforming Kings*, 206–7) that "there is no reason to

V. 5a does not explain how the komer-priests were "given rest," encouraging scholarly guesswork[19] or evasion.[20] Vv. 8a + 9, more interested in the fate of the clergy at the bamoth, gives a clear explanation: they were "recycled" by being brought to Jerusalem where their priestly status was redefined.[21]

Who, then, are the "offerers to Baal, to the sun and to the moon and to the *mazzālôt* and to all the host of heaven" who also were "given rest"? Either priests or worshippers are possible. The latter would recall Huldah's oracle (22:16–17): Yahweh "will bring evil upon this place and its inhabitants ... because they have forsaken me *wayĕqaṭṭĕrû* to other gods." These would be "the inhabitants" (also v. 19) of Jerusalem who will participate with "the men of Judah" and "the priests and the prophets" in making the covenant (23:2–3), and are the only other people in the Josiah narrative said to "burn offerings" (*QṬR* in Piel) to deities other than Yahweh. Similarly, Jer. 8:1–3 identifies the worshippers of "the sun and the moon and all the host of heaven" as "the kings of Judah, ... its princes, ... the priests, ... the prophets, and ... the inhabitants of Jerusalem," the entire "evil family" of Judah.

The astral phenomena mentioned in v. 5b also pose difficulties. Surely "all the host of heaven" (*kol ṣĕbāʾ haššāmāyim*) mentioned in v. 4aβ, presumably "the totality of the celestial bodies and the signs of the zodiac," includes the "sun," the "moon," and the "mazzaloth" of v. 5b which are not mentioned there.[22] V. 4aβ is reminiscent of Deut. 17:3 (and Jer. 8:2) if *ʾăšērâ* is equated with *yārēaḥ*, and v. 5b approximates Deut. 4:19 if *mazzālôt* is equated with *kôkābîm*, but neither is truly "deuteronomic" or "deuteronomistic":

---

suppose that v. 5 and vv. 8–9 have different kinds of priests in mind." For J. Robinson they are "local village priests, the country clergy of the day, who doubtless regarded themselves as faithful followers of Yahweh," denigrated by being called "komer-priests" (*Second Book of Kings*, 219).

[19] E.g., T. H. Robinson supposes that they "were simply suppressed, being left, apparently, without means of sustenance except what they might obtain from land which some of them almost certainly held" (*History of Israel*, 421), while Hermann imagines that they were subjected to forced labor (*History*, 266).

[20] Evident in the frequent recourse to noncommittal translations: e.g., RSV ("deposed"); NEB and NJPSV ("suppressed"); Gray, *I–II Kings*, 730 ("suspended"); Ahlström, *Royal Administration*, 68 ("dismissed"); Halpern, "Yhwh's Retainers Retired," 139 ("cashiered"); Provan, *1–2 Kings*, 276 ("removed from office").

[21] On the nature of this status see Chapter 9.B below.

[22] E. T. Mullen, in *ABD* (1992) 3.301–4 (quotation from p. 302). Cf. H. Niehr, in *DDD* (1995) 811–4.

2 K 23:4aβ	Deut. 17:3	2 K 23:5b	Deut. 4:19
ba'al	——	*ba'al*	——
——	*šemeš*	*šemeš*	*šemeš*
'ăšērâ	*yārēaḥ*	*yārēaḥ*	*yārēaḥ*
——	——	*mazzālôt*	*kôkābîm*
kol ṣĕbā'	*kol ṣĕbā'*	*kol ṣĕbā'*	*kol ṣĕbā'*
haššāmāyim	*haššāmāyim*	*haššāmāyim*	*haššāmāyim*

There would be little meaningful semantic difference between *kôkābîm* and *kol ṣĕbā' haššāmāyim* in Deut. 4:19 unless it is supposed that *kôkābîm* is a generalizing euphemism for a more specific astral phenomenon such as whatever *mazzālôt* identifies in 2 Kgs. 23:5b. The meaning of *mazzālôt* (occurring only here, but cf. *mazzārôt* in Job 38:32) is very uncertain. If it is an Akk. loan-word meaning "constellations" or the like (cf. Bab. Akk. *manzaltu*), it would be "virtually synonymous" with *kol ṣĕbā' haššāmāyim* and not materially different from *kôkābîm*,[23] but both the derivation and identification are doubtful; it seems more likely that *mazzālôt* entered the language by way of Aramaic (cf. *mazzāl*, "planet, constellation, luck") as a reference to a more specific configuration of stars, such as the Pleiades (Akk. *zappu*, "bristle")[24] which was of cultic significance in the region,[25] or

---

[23] For discussion of *mazzālôt/mazzārôt* see the commentaries and, e.g., McKay, *Religion in Judah*, 38–9 and accompanying notes (quotation from p. 39); Spieckermann, *Juda unter Assur*, 271–3; M. Delcor, "Les cultes étrangers en Israël au moment de la réforme de Josias d'après 2R 23: Étude de religions sémitiques comparées," *Environnement et Tradition de l'ancien Testament* (AOAT 228; Kevelaer/Neukirchen-Vluyn: Butzon & Bercker/Neukirchener, 1990) 109–13) (= *AOAT* 212 [1981] 95–9]); I. Zatelli, "Astrology and the Worship of the Stars in the Bible," *ZAW* 103 (1991) 94–5; Eynikel, *Reform of King Josiah*, 210–1.

[24] For the Akkadian terminology see E. Reiner, *Astral Magic in Babylonia* (Transactions of the American Philosophical Society 85/4; Philadelphia: American Philosophical Society, 1995) ch. 1 (especially p. 17 n. 49), and cf. W. Horowitz, "The Reverse of the Neo-Assyrian Planisphere CT 33,11," *Die Rolle der Astronomie in den Kulturen Mesopotamiens: Beiträge zum 3. Grazer Morgenländischen Symposiun (23.–27. September 1991)* (ed. by H. D. Galter; Grazer Morgenländische Studien 3; Graz: n. pb., 1993) 149–59. That Hebr. *kîmâ* (Amos 5:8; Job 9:9; 38:31) denotes the Pleiades is traditional (cf. Akk. *kimtu*, "family"); it only occurs with *kĕsîl*, "Orion" or "Sirius" (the dog of Orion), duplicating the juxtaposition in Mesopotamian sources of *zappu* and *šitaddar/lu* ("Orion") or *bālu/balli* (a nearby star ["Sirius"?]) (see Horowitz, "Reverse," 152 n. 6): for recent discussion and other opinions see S. M. Paul, *Amos* (Hermeneia; Minneapolis: Augsburg Fortress, 1991) 168 and ns. 88–89.

[25] Cf. a 7th-century silver medallion from neighboring Ekron inscribed with a crude rendition of the familiar Neo-Assyrian cult scene of a figure praying toward the goddess Ishtar (cf. the Judahite "Queen of Heaven") standing on the back of a striding lion and beneath the sun (a winged sun-disk), the moon, and the Pleiades

perhaps the 12-sign "ecliptic" zodiac or the more general "zodiacal belt" (first attested in 5th- and late 8th-century cuneiform sources, respectively),[26] or even "planets."[27] Whatever the semantic relationship between *mazzālôt* and *kol ṣĕbā' haššāmāyim*, stylistically the occurrence of the latter both in v. 4aβ and at the end of v. 5b can be seen as a *Wiederaufnahme* bracket by which at least some of the intervening material was grafted into an earlier version of the reform report.

As v. 5a is a doublet of vv. 8a + 9, v. 5b can be seen as a doublet (of a sort) of v. 4aβ: whether the "offerers" are to be understood as priests or worshippers, if they were associated with Jerusalem (cf. Jer. 8:1–3) rather than "the cities of Judah," they would be the human counterparts of the equipage for "Baal, Asherah, and all the

---

(seven circular "stars"): S. Gitin, "Tel-Miqne-Ekron in the 7th Century BCE: The Impact of Economic Innovation and Foreign Cultural Influences on a Neo-Assyrian Vassal City-State," *Recent Excavations in Israel: A View to the West* (ed. by S. Gitin; Archaeological Institute of America Colloquia and Conference Papers 1; Dubuque, IA: Kendall/Hunt, 1995) 69–71 and fig. 4.14, and *idem*, "The Neo-Assyrian Empire and its Western Periphery," *Assyria 1995: Proceedings of the 10th Anniversary Symposium of the Neo-Assyrian Text Corpus Project, Helsinki, September 7–11, 1995* (ed. by S. Parpola and R. M. Whiting; Helsinki: Neo-Assyrian Text Corpus Project at the University of Helsinki, 1997) 93 and n. 58, 101 fig. 21; A. Golani and B. Sass, "Three Seventh-Century BCE Hoards of Silver Jewelry from Tel Miqne-Ekron," *BASOR* 311 (1998) 70–2 and fig. 14:2. All known examples of this scene are also dated to the 7th century. For the same representation of the Pleiades on a Late Babylonian tablet see Reiner, *Astral Magic in Babylonia*, 11, Fig. 5. Could the Pleiades, a very distinctive and readily observable cluster of seven stars, be echoed in the 7-spouted bowl-lamps "typically found in cultic contexts" in IA II Palestine (quotation from C. Meyers, in *ABD* [1992] 4.142)?

[26] So, hesitantly, S. W. Holloway: "then we are in the world of the Persian Period, for the *concept* of the zodiac cannot be found in Assyro-Babylonian thought, or anywhere else, before the 5th century" (personal correspondence, 26 May 1999). The earliest cuneiform evidence for the 12-sign "ecliptic" zodiac comes from 5th-century astronomical diary texts: see now F. Rochberg-Halton, *Babylonian Horoscopes* (Transactions of the American Philosophical Society 88/1; Philadelphia: American Philosophical Society, 1998) 30; cf. x, 3. Babylonian familiarity with the "zodiacal belt" ("a belt of some 12° breadth in which the planets [including Sun and Moon] move, with its *constellations*, the number of which need not be restricted to 12") is documented "as early as 700 BC": see B. L. van der Waerden, "History of the Zodiac," *AfO* 16 (1952) 216–230 (quotations from p. 216, 218), followed lately by A. Lemaire, "Coupe astrale inscrite et astronomie araméenne," *Michael: Historical, Epigraphical and Biblical Studies in Honor of Prof. Michael Heltzer* (ed. by Y. Avishuir and R. Deutsch; Tel Aviv-Jaffa: Archaeological Center, 1999) 197–8.

[27] Cf., e.g., H. Mesnard, "Les Constellations du Livre de Job," *Revue belge de philologie et d'histoire* 30 (1952) 142 and n. 1, disassociating *mazzālôt* from *mazzārôt* ("l'idée de Courone ou Ceinture, les Constellations zodiacales" [from *NZR*]).

host of heaven" removed from the Temple which they certainly would have patronized.

5.B. Bringing Ashes to Bethel (v. 4bβ)

wĕnāśāʾ ʾet-ʿăpārām bêt-ʾēl;

and he brought their ashes to Bethel.

This may be the most puzzling statement in the entire pericope. Although its originality has been defended,[28] most commentators consider it a secondary addition. *In situ*, the antecedent of *ʿăpārām* is the "equipage" taken from the Temple in v. 4a and burned in v. 4bα. A plausible motive for this act has thus far escaped detection: e.g., R. D. Nelson can find "no conceivable reason why Josiah would have done this,"[29] while J. Gray finds it "a rather impracticable operation," whatever its purpose;[30] others dismiss it as "a ludicrous editorial touch,"[31] "an absurd intrusion."[32] But an analogous episode is reported following Sennacherib's destruction of Babylon in 689:[33]

> To quiet the heart of Assur, my lord, that peoples should bow in submission before his exalted might, I removed the dust of Babylon for presents to (the most) distant peoples, and in that Temple of the New Year's Feast, I stored up (some) in a covered bin (?).

As Sennacherib sends the dust of the enemy (Babylon) as a warning to other potential rebels and deposits some in the Akitu House at Assur as a sign of the god Assur's dominance, Josiah brings the dust of the enemy (the other gods in the Temple) to Bethel and

---

[28] Lately by Washburn, "Perspective and Purpose," 68: if "and he burned them" is consecutive, then the perfect in v. 4d is a "parenthesis"—"he burned them . . . (now, he carried the ashes to Bethel)"—but if the *waw*-consecutive "introduces another new topic," then v. 4c and v. 4d are a self-contained unit that deals with the disposition of the vessels."

[29] Nelson, *Double Redaction*, 81. For a utilitarian use of the ashes of organic material in the "paving" of streets at Beer-sheba see A. F. Rainey, "Dust and Ashes," *TA* 1 (1974) 77–83. The materiel of the "equipage" is unknown.

[30] Gray, *I–II Kings*, 732.

[31] E. W. Heaton, *The Hebrew Kingdoms* (The New Clarendon Bible; London: Oxford University, 1968) 122.

[32] Jones, *1–2 Kings*, 618; similarly Montgomery, *Kings*, 529.

[33] D. D. Luckenbill, *The Annals of Sennacherib* (OIP 2; Chicago: University of Chicago, 1924) 138.44–47.

presumably deposits it in the Yahweh sanctuary there. Josiah's motive
nonetheless is unclear.

2 Kgs. 23:4 seems to parallel v. 6 closely and v. 12 more distantly. They report the disposition of objects removed from the Temple:

v. 4	v. 6	v. 12
equipage	asherah	altars
——	——	pulled down
burned (*ŚRP*)	burned (*ŚRP*) (*NTṢ*)	broke in pieces
outside Jerusalem	outside Jerusalem	——
in Kidron "fields"	in Kidron	——
——	ground to dust[34]	*wyrṣ mšm*[35]
"ashes" to Bethel	"ashes/dust" on graves/tombs	"ashes/dust" into Kidron

In each case the burnt residue (*ʿăpārām; ʿāpār* and *ʿăpārāh*)[36] of the
offensive object(s) is deposited somewhere unusual. For D. J. Wiseman, "casting the [pulverized] ashes" of the asherah on the Kidron
tombs likely "served to despise both the god and its worshippers,"[37]
a final desacralization of the asherah and an affront to the occupants of the tombs and their living descendants who had patronized
her cultus in the Temple. The parallel would suggest a similar motive
in dispatching the "ashes" of the cultic equipage to Bethel, perhaps
a symbolic affront like the Dauphin's tennis balls[38] (directed against

---

[34] For *wydq l'pr* see Chapter 3 n. 66 above.

[35] MT's *wĕyyāroṣ miššām/wayyāraṣ miššām*, "and broke in pieces from there"/"he
ran from there," is text-critically problematic. According to Washburn ("Perspective and Purpose," 74 n. 52), "*min* has no purpose here, and appears to have arisen
from an erroneous word-division"; he reads *wayyĕraṣēm šām*, "and he crushed them
there" ("i.e., right where he found them"). Cf., e.g., Montgomery, *Kings*, 533, 540;
Eynikel, *Reform of King Josiah*, 137, 257–8, favoring "mistreat, oppress" (e.g., Deut.
28:33; Judg. 10:8; Hos. 5:11; Amos 4:1; cf. Judg. 9:53 and Ps. 74:14; 2 Kgs. 18:21
[Isa. 36:6] might suggest "broken"). Gray prefers *wayĕdiqqēm šām*, "and [he] beat
them up small on the spot" (*I–II Kings*, 731 n. h); cf. also Jones, *1–2 Kings*, 623.
Cogan-Tadmor propose *wayyĕriṣēm šām*, "he hastened them, kept them distant" (*II
Kings*, 289). The parallel with v. 6 is not a reliable guide in the matter.

[36] Cf. D. R. Hillers, "Dust: Some Aspects of Old Testament Imagery," *Love &
Death in the Ancient Near East: Essays in Honor of Marvin H. Pope* (ed. by J. H. Marks
and R. M. Good; Guilford, CT: Four Quarters, 1987) 105–9. On the relationship
of *ʿapār*, "dust," and *ʾāpār*, "ash(es)" see Rainey, "Dust and Ashes," 79–81.

[37] Wiseman, *1–2 Kings*, 301.

[38] Reversing Sennacherib's motive: the Dauphin, expected to send a gift flatter-

the sanctuary or, conceivably, Assyria through its provincial authorities)[39] or perhaps one with more ritualistic potency.

J. Robinson takes 23:4bβ as "an addition made by a later scribe
to link the reform in Jerusalem with the reform later carried out at
Bethel."[40] The "cemetery scene" (23:16–18) makes reference to "these
things" (v. 16b)/"these things which you [Josiah] have done against
the altar at Bethel" (v. 17). In the final version of the account "these
things" are defined contextually as the destruction of the altar and
other appurtenances of the Bethel sanctuary (v. 15) and the desecration of the tombs and burning of the bones on its altar (v. 16a)
when the comment is uttered. If vv. 16b + 17 were part of an earlier version which lacked v. 15 and located the cemetery scene elsewhere, there would have been no contextual indicators of what
"things" Josiah did at Bethel unless (1) something in the "original"
version has dropped out of the text in the course of its evolution,[41]
or (2) v. 4bβ provided the reader with that information proleptically,
regardless of what Josiah may actually have done or was said to
have done at Bethel. Although "doublet" may be too strong a term
to describe the relationship between v. 4bβ and vv. 16b–18, they do
reverberate, being linked locationally (mention of the sanctuary at
"Bethel") and probably functionally (the desecration of something
there), giving merit to Robinson's suggestion. If v. 4bβ was part of
the "original" reform report, it alludes to the "things" of vv. 16b–17
independent of the prediction in 1 Kgs. 13:2.[42] Alternatively, since
v. 16b (including *wayyĕṭammĕ'ēhû* at the end of v. 16a) probably is a
secondary amplification of the action in v. 16a based on 13:1–32
(see Chapter 3.F above), the corresponding notice in v. 17 could
also be secondary, in which case v. 4bβ would have been the only

---

ing the new English king, sends instead a snide reminder of Henry's seemingly mis-
spent youth and the superiority of his own dynastic claim to the French throne (see
Shakespeare's *Henry V*, Act 1, Scene 2).

[39] Cf. Wiseman, *1–2 Kings*, 301.

[40] Robinson, *Second Book of Kings*, 219; cf. similarly, e.g., Montgomery, *Kings*, 529.

[41] *hā'ēlleh* would have been explained by this deleted material, or may be part
of the secondary adjustment.

[42] Cf. the similar conclusion, reached through a very different compositional analysis, of G. S. Ogden, "The Northern Extent of Josiah's Reforms," *Australian Biblical
Research* 26 (1978) 26–34. As to the purpose of the action he speculates (p. 29): "Is
he returning the remains of these alien cult objects to the nearest 'foreign' sanctuary? Is he seeking to defile Bethel? Or are there multiple motives?"

mention of Bethel in the "original" report—and the augmented "cemetery scene" a secondary doublet of it.

5.C. The Remains of the Roof-Top Altars (v. 12bβ)

wĕhišlîk ʾet-ʿăpārām ʾel-naḥal qidrôn;

and he threw their dust into the Wadi Kidron

The first half of this verse has probably been expanded secondarily (a marginal annotation?) by specifying that "the roof" (*haggāg*) was that of "Ahaz's upper-chamber" somewhere in the palace-complex (cf. 20:11).[43] The effect of this addition was to disrupt the locational continuity with v. 11 and v. 12aβ, both of which deal with the (outer) precincts of the Temple.[44] The verse resembles v. 4 and v. 6 only superficially, the sequence of actions being very different (see above). The author-compiler responsible for v. 12bβ obviously thought that these altars were disposed of in the same location as were the equipage and the asherah, which is certainly plausible but need not be original: it is equally plausible that the redactor responsible for the reference to "Ahaz's upper-chamber" added v. 12bβ to "correct" this omission in his *Vorlage*, and the dissimilarities with v. 4 and v. 6 suggest that this very likely is the case;[45] the expansion makes v. 12 a virtual doublet of v. 4 and v. 6. And if v. 12bβ is secondary, the dissimilarities with v. 4 might indicate that v. 4bβ may not be.

5.D. The "Bamoth of the Gates" (v. 8b)

wĕnātaṣ ʾet-bāmôt haśśĕʿārîm ʾăšer-petaḥ šaʿar yĕhôšuaʿ sar-hāʿîr ʾăšer-ʿal-śĕmōʾwl ʾîš bĕšaʿar hāʿîr;[46]

and [Josiah] tore down *bāmôt haśśĕʿārîm* (at the) entrance of the gate of Joshua, governor of the city, (at) one's left in the gate of the city.

---

[43] In addition to the commentaries (note Montgomery's opinion that, if secondary, it is "a worthy historical gloss" [*Kings*, 533]), see, e.g., Knoppers, *Two Nations under God 2*, 178 n. 9, and Eynikel, *Reform of King Josiah*, 254–5, 347.

[44] Cf. Eynikel, *Reform of King Josiah*, 254–5, 347.

[45] *Contra* Eynikel who disregards the dissimilarities with v. 4 and v. 6 (*ibid.*, 347).

[46] Some commentators emend *bĕšaʿar hāʿîr* to *bāʾ šaʿar hāʿîr* (cf. LXX[L], Targ.): e.g., Skinner, *I–II Kings*, 420; F. Delitzsch, *Die Lese- und Schreibfehler im Alten Testament* (Berlin: Vereinigung Wissenschaftlicher, 1920) 22; Gray, *I–II Kings*, 730 n. k. Montgomery rightly regards this as interpretive (*Kings*, 539); see the recent critique by

The reference evidently is to bamoth associated with a particular gate at a particular city, usually assumed to be Jerusalem[47] despite the difficulties with that identification: no "gate of Joshua, governor of the city," is otherwise known to have existed at Jerusalem, and no "Joshua" is known to have been "governor" of Jerusalem.[48] Since v. 8b immediately follows v. 5 in this compositional cluster, it might be supposed that the gate in question was located in one of "the cities of Judah" (e.g., Beer-sheba, mentioned in v. 8a),[49] but v. 5 could just as well imply that these were among the bamoth "around

J. A. Emerton, "'The High Places of the Gates in 2 Kings xxiii 8," *VT* 44 (1994) 460–1.

[47] Thus D. R. Ap-Thomas's imagination connects it with a small walled chamber containing two stone pillars adjacent to two shallow caves and an altar base (?) on the eastern slope of Jerusalem below the city wall ("Jerusalem," *Archaeology and Old Testament Study* [ed. by D. W. Thomas; Oxford: Clarendon, 1967] 288, relying on the work of K. M. Kenyon: "Excavations in Jerusalem, 1963," *PEQ* 99 [1964] 7–18; cf. also *idem, Jerusalem: Excavating 3000 Years of History* [London: Thames & Hudson, 1967] 66, and *idem,* "Israelite Jerusalem," *Near Eastern Archaeology in the Twentieth Century: Essays in Honor of Nelson Glueck* [ed. by J. A. Sanders; Garden City: Doubleday, 1970] 245–6). The "cultic" nature of the walled chamber and its functional relationship to the caves are dubious: see now H. J. Franken and M. L. Steiner, *Excavations by K. M. Kenyon in Jerusalem 1961–1967, 2: The Iron Age Extra-Mural Quarter on the South-East Hill* (British Academy Monographs in Archaeology 2; Oxford: Oxford University, 1990); cf. S. Bourke, "Excavations in the Iron Age Extra-Mural Quarter on the South-East Hill of Jerusalem: Review Article," *PEQ* 124 (1992) 59–62. The function of the caves is also disputed: see now I. Eshel and K. Prag, eds., *Excavations by K. M. Kenyon in Jerusalem 1961–1967, 4: The Iron Age Cave Deposits on the South-east Hill and Isolated Burials and Cemeteries Elsewhere* (British Academy Monographs in Archaeology 6; Oxford: Oxford University, 1995), and cf. H. J. Franken, "Cave I at Jerusalem—An Interpretation," *Trade, Contact, and the Movement of Peoples in the Eastern Mediterranean: Studies in Honour of J. Basil Hennessy* (ed. by S. Bourke and J.-P. Descœudres; Mediterranean Archaeology Supplement 3; Sydney: Mediarch, 1995) 233–40, and M. Steine, "Two Popular Cult Sites of Ancient Palestine: Cave 1 in Jerusalem and E 207 in Samaria," *SJOT* 11/1 (1997) 16–28. Activity at the installation ended c. 700; see further Chapter 7 n. 102 below.

[48] Although during Josiah's reign that post evidently was held by one Maaseiah (2 Chron. 34:8; cf. R. de Vaux, *Ancient Israel: Its Life and Institutions* [trans. by J. McHugh, New York: McGraw-Hill, 1961] 137), this datum is irrelevant to the question because the gate could well have been named after an earlier "governor."

[49] The case for Beersheba was argued by Y. Yadin ("Beer-Sheba: The High Place Destroyed by King Josiah," *BASOR* 222 [1976] 5–17, and [H. Shanks,] "Yadin Answers Beer-Sheva Excavator: Reply to Rainey's 'No Bama at Beer-Sheva'," *BARev* 3/4 [1977] 3–4; cf. H. Shanks, "Yigael Yadin Finds a Bama at Beer-Sheva," *BARev* 3/1 [1977] 3–12) and successfully refuted, in particular, by A. F. Rainey ("No Bama at Beer-Sheva," *BARev* 3/3 [1977] 18–21, 56, and cf. *idem,* "Hezekiah's Reform," 333–54); see the recent recapitulation by Emerton, "'High Places of the Gates'," 458–60. Nonetheless, Miller-Hayes still assert that the city was Beersheba (*History of Ancient Israel and Judah,* 399), without explanation.

Jerusalem." Many commentators, following the Versions (unambiguously only Pesh., however), see a single installation at this particular gate,[50] and this is not impossible. But the Versions plainly
had as much difficulty making sense of this passage as have modern commentators,[51] and this compromises their text-critical value;
the MT's *bāmôt* is not in itself implausible if one supposes that bamoth
were small installations or objects which could be clustered in one
place such as a gate.

The archaeological record contains several different examples of
possible cultic installations associated with some city-gates which
might illustrate this phenomenon.[52] One of these, found *between* the
double-gates at Dan,[53] is the basis of a proposal recently advanced

---

[50] So, e.g., Stade-Schwally, *Kings*, 294; Gray, *I–II Kings*, 730 n. i; N. H. Snaith,
"The Meaning of *śĕ'îrîm*," *VT* 25 (1975) 116. Cf. Burney, *Notes*, 359; Montgomery,
Kings, 532. Vaughan speculates that *bāmôt* may be correct as a "plural of local exten-
sion" or "a variant (but correct) vocalization of the feminine singular construct,
under the influence of Phoenician" (*Meaning*, 14; cf. also 61 nn. 39–41); cf. Cogan-
Tadmor, *II Kings*, 286–7.

[51] See the full discussion by Emerton, "'High Places of the Gates'," 455–6, and
T. H. Blomquist, *Gates and Gods: Cults in the City Gates of Iron Age Palestine—An Investigation of the Archaeological and Biblical Sources* (CBOT 46; Stockholm: Almqvist & Wiksell International, 1999) 153–4.

[52] See the 14 possible archaeological examples recently surveyed by Blomquist,
Gates and Gods, ch. 3. Notable of these are the well-known podium with canopy-
bases (?) to the right of the entrance of the Israelite gate complex at Dan (see the
preliminary excavation reports by A. Biran ["Tel Dan," *IEJ* 19 (1969) 239; "Tel
Dan," *BA* 37 (1974) 45–8; *Biblical Dan*, 238–41; "Tel Dan: Biblical Texts and
Archaeological Data," 8–11] and the summary by Blomquist [*Gates and Gods*, 57–67,
122–3 Figs. 2a–2b]) and the similarly-located podium and cultic objects recently
uncovered at Bethsaida (see Blomquist, *Gates and Gods*, 49–57 and the literature
cited there, and p. 121 Fig. 1). Y. Aharoni reports finding a round stone incense-
altar (?) just outside the Stratum V–IV gate at Beer-sheba; in view of the similarities between the gates, Aharoni infers from this object that there was a similar
bamah installation here as well ("Excavations at Tel Beer-Sheba," *BA* 35 [1972]
119; *idem*, "Excavations at Tel Beer-Sheba: Preliminary Report of the Fourth Season, 1972," *TA* 1 [1974] 38 and pl. 6:1), but this is far from certain (cf. Blomquist,
Gates and Gods, 83–5). See further J. T. Whitney, "'Bamoth' in the Old Testament,"
TynBul 30 (1979) 140–1, and Emerton, "'High Places of the Gates'," 462–3. The
Bethsaida podium served a cultic purpose as the base of a stele of a lunar deity;
the Dan podium might have had a similar function, but might as well be associated with the documented judicial and political functions of city-gates (on which
see now B. Halpern, "Eli's Death and the Israelite Gate: A Philological-Architectural Correlation," *E-I* 26 (1999) 52*–63*, and Blomquist, *Gates and Gods*, *passim*,
both with earlier literature).

[53] Biran, *Biblical Dan*, 243–245; *idem*, "Tel Dan: Biblical Texts and Archaeological Data," 8–11; and *idem*, "Sacred Spaces," 41–5, 70; Blomquist, *Gates and Gods*,
61. The installation (locus 5122), characterized by five standing stones, stands against

by J. A. Emerton:[54] he draws the reasonable inference that *haššĕʿārîm* in v. 8b could well indicate that the "gate" (*šaʿar*) of the city/of Joshua was such a double-gate complex (cf. 2 Sam. 19:9 with 18:24) and that the bamah (accepting the **bāmat* reading)—whatever it was—was situated between the main (inner) gate and the outer gate. Emerton's proposal is attractive enough, but it does not explain what was objectionable about the installation(s) at this particular gate or why they are said to have been "demolished" (*NTṢ*) rather than "defiled" (*ṬMʾ*) as are the bamoth in "the cities of Judah" (v. 8a) and on the Mount of Olives (v. 13). Since only v. 8b associates bamoth with gates, it cannot be inferred from this ambiguous reference alone that gate-bamoth were typical of IA cities in Palestine generally.[55] To date nothing really comparable to the Dan installation[56] is reported in conjunction with other contemporary double gates.[57]

---

the perpendicular wall to the right as one enters the city through the outer gate of the Lower Gate complex and connecting it to the outer wall of the main gate where the podium (see preceding note) is situated, both being between the two gates: see *Biblical Dan*, 248 fig. 206, 249 fig. 206a. See further n. 56 below.

[54] Emerton, "'High Places of the Gates'," 464–6.

[55] As in Yadin's understanding of *bāmôt haššĕʿārîm* as "bamah of the gate-type" ("Beer-Sheba: The High Place Destroyed by King Josiah," 8); similarly Blomquist, *Gates and Gods*, 157 ("a type of bamah that could be placed in a variety of ways in connection with a city gate, assumingly according to e.g. local traditions, functional needs and typographical conditions"). Blomquist's assessment of the archaeological record finds (*ibid.*, 209–12) the only assured examples of this "type of bamah" to be the podia at Bethsaida and Dan, both northern sites and both with north Syrian analogues.

[56] The archaeological picture at Dan is more complicated than Emerton's representation of it: a total of four such installations have thus far been found in conjunction with the gate, two (loci 5188 and 5181) *outside* the outer gate of the Lower Gate complex and one to the right of the entrance in the Upper Gate a considerable distance from the Lower Gate (Biran, "Sacred Spaces," 41–5, 70; Blomquist, *Gates and Gods*, 60–1). Biran speculates that these installations may have served the cultic needs of "merchants and travelers, many of whom were not indigenous inhabitants of Dan" (p. 45); cf. Blomquist, *Gates and Gods*, 65–6.

[57] Cf. Blomquist, *Gates and Gods*, ch. 3. For a 9th-century double gate at Tell en-Nasbeh/Mizpeh? which apparently remained in use until 586 see J. R. Zorn, "An Inner and Outer Gate Complex at Tell en-Nasbeh," *BASOR* 307 (1997) 53–66; other examples are found at Megiddo (Mazar, *Archaeology of the Land of the Bible*, 414 fig. 10.7) and Lachish (D. Ussishkin, *The Conquest of Lachish by Sennacherib* [Tel Aviv University Publications of the Institute of Archaeology 6; Tel Aviv: Tel Aviv University, 1982] 29 fig. 9, 30–1 and fig. 11). Cf. n. 55 above.

Some commentators read *bāmat/bāmôt-haśśĕʿārîm*, "the bamah/bamoth of he-goats,"[58] thought to be "demonic creatures of the desert" (cf. NEB),[59] a "shaggy, hirsute being that inhabits uninhabitable places and that malignantly threatens people with storms."[60] Reading *haśśĕ-ʿîrîm* for *haśśĕʿārîm* has the advantage of providing a motivation for the attack. Slight support for this reading is found in 2 Chron. 11:15 which asserts that Jeroboam b. Nebat "appointed for himself priests for the bamoth and for the he-goats and for the calves which he made"; this passage, the only attestation of the worship of he-goats prohibited in Lev. 17:7, anachronistically associates the practice with (North-)Israelite religiosity and the resettling of northern cultic personnel in Judah.[61] If the emendation is correct, these two passages might suggest a correspondingly late (post-Exilic) date for v. 8b when "pronounced but variant demonic conceptions" were evolving;[62] if v. 8a is a secondary addition to the reform report, perhaps an "aetiological note explaining some feature at the city gate [of post-Exilic Jerusalem] that was associated with Josiah's reform,"[63] this would account for the anomalous use of *NTS* (as in v. 15 which also is compositionally suspect: see Chapter 3.D above) rather than the expected *TM*'. It is worth noting that an incense altar found at Beersheba (Locus 532), bearing drawings of several animals, including an "animal with large horns (mountain-goat?)," shows a "surprising resemblance to" an altar from Samaria, and on the strength of the

---

[58] For discussion, in addition to many commentaries (by, e.g., Skinner, Benzinger, Burney, Stade-Schwally, Montgomery, J. Robinson), see, e.g., G. Hoffmann, "Kleinigkeiten," *ZAW* 2 (1882) 175; Delitzsch, *Lese- und Schreibfehler*, 80; W. F. Albright, "The High Place in Ancient Palestine," *VTSup* 4 (1957) 245; Snaith, "Meaning of *śĕʿîrîm*," 115–8; Vaughan, *Meaning*, 61 n. 41; Spieckermann, *Juda unter Assur*, 99–101; Eynikel, *Reform of King Josiah*, 137 n. 2, 236–8. Cf. Barthélemy, *Critique textuelle de l'Ancien Testament 1*, 419, and Emerton, "'The High Places of the Gates'," 458, and Blomquist, *Gates and Gods*, 154–7. Gray (*I–II Kings*, 730 n. j) reads *śōʿārîm*, "gatekeepers" (i.e., gate genii).

[59] Jones, *1–2 Kings*, 621 (cf. Isa. 13:21, 34:14); "goat-like ones/*śyrym* means nothing other than demons/*šdym*" (Sifre Lev. 17:7; cf. Deut. 32:17). For full discussion of the term see now B. Janowski, in *DDD* (1995) 1381–4, with earlier literature.

[60] An etymological composite offered by Eynikel, *Reform of King Josiah*, 238.

[61] For the possible connection to Azazel ("the demonic ruler of the wilderness") and the scapegoat ritual see, e.g., B. A. Levine, *Leviticus* (JPSTC; Philadelphia/New York/Jerusalem: Jewish Publication Society, 1989) 102, 250–3 (quotation from p. 251).

[62] Janowski, in *DDD*, 1383. G. R. Berry cites this as one indication that the Holiness Code was Josiah's "book" ("The Code Found in the Temple," *JBL* 39 [1920] 51).

[63] Jones, *1–2 Kings*, 621.

parallel is dated to the 6th–5th centuries.[64] Without supporting text-critical evidence, however, the emendation is no more than an attractive educated guess.

5.E. THE TOPHET IN THE BEN-HINNOM VALLEY (v. 10)

wĕṭimmēʾ ʾet-hattōpet ʾăšer bĕgê beny-hinnōm, lĕbiltî lĕhaʿăbîr ʾîš ʾet-bĕnô wĕʾet-bittô bāʾēš lammōlek;

and he defiled *hattōpet* which (was) in the Ben-Hinnom Valley, to prevent (any)one from passing his son or his daughter through fire to Molek.

Unlike "the gate of Joshua" in v. 8b, the location of the tophet in v. 10 is not in doubt: somewhere in the Ben-Hinnom Valley, usually identified with the Wadi er-Rababeh immediately southwest of Jerusalem (see Illustration), although some late biblical passages and certain post-biblical writers suggest that it was not always sharply differentiated from the Wadi Kidron.[65] The *waw*-conjunctive + Perfect construction casts doubt on the compositional integrity of the verse,[66] and mention of the Ben-Hinnom Valley at this point in the narrative interrupts the geographical sequence of the narrative, as does v. 5; if it is deleted as a secondary addition, "the geographic movement is even more obvious":[67] starting from the entrance of the Temple (v. 11, 12a–bα) through the Kidron valley (v. 12bβ) to the Mount of Olives (v. 13–14) beyond.

---

[64] E. Stern, "Limestone Incense Altars," in Y. Aharoni *et al.*, *Beer-Sheba I: Excavations at Beer-Sheba, 1969–1971 Seasons* (Institute of Archaeology Publications 2; Tel Aviv: Tel Aviv University Institute of Archaeology, 1973) 52 and pls. 29:1–2, 52:6; for the Samaria example see G. A. Reisner *et al.*, *Harvard Excavations at Samaria: 1908–1910* (Cambridge: Harvard University, 1924) 2. pl. 80:a–c. For further discussion see Stern, *Material Culture*, 182–95 (especially pp. 185, 194); S. Gitin, "Incense Altars from Ekron, Israel and Judah: Context and Typology," *E-I* 20 (1989) 52*–67* (especially p. 64*), and *idem*, "New Incense Altars from Ekron: Context, Typology and Function," *E-I* 23 (1992) 43*–9*. This style of portable altar, "found by the hundreds in Israel and throughout the ancient Near East" from the 6th century onward, "most probably represents the influence of a foreign cult" (Gitin, "Incense Altars from Ekron, Israel and Judah," 64*).

[65] See Chapter 3 n. 29 above.

[66] Note Gibson's observation that if *wĕṭimmēʾ* is sequential in 23:10 ("and [next] he defiled the Tophet") "it is not easy to see why [the *waw*-consecutive + Imperfect] was not used" ("Coordination by Vav," 274).

[67] Eynikel, *Reform of King Josiah*, 157; cf. also 155–6 n. 29, 245–9.

If the general location of the tophet is clear enough, nothing else about v. 10 is. The scholarly consensus has long considered the verse historically credible, but the activity which Josiah is said to have ended is much debated.

An Overview of the Biblical Evidence

There are five other references in the Kings History to cultic acts involving the burning of children.[68] 2 Kgs. 3:27a reports, without comment, that King Mesha of Moab "took his eldest son who was to reign after him *wayyăʿălēhû ʿōlâ* on the wall" of a besieged city. This act is represented by a neutral narrator as a desperate—and successful—military tactic conducted on one occasion under a particular set of circumstances; Ugaritic and Egyptian sources suggest that the ritual death of a child as an emergency measure in time of war (and other national calamities?) probably was part of the traditional Syro-Palestinian cultic arsenal.[69] The notice, also without comment, that the Sepharvites transplanted to the territory of (North-) Israel "burned their sons/children in fire to Adrammelek and Anammelek, the Sepharvamian gods" (17:31b) reveals nothing about the rite except that it involved the "burning" (*ŚRP*) of children; the identity of this people is disputed and the veracity of the notice cannot be checked.[70] Linguistically distinct from these two, the three remaining occurrences use the *ʿBR* (in Hiphil) + *bāʾēš* idiom, as in 23:10: both Ahaz (16:3) and Manasseh (21:6a; cf. v. 2) are accused of having "passed his son through fire," emulating "the abominations of the nationalities whom Yahweh dispossessed before the children of Israel," and this is among the perverse practices attributed to the

---

[68] 1 Kgs. 16:34 probably concerns foundation sacrifices but there is no explicit mention of the means of ritual execution.

[69] Cf. P. Derchain, "Les plus ancien Témoignages de Sacrifices d'Enfants chez les Sémites occidentaux," *VT* 20 (1970) 351–5; A. J. Spalinger, "A Canaanite Ritual Found in Egyptian Military Reliefs," *Journal of the Society for the Study of Egyptian Antiquities* 8 (1978) 47–60; B. Margalit, "Why Mesha of Moab Sacrificed his Oldest Son," *BARev* 12/6 (1986) 62–3, 76 (and cf. J. M. Sasson's "Letter to the Editor," *BARev* 13/2 [1987] 12, 60); J. K. Hoffmeier, "Further Evidence for Infant Sacrifice in the Ancient Near East," *BARev* 13/2 (1987) 60–1; M. S. Smith, *The Early History of God: Yahweh and the other Deities in Ancient Israel* (San Francisco: Harper & Row, 1990) 135–6; V. A. Donohue, "A Gesture of Submission," *Studies in Pharaonic Religion and Society in Honour of J. Gwyn Griffiths* (ed. by A. Lloyd; London: Egypt Exploration Society, 1992) 82–114.

[70] For recent discussion see H. Avalos, in *ABD* (1992) 5.1090, with earlier literature.

(North-)Israelites which led to their exile (17:17aα, reading "their sons and their daughters" as in 23:10). The Jeremiah corpus mentions *bāmôt-hattōpet* (7:31a) and *bāmôt-habbaʿal* (19:5a; 32:35aα) in the Ben-Hinnom Valley and describes the actions performed there as "passing through" (*ʿBR*: 32:35aα) and "burning" (*ŚRP*: 7:31; 19:5a) children.

ŚRP is a straightforward indication that the act(s) in question included the physical burning, but not necessarily incinerating, of children. Although *ʿBR* (in Hiphil) + *bāʿēš* has been somewhat controversial in this context,[71] in biblical usage the *ʿBR* (in Hiphil) + *B* idiom always implies that the prepositional object is penetrated and traversed in the course of the verbal action,[72] meaning that one would have been passed literally "through fire."[73] That such an operation could/would have resulted in the physical endangerment of a living child—a painful singeing at the least—is beyond doubt (cf. Num. 31:21–24);[74] "burning" (*ŚRP*), but not necessarily incinerating, would aptly describe the physical consequences of it.

Deuteronomic legislation contains two references to the ritualistic burning of children. The reference in 18:10 (*maʿăbîr bĕnô ûbittô bāʾēš*) is the first item in a list of various means of "mediation with the other world—the world of the gods, spirits and the dead" (vv. 9–14, quoted in part below),[75] "abominations" of the nationalities which Yahweh is "dispossessing" for the Israelites who are enjoined from

---

[71] For the interpretational history of this and other issues relating to the question of *mlk*/"Molek" see G. C. Heider, *The Cult of Molek: A Reassessment* (JSOTSup 43; Sheffield: JSOT, 1985) ch. 1 (especially pp. 66–81).

[72] Cf. Ex. 36:6; Lev. 25:9; Deut. 2:30; Ezek. 14:15; 47:3–4; Ezra 1:1; 10:7; Neh. 8:15; 2 Chron. 30:5; 36:22. See also H. J. Austel, *Prepositional and Non-Prepositional Complements with Verbs of Motion in Biblical Hebrew* (unpublished dissertation, University of California at Los Angeles, 1969) ch. 6 (especially pp. 193ff.).

[73] And not "between rows of fire," as M. Weinfeld contends ("The Worship of Molech and of the Queen of Heaven and its Background," *UF* 4 [1972] 133–154 [especially pp. 141–3]), which would require *ʿBR* (in Hiphil) + *BN*: cf. Gen. 15:17 and Jer. 34:19.

[74] Cf. M. Smith, "A Note on Burning Babies," *JAOS* 95 (1975) 477–9, and the response by M. Weinfeld, "Burning Babies in Ancient Israel," *UF* 10 (1978) 411–3. See also more fully J. Day, *Molech: A God of Human Sacrifice in the Old Testament* (University of Cambridge Oriental Publication 41; Cambridge: Cambridge University, 1989), 15–20.

[75] J. Blenkinsopp, "Deuteronomy and the Politics of Post-Mortem Existence," *VT* 45 (1995) 11–5 (quotation from p. 11).

adopting them (cf. 2 Kgs. 21:2). The reference in 12:31 occurs in
an injunction to the Israelites (vv. 29–31) to

> take care that you are not ensnared by [the indigenous nationalities]
> after they have been destroyed before you, and that you do not inquire
> about their gods saying: "How did these nationalities serve their gods,
> so I too may do likewise?" You shall not do so for Yahweh your god,
> for every abomination which Yahweh hates they have done for their
> gods, *kî gam 'et-běnêhem wě'et-běnōtêhem yiśrěpû bā'ēš lē'lōhêhem.*

Contextually, the distinction made by these two passages would seem
to be between a ritual act of mediation (*'BR* + *bā'ēš*) and an act of
(sacrificial?) worship (*ŚRP*). 12:31 looks like a secondary afterthought—
it has the same distinctive grammatical structure as 2 Kgs. 23:19a
and 23:24a which are secondary to the "Josianic" edition of the
reform report—perhaps an inter-textual allusion to the especially
loath-some Shepharvamian practice of 17:31b to exemplify these
"abominations."

Although the context of 2 Kgs. 17:31b and Deut. 12:3 leave no
doubt that *ŚRP* there does refer to a form of (sacrificial?) worship,
neither *'BR* nor *ŚRP* alone necessarily implies a "sacrificial" act of
worship. The "passing through fire/water" of certain metal objects
in Num. 31:21–24 constitutes a purification procedure. In Ex. 13:12
"the passing through to Yahweh" of "all [males] that first opens the
womb" is understood as an act of "consecration" (*QDŠ* [v. 2]);[76] similarly, contemporary Assyro-Aramean documents tell of "burning"
(*šarāpu*) or "sacrificing" (*ramu*) one's children to a deity, perhaps also

---

[76] First-born human males are included (vv. 2, 13b), raising the possibility that
human sacrifice is envisioned. The method of "consecration" is not specified here:
first-born male cattle and sheep "shall be Yahweh's" (v. 12b; cf. 34:19) presumably
by sacrifice, but both first-born male asses and humans are "redeemed" (v. 13; cf.
34:20) in lieu of death. The alternative for an ass is a lamb which presumably is
sacrificed; if no substitute is provided the ass is killed (by breaking its neck and not
sacrificial slaughter). Although no sacrificial alternative for humans is specified, Gen.
22:1–19 implies that a ram could have been used; but it is quite possible that there
were "service" alternatives as well (e.g., Hannah's vow to dedicate her first-born
son, Samuel, to Yahweh for having "opened her womb" after years of barrenness
[1 Sam. 1:11, 21–28]). See S. Ackerman, "Child Sacrifice: Returning God's Gift—
Barren Women Give Birth to Exceptional Children," *BRev* 9/3 (1993) 20–28, 56.
Weinfeld ("Worship of Molech," especially 140ff., and *idem*, "Burning Babies in
Ancient Israel," 413 n. 4), followed lately by Albertz (*History of Israelite Religion 1*,
190–3), maintains that the expression identifies the rite as an initiatory consecration (cf. Lev. 18:21; 20:3–5; see further below) rather than cultic killing, the texts
which suggest otherwise being polemical exaggerations or references to different rituals. Cf. N. H. Snaith, "The Cult of Molech," *VT* 16 (1966) 123–4, and *idem*,
Leviticus and Numbers (London: Nelson, 1967) 125.

a consecration/dedication act rather than an immolation, as a ritualistic punishment for desecrating a stele or violating contract obligations, meted out at a special installation (*bīt ḥamri*) evidently outside the city.[77] 2 Kgs. 23:10 likewise localizes the Judahite practice at an installation called *hattōpet* below the walls of Jerusalem. The word probably means something like "fireplace" (cf. Isa. 30:33), either cognate with Aram. *tapyā* (cf. Syr. *tĕpa/āyā*) with a similar meaning or possibly an Aramaic loan-word.[78] In 23:10 it is usually understood as a *termus technicus* for the entire installation—the actual "fireplace" apparatus[79] and any other architectural accouterments associated with it.[80] 23:10 gives no indication of the purpose of the "passing" done here,

---

[77] See K. Deller, in *Or* 34 (1965) 382–6; Weinfeld, "Worship of Molech," 144ff.; Cogan, *Imperialism and Religion*, 82–3; Smith, "Note on Burning Babies," 479; Albertz, *History of Israelite Religion 1*, 192, 342 n. 34.

[78] See the recent discussion and review of alternatives by Day, *Molech*, 24–8. Cf. the noun *tōpet*, "(act of) spitting," in Job 17:6: although usually considered a homonym, "spitting" would aptly describe the hiss and crackle of a hot wood or charcoal fire or of a piece of roasting meat (thus a synonym for "to spit" in English is "to sputter," as a candle flame or a roasting sausage: *OED* [1971] 629–30), as any backyard barbecuer can attest. For an Egyptian derivation—"city of Ptah"> "city of fire"—see now M. Görg, "*Topaet* (Tofet): 'Die (Stätte) des Feuergottes'?" *BN* 43 (1988) 12–3.

[79] For an archaeologically-known example, an oven-like burning apparatus, at Akhzib see Chapter 8 n. 17 below.

[80] If the Phoenician practice of (presumed) child-sacrifice is germane, as is commonly assumed (see below), the archaeological evidence from Carthage may be instructive in this regard (S. Brown, *Late Carthaginian Child Sacrifice and Sacrificial Monuments in their Mediterranean Context* [JSOT/ASOR Monograph 3; Sheffield: JSOT, 1991] 170; see also pp. 72, 142–5): "The vessels and other paraphernalia depicted on [commemorative] stelae indicate as well that there were rituals associated with killing and burying a child victim that required planning, preparation, and, presumably, professional assistance. Associated with and probably preceding the sacrifice proper were other ritual acts, depicted in full and in schematic form on stelae such as the greeting of the god(s) with right hands raised and palms facing outward, the pouring of libations from pitchers, and the burning of incense. Holy liquids may have been stored in very large, open kantharoi or kraters and scooped out with special, deep ladles. These ritual acts took place by small gabled shrines and at altars located outside the [burial ground] proper (or not yet found in context inside any known [burial-ground])." Classical sources do not mention a temple or cult-building in connection with the Phoenician practice; the "gabled shrines" are known only from the stelae. J. A. Dearman sees the matter differently ("The Tophet in Jerusalem: Archaeology and Cultural Profile," *JNSL* 22 [1996] 62): "A Mediterranean tophet was an open-air cult-place located at the edge of town and/or near a cemetery.... Apparently a tophet did not require a temple or even a stone altar. A wooden pyre or stone pit would suffice for the fire, although personnel were available to perform the rituals. Typically there was only one tophet per town, with a perimeter wall or similar means of demarcation where the cultic rites took place." Similarly, e.g., M. Gras, P. Rouillard, and J. Teixidor, "The Phoenicians and Death," *Berytus* 39 (1991) especially 161–73.

except that it was done "to/for" *mōlek*, a word of disputed meaning but more likely a deity-name or epithet (of Baal?) than a type of offering (cf. Phoen. *mulk*).[81] Use of the *'BR* (in Hiphil) + *B* idiom and mention of both "sons" and "daughters" as victims of the ritual, suggest a link with Deut. 18:10 and thereby also to 2 Kgs. 17:17aα and 21:6a, all passages which place the practice firmly within the rich and eclectic category of divination and magic.[82] These lists, together with such passages as Isa. 57:9[83] and the chthonic associations of the Ben-Hinnom Valley[84] (cf. also the enigmatic "Valley of Vision" in Isa. 22:1, 5),[85] point to some sort of necromantic divination rite involving the burning of children.

Is this understanding of 2 Kgs. 23:10 compatible with the three prose references in the Jeremiah corpus? The vocabular similarities among the four verses are clear enough, but none are identical:

---

[81] See the recent discussion of this issue by Heider, *Cult of Molek*, in *ABD* (1992) 4.895–8, and in *DDD* (1995) 1090–7; D. Edelman, "Biblical Molek Reconsidered," *JAOS* 107 (1987) 727–31; Day, *Molech*; S. Ackerman, *Under Every Green Tree: Popular Religion in Sixth-Century Judah* (HSM 46; Atlanta: Scholars, 1992) 126–38. Advocates of the view that the term refers to a type of sacrifice (classically O. Eissfeldt, *Molk als Opferbegriff im Punischen und Hebraischen und das Ende des Gottes Moloch* [Beitrage zur Religionsgeschichte des Altertums 3; Halle: Niemeyer, 1935]) must explain the image of "whoring after" a sacrifice in Lev. 20:5. Cf. K. A. D. Smelik, "Moloch, Molekh or Molk-Sacrifice?" *SJOT* 9/1 (1995) 133–42 ("an idol named 'the *Molekh*' was deliberately introduced into the biblical text during the Persian period in order to conceal the fact that Judahite worship of YHWH in the eighth and seventh century BCE also included child sacrifice" [p. 141]). B. Margalit reconstructs a reference in the Bar-Rakib inscription (KAI 215.21)—*ysb' mlk* [*mn dmh*], "'Molech' drank [of his (i.e., a child's) blood] to excess" ("Studies in NW Semitic Inscriptions," *UF* 26 [1994] 304, 305)—which he considers "confirmation of the view which identifies the Biblical 'Molech' with the god of the Netherworld known (from Ugaritic) as *mt/Môtu*, and possibly related to the Ammonite national god 'Milkom' (Ammonite: *mlkm*)" (p. 312), but this reading is uncertain. An 8th-century Phoenician inscription, recently discovered at Incirli in Turkey, reportedly mentions human sacrifice in a military context apparently to a god Molek ([H. Shanks,] "Who—or What— Was Molech?" *BARev* 22/4 [1996] 13), but the text is as yet unpublished.

[82] Tigay suggests that the placement of the ritual "passing" of children among "magical and divinatory practices" in 18:10 may be due to an interpretation of Mesha's action (2 Kgs. 3:27) as a "magical act designed to produce some kind of supernatural outburst against the enemy" (*Deuteronomy*, 465); that interpretation, for all we know, may be historically accurate (see further below).

[83] See especially W. H. Irwin, "The Smooth Stones of the Wadi? Isaiah 57,6," *CBQ* 29 (1967) 31–40; T. J. Lewis, "Death Cult Imagery in Isaiah 57," *HAR* 11 (1987) 267–84; Day, *Molech*, 50–2; Ackerman, *Under Every Green Tree*, ch. 3. Differently, cf. B. B. Schmidt, *Israel's Beneficent Dead: Ancestor Cult and Necromancy in Ancient Israelite Religion and Tradition* (2nd edn.; Winona Lake: Eisenbrauns, 1996) 254–9.

[84] See Chapter 3 n. 26 above.

[85] According to R. B. Y. Scott, "the reference is probably to divination at an

2 Kgs. 23:10	Jer. 7:31	Jer. 19:5a	Jer. 32:35aα
haṭṭōpet	*bāmôt-haṭṭōpet*	*bāmôt habbaʿal*	*bāmôt habbaʿal*
lĕhaʿăbîr	*liśrōp*	*liśrōp*	*lĕhaʿăbîr*
bāʾēš	*bāʾēš*	*bāʾēš*	———
benô/ bittô	*bĕnêhem/ bĕnōtêhem*	*bĕnêhem*	*bĕnêhem/ bĕnōtêhem*
lammōlek	———	(*ʿōlôt*) *labbāʿal*	*lammōlek*

On the assumption that *haṭṭōpet* in 2 Kgs. 23:10 refers to a single cultic installation, most commentators read **bāmat* in Jer. 7:31 (cf. LXX and Targ.),[86] and some also apply this reading to 19:5a and 32:35aα even though there is no text-critical warrant for doing so.[87] In Jeremiah *haṭṭōpet* seems to be used as a toponym comparable to *gêʾ ben-hinnōm* (cf. 7:32; 19:6, 11–12); in 7:31a, therefore, **bāmat/ bāmôt-haṭṭōpet* would mean "the bamah/bamoth of [i.e., in/at the place called] Tophet." 19:5a and 32:35aα, however, identify the installation(s) by the deity to whom the practice there was directed: **bāmat/ bāmôt habbaʿal*, "the bamah/bamoth of Baal." The nomenclature is interpretive, since 32:35aα identifies *habbaʿal* as Molek, as in 2 Kgs. 23:10. Both 7:31a and 19:5a use *ŚRP* to define the practice, but identify the victims and the practitioners differently.

There is considerable agreement regarding the compositional history of the Jeremiah passages. 32:35aα is part of what is almost cer-

---

altar in the 'Valley of Hinnom'" ("The Book of Isaiah, Chapters 1–39: Introduction and Exegesis," *IB* [1956] 5.290); see further Heider, *Molech*, 355–6.

[86] So, e.g., B. Duhm, *Das Buch Jeremiah* (KHCAT 11; Leipzig/Tübingen: Mohr, 1901) 84; S. R. Driver, *The Book of the Prophet Jeremiah* (London: Hodder & Stoughton, 1906) 46; A. S. Peake, *Jeremiah and Lamentations* (New-Century Bible 16; New York: Frowde, [1910]) 1.155; F. Nötscher, *Das Buch Jeremias* (HSAT 7.2; Bonn: Hanstein, 1934) 88; J. P. Hyatt, "The Book of Jeremiah: Introduction and Exegesis," *IB* (1956) 5.878; E. A. Leslie *Jeremiah* (New York: Abingdon, 1954), 129–3; J. Bright, *Jeremiah* (AB 21; Garden City: Doubleday, 1965) 57; E. W. Nicholson, *The Book of the Prophet Jeremiah* (CBC; Cambridge: Cambridge University, 1973) 1.82–3; Vaughan, *Meaning*, 14, 61 n. 42; J. A. Thompson, *The Book of Jeremiah* (NICOT; Grand Rapids: Eerdmans, 1980) 291; W. McKane, *A Critical and Exegetical Commentary on Jeremiah 1* (ICC; Edinburgh: Clark, 1986) 178–9; Carroll, *Jeremiah*, 220; Ackerman, *Under Every Green Tree*, 118 and n. 42. Cf. Holladay, *Jeremiah 1*, 264. Rudolph suggests that the MT may be a "Plural der Ausdehung" because presumably only one cult place is involved (*Jeremia* [HAT 12; Tübingen: Mohr, 1947] 48); cf. P. C. Craigie's translation "they have built high places, Tophet which is in the Valley of [B]en-Hinnom" (*Jeremiah 1–25* [with P. H. Kelley and J. F. Drinkard, Jr.; WBC 26; Waco: Word, 1991] 115). See further below.

[87] E.g., Duhm, Voltz, Rudolph, Leslie, followed by Vaughan, *Meaning*, 14, 61 n. 42. According to Nötscher, the pl. form "ist vielleicht absichtliche rhetorische Verallgemeinerund für das eine Tophet" (*Jeremias*, 154). See further below.

tainly a secondary insertion (minimally vv. 30–35, missing in LXX).[88] V. 32 recalls 2:26, 8:1, 11:17, and 17:25, all late interpolations, while vv. 34–35 "reflect, with few changes of wording, 7:30–31";[89] these changes include the verb ʿBR and the nomenclature "bamah/bamoth of Baal" (from 19:5a?). 19:5a is part of what is widely considered a secondary expansion of the broken-flask episode (vv. 2b–9 + 11b–13),[90] although W. L. Holladay attributes the entire pericope to Baruch, as "a narrative version of 7:30–34."[91] Mention of "filling this place" with "innocents' blood" (*dam nĕqîyīm* [v. 4b]), contextually identified as that of the "sons" burned as offerings to/for Baal (*ʿōlôt labbāʿal* [missing in LXX]) in the Ben-Hinnom Valley" (v. 6; cf. Ps. 106:37–38), links the passage to 2 Kgs. 21:16 and especially 24:4a, two late interpolations which add this item to the heap of Manasseh's abominations;[92] they shift the responsibility for the offense from "the people" to Manasseh and enlarge the "place" which was "filled" from the valley to all of Jerusalem, differences suggesting that they may be secondary applications of the Jeremiaic prototype (cf. also Jer. 22:17 in reference to Jehoiakim).[93] In its use of ŚRP and

---

[88] Recently, e.g., Holladay, *Jeremiah 2*, 205, 207, 219; Carroll, *Jeremiah*, 386–9; J. R. Lundbom, in *ABD* (1992) 3.715; W. McKane, *A Critical and Exegetical Commentary on Jeremiah 2* (ICC; Edinburgh: Clark, 1996) 847–9.

[89] Holladay, *Jeremiah 2*, 219.

[90] Cf., e.g., Rudolph, *Jeremia*, 109; Leslie, *Jeremiah*, 318–9; Hyatt, "Jeremiah," 5.966–7; Bright, *Jeremiah*, 131; Weinfeld, *Deuteronomy and the Deuteronomic School*, 28–9; Nicholson, *Jeremiah*, 1.162–3; Carroll, *Jeremiah*, 386–9; McKane, *Jeremiah 1*, 451–59 (especially p. 455); Craigie, *Jeremiah 1–25*, 256–8.

[91] Holladay, *Jeremiah 1*, 536–9 (quotation from p. 539). Cf. also Thompson, *Jeremiah*, 446–7; Craigie, *Jeremiah 1–25*, 258; Lundbom, *Jeremiah 1–20*, 836–8, 841–2.

[92] *wĕgam dām nāqî šāpak mĕnaššeh harbēh mĕʾōd ʿad ʾăšer-millēʾ ʾet-yĕrûšālaim peh lāpeh, lĕbad mēhaṭṭāʾtô ʾăšer heheṭîʾ ʾet-yĕhûdâ laʿăśôt hāraʿ bĕʿênê yhwh* (2 Kgs. 21:16); *wĕgam dam-hannāqî ʾăšer šāpāk wayĕmallēʾ ʾet-yĕrûšālaim dām nāqî* (24:4): cf., e.g., Montgomery, *Kings*, 552–3.; Dietrich, *Prophetie und Geschichte*, 30–1; Gray, *I–II Kings*, 757; Nelson, *Double Redaction*, 66; Jones, *1–2 Kings*, 594, 634–5; McKenzie, *Trouble with Kings*, 192–3; Provan, *Hezekiah*, 146 n. 40, 151 n. 62; Lowery, *Reforming Kings*, 175–6; Smelik, "Portrayal of King Manasseh," 151–3 ("bloody oppression of the poor" [cf. Jer. 22:3, 17]; 167); Schmid, "Manasse und der Untergang Judas," 92–3. Van Keulen's defense of the authenticity of 21:16 (*Manasseh*, 173, 181–3, 189–90) is not convincing: see the rebuttal by Eynikel, "Portrait of Manasseh," 258–61 (especially n. 97). Some commentators suggest that 24:4aβ is secondary to 24:4aα because of "the awkwardness and repetitiveness of the phrase" (Jones, *1–2 Kings*, 635); cf. Dietrich, *Prophetie und Geschichte*, 29ff.

[93] Holladay considers it "probable" that 2 Kgs. 24:4 is dependent of Jer. 19:4 (both use *MLʾ*), while it is "possible" that Jer. 22:17 is dependent on 2 Kgs. 21:16 (*Jeremiah 1*, 540; cf. also p. 537). See further now Halpern, "Why Is Manasseh Blamed?" 505–14.

identification of the victims as the "sons" of the practitioners and "burnt offerings" to/for Baal, Jer. 19:4–5 could be an interpretative application of 2 Kgs. 21:6 melded with Jer. 7:30–32.

The heart of the matter, therefore, is 7:29–34. Since the passage is post-Josianic,[94] it cannot speak of cultic activity eliminated by Josiah unless it is supposed, with Holladay (and many others), that it describes "the renewed practice of pagan rites in the temple area during the reign of Jehoiakim," including the "reinstate[ment], overtly or covertly," of the Molek rites in the Ben-Hinnom Valley.[95] There are ample indications that the cultic burning of children occurred in post-Josianic Judah and post-Exilic Yehud: "You took your sons and your daughters that you bore me and sacrificed [*ZBH*] them to [male idols] for food. As if your harlotry was not enough, you slaughtered [*ŠHT*] my sons as an offering and passed them through ['*BR*] to them" (Ezek. 16:20–21; cf. 20:31a [with '*BR* + *bā'ēš*]); "with their idols they have committed adultery, and blood is on their hands; and they have even passed through ['*BR*] to them to eat the sons whom they had borne to me" (23:37aβ–b); "[you] who slay [*ŠHT*] your children in the valleys, under the clefts of the rocks; among the smooth stones of the valley is your portion . . . to them you have poured out a drink offering, you have brought a cereal offering" (Isa. 57:5b–6a); "they sacrificed [*ZBH*] their sons and their daughters to the demons; they poured out innocent blood, the blood of their sons and daughters whom they sacrificed [*ZBH*] to the idols of Canaan, and the land was polluted with blood" (Ps. 106:37–38). Even with due allowance for polemic hyperbole, there is little doubt that the references are to sacrificial immolation providing sardonic "food for the gods." Except for Isa. 57:5b–6a (cf. vv. 9–10), there is nothing

---

[94] Holladay dates it to c. 600 (*Jeremiah 1*, 265–6 ["made public in 600 or soon thereafter" (p. 266)], 268), while commentators who consider Jeremiah's career to have begun in Josiah's reign date it earlier (e.g., Thompson, *Jeremiah*, 445–6, and Lundbom, *Jeremiah 1–20*, 502 [c. 609–605]).

[95] Holladay, *Jeremiah 1*, 268. He maintains that "Josiah had rid Judah of pagan practices which were specifically associated with foreign powers, and what reappeared in Jehoiakim's reign was the fertility worship which had always been associated with Canaanite Palestine" (p. 80; see also *idem*, "A Coherent Chronology of Jeremiah's Early Career," *Le Livre de Jérémie: Le Prophète et son Milieu, les Oracles et leur Transmission* [ed. by P.-M. Bogaert; BETL 54; Leuven: Leuven University 1981] 67–8), but there is nothing in the reform report to support such a differentiation. More typical is Lundbom's assertion that "subsequent to the Temple Oracles [or Sermon] . . . idol worship had been reintroduced into the Temple and the Topheth had been rebuilt" (*Jeremiah 1–20*, 502; cf. also pp. 116–7).

suggestive of divination here or in the Jeremiah texts, raising the possibility that these references may be to an entirely different practice than that represented in the Kings History, something more akin to the sacrificial "burning" of children in Deut. 12:31 than to the divinatory "passing" of children in Deut. 18:10. If Josiah did suppress the divinatory practice in the Ben-Hinnom Valley, a *different* cultic practice with a similar methodology soon took its place;[96] and if 2 Kgs. 23:10 is also post-Josianic, it too could refer to that sacrificial activity.

Levitical legislation further complicates matters: "You shall not give [*NTN*] any of your children to pass them through [*'BR*] to Molek, and so profane the name of your god: I am Yahweh" (Lev. 18:21). This proscription and the elaborated version in 20:2–5 are found in the midst of legislation concerning illicit sexual couplings, the incongruity of the juxtaposition demonstrated by the ingenuity of the ancient Jewish attempts to explain it.[97] Perhaps the reference is to some sort of ritual dedication (cf. Ex. 13:12) to Molek.[98] Lev. 20:6 + 27 presents another anomaly by interpolating a prohibition of the two forms of divination included in the late appendix to the reform report (2 Kgs. 23:24a: *'et-hā'ōbōt wĕ'et-hayyiddĕʿōnîm*).[99]

Compositional and Historical Considerations

Scholarly speculation on this topic has proceeded, for the most part, on the assumptions that (1) all of these passages refer to one and the same cultic praxis which is related in some way to the child sacrifice practices castigated by later Classical writers[100] and the exten-

---

[96] See, e.g., Cogan, *Imperialism and Religion*, 77–83, who supposes that "defiled by Josiah, the Tophet may have been rededicated after his death to serve a popular sacrificial cult in which royalty no longer had a part" (p. 78); cf. Cogan-Tadmor, *II Kings*, 288.

[97] See the compilation and discussion of this material by G. Vermes, "Leviticus 18:21 in Ancient Jewish Bible Exegesis," *Studies in Aggadah, Targum and Jewish Liturgy in Memory of Joseph Heinemann* (ed. by J. J. Petuchowski and E. Fleischer; Jerusalem: Magnes/Hebrew Union College, 1981) 108–24; cf. also J. E. Hartley and T. Dwyer, "An Investigation into the Location of the Law on Offerings to Molek in the Book of Leviticus," *Go to the Land I Will Show You: Studies in Honor of Dwight W. Young* (ed. by J. E. Coleson and V. H. Matthews; Winona Lake: Eisenbrauns, 1996) especially 84–5.

[98] See n. 76 above.

[99] Lev. 20:6a: *wĕhannepeš tipnâ 'el-hā'ōbōt wĕ'el-hayyiddĕʿōnîm liznōt 'aḥărêhem*; v. 27a: *wĕ'iš 'ô-'iššâ kî-yihyeh bāhem 'ôb 'ô yiddeʿōnî môt yûmātu*.

[100] See the collection by Day, *Molech*, 86–91. Cf. Gras-Rouillard-Teixidor, "Phoeni-

sive physical and epigraphic evidence of the immolation of children at Carthage,[101] Tyre,[102] and elsewhere in the Phoenician/Punic cultural world;[103] that (2) this praxis "became prevalent as an established practice during the reign of Manasseh";[104] and that (3) it was suppressed by Josiah in accordance with the deuteronomic proscription. In point of fact, none of these assumptions is necessary nor even very likely.

The homogenizing impulse is contrary to the biblical record which, as shown above, suggests *prima facie* that we may be dealing with three different ritual activities: (1) a special emergency rite involving the sacrifice of a child performed by a king or his representative (Mesha [2 Kgs. 3:27a], reinforced by comparable Ugaritic, Egyptian, and certain Phoenician/Punic literary materials)[105] and reported without criticism; (2) a ritual "passing" of children for divinatory purposes and not confined to the king (Deut. 18:10 and the Kings History references); and (3) a sacrificial "burning" of children (Deut.

---

cians and Death," especially 154–9, characterizing these sources as "the defamatory propaganda of the enemies of Carthage" (p. 157) and finding that "the only conclusion to be drawn from [these sources] is that child sacrifice was not a regular but an exceptional practice among the Phoenicians of the western Mediterranean" (p. 159).

[101] See L. E. Stager, "The Rite of Child Sacrifice at Carthage," *New Light on Ancient Carthage* (ed. by J. G. Pedley; Ann Arbor: University of Michigan, 1980) 1–11; *idem*, "A View from the Tophet," *Phönizier im Westen* (ed. by H. G. Niemeyer; Madrider Beiträge 8; Mainz: von Zabern, 1982) 155–66; *idem* and S. R. Wolff, "Child Sacrifice at Carthage—Religious Rite or Population Control?" *BARev* 10/1 (1984) 30–51; Brown, *Late Carthaginian Child Sacrifice*.

[102] See H. Seeden, "A Tophet in Tyre?" *Berytus* 39 (1991) 39–87. Cf. H. Sader, "Phoenician Stelae from Tyre," *Berytus* 39 (1991) 101–26, and *idem*, "Phoenician Stele from Tyre (continued)," *Studi epigrafici e linguistici* 9 (1992) 53–79.

[103] Cf. also, e.g., A. Gianto, "Some Notes on the Mulk Inscription from Nebi Yunis (RES 367)," *Bib* 68 (1987) 397–401; Ackerman, *Under Every Green Tree*, 121 and n. 54, 123 and n. 61, 123–5; Gras-Rouillard-Teixidor, "Phoenicians and Death," 127–76; F. M. Cross, "A Phoenician Inscription from Idalion: Some Old and New Texts Relating to Child Sacrifice," *Scripture and Other Artifacts: Essays on the Bible and Archaeology in Honor of Philip J. King* (ed. by M. D. Coogan *et al.*; Louisville: Westminster John Knox 1994) 93–107; A. Kempinski, "From Death to Resurrection: The Early Evidence," *BARev* 21/5 (1995) 56–65, 82.

[104] L. E. Fuller, *The Historical and Religious Significance of the Reign of Manasseh* (Leipzig: Drugulin, 1912) 79; similarly of late, e.g., B. A. Levine, *Leviticus* (JPSTC 3; Philadelphia/New York/Jerusalem: Jewish Publication Society, 1989) 260 ("it can be reliably stated that this cult was sponsored by Manasseh and Amon, kings of Judah during the seventh century BCE, and that it involved the burning of children as sacrifices").

[105] E.g., Philo of Byblos and Porphyry (both *apud* Eusebius), quoted by Day, *Molech*, 86–7.

12:31, the Shepharvamian practice of 2 Kgs. 17:31b, and the post-Josiah references), both of which are vociferously castigated. In each, adults manipulate children (of unspecified ages) for a supranormal purpose beneficial to the adults at the expense of the child's well-being and—like the sexual offenses with which Molek praxis is paired in Leviticus—of normal, proper kinship relations.[106] But the manifestations of this manipulation appear to be different, as is suggested by the linguistic distinctions noted above.[107]

The Phoenician/Punic archaeological evidence, although abundant and evocative, is not as helpful as it might seem. It is not completely certain that the Phoenician/Punic evidence *in toto* testifies to more than an extra-ordinary Mesha-like practice alongside the routine funerary immolation of very young children.[108] Since the killing of a child as an emergency measure performed by a king (or on his behalf) apparently was a component in the cultic culture of Syria-Palestine generally, including the Phoenician/Punic orbit, it would not be surprising to find it in Judah, but all of the references cannot be so explained.[109] Although the rationale of this rite—how and

---

[106] This could include dedicating children to unacceptable "service" to Yahweh or to unacceptable deities (cf. n. 76 above). Whatever else Molek praxis entailed, Hartley-Dwyer have rightly seen the commonality with the sexual offenses in Leviticus to be kinship violations ("Investigation," 90–3).

[107] The archaeological record also contains evidence of some differences, if the Amman airport installation is to be interpreted along the lines advocated by J. B. Hennessy, "Excavation of a Late Bronze Age Temple at Amman," *PEQ* 98 (1966) 155–62, and *idem*, "Thirteenth Century BC Temple of Human Sacrifice at Amman," *Phoenicia and Its Neighbors* (ed. by E. Lipinski and E. Grubel; Studia Phoenicia 3; Leuven: Peeters, 1985) 85–104; cf. L. G. Herr, "Stratigraphy," The *Amman Airport Excavations, 1976* (ed. by L. G. Herr; ASOR 48; Winona Lake: Eisenbrauns, 1983) 11–31.

[108] Gras-Rouillard-Teixidor, "Phoenicians and Death," 127–76, concluding that "the tophet was very likely a child cemetery (for stillborn, premature, deformed infants) but also a sacred place, a sanctuary where animals were sacrificed to request another child from Baal-Hamon in the place of the one that was being buried" (p. 173); the incineration of dead infants was considered barbaric by the Greeks and their successors who transformed it into gruesome child sacrifice for propaganda purposes (see also n. 100 above). This conclusion is based, in part, on the rarity of child burials outside the "Tophet" in Carthage, but cf. S. R. Wolff, in *BASOR* 265 (1987) especially 92. For similar skepticism about the findings at Tyre (see n. 102 above) see S. Moscati, "Non è un Tofet a Tiro," *Rivista di Studi Fenici* 21 (1993) 147–52.

[109] As in M. S. Smith's synthesis (*Early History of God*, 132–8 [quotation from p. 138]): "[D]escriptions of child sacrifice in Canaan and Israel specify their largely royal character, as undertaken in moments of crisis. A city under siege seems to be the most characteristic setting; child sacrifice was designed to enlist the aid of a god to ward off a threatening army. If this does represent the customary setting for child sacrifice, then it belonged to urban, royal religion; it was reserved for special occasions and not part of regular cultic offerings."

why it "worked"—is unknown,[110] it may well have overlapped phenomenologically with the rationale of necromantic divination generally, or at least of an extreme form which entailed the burning of children and which presumably was not resorted to by the populace for mere routine concerns; if so, the two practices may not have been as distinct in the doing of them as they appear in the biblical record.[111] But it is a much greater speculative leap from here to the gruesome contents of the "tophet"-cemeteries of Carthage and elsewhere which seem to reflect a more widespread and commonplace activity. If the scholarly consensus is accepted and this evidence does attest to the practice of child-sacrifice, the religio-social circumstances surrounding this practice are not at all clear: were these children burned as sacrificial "food" for a god, or as a "redemption" for a debt owed to a god, or as a "present" to entice a particular action from god, or were there multiple motives? And how does any of this relate to Josiah's Judah, if at all?

The more relevant question for the present inquiry is whether 2 Kgs. 23:10 refers to actual pre-Josianic cultic activity which was terminated in his religious reform, or is a post-Josianic interpolation anachronistically attributing that activity to Judahites before the reform. There are several factors to consider:

• It is simply not the case that the biblical record represents the practice as having been "rampant under Ahaz and Manasseh."[112] Only these two kings themselves are said to have engaged in it in the Kings History, and each only once (both 16:3b and 21:6aα mention only one son); Chronicles darkens both portrayals by pluralizing the victims (2 Chron. 28:3; 33:6),[113] consistent with the secondary charge in 2 Kgs. 22:16 (without an equivalent in Chronicles) that Manasseh filled Jerusalem with "innocents' blood."

---

[110] For discussion see the references cited in n. 69 above.

[111] Cf. Ackerman, *Under Every Green Tree*, 138–41.

[112] O. Margalith, "Religious Life in Jerusalem on the Eve of the Fall of the First Temple," *Fucus: A Semitic/Afrasian Gathering in Remembrance of Albert Ehrman* (ed. by Y. L. Arbeitman; Amsterdam Studies in the Theory and History of Linguistic Science 4.58; Philadelphia/Amsterdam: John Benjamins, 1988) 343. Similarly, e.g., according to Day (*Molech*, 62), "it was precisely during the period of Assyrian hegemony that [the Molek] cult particularly flourished, as the offering up of their children by Ahaz and Manasseh testifies."

[113] Note that 2 Chron. 28:3b also intensifies 2 Kgs. 16:3b by using *BʿR* in place of *ʿBR*: see Ackerman, *Under Every Green Tree*, 129 n. 86.

This is not to deny the possibility or even likelihood that the phenomenon of necromantic divination, if that is what these passages are referring to,[114] had been a factor in Israelite and Judahite society since the time of Saul (if 1 Samuel 28 is credible),[115] but the possible allusions to the practice in Proto-Isaiah[116] and Micah[117] do not mention the burning of children by Ahaz or any-

---

[114] Ahaz might have resorted to an act of desperation, like Mesha's, in the course of the Syro-Ephraimitic War (e.g., Šanda, *Könige*, 2.24, 195; Montgomery, *Kings*, 363; Ackroyd, *I & II Chronicles, Ezra, Nehemiah*, 174–5; cf. Wiseman, *1–2 Kings*, 260), but it is difficult to imagine a comparable occasion for Manasseh to have done so. The different verbs argue against this surmise, although it is conceivable that the Mesha reference derives from a (northern?) source which did not use the ʿBR (in Hiphil) + *bāʾēš* idiom.

[115] Apart from the question of its historicity, the pericope does give a very credible representation of a necromantic practice that *worked*, which in itself demonstrates the appeal of such practices to those for whom the later proscriptions were intended: see now M. Cogan, "The Road to En-Dor," *Pomegranates and Golden Bells: Studies in Biblical, Jewish, and Near Eastern Ritual, Law, and Literature in Honor of Jacob Milgrom* (ed. by D. P. Wright *et al.*; Winona Lake: Eisenbrauns, 1995) 319–26.

[116] (1) Isa. 8:19–22 attests to the prophet's disapproval of certain necromantic divination practices in Judah (cf. also 2:6; 29:4; and for Egypt 19:3); there is no indication that these might have involved the burning of children unless "Molek" is read into *melek* in v. 21, but this is unnecessary to make acceptable sense of the passage: see, e.g., Heider, *Cult of Molek*, 328–12, and Lewis, *Cults of the Dead*, 128–32. (2) The "covenant with death" (28:15, 18), like the pericope as a whole, is very likely a reflex of ritual practices, including divination, concerning the ancestors, but again there is no hint of burning children: see, e.g., B. Halpern, "'The Excremental Vision': The Doomed Priests of Doom in Isaiah 28," *HAR* 10 (1986) 109–21; K. van der Toorn, "Echoes of Judaean Necromancy in Isaiah 28,7–22," *ZAW* 100 (1988) 199–217; Day, *Molech*, 58–62; Lewis, *Cults of the Dead*, 134–5. (3) Isa. 30:33 uses immolation imagery in an oracle against Assyria (c. 701): "For *topteh* has long been prepared, *lammelek* it is made ready, its pyre made deep and wide . . .; the breath of Yahweh . . . kindles it." There is no reason that *melek* should not be accepted as the Assyrian "king" (with Heider, *Cult of Molek*, 320–4, against Day, *Molech*, 17 and n. 6). If *topteh* is a variant of *topet* ("fireplace" or the like; see above) and refers to a Molek installation in the Ben-Hinnom Valley (cf. 2 Kgs. 23:10; Jer. 7:31, 32; 19:6, 11–14) the prophet's benign attitude toward the practice is remarkable, especially in the reign of the reform-minded Hezekiah (cf. Heider, *Cult of Molek*, 325–8). But it is more likely, in view if the form *topteh* and the parallelism with *mĕdurâ* ("pile of fuel, pyre"), that the reference is more general; if so, the imagery could be drawn from certain funerary customs involving burning (cf. 2 Chron. 16:14; 21:19–20), if not cremation (on which cf. Chapter 8 nn. 7 and 19 below), perhaps a faddish Syrian-inspired innovation which would not be surprising in this era (cf., e.g., Cogan-Tadmor, *II Kings*, 193). For Zeph. 1:4–5 see nn. 127–128 below. B. B. Schmidt discounts the relevance of 8:19–22, 19:3, 28:15, 18, and 29:4 by attributing them to "a post-Isaianic redactor with a dtr orientation" (*Israel's Beneficent Dead: Ancestor Cult and Necromancy in Ancient Israelite Religion and Tradition* [2nd edn.; Winona Lake: Eisenbrauns, 1996] 147–65 [quotation from p. 164]); see further below.

[117] The testimony of Mic. 6:6–7 is ambiguous at best: see the review by Heider,

one else. The possibility that such practices involving the burning of children were introduced to Judah under Manasseh cannot be rejected out-of-hand, but there is no unambiguous evidence for this contention.[118]

• The Manasseh attribution (21:6a, duplicated in 2 Chron. 33:6) is part of a list of practices which he is said to have done. This list is virtually identical to the list in Deut. 18:10−11, whence 2 Kgs. 17:17 also derives (*):

Deut. 18:10−11	2 Kgs. 21:6a
maʿăbîr bĕnô-ûbitô bāʾēš [*]	*wĕheʿĕbîr ʾet-bĕnô bāʾēš*
qōsēm qĕsāmîm [*]	——
mĕʿônān	*weʿônān*
ûmĕnaḥāš [*]	*wĕniḥāš*
ûmĕkaššēp	*wĕkiššēp* (from 2 Chron. 33:6)
wĕḥōbēr ḥaber	——
wĕšōʾēl ʾōb wĕyiddĕʿōnî	*wĕʿāśâ ʾōb wĕyiddĕʿōnîm*
wedoreš ʾel-hammetîm	——

Manasseh thus personifies the individual Israelites who are enjoined from engaging in these practices in deuteronomic legislation and those whose practice of them brought about the fall of (North-) Israel and their exile—coincidences certainly more rhetorical than historical. Deut. 18:10−11 would seem to be the prototype of which the others are abbreviations. 2 Kings 17 consists of a basic narrative which has been expanded over time by the successive

---

Cult of Molek, 316−9, concluding that "it is impossible to know whether the prophet obtained his roster of proposed offerings purely from the contemporary cultic life of the people, or included a more theoretical construct of the most valuable sacrifices which one might offer on the basis of the law" (p. 318). Cf. the commentaries (e.g., H. W. Wolff, *Micah* [trans. By G. Stansell; CC; Minneapolis: Augsburg, 1990] 177−9).

[118] Schmidt's recent sifting of the evidence (*Israel's Beneficent Dead*, especially 220−45) concludes: "*If* Israelite necromancy owes its historical origins to mid first century Mesopotamia, then the dtr tradition *might* preserve—whether by accident or intent—a recollection of an historical development in which necromancy took hold in Judah during Manasseh's reign *or thereafter*" (p. 241 [emphasis supplied]). His tentativeness here is noteworthy. Aside from 2 Kgs. 21:16a (see n. 123 below), his argumentation rests largely on circumstantial evidence, much of which derives from the application of the "Assyrian Vassalship Hypothesis" (on which see Chapter 1 above) to the reform measures inventoried in 2 Kgs. 23:4−20 (on which see Chapter 7.B below); cf. J. Scurlock, "Ghosts in the Ancient Near East: Weak or Powerful?" *HUCA* 68 (1997) 77−96. Note that Schmidt considers the "passing through fire" of one's children to have been child-sacrifice and not a necromantic divinatory act, despite their juxtaposition in 2 Kgs. 21:16a.

addition of different blocks of theological commentary.[119] Vv. 12–17 encompasses both "Israel and Judah" (v. 13) and enumerate specific cultic offenses, most of which are elsewhere associated with both kingdoms or uniquely with Judah.[120] The scatological euphemism *gillûlîm* ("shit-gods"), "all but peculiar to Ezekiel," in v. 12 is indicative of a relatively late date;[121] the repetition of *lehakʿîs* in v. 11b

---

[119] The basic narrative probably consists of vv. 1–7aα + 18aβ + 21–34a. In addition to the commentaries see, e.g., Dietrich, *Prophetie und Geschichte*, especially 41–2; Hoffmann, *Reform und Reformen*, 127–39; M. Cogan, "Israel in Exile: The View of the Josianic Historian," *JBL* 97 (1978) 40–4; Nelson, *Double Redaction*, 53–69; Mayes, *Story of Israel*, 125–7; B. Oded, "II Kings 17: Between History and Polemic," *Jewish History* 2 (1987) 37–50; P. Viviano, "2 Kings 17: A Rhetorical and Form-Critical Analysis," *CBQ* 49 (1987) 548–59; Provan, *Hezekiah*, 70–3; Brettler, "Ideology, History and Theology," 268–82, and especially *idem*, *Creation of History in Ancient Israel*, ch. 7; McKenzie, *Trouble with Kings*, 140–2; C. Frevel, "Vom Schreiben Gottes: Literarkritik Komposition und Auslegung von 2 Kön 17,34–40," *Bib* 72 (1991) 23–48; S. Talmon, "Polemics and Apology in Biblical Historiography—2 Kings 17:24–41," *Literary Studies in the Hebrew Bible: Form and Content—Collected Studies* (Leiden/Jerusalem: Brill/Magnes, 1993) 134–59 (= a somewhat different version in *The Creation of Sacred Literature: Composition and Redaction in the Biblical Text* [ed. by R. E. Friedman; University of California Publications, Near Eastern Studies 22; Berkeley/Los Angeles/London: University of California, 1981] 57–68); Knoppers, *Two Nations Under God 2*, especially 64 n. 36; B. Becking, "From Apostasy to Destruction: A Josianic View on the Fall of Samaria (2 Kings 17,21–23)," *Deuteronomy and Deuteronomic Literature: Festschrift C. H. W. Brekelmans* (ed. by M. Vervenne and J. Lust; BETL 133; Leuven: University, 1997) 279–97.

[120] *gillûlîm* (v. 12; cf. Deut. 29:16): North (1 Kgs. 21:26)/South (1 Kgs. 15:12; 2 Kgs. 21:11, 21; 23:24). *'ăšērâ* (v. 16b; cf. Deut. 16:21): North (1 Kgs. 21:33a)/South (1 Kgs. 15:13; 2 Kgs. 21:3, 7; 23:6–7). *ṣĕbā' haššāmāyim* (v. 16b; cf. Deut. 17:3): North (Ø)/South (2 Kgs. 21:3, 5; 23:4, 5, 12). *baʿal* (v. 16b): North (1 Kgs. 16:31; 18:18–40; 22:54; 2 Kgs. 10:18–28)/ South (2 Kgs. 11:18; 21:3; 23:3, 4). *ʿBR + bā'ēš* (v. 17a; cf. Deut. 2:31; 18:10a): North (Ø)/South (2 Kgs. 16:3; 21:6; 23:10). *qesem* (v. 17a; cf. Deut. 18:10–14): North (Ø)/South (2 Kgs. 21:6). As Viviano has seen, the inventory "actually highlights Judah's failings" even though the items are drawn from both (North-)Israel and Judah ("2 Kings 17," 552). The most distinctively northern item mentioned actually misrepresents Jeroboam's two calf images in two different locations (1 Kgs. 12:28–30; 2 Kgs. 10:29) as "a (single) image of two calves: (v. 16aβ: *massēkâ šĕnêm ʿăgālîm*, recalling the two cherubim attached to the Ark (Ex. 25:18–22) and the two standing over it in the Temple (1 Kgs. 6:23–28; 8:6–9). In view of this, it is hardly likely that *ûbîhûdâ* in v. 13a is a gloss as many commentators maintain.

[121] J. Skinner, *The Book of Ezekiel* (Expositor's Bible; New York/Cincinnati: Eaton & Mains/Jennings & Graham, n.d.) 70 n. 1. As intimated by Skinner's remark, the general distribution of the term and the extraordinarily large number of occurrences (39 of 48) in the Book of Ezekiel have led some scholars to imagine that the prophet may have actually coined the neologism: e.g., C. R. North, "The Essence of Idolatry," *Von Ugarit nach Qumran: Festschrift O. Eissfeldt* (2nd edn.; ed. by J. Hempel and L. Rost; BZAW 77; Berlin: Töpelmann, 1961) especially 155; H. D. Preuss, in *TDOT* (1978) 3.1–5. W. Zimmerli suggests that the term was coined, perhaps in "the period of the reform," within "the circles of the Jerusalem priesthood" to which

and v. 17b is recognizable as a *Wiederaufnahme* bracket by which
vv. 11aβ–b + 12–17 was grafted into vv. 7aβ–11aα + 18aα, itself
a graft into vv. 1–7aα + 18aβ. Thus the list in v. 17 is at least
two redactional generations later than the "original" narrative
(KH-1) and probably was inspired by the "sins of Manasseh."[122]
The *waw*-copulative + Perfect construction in 2 Kgs. 21:6a raises
the possibility that Manasseh's list is a secondary interpolation
derived from Deut. 18:10–11 to make necromantic divination one
of those "sins" which caused Judah's downfall.[123] The Ahaz attribution (16:3bα), in turn, could also be an addition—it interrupts
the conventional evaluation formula (vv. 2b + 4) and stylistically
(*wĕgam . . .*) looks like an afterthought—perhaps inspired by the
Manasseh attribution.[124]

• The only documentary evidence for connecting 2 Kgs. 23:10 to
the rite(s) practiced by Ahaz and Manasseh, other than the '*BR*

Ezekiel belonged (*Ezekiel 1* [trans. by R. E. Clements; ed. by F. M. Cross *et al.*;
Hermeneia; Philadelphia: Fortress, 1979] 187). See now the full discussion by
D. Bodi, "Les *gillûlîm* chez Ézéchiel et dans l'Ancien Testament, et les différentes
pratiques cultuelles associées à ce terme," *RB* 100 (1993) 481–510, and M. I.
Gruber, in *DDD* (1995) 655–8.

[122] Cf. Brettler, *Creation of History in Ancient Israel*, 123–4.

[123] See recently Eynikel, "Portrait of Manasseh," 244–5, 255. Schmidt reverses
the influence (*Israel's Beneficent Dead*, 182), asserting but not arguing for the priority
of 2 Kgs. 21:6a over Deut. 18:10b–12a which he considers "a late expansion on a
dtr inventory proscribing various mantic practices" (p. 189). The latter reflects "a
rhetorical strategy designed to polemicize against contemporary cults competing with
dtr-Yahwism" (*ibid.*) which was spawned by "Manasseh's unique association with
necromancy" (p. 244). But the only textual evidence of this "unique association" is
2 Kgs. 21:6a which is completely compatible with this same rhetorical strategy and
also with the rhetorical Blame-the-Exile-on-Manasseh strategy—further indications
that 2 Kgs. 21:6a is an ahistorical secondary embellishment.

[124] Cogan-Tadmor's explanation that "the most serious of the cultic offenses of
the king is set at the head of the list" (*II Kings*, 186) is possible, but ignores the
anomalous placement of the notice in the middle of the evaluation formula. (The
Chronicler understood the word-order as do Cogan-Tadmor: he changed *wĕgam 'et-
bĕnô he'ĕbîr bā'eš* to *wayyab'ēr 'et-bānāyw bā'eš*, but appends this to a sentence of his
own beginning *wĕgam massēkôt 'āśâ labbĕ'ālîm* [2 Chron. 28:2b].) It is equally possible that the inverted word-order in 16:3b is indicative of a quotation of 21:6aa
(*wĕhe'ĕbîr 'et-bĕnô bā'eš*); on this device see Beentjes, "Inverted Quotations," 506–23,
and Peckham, "Writing and Editing," especially 366–71. Note also that the comparison to the "abominations" of the indigenous inhabitants (v. 3bβ) duplicates 21:2b
and may emanate ultimately from Deut. 18:9–14; cf. Halpern-Vanderhooft, "Editions of Kings," 211–2. On the extraordinary charge that Ahaz "walked in the way
of the kings of Israel" (v. 3a) as originally a political reference which has been reinterpreted redactionally in a religious sense see S. A. Irvine, *Isaiah, Ahaz, and the Syro-
Ephraimitic Crisis* (SBLDS 123; Atlanta: Scholars, 1990) 76–9.

(in Hiphil) + *bā'ēš* idiom, comes from the Chronicler who asserts
that Manasseh's "passing" had been done "in the Ben-Hinnom
Valley" (2 Chron. 33:8). He makes the same connection with Ahaz
by inserting *wĕgam massēkôt 'āśâ labbĕ'ālîm; wĕhû' hiqṭîr bĕgē' ben-hinnōm*
(2 Chron. 28:2b–3a; note the use of *QṬR* in Hiphil, characteristic
of the Chronicler) immediately ahead of the notice of his "passing"
(v. 3bβ).[125] But these surely are cases of intertextual exegesis
and not actual knowledge. One might suppose that the Chronicler (like modern commentators) interpreted 2 Kgs. 16:3 and 21:6
in light of 23:10, a natural synchronic reading of the accounts of
the three reigns. But if he did so, it is remarkable that he saw fit
to eliminate all trace of his source in his version of Josiah's reform:
either his additions to the accounts of Ahaz and Manasseh were
meant to compensate for this omission (leaving the impression that
the practice was confined to these kings alone, and/or was abolished by a repentant Manasseh), or his Kings *Vorlage* did not include
23:10—as it may not have included 23:15 and the other passages
locating the "cemetery scene" in Bethel (see Chapters 2–4 above)—
and his intertextual allusions were drawn from some other source,
perhaps Jeremiah.[126] A bona fide historical link between the rite
attributed to Ahaz and Manasseh and the installation mentioned
in 23:10 does not exist.

• Other than the testimony of 2 Kgs. 23:10, there is practically no
evidential basis for supposing that the ritual burning of children
was a common practice in Josiah's reign or that there was an
installation for this purpose in the Ben-Hinnom Valley during his
reign. Zephaniah's criticism of those who "bow down, swearing
loyalty to Yahweh but swearing by *mlkm*" (1:5b) might refer to
some chthonic practice involving "Molek,"[127] although "Milkom"
(cf. 2 Kgs. 23:13) and "their king [Baal?]" (MT, LXX) are also
possible;[128] the juxtaposition with "bowing down on the roofs to

---

[125] See also Chapter 3 n. 108 above.
[126] See p. 105 and n. 6 above.
[127] E.g., Heider, *Cult of Molek*, 332–6; Day, *Molech*, 1, 13 n. 33, 34 n. 13, 69
("perhaps"), 82; Berlin, *Zephaniah*, 75–7.
[128] Favoring Baal: e.g., Weinfeld, "Worship of Molek," 149; L. Sabottka, *Zephanja:
Versuch einer Neuuersetzung mit philologischem Kommentar* (Biblica et Orientalia 25; Rome:
Biblical Institute, 1972) 24–5; A. S. Kapelrud, *The Message of the Prophet Zephaniah:
Morphology and Ideas* (Oslo: Universitets, 1975) 23–4. Roberts concludes (*Nahum,
Habakkuk, and Zephaniah*, 168; cf. 172–3) that whether the reference is to "the
Ammonite Milkom or the Canaanite Molech . . . is impossible to decide." Accord-

the host of heaven" (v. 5a) would seem to point to an astral connection. Moreover, it is improbable at the very best that a prophet who complains about the comparatively trivial matter of "foreign" clothing and the seemingly innocuous practice of "leaping over the threshold" (vv. 8–9) should fail to mention that "swearing by *mlkm*" included parents burning their own children. Of special significance is Jer. 2:23, a poetic passage in which the prophet refutes the people's claim to "never have followed the Baals" by pointing to their "behavior"[129] in the [Ben-Hinnom] Valley."[130] If this represents a genuine Jeremiah polemic, it could have been delivered during Josiah's reign if his prophetic career began that early;[131]

---

ing to Ben Zvi (*Zephaniah*, 74–8): *mlkm* "is probably nothing but the exact parallel of *'lhyk*. Since YHWH was considered and referred to as mlk, malkam here may be understood as something representing YHWH. From the negative context in which the term occurs, it has to be concluded that this form of representation was considered illegitimate after the deuteronomic reform."

[129] Or "path" (consistent with the metaphor): see K. E. Bailey and W. L. Holladay, "The 'Young Camel' and the 'Wild Ass' in Jer. II 23–25," *VT* 18 (1969) 256–60. See Holladay, *Jeremiah 1*, 53, 100; McKane, *Jeremiah 1*, 45; Carroll, *Jeremiah*, 132–4; Lundbom, *Jeremiah 1–20*, 281.

[130] This is the only occurrence of *gē'* in the book which is not expressly identified as the Ben-Hinnom "valley" (cf. the "Valley Gate" [2 Chron. 26:9; Neh. 2:13, 15]). Most commentators make the connection: e.g., Driver, *Jeremiah*, 10; Peake, *Jeremiah and Lamentations*, 1.96; Hyatt, "Jeremiah," 5.819; Bright, *Jeremiah*, 15–16; Nicholson, *Jeremiah*, 1.73; Rudolph, *Jeremia*, 17; J. A. Soggin, "'Your Conduct in the Valley': A Note on Jeremiah 2,23a," *Old Testament and Oriental Studies* (Biblica at Orientalia 29; Rome: Biblical Institute, 1975) 78–83 (= *RSO* 36 [1961] 207–11); Thompson, *Jeremiah*, 179; Heider, *Molek*, 341–2; Holladay, *Jeremiah 1*, 100, 268; Lundbom, *Jeremiah 1–20*, 281. For the view that the reference is to other illicit cultic activity in the Ben-Hinnom or *any* valley cf., e.g., Duhm, *Jeremiah*, 26; J. Skinner, *Prophecy and Religion: Studies in the Life of Jeremiah* (Cambridge: Cambridge University, 1926) 57 n. 1, 62–3 n. 1; W. McKane, "Jeremiah II 23–25: Observations on the Versions and History of Exegesis," *OTS* 17 (1972) 73–88 (especially 82), and *idem*, *Jeremiah 1*, 45 ("a more general pattern of idolatry is indicated"); Carroll, *Jeremiah*, 133 ("a non-specific reference to baalistic worship [which] becomes shorthand for involvement with baalism throughout Israel's history").

[131] Cf. the commentaries (lately Lundbom, *Jeremiah 1–20*, 109–117, 285 [on 2:23–25a]; cf. *idem*, in *ABD*, 3.686–8, 713), and classically H. H. Rowley, "The Early Prophecies of Jeremiah and their Setting," *Men of God: Studies in Old Testament History and Prophecy* (London: Nelson, 1963) 133–68 (= *BJRL* 45 [1962–1963] 198–234), with earlier literature For good defenses of the traditional view that Jeremiah was active during the reign of Josiah (cf. 1:2; 3:6; 25:3; 36:2) see also T. W. Overholt, "Some Reflections on the Date of Jeremiah's Call," *CBQ* 33 (1971) 165–184, and more recently, e.g., H. Cazelles, "La Vie de Jérémie dans son Contexte National et International," *Le Livre de Jérémie: Le Prophète et son Milieu, les Oracles et leur Transmission* (ed. by P.-M. Bogaert; BETL 54; Leuven: University, 1981) 21–39 (especially 25–32); Lohfink, "Junge Jeremia," 351–68. The polemic is dated to c. 627–616 by J. Milgrom, "The Date of Jeremiah, Chapter 2," *JNES* 14 (1955) 65–9.

if his career did not begin until the ascension of Jehoiakim (in 609) or shortly before, however,[132] and the polemic refers to an installation Josiah actually had "defiled," it would indicate that the practice resumed immediately after Josiah's death. But the polemical charge in this pericope is willful defection from Yahweh to "the Baals," gods "which you made yourself" and are really "no-gods" at all (2:8, 11, 13, 20, 23a, 25b, 27, 28, 29, 31b, 32b); there is nothing here to indicate that the deplorable "behavior" included the burning of children—a breathtaking instance of prophetic understatement if that was, in fact, what was going on there, and Jeremiah does not seem to have been given to understatement.[133]

• The MT of Jer. 7:31 speaks of many installations (bāmôt, as in 19:5a and 32:35aα) in the Ben-Hinnom Valley. As with bāmôt in 2 Kgs. 23:8b, the preponderance of text-critical evidence favors the plural.[134] The only reason for abandoning the plural in the Jeremiah passages is the assumption that hattōpet in 23:10 refers to a single installation which was reestablished after Josiah's death. But it is equally possible that the term has the same topographical connotation in 23:10 that it has in Jer. 7:31–33 and 19:4–6. In light of the probable literary relationship between these passages and 2 Kgs. 21:16 and 24:4a (noted above), the possibility that 23:10 is also dependent on them must be seriously entertained.

• Although 2 Kgs. 23:10 uses neither bāmâ nor bāmôt (an omission which commentators have generally ignored),[135] the plural in the Jeremiah passages is consistent with 23:8a in representing "bamoth" as installations or objects small enough to be found in groups in

---

[132] Cf., e.g., C. F. Whitley, "The Date of Jeremiah's Call," VT 14 (1964) 467–83; J. P. Hyatt, "The Beginning of Jeremiah's Prophecy" ZAW 78 (1966) 204–14 [cf. idem, in IB 5.778–80]; W. L. Holladay, "A Fresh Look at 'Source B' and 'Source C' in Jeremiah," VT 25 (1975) 409–12, idem, "Coherent Chronology," 58–73, and idem, Jeremiah 1, 63, 67 ("the time of the Battle of Carchemish" in 605), 78–81 ("between 608 and 605" [p. 81]). On the other hand, cf. Carroll, Jeremiah, 115–8 ("it is arguable that . . . the discourse in ch. 2 is exilic, if not later" [p. 116]).

[133] If, with R. R. Wilson ("Poetry and Prose in the Book of Jeremiah," Ki Baruch Hu: Ancient Near Eastern, Biblical, and Judaic Studies in Honor of Baruch A. Levine [ed. by R. Chazan et al.; Winona Lake, IN: Eisenbrauns, 1999] 412–27), 7:1–8:3 is a secondary prose explanation, clarification, and amplification of the poetic ambiguities of the preceding material (especially 4:13–6:30 [pp. 420–3]), 7:29–34 could be seen as a gloss of 2:23 but not necessarily an accurate one.

[134] 4QJerᵃ supports MT (apud Holladay, Jeremiah 1, 264).

[135] E.g., Whitney includes 23:10 as evidence of bamoth in the late monarchy on the strength of the Jeremiah passages, and observes only that "the writer of Kings does not call this shrine a bamah" ("'Bamoth' in the Old Testament," 137–8).

narrowly defined areas, such as altars or small shrines,[136] and belonging to the sphere of "popular" religiosity (the "bamoth" in Jer. 7:30 are said to have been built by the "sons of Judah"). This is not the impression one gets of the "bamoth" in "the cities of Judah" and reportedly staffed by "the kings of Judah" (23:5, cf. v. 8a) and those on the Mount of Olives built by Solomon (23:13; cf. 21:3), and both thus part of the "official" religiosity of the state. Unfortunately, our current understanding of the bamah phenomenon(a) is too imperfect for these impressions to be verified (or refuted),[137] but some evolution in the semantics of *bāmâ/bāmôt* in the development of the lexicon of Biblical Hebrew would not be surprising and is tacitly allowed in the scholarly discussion of the term.[138]

---

[136] Cf. the "small gabled shrines" associated with the immolations at Carthage (see n. 80 above). Surprisingly, Lundbom resurrects the theory popularized by W. F. Albright (in "High Place in Ancient Palestine," 242–58) that *bāmâ/bāmôt* refer to "funerary shrines built on hills or mountain ridges [which] came to refer more generally to any funerary shrine" (*Jeremiah 1–20*, 495–6); against this theory see W. B. Barrick, "The Funerary Character of 'High-Places' in Ancient Palestine: A Reassessment," *VT* 25 (1975) 565–95 (unmentioned by Lundbom).

[137] Since the appearance of the watershed works on the subject by Vaughan (*The Meaning of "bāmâ" in the Old Testament* [1974]) and Whitney ("'Bamoth' in the Old Testament," [1979], a growing number of scholars have begun to question the traditional positions recapitulated in those works and repeated in many others: for the view that *bāmâ*-installation should be understood in architectural terms as a temple-like structure *in* which certain activities were performed, see, e.g., W. B. Barrick, "What Do We Really Know about 'High Places'?" *SEÅ* 45 (1980) 50–7, and *idem*, in *ABD* (1992) 3.196–200; R. L. Omanson, "Translating *Bamoth*," *BT* 46 (1995) 309–20; J. E. Catron, "Temple and *bāmāh*: Some Considerations," *The Pitcher is Broken: Memorial Essays for Gösta W. Ahlström* (ed. by S. W. Holloway and L. K. Handy; JSOTSup 190; Sheffield: Sheffield Academic, 1995) 150–65. Cf. the very conventional treatment by Dever, "Silence of the Text," 148–9. Furthermore, the new survey of "The Biblical High Place in the Light of Recent Study" by J. A. Emerton (*PEQ* 129 [1997] 116–32) concludes (p. 130): "We do not know whether the word could be used of any local sanctuary, or whether there was something that differentiated *bāmôt* from other sanctuaries." Cf. now M. Gleis, *Die Bamah* (BZAW 251; Berlin/New York: de Gruyter, 1997), and my review in *JBL* 118 (1999) 532–4. See further Chapter 8 below.

[138] E.g., Whitney's assertion that bamoth were "different things in different places at different times" ("'Bamoth' in the Old Testament," 147); the earliest references may be to cult places with a particular architectural configuration and characteristic location, but by the late monarchy *BMH* had become an all-purpose label for "local shrines" in general and with no architectural specificity at all (p. 138). Thus, and most notably, 2 Kings 23 reports that in the course of a reorganization of the religious life of the realm King Josiah took action against various cultic installations which the narrator calls "bamoth" and, as Whitney points out, more than one type of installation seems to be so identified (*ibid.*, 137–8): small gate shrines, royal chapels dedicated to foreign gods, large public sanctuaries, and local cult places in both urban areas and the countryside (vv. 5, 8, 9, 13, 15, 19, 20).

- Jer. 7:30–31 states that the "sons of Judah" "*ûbānû*" the bamoth in the Ben-Hinnom Valley. How is the verb to be translated? Holladay argues for "they *keep building*," consistent with his synchronic understanding of the pericope.[139] If "they *have built*" is preferred (so, e.g., RSV, NJPSV, and most commentators) this would be another example of the *waw*-copulative + Perfect construction used in place of the expected *waw*-consecutive.

- Finally, 2 Kgs. 23:10, unlike the other three *'BR* (in Hiphil) + *bā'ēš* passages in Kings and Deut. 18:10, specifically associates the ritual "passing" with Molek, linking it linguistically more closely to Lev. 18:21 and 20:2–5 than to Deut. 18:10. The other texts which associate the rite with Molek are all post-Josianic and, like 23:10, also represent the practitioners as the populace at large rather than kings. Indeed, the fact that 23:10 is the only biblical passage to combine the idiom *'BR* (in Hiphil) + *bā'ēš* and *mōlek* might indicate that the verse actually is a late inter-textual harmonization of Lev. 18:21 and 20:2–5 with Deut. 18:10.

What can be made of all of this? At the very least, these factors are sufficient to cast "reasonable doubt" on the assumption that 2 Kgs. 23:10 is factual reportage of an event in Josiah's reign. If it is a secondary addition to the reform report,[140] it need not have been in the Chronicler's Kings *Vorlage*: assuming that he had no independent information on the subject, his claim that Ahaz "made idols for the Baals and he burned incense to them in the Ben-Hinnom Valley" (2 Chron. 28:2b–3a), juxtaposed with his "passing his sons through the fire" (v. 3b) could well have been inspired by the polemical charge in Jeremiah 2 that the "house of Jacob" (v. 4) had gone after "the Baals" (v. 23a) "in the [Ben-Hinnom V]alley" (v. 23b), and this location was then applied to the "passing" of Ahaz's and Manasseh's sons; this would be consistent with his use of Jer. 8:1–2 in his representation of Josiah's reform (34:4b–5a: see Chapter 2.C–D and Chapter 4 above). Since the Chronicler has an equivalent of both 2 Kgs. 16:3 (concerning Ahaz) and 21:6 (concerning Manasseh), these passages presumably were in his *Vorlage*. If the Ahaz attribution is a secondary addition to that regnal account, the Chronicler's

---

[139] Holladay, *Jeremiah 1*, 264, 267 (cf. 37:15).
[140] Cf. Eynikel, *Reform of King Josiah*, 245–9, 346–7.

Kings *Vorlage* must have been at least the "Josianic" second edition of the Kings History.

Exactly what cultic activity is envisioned by its author-compiler remains uncertain, other than that it involved the burning of persons identified as the "sons and daughters" of the participants. Whether some sort of necromantic divination as in Deut. 18:10 and attributed homiletically to Manasseh, or child sacrifice on the Phoenician model, or some hybrid of the two, or something else entirely,[141] it undoubtedly involved death and the nether-world in some way, consistent with its location in the Kidron/Hinnom Valley complex and with the post-Josiah references generally. It could be considered a doublet of 23:16a if the original version of the reform report did locate that episode in this same general area beneath the Mount of Olives where, the better evidence suggests, cultic activity associated with "the Baals" and probably involving at least one altar—but not (necessarily) the burning of children—apparently did take place during Josiah's reign (see further Chapter 8.C below).

5.F. THE MASSEBOTH AND ASHERIM (v. 14a)

wĕšibbar ᵓet-hammaṣṣēbōt wayyikrōt ᵓet-hāᵓăšērîm

and he shattered the masseboth and cut down the asherim

The language of v. 14a is stereotypical, but not "deuteronomic":

Deut. 7:5	Deut. 12:3 2	Kgs. 23:14a
NTṢ altars	*NTṢ* altars	——
ŠBR masseboth	*ŠBR* masseboth	*ŠBR* masseboth
GDᶜ asherim	*ŚRP* asherim	*KTR* asherim
ŚRP pesel-images	*GDᶜ* pesel-images	——

Not only is there no mention of altars or pesel-images in v. 14a, but there is no (explicit) mention of bamoth in the two "deuteronomic" passages. By contrast, the resemblance to 18:4a is virtually exact:

---

[141] Cf. M. Malul, "Some Measures of Population Control in the Ancient Near East," *Michael: Historical, Epigraphical and Biblical Studies in Honor of Prof. Michael Heltzer* (ed. by Y. Avishuir and R. Deutsch; Tel Aviv-Jaffa: Archaeological Center, 1999) 221–36.

2 K18:4a: *hû' hēsîr habbāmôt wĕšibbar 'et-hammaṣṣēbōt wĕkārat 'et-hā'ăšērâ*

2 K 23:13–14a: *'et-habbāmôt . . . ṭimmē' hammelek; wĕšibbar 'et-hammaṣṣēbōt wayyikrōt 'et-hā'ăšērîm*

23:14 can be seen as "a generalizing summary statement repeating what precedes and in turn anticipating v. 16"; since at least 23:14a seems to give "no specific information as an actual annalistic source would," it may well be the editorial work of the "original" author-compiler or a later hand.[142] There is no contextual reason for considering it secondary, particularly if v. 14a, like v. 14b, is thought to be related in some way (literary or historical) to the Solomonic bamoth defiled in v. 13.[143] This relationship may well be editorial and secondary, however, a "literary reflex" prompted by the mention of bamoth in v. 13 which 18:4a associates with masseboth and asherim.[144]

5.G. Summary

This review of the *waw*-copulative + Perfect passages in the reform report has found little to justify the natural synchronic assumption that they must be original, and much to warrant the diachronic suspicion that they are not. External literary or historical considerations do not require their originality. Three (vv. 5, 8b, 10) are intrusive in the larger context of the pericope, and four (vv. 4bβ, 5, 10, 12bβ) can be seen as doublets or echoes of material in the "original" report. When added to the abnormal verbal construction, there is ample reason to consider these passages as supplementary and not part of the "original" reform report. The secondary status of v. 4bβ is suggested only by the verbal construction, however, and it alone may well be original.

While some of these passages can be seen as editorial "fine-tuning" (vv. 12bβ, 14a), most convey very specific information, often using unique, technical language: "*kōmer*-priests" (v. 5a) "*mazzālôt*-stars"

---

[142] Nelson, *Double Redaction*, 82, considering it "probably part of the historian's editorial work"; the same thing could be said of 18:4aβ. Jones considers the verse "a general comment to conclude the additions made by the reviser" (*1–2 Kings*, 624; but such views about 18:4a "can be dismissed" [561]). For Montgomery, 23:14 is "another generalizing addition" (*Kings*, 534).

[143] Eynikel, *Reform of King Josiah*, 348 and n. 49; cf. 268–71.

[144] "Best explained as a literary reflex prompted by the Deuteronomist's description of these sites as 'high places'" (Lowery, *Reforming Kings*, 207–8).

(v. 5b), bamoth installations at a certain location adjacent to a certain gate identified by name (v. 8b); activity at the "*tōpet*-installation" in the Ben-Hinnom Valley (v. 10). These do not look at all like rhetorical flourishes or generalizations. Presumably this information is not completely imaginary, but has some basis in the realities known to the author-compiler responsible for the items to be comprehensible to his intended audience. Although Chronicles has nothing corresponding to these particular passages, it does contain many such unique details (often in accounts of royal reforms) which derive from a source other than our version of the Kings History or from his own experience or imagination; the historical credibility of these notices probably varies and is much debated.[145]

---

[145] In addition to the commentaries cf. recently the complementary studies in *The Chronicler as Historian* (ed. by M. P. Graham *et al.*; JSOTSup 238; Sheffield: Sheffield Academic, 1997), especially Barnes, "Non-Synoptic Chronological References," 106–31; E. Ben Zvi, "The Chronicler as Historian; Building Texts," 132–49; J. W. Wright, "The Fight for Peace: Narrative and History in the Battle Accounts in Chronicles," 150–77; G. N. Knoppers, "History and Historiography: The Royal Reforms," 178–203 (excluding the Josianic materials). On 2 Chron. 11:5–11 see further T. R. Hobbs, "The 'Fortresses of Rehoboam': Another Look," *Uncovering Ancient Stones: Essays in Memory of H. Neil Richardson* (ed. by L. M. Hopfe; Winona Lake: Eisenbrauns, 1994) 41–64 (with earlier literature).

CHAPTER SIX

JOSIAH'S REFORM IN KINGS (III): COMPOSITIONAL IMPLICATIONS

This chapter considers the compositional history of the accounts of Josiah's reform activities in the Kings History, building upon the insights gained from the preceding five chapters.

6.A. The "Original" Reform Report in Kings

From a comparative analysis of plot structuring in the presentation of Josiah's reign in Kings and Chronicles L. Eslinger concludes:[1]

> The Chronicler's handling of the Kings text suggests that he may have been dealing with a text that had already attained an authoritative status in the community. Given that his own views differed from those of the author of Kings, the Chronicler expressed his views in subtle alterations to the plot structure, and by deleting Kings' material or adding new expansionistic details. That he was constrained to leave the Kings text as it stood, however, is evidenced by those places in his narrative where he has to maneuver. . . .

The preceding analyses support this finding. The Chronicler has followed the reform report in Kings very closely. The purging of the Temple and its precincts which Kings attributes to Josiah (2 Kgs. 23:4a–bα, 6–7, 9, 11–12) the Chronicler credits to Manasseh (2 Chron. 33:15–17) and depicts in terms of the cultic innovations which he introduced after the comprehensive pogrom executed by Hezekiah (vv. 4–5, 7). The Chronicler's representation of Josiah's pogrom consists of consolidations or paraphrases of the Kings account. 34:4–5a provides independent support for the contention that the original locale of the cemetery scene in 2 Kgs. 23:16–18 was the vicinity of the Mount of Olives adjacent to Jerusalem; that the Chronicler's

---

[1] Eslinger, "Josiah and the Torah Book," 60. Cf. W. M. Schniedewind, "The Chronicler as an Interpreter of Scripture," *The Chronicler as Author: Studies in Text and Texture* (ed. by M. P. Graham and S. L. McKenzie; JSOTSup 263; Sheffield: Sheffield Academic, 1999) 158–180.

report contains no trace of 23:15—the contextual basis for locating the cemetery at Bethel—suggests that this verse may not have been in his *Vorlage*. There is also no trace of 23:4bβ, 5, 8b, 10, 12bβ, 14a—the *waw*-conjunctive + Perfect passages of uncertain compositional status. Except for v. 4bβ (which pertains to the Temple, already purged by Manasseh in Chronicles), there is nothing in the content of these passages, the Chronicler's literary strategies in dealing with his *Vorlage*, or his ideological *Tendenz*, which would explain their omission; indeed, the omission of 23:10 is surprising in view of his references to the "passing of children through fire" by Ahaz and Manasseh which he explicitly connects with the Ben-Hinnom Valley (28:3b; 33:6aα). The absence of the *waw*-conjunctive + Perfect passages in Chronicles is further support for the contention that they are secondary to the "original" reform report and perhaps also to whatever edition of the Kings History was among the Chronicler's sources.

The compositional history of the story of the man-of-god from Judah (1 Kings 13) and the Kings account of Josiah's reform can be tentatively reconstructed as follows:

KH-1 ("Hezekian")	KH-2 ("Josianic")	KH-3 (post-"Josianic")	KH-4 (post-Exilic)
1 K 12:26–32	1 K 12:26–32	1 K 12:26–32	1 K 12:26–32
			+ 12:33a
		+ 12:33b–13:1–2a	12:33b–13:1–2a
		+ 13:2bα	13:2bα
			+ 13:2bβ
		+ 13:2bγ	13:2bγ
			+ 13:3
		+ 13:4	13:4
			+ 13:5
		+ 13:6	13:6
			+ 13:7–9
		+ 13:10a	13:10a
			+ 13:10b–32
		+ 13:33–34	13:33–34
	+ 2 K 23:4a–bα	2 K 23:4a–bα	2 K 23:4a–4bα
	[+ 23:4bβ?]	[+ 23:4bβ?]	[+ 23:4bβ?]
		[+ 23:5?]	[+ 23:5?]
	+ 23:6–8a	23:6–8a	23:6–8a
		[+ 23:8b?]	[+ 23:8b?]
	+ 23:9	23:9	23:9
		[+ 23:10?]	[+ 23:10?]
	+ 23:11–12bα	23:11–12bα	23:11–12bα
		[+ 23:12bβ?]	[+ 23:12bβ?]

Table (*cont.*)

KH-1 ("Hezekian")	KH-2 ("Josianic")	KH-3 (post-"Josianic")	KH-4 (post-Exilic)
	+ 23:13	23:13	23:13
		[+ 23:14a?]	[+ 23:14a?]
	+ 23:14b	23:14b	23:14b
		[+ 23:15?]	[+ 23:15?]
	+ 23:16 + 18	23:16a + 18	23:16a + 18
			+ 23:16b–17
			+ 23:19–20
	+ 23:21a	23:21a	23:21a
		+++++++	+++++++
			+ 23:24

The basic narrative of the reform report (KH-2), bracketed by 23:4 and 23:21a, dealt with actions conducted entirely in Judah and Jerusalem and possibly Bethel (v. 4bβ). The "original" story of the man-of-god's visit to Bethel first appears in the next edition (KH-3); it is possible that some portion of 23:15 was added simultaneously to suggest that the activity in v. 16a took place at Bethel. Subsequently (KH-4), the story of the man-of-god was "fine-tuned" (including the prediction of bamoth-priests being slaughtered on the Bethel altar in 13:2bβ) and transformed into a parable on the theme of obedience; the reform report was expanded concomitantly with the invention of Josiah's "northern crusade" (23:19–20) and the direct allusion in vv. 16b–18 to confirm the final words of the old prophet from Bethel. The *waw*-copulative + Perfect supplements were added to the reform report either in KH-3 or, more likely, in KH-4.

This compositional history raises the possibility that 2 Kgs. 23:19–20 may not have been in the Chronicler's *Vorlage*. 2 Chron. 34:6 reads: *ûbĕʿārê mĕnaššeh wĕʾeprayim wĕšimeʿôn wĕʿad-naptālî, bḥr btyhm sābîb*; "and in the cities of Manasseh, Ephraim, and Simeon and as far as Naphtali, *bḥr btyhm* round about." The only evidential reason for assuming that the Chronicler knew of 23:19–20 is an emendation with no text-critical foundation: reading *biʿēr bātêhem*, "he destroyed their sanctuaries," for MT's *bāhar bātēhem* (K), "their houses in the mountain(s)," or *bĕḥarbōtêhem* (Q), "with their swords." Of the Ketib reading S. Japhet finds "the relevance of 'mountain' (*bāhar*) in the context [to be] attested in II Kings 23:16."[2] The present analyses

---

[2] Japhet, *I–II Chronicles*, 1025.

support Japhet's observation: vv. 6–7 are not the Chronicler's version of 23:19–20, but are his own invention consistent with his *Tendenz*, a midrashic fiction constructed from a version of the reform report in Kings very similar to the "original" KH-2 version proposed here which lacked Josiah's "northern crusade" and located the "cemetery scene" (23:16–18) in the Wadi Kidron and on the slopes of the Mount of Olives. If this is so, it would seem to support McKenzie's contention that the Chronicler's *Vorlage* was the unrevised "Josianic" version of Kings (his Dtr[1]), which in other respects may have retained much of the earlier "Hezekian" version (KH-1) as Halpern and Auld contend[3] (cf. the discussion of 1 Kings 11 in Chapter 9.B below).

The "original" version of the reform report can be outlined as follows:

1. Equipage in the Temple[-building?] (v. 4a–bα [+ bβ?])
　2. Asherah and Accouterments in the Temple[-courtyard?] (vv. 6–7)
　　3.a. Bamoth and bamoth-priests in "the cities of Judah" (v. 8a)
　　3.b. Elaboration: the Temple clergy (v. 9)
4. Horses/chariots of the sun at entrance to Temple (v. 11)
　5. Rooftop and courtyard altars in Temple/palace (v. 12a–bα)
　　6.a. Solomon's bamoth on Mount of Olives (vv. 13 + 14b)
　　6.b. Elaboration: cemetery scene (vv. 16a + 18)

The first section of the report (#1–3) deals specifically with the Temple itself—divine "residents," now unwelcome in the eyes of the reformers, are evicted along with their baggage—and concludes with the realignment of state-sponsored worship of Yahweh in terms of location and personnel. The second section (#4–6) deals with collateral cultic concerns, and concludes with the despoiling of the Kidron/Hinnom tombs, the disposition of their osteal contents, and the preservation of one tomb with its identifying monument. Both sections envision a locational progression outward from the Temple-building. The parallel structure implies both a possible connection between Solomon's bamoth and the tombs, and the comparable importance of cultic "centralization" and the desecration of the tombs and their contents.

If this reconstruction approximates the actual compositional history of this material, that history has been informed by four external historical realities. Three are obvious enough: the actions actually

---

[3] For references see Chapter 1 n. 47 above.

undertaken by Josiah and his supporters to alter the religious life of
the kingdom; the aftermath of Josiah's reign, including the final
downfall of the kingdom and the physical destruction of Jerusalem
in 587/6; and the continuing political and religious turmoil in the
Exilic and post-Exilic periods (exemplified by the passages from
Jeremiah, Ezekiel, and Deutero-Isaiah concerning the Molek cultus
examined in Chapter 5.E above). The fourth may not be so apparent. Concerning a post-Josianic dating of the man-of-god pericope
one recent critic has observed:[4] "Ultimately, it is difficult to explain
why this story should be assigned to an exilic redactor when it explicitly looks forward to the birth of Josiah and his reforms." But "Josiah
and his reforms" had an afterlife of sorts. The explanation lies, in
my view, in the ongoing theological and political dilemma of the
north. Ezra 4:1–2 reports that northern "adversaries of Judah and
Benjamin" sought membership in the post-Exilic Temple community on the grounds that they had been worshipping Yahweh since
the days of Esarhaddon "who brought us here"; Zerubbabel and
company reject this claim (v. 3).[5] Whatever the factuality of this
report,[6] the claim is no doubt real: some northerners believed themselves to be good Yahwists and thus deserving of membership in the
reconstituted Yahwist community headquartered in Jerusalem, long
after Josiah's time. 2 Kgs. 17:24–34a (without vv. 34b–41, and probably KH-1) actually supports that claim.[7] The claim would have been
invalidated had Josiah actually destroyed the Bethel priesthood and
their sanctuary, to say nothing of a wholesale slaughter of northern
priests and destruction of northern sanctuaries: such a bold-faced lie
by the northerners could only have alienated the southern elites
whom it was meant to persuade but who would have known better

---

[4] Schniedewind, "Problem with Kings," 24, concerning McKenzie's treatment of
this material (*Trouble with Kings*, 51–6).

[5] Ackroyd concludes from Zerubbabel's response that the pericope advocates "a
separation between those commissioned to build by the royal authority of Cyrus
[i.e., by Yahweh] and all others" ("A Subject People," 232; see also p. 214).

[6] For discussion see, in addition to the commentaries and standard histories,
H. G. M. Williamson, "The Composition of Ezra i–iv," *JTS* 34 (1983) 1–30 (espe-
cially pp. 25–6; M. Cogan, "For We, like You, Worship your God: Three Biblical
Portrayals of Samaritan Origins," *VT* 38 (1988) 286–92; O. Margalith, "The Political
Background of Zerubbabel's Mission and the Samaritan Schism," *VT* 41 (1991)
312–23. Cf. also Chapter 3 n. 56 above.

[7] See Barrick, "On the Meaning of *bêt-hab/bāmôt*," 631, 633–5, 636, 638–40 (with
earlier literature).

from (at least) the Kings History itself. As literary fictions, however, these exploits would have made good southern propaganda against this northern claim of uninterrupted Yahwism promulgated from Bethel.[8] The author-compiler of the KH-3 edition undermined that claim with the fictive report that Yahweh had ordained the decommissioning of the Bethel altar in Josiah's day (1 Kgs. 13:1–2a + 2bγ), possibly embellishing an actual incident in his reign (reflected in 2 Kgs. 23:4bβ). The author-compiler of the KH-4 edition went further, adding Josiah's equally fictive slaughter of the Bethel priesthood also predicted by the man-of-god (13:2bβ; 23:19b), the destruction of the Bethel sanctuary and its altar (23:15 + 16b–17) and his attack on the bamoth-houses in the cities of Samaria (23:19a + 20a), repudiating their cultic calendar (by adding 1 Kgs. 12:33a), and parabolically representing their prophets as treacherous liars liable to lead faithful and unsuspecting southern Yahwists astray (by adding 13:11–32).[9] The invalidation of the etiological warrant for the northern claim (by adding 2 Kgs. 17:34b–41, a literary composite) probably began in KH-2 and reached its present form in either KH-3 or KH-4.[10] The Chronicler's "all-Israel" purge (2 Chron. 34:6–7) served the same purpose.

6.B. THE REFORM REPORT AND ITS LITERARY CONTEXT

The "Deuteronomistic History Hypothesis," in the several models spun out of Noth's pioneering work, assumes that the basic principles informing the historiographical books of Joshua, Judges, 1–2 Samuel and 1–2 Kings are enunciated in the Book of Deuteronomy and tied, directly or indirectly, to Josiah's reform pogrom. This proposition presupposes the "Deuteronomic Book Hypothesis" which identifies the "book" (*sēper*) said to have been found in the Temple (2 Kgs. 22:3–23:3) with some form of the Book of Deuteronomy, either as

---

[8] For the occupational history of Bethel (mod. Beitin) see Chapter 3.B above.

[9] Josephus even attributes "the sin(s) of Jeroboam" to the old prophet's pernicious influence on the well-intentioned king (*Ant.* 8.9). For the larger context of the attribution see L. H. Feldman, "Prophets and Prophecy in Josephus," *JTS* 41 (1990) especially 407–11 (= *Society of Biblical Literature 1988 Seminar Papers* [ed. by D. J. Lull; SBLSP 27; Atlanta: Scholars, 1988] especially 433–5).

[10] See the works cited in Chapter 5 n. 119 above, especially Frevel, "Vom Schreiben Gottes," 23–48.

an historical fact of Josiah's reign or as a literary construct produced by a "Deuteronomistic Historian." If this is the present, final literary context in which the reform report is found, the relationship between this larger context and the reform report itself now must be considered.

The "Deuteronom(ist)ic" Connection

In a recent paper T. C. Römer has shown the importance of the "book" as a "leitmotiv for dtr. historiographical writing" after 597/586, evident in the overall structure of the work: the "book of the law" (*sēper hattôrâ*), first identified in Moses's sermonic introduction as "the dtn. law code" (Deut. 17:18; 28:58, 61; 29:19–20, 26; 30:10; 31:24, 26; cf. also Josh. 1:8; 8:31, 34; 23:6; 24:26) and then as "the impetus of Josiah's reform" toward the end of the history (2 Kgs. 22:8a, 11; 23:24b), form a literary *inclusio* for the entire work.[11] Two of the three latter occurrences of the phrase—in the notice of the discovery of the "book" by Hilkiah in 22:8, and in the summary of Josiah's reform activities in 23:24b—likewise form an *inclusio* for the central structural unit of final literary form of that account.[12] But neither *inclusio* is original. The contents of Hilkiah's "book" in the account are referred to as *hattôrâ* (22:8a, 11; 23:24b) or *habbĕrît* (23:2, 3, 21) with no obvious difference in meaning or literary nuance:[13] e.g.,

> 2 K 23:3:   ... 'et-dibrê-habbĕrît hazzō't hakkĕtubîm 'al-hassēper hazzeh ...
> 2 K 23:24b: ... 'et-dibrê hattôrâ   hakkĕtubîm 'al hassēper ...

While it is true, with McKenzie, that v. 24, with the "patently Deuteronomistic" expression *hāqîm 'et-dibrê hattôrâ* and the explicit reference to Hilkiah's finding of the book, functions as "a fulfillment remark showing that Josiah carried out all the prescriptions of the law book to their fullest extent,"[14] the gratuitous variation in nomenclature, the all-Israel scope of v. 24a, its grammatical resemblance to v. 19a, and

---

[11] Römer, "Transformations in Deuteronomistic and Biblical Historiography," 1–11 (quotations from pp. 5–6).

[12] C.1–C.1′ in the outline given above (p. 2).

[13] According to Long (*2 Kings*, 269), "the change in nomenclature signals a shift to the ceremonial context, and also does its part to surround subsequent reformative acts with the suggestion that Josiah's behavior conforms to a deeply traditional model" (whatever that may mean). This strikes me as grasping at synchronic straws in the face of a plainly diachronic problem. See further n. 53 below.

[14] McKenzie, *Trouble with Kings*, 114.

its violation of the *wayēṣaw hammelek inclusio* (v. 4a and v. 21a) support the contention, endorsed by the present analyses, that v. 24 is a very late addition, probably attributable to the post-Exilic KH-4 edition.[15] If the other occurrences of *sēper hattôrâ* (22:8a, 11) also are attributed to that edition, the compositional link with Deuteronomy must be correspondingly late as well.[16] The distinctive phrase *sēper-habĕrît* (23:2, 21), recurring only at Ex. 24:7, reflects a different tradition and could well belong to an earlier Josiah narrative (see further below).

Two other elements of the Josiah narrative reinforce this post-Exilic connection. The narrative presupposes that the "book" found in the Temple had been there for some time—and consequently should be taken seriously—but had been "lost" or forgotten. 2 Kgs. 23:22 implies that it had been "lost" since "the days the judges ruled Israel." This is a clear cross-reference to the Passover conducted by Joshua at Gilgal (Josh. 5:10–12), the first and, until Josiah's, the last reported Passover held in Cisjordanian Palestine. The Gilgal Passover followed the people's crossing of the Jordan with the "Ark of the Covenant" (3:3, 6, 8, 11, 14–17; 4:7, 9, 18). The Ark is the inter-textual nexus conjoining Passover, covenant, "book," and Temple in the "Deuteronomistic History." According to Deut. 10:1–5, its religious significance is as the reliquary of the Mosaic tablets of the "Ten Words."[17] Deut. 31:24–26 reports that

> [w]hen Moses had finished writing the words of this law in a book, to the very end, Moses commanded the Levites who carried the Ark of the Covenant of Yahweh: "Take this book of the law and put it by the side of the Ark of the Covenant of Yahweh your god, that it may be there as a witness against you."

Solomon's installation of the Ark of the Covenant in the Holy-of-Holies of the Temple (1 Kgs. 8:1–11) provides the occasion for the

---

[15] See also Chapter 1 n. 9 above, and cf. Eynikel's observation that "only for 2 Kgs. 23:24, missing in Chronicles and added very late to Kings, can Chronicles function as an additional argument for the dating" (*Reform of King Josiah*, 341).

[16] Cf. J. D. Levenson, "Who Inserted the Book of the Torah?" *HTR* 68 (1975) 203–33.

[17] Perhaps displacing a divine image of some sort as the original embodiment of Yahweh's presence: see K. van der Toorn, "The Iconic Book: Analogies between the Babylonian Cult of Images and the Veneration of the Torah," *The Image and the Book: Iconic Cults, Aniconism, and the Rise of Book Religion in Israel and the Ancient Near East* (ed. by K. van der Toorn; Contributions to Biblical Exegesis & Theology 21; Leuven: Peeters, 1997) 229–48 (especially pp. 241–2).

"book" to have gotten there as well. And it is Hilkiah, as high-priest the only person allowed to enter the "Holy-of-Holies" (cf. Leviticus 16), who finds the "book" there (*sēper hattôrâ māṣā'tî bēbêt yhwh*; "*I* have found *the* book of the Torah [which is/was?] in the House of Yahweh" [22:8a]).[18] This chain of inferences makes it plausible for the reader to believe the narrative's assumption that the "book of the law" which he found in "the House of Yahweh" (22:8) was, in fact, *that* "book of the law." Both of these intertextual allusions presuppose a literary work which encompasses the Books of Deuteronomy and Joshua as well as the Kings History, and such a work in its entirety is not likely to have existed before the Exile (with Noth and many others).

These considerations sever any necessary direct connection between the reform report and Deuteronomy, implicit in both the "Deuteronomistic Book Hypothesis" and the "Deuteronomistic History Hypothesis," by making that connection a post-"Josianic," probably post-Exilic, literary invention. It may be the case that the "decisive redaction" of much, if not all, of the Book of Deuteronomy was not much earlier.[19] The "original" reform report must be earlier still: indeed, as Römer points out, "the restoration and the 'yahwisiation'" of Solomon's Temple, the bulk of the "original" report's content, was not particularly relevant in a post-587/6 context in which that edifice and the socio-political world of which it was a part no longer existed and the self-proclaimed "real Israel" in exile was alienated from the population which had remained in the land;[20] on the contrary:[21]

> the post-587 Dtrs. knew that they could not reactivate the former institutions, and they did not share the prophetic enthusiasm as expressed for instance by the Second Isaiah. But they did undertake a most

---

[18] Cf. N. Lohfink, "Die Bundesurkunde des Königs Josias," *Bib* (1963) 280–2, and *idem*, "Was there a Deuteronomistic Movement? 48 (= "Gab es eine deuteronomistische Bewegung?" 326).

[19] Cf., e.g., N. Lohfink, "Distribution of the Functions of Power: The Laws Concerning Public Offices in Deuteronomy 16:18–18:22," *A Song of Power and the Power of Song: Essays on the Book of Deuteronomy* (ed. by D. L. Christensen; Sources for Biblical and Theological Study 3; Winona Lake: Eisenbrauns, 1993) especially 339–46 (quotation from p. 346) (= *Great Themes from the Old Testament* [trans. by R. Walls; Chicago: Franciscan Herald, 1981] especially 58–68 [quotation from p. 68]).

[20] Römer, "Transformations in Deuteronomistic and Biblical Historiography," 1–11 (quotation from p. 6). Note that of the six supplementary *waw*-copulative + Perfect passages only 23:12bβ and arguably 23:8b deal with the Temple precincts and none with the Temple itself.

[21] *Ibid.*, 5.

important transformation in substituting the "book" [for] the temple and the prophet.

This same impulse is probably reflected in the Chronicler's generalizing and minimizing of the reform *per se*. The "deuteronom(ist)ic" connection in the Kings History belongs to a compositional strand which is not coterminous with the basic literary structure of the reform narrative, but has been added to and intercalated with it. This strand understands the "book" to be the "Torah of Moses"— i.e., Deuteronomy 12–28—perhaps the same "book of the Torah of Moses" read in a morning by Ezra from "upon a wooden platform" (*ʿal-migdal-ʿēṣ*) to "the men and the women and those who could understand" (Neh. 8:1–8), an episode plainly evocative of the scene of Josiah reading his "book" from "upon the standing-place/podium" (*ʿal-hāʿammûd*) to "all the people, both small and great" (2 Kgs. 23:1–3).[22] Later still, Jewish tradition would understand both "books" to be the entire Torah while early Christian tradition would revert to Deuteronomy.[23]

Complementing the "book" is the place where it was found: not the Temple edifice and its contents but, in the "deuteronom(ist)ic" idiom, "the [one] place where Yahweh will choose to put his name" (and its several variations), i.e., Jerusalem. The cornerstone of the abiding popular and scholarly consensus concerning the Josianic "reform" is a connection between Josiah's treatment of the "bamoth" and the proscriptions in Deuteronomy 12: the "altar law" stipulates the exclusivity of the chosen "place," implicitly Jerusalem, for the correct Yahweh cultus, in contrast to the "places" where the dispossessed indigenous peoples "served their gods, upon the high mountains and upon the hills and every green tree" with altars, masseboth, and asherim which the Israelites are enjoined to destroy (vv. 2–5). This is arguably "the most unique and far-reaching law in Deuteronomy."[24] Theoretically, the claim of locational exclusivity could have been advanced by or on behalf of the Temple at any time from Solomon to Ezra—the Josianic period has no *a priori* claim on the concept—and the compositional history of the "altar law" may well

---

[22] Cf. Ahlström, *History of Ancient Palestine*, 777, and Coggins, "What Does 'Deuteronomistic' Mean?" 25 (= *Words Remembered, Texts Renewed*, 138).

[23] For references and discussion see L. K. Handy, "Josiah after the Chronicler," *PEGLMWBS* 14 (1994) 95–103.

[24] Tigay, *Deuteronomy*, 118.

cover nearly that entire time-span.[25] If the phrase "upon the high mountains and upon the hills and every green tree" (v. 2) is, in fact, "a prosaicized form of Hos. [4:]13, and thus dependent on it,"[26] that portion of the pericope—perhaps 12:1–12 + 20–28, which may, in fact, be secondary to vv. 13–19—cannot antedate Hezekiah's reign at the earliest. The formulaic complaint about "removing" (*SWR*) the "bamoth" to prevent "the people" from worshipping there, characteristic of the KH-1 regnal accounts, concludes with Hezekiah who is credited with having done so (2 Kgs. 18:4a, 22);[27] whatever its historical basis may be,[28] this literary motif associates the concept of cultic centralization with the reign of Hezekiah, reinforcing the linguistic connection implied by Deut. 12:2.[29] On the other hand, there is a growing recognition that "the demand for cultic exclusiveness on anything like the scale and seriousness that the Deuteronomic authors insisted upon had never been effectively enforced until the events of 587 BCE overtook the nation."[30] With Solomon's Temple in ruins, many Judahites at home and abroad found alternative locational foci for their Yahwism;[31] the cultic resurgence of nearby Bethel

---

[25] The compositional history of Deuteronomy 12 is as controversial as is that of 2 Kgs. 22:1–23:30 with no real consensus: see the comprehensive study by E. Reuter, *Kultzentralisation: Zur Entstehung und Theologie von Dtn 12* (Athenäums Theolische Monografien, Theologie; BBB 87; Frankfort am Main: Hain, 1993), with earlier literature.

[26] W. L. Holladay, "'On Every High Hill and Under Every Green Tree'," *VT* 11 (1961) 170–6 (quotation from p. 175).

[27] Cf. Barrick, "On the 'Removal of the "High-Places"'," 57–9; Provan, *Hezekiah*, chs. 2–3 and pp. 84–5; Halpern-Vanderhooft, "Editions of Kings," especially 199–212; Eynikel, *Reform of King Josiah*, ch. 2. McKenzie's claim that "Josiah's reign is . . . the real climax of the *bmwt* motif" (*Trouble with Kings*, 125) disregards the presentational difference: brief, unadorned formulaic notices ending with Hezekiah (2 Kgs. 18:4a) and descriptive passages using different vocabulary thereafter.

[28] See Chapter 7 n. 27 below.

[29] But Reuter sees vv. 1–7 as a later, Exilic augmentation (*Kultzentralisation*, 259).

[30] Clements, "Deuteronomic Law of Centralisation and the Catastrophe of 587 BCE," 5–25 (quotation from p. 19). According to Coggins, "the exilic and even post-exilic periods are now regarded as the age at which Deuteronomistic influence was at its height" ("What Does 'Deuteronomistic' Mean?" 25 (= *Words Remembered, Texts Renewed*, 138). Cf. L. J. Hoppe, "Jerusalem in the Deuteronomistic History," *Das Deuteronomium: Entstehung, Gestalt, und Botschaft* (ed. by N. Lohfink; BETL 68; Leuven: University, 1985) 107–10 ("Deuteronomy's cult centralisation is a reflection of the exilic situation and is an attempt to make virtue out of necessity" [p. 106]).

[31] Note that the temple of Yahu at Elephantine was the locus of meal-offerings (*minḥâ*), incense (*lĕbônâ*), and burnt-offerings (*'ôlâ*) until its destruction in 410, while only meal-offerings and incense would be offered at its successor (see *ANET*, 491–2, and cf. B. Porten, in *ABD* [1992] 2.445–55 [especially p. 449], with earlier literature). Since the change probably is due to the implementation of the deuteronomic "altar law" through the influence of the Jerusalem authorities (see D. Jones, "The

and its literary disparagement by later biblical writers betoken its great appeal in this period. Solomon's prayer at the dedication of the Temple, projecting its future function, counters this natural (and probably inevitable) tendency by representing it not as a place of sacrifice, but as a place of prayer, and especially prayer from afar (1 Kgs. 8:14–53).[32] Yet none of the functions of the "place" of Deuteronomy 12—burnt offerings and sacrifices, tithes and contributions, votive and freewill offerings, and sacred meals (vv. 6–7, 11–12, 13–14, 17–18, 26–27)—are anticipated, suggesting that these provisions may have originally pertained to different circumstances.

Between these chronological extremes lies the report of Josiah's reform which seems at odds with both.[33] Little in the language or content of the report, least of all in the "original" version, can be called "deuteronom(ist)ic" except in the most general and unhelpful of terms, especially when compared to the surrounding narrative;[34] the absence of any mention of or allusion to Yahweh's "name," a linguistic and theological touchstone of "deuteronomism"—and entirely

Cessation of Sacrifice after the Destruction of the Temple in 586 BC," *JTS* 14 [1963] especially 14–6), the episode provides a *terminus ad quem* for that provision. The relevance of Jer. 41:5 (pilgrims bringing only meal-offerings and incense to the "house of Yahweh") to this question is unclear: (1) If the "house of Yahweh" was the Temple in Jerusalem, the absense of burnt-offerings could be due to the fact that they could not be offered there because the altar was no longer functional. (2) The "house of Yahweh" could have been elsewhere (see Chapter 3 n. 58 above).

[32] See recently Y. Hoffman, "The Deuteronomist and the Exile," *Pomegranates and Golden Bells: Studies in Biblical, Jewish, and Near Eastern Ritual, Law, and Literature in Honor of Jacob Milgrom* (ed. by D. P. Wright et al.; Winona Lake: Eisenbrauns, 1995) 659–75. For the pericope as a whole see J. R. Levenson, "From Temple to Synagogue: 1 Kings 8," *Traditions in Transformation* (ed. by B. Halpern and J. D. Levenson; Winona Lake: Eisenbrauns, 1981) 143–66. For the dependency of 1 Kgs. 8:46–53 on Deut. 29:17–27 and 30:1–10 cf. J. G. McConville, "1 Kings viii 46–53 and the Deuteronomic Hope," *VT* 42 (1992) 67–79.

[33] The reform report, if read in light of 1 Kgs. 8:14–53, could give the impression that by emptying the Temple of the cultic paraphernalia of deities other than Yahweh Josiah was, in fact, preparing it for this non-sacrificial function. The wealth of detail in the "original" version suggests that this inference would be secondary to the intent of its author-compiler.

[34] Contrast, e.g., M. Rose, "Bemerkungen zum historischen Fundament des Josia-Bildes in II Reg 22f.," *ZAW* 89 (1977) 50–63; Hoffmann, *Reform und Reformen*, especially 220ff., 315ff., 327ff.; A. D. H. Mayes, *Deuteronomy* (NCB; Grand Rapids/London: Eerdmans/Marshall, Morgan & Scott, 1979) 96–8 (cf. the abbreviated version in "King and Covenant: A Study of 2 Kings Chs. 22–23," *Hermathena* 125 [1978] 42–3), and *idem, Story of Israel between Settlement and Exile*, 130–2 and accompanying notes ("of the strongly deuteronomic/deuteronomistic character of the story there can be no doubt" [p. 131]); Eynikel, *Reform of King Josiah*, 353, but see n. 109 below.

compatible with Exilic and post-Exilic realities[35]—is especially conspicuous in view of 21:4 + 7 (contrast 23:6 + 12). That it can be
read "deuteronom(ist)ically," as the exegetical history of the pericope
amply demonstrates, does not mean that that reading was intended
by the author—i.e., that its author was a "deuteronomist." Nothing
in the rhetoric or content of the report requires the any part of the
Book of Deuteronomy in order to be understandable. Nothing in
the rhetoric or content of the report presupposes the story of the
"book" which leads naturally to the covenant ceremony and thence
to the Passover.[36] Indeed, in terms of narrative continuity the reform
report fits into this context uncomfortably: a renovation of the Temple
is itself an act of cultic reform and would more logically be the consequence of the covenant and the occasion of many of the measures
cited in the reform report;[37] as it is, the covenant ceremony takes
place amid the clutter of a Temple already under renovation but
still full of offensive cultic paraphernalia and persons. The date notices
with the repeated nomenclature "of King Josiah" (22:3; 23:22–23)
create an *inclusio* bracketing a discrete literary cluster and if taken
literally imply that all of Josiah's undertakings within that cluster,
including the Temple repairs and his "northern crusade," occurred
in the course of a few weeks of his 18th regnal year;[38] such a timetable
is dubious as history. These discontinuities, and the interrupted
"sent"/"commanded" alternation at 23:4 or 23:21, make the proposition that the author of the reform report also composed the surrounding narrative less likely than the proposition that an inventory
of reform measures which originated elsewhere was incorporated into
the surrounding narrative by either the author of the narrative or a
later author-compiler.

---

[35] On the "Name Theology" see T. N. D. Mettinger, *The Dethronement of Sabaoth:
Studies in the Shem and Kabod Theologies* (CBOT 18; Lund: Gleerup, 1982), and *idem*,
"The Name and the Glory: The Zion-Sabaoth Theology and its Exilic Successors,"
JNSL 24 (1998) 1–24; Clements, "Deuteronomic Law of Centralisation and the
Catastrophe of 587 BCE," 16–8.

[36] Classically Lohfink, "Bundesurkunde des Königs Josias," 261–88, 461–98. This
narrative continuity argues against taking the Passover unit as secondary.

[37] As often pointed out by scholars favoring the Chronicler's sequence of events
(see, e.g., the references cited in Chapter 2 n. 2 above); see further below.

[38] As Cogan points out, the Kings account implies that "all of Josiah's reform
program was executed within the short period from New Year's until Passover"
("Chronicler's Use of Chronology," 204 n. 27); similarly Eynikel, *Reform of King
Josiah*, 320–1 and n. 12 ("an interval of but two weeks between New Year [1 Abib]
and the Passover feast [15 Abib]").

The Reform Report and the Story of the "Book"

The compositional history of the larger narrative has generated much scholarly disputation and little agreement.[39] For the purposes of the present inquiry, the relevant issue is when the reform report and the narrative were conjoined: was the report inserted into the narrative secondarily, or was it part of the account of Josiah's reign from the beginning with or without the surrounding narrative? If the reform report evolved basically in two stages (as summarized in Section 6.A above), it could not have entered the Josiah narrative in the "post-Exilic" KH-4 edition unless that author-compiler revised a pre-existing document at the time he incorporated it; that prospect, of course, begs the questions of the origin of this document dealing with specific cultic modifications of a now-defunct Temple and why it was thought desirable to incorporate an elaborated version of it rather than invent something simpler. Alternatively, and I think preferably, the "original" reform report either (1) was in the "Josianic" KH-2 account of Josiah's reign and was revised as that account was revised in KH-4, with or without an intermediate KH-3 stage, or (2) was added to a pre-existing narrative in KH-3 and revised in KH-4. In either case, what else concerning the reform might have been in the KH-2 account? There are a limited number of possibilities:

- The complete narrative sequence within the 18th-year *inclusio*, including the reform report and chiastic structure centered on the covenant, could have existed already in KH-2. According to Lohfink, for example, that sequence consists of an "historical short-story" ("historischen Kurzgeschichte") about Josiah and the "book" which was composed by the KH-2 author-compiler and into which he "skillfully inserted" the reform report;[40] it was composed in "Josiah's last years, just a few years removed from the events it reports."[41] This scenario requires two dubious propositions: (1) that someone

---

[39] For reviews of scholarly opinion on the compositional history of this material see the recent commentaries (e.g., Hobbs, *2 Kings*, 215–21), Knoppers, *Two Nations under God 2*, ch. 6, and the references cited in Chapter 1 n. 4 above.

[40] Lohfink, "Cult Reform of Josiah," 463–4. See further *idem*, "Die Gattung 'Historischen Kurzgeschichte' in den letzten Jahren von Juda und in der Zeit des Babylonischen Exils," *ZAW* 93 (1978) 319–47. His other examples are Jeremiah 26, 36, and 37–43. Cf. C. D. Isbell, "2 Kings 22:3–23:24 and Jeremiah 36: A Stylistic Comparison," *JSOT* 8 (1978) 33–45.

[41] Lohfink, "Cult Reform of Josiah," 462–3.

in Josiah's lifetime, who may well have witnessed or even participated in the reform, composed an account of the reform in which
the chronology—everything taking place in Josiah's 18th year—
was recognizably erroneous to the contemporary readers; and (2)
that someone capable of artfully structuring a narrative by alter-
nating episodes initiated by the king "sending" (22:3; 23:1) and
"commanding" (22:12; 23:21) would have artlessly interrupted this
neat alternation by inserting a misplaced "commanding" with the
reform report, when he could easily have adjusted the alternation
to accommodate the insertion. The alternation alone would suggest,
prima facie, that the conjoining of the two units was not original.

- The 18th-year *inclusio* could have existed in KH-2, but without the
  reform report which was added to it in KH-3. This scenario begs
  the question why a post-"Josianic" redactor would have seen fit
  to enlarge the narrative in this way—especially if this redactor was
  working after the Temple was destroyed and the country was in
  ruins. In the version of this scenario lately advocated by Eynikel,[42]
  the KH-2 author-compiler (his RII/Dtr1) worked "shortly after
  Josiah's death," and "a second redactor, or perhaps the same but
  at a later date, but in any case someone from the same dtr 1
  movement," added the reform report,[43] and yet another redactor
  (perhaps to be sought "among the 'Jeremian redactors'") inserted
  "several additions" of *waw*-conjunctive + Perfect passages,[44] all *before*
  the exilic KH-3 (his RIII/Dtr2) edition. In this reconstruction the
  unanswered question of motivation is exacerbated by the political
  and social tumult of the scant two decades separating Jehoiakim's
  accession, the first capitulation and deportation, and the final fall
  of Jerusalem when all this creative redacting supposedly was done.

- Only certain portions of the narrative sequence, in addition to the
  reform report, may have been part of the KH-2 account of Josiah's
  reign. A. D. H. Mayes, for example, maintains that "there is a
  layer constituted by the [T]emple repair story in 22:3–7, 9 and
  Josiah's reform measures in 23:4–20, to which has been added a
  story setting [those events] within the context of the finding of a

---

[42] Eynikel, *Reform of King Josiah*, 343, 351, 359–62.
[43] *Ibid.*, 359–60. Cf. Halpern's "pre-exilic touch-up to the Josianic DtrH" ("Why
Is Manasseh Blamed for the Exile?" 510).
[44] *Ibid.*, 355.

lawbook and the making of a covenant."[45] If this earlier layer belongs to the "Josianic" KH-2 edition, it could be claimed that it approximates historical reality and, concomitantly, that the evident literary connection between this unit and the account of Joash's earlier Temple renovations (12:5–17) is due to the influence of the former on the latter;[46] indeed, Lohfink considers the Temple renovations unit to be "the oldest, historically reliable level" of this material.[47] But there is absolutely no evidential basis for assuming the historicity of that unit. The description of Josiah's Temple renovations merely creates a literary setting for the finding of the "book" (22:8, 10) and a prologue to the Huldah and covenant episodes which it precipitates: the unit does *not* report the launching of the renovation project or the motivation behind it,[48] but merely provides the reason for Shaphan to be in the Temple on the king's business, the first link in the chain of events by which Josiah learns of Yahweh's displeasure; it cannot stand without at least the "book" and Huldah episodes which it initiates. By contrast, the representation of Joash's Temple renovations is a complete narrative in its own right, and it is more reasonable to suppose that the Josianic episode is an adaptation of it rather than the reverse[49] (but see further below). And if the KH-2 account did, in fact, record that Josiah undertook extensive renovations of the Temple, it is hard to fathom why a "Josianic" author-compiler would have cribbed his account of it.[50]

---

[45] See Mayes, "King and Covenant," especially 38–46 (= *Deuteronomy*, 90–103); *idem, Story of Israel between Settlement and Exile*, 128–31 (quotation from p. 130). Cf. Hoffmann, *Reform*, 192–7; Knoppers, *Two Kingdoms Under God 2*, 125–35.

[46] Mayes does not make these claims, but cf. Spieckermann, *Juda unter Assur*, 48–53, 179–82.

[47] Lohfink, "Cult Reform of Josiah," 473 n. 29, following Spieckermann. Edelman speculates that "the earliest form of the chapter [possibly] mentioned only the temple repairs undertaken by Josiah, written to recall to mind the repairs done by Jehoash . . ., and that the section dealing with the finding of the law scroll and the related consultation of Huldah was added secondarily" ("Huldah the Prophet," 249).

[48] *Pace* Knoppers, *Two Kingdoms Under God 2*, 132.

[49] Cf., e.g., W. Dietrich, "Josia und das Gesetzbuch (2 Reg. xxii)," *VT* 27 (1977) 18–27; Hoffmann, *Reform und Reformen*, 192–7; C. Minette de Tillesse, "Joiaqim, Repoussoir de 'Pieux' Josias: Parallélismes entre II Reg 22 et Jer 36," *ZAW* 105 (1993) 355–9.

[50] It could be supposed that both accounts draw upon a common literary topos for temple-renovation. Cf. the very fragmentary Horonaim/"House of David" section of Mesha's memorial inscription (KAI 181.31–34), perhaps added in a "second edition," in which "phrases and compositional techniques from earlier in the

- It is conceivable that the 18th year cluster of "book"/Huldah-covenant-Passover existed in KH-2 without a Temple renovations unit.[51] Since there appears to be at least two redactional levels in this cluster (especially the Huldah unit where the evidence seems clear),[52] unlike the Temple renovations unit where there is no shadow of compositional stratification, an earlier version must have existed in the post-"Josianic" KH-3 edition or already in the "Josianic" KH-2 edition. If this account also included the reform report, a logical place for it would be its present position between the covenant and the Passover units.[53] Alternatively, the KH-2 account could have contained the "book"/Huldah-covenant-Passover cluster *preceded* by the reform report. The Chronicler's presentation of Josiah's reign has this arrangement, but includes the Temple renovations unit in the 18th-year cluster.

- It is also conceivable that the KH-2 account contained little beyond the "original" reform report, with nothing to explain the motivation behind Josiah's actions.[54] Precedents for this arrangement in

---

inscription have been recast to compose a new narrative about a different town and campaign": see S. B. Parker, *Stories in Scripture and Inscriptions: Comparative Studies on Narratives in Northwest Semitic Inscriptions and the Hebrew Bible* (New York/Oxford: Oxford University, 1997) 52–55 (quotation from p. 53), and for the Mesha inscription see further Section 6.C below. The specificity of the account of Joash's Temple renovations (2 Kgs. 12:5–17), which gives the impression of a unique, one-time-only episode, argues against this possibility.

[51] There is no *a priori* necessity to posit one, since other, equally plausible circumstances for the finding of a "lost" document in the Temple can be imagined (e.g., in an archival collection of some sort: cf. Ezra 5:19–20; 6:1–5), and there is no reason to assume that anything would have been mentioned other than the essential fact that it was found "in the House of Yahweh" (22:8), if that (cf. v. 10a).

[52] See especially Knoppers, *Two Nations Under God 2*, 140–56, and the literature cited there; cf. also Chapter 1 n. 29 above. Knoppers makes a strong case for the secondary status of Huldah's first oracle (22:16–17), accompanied by considerable reworking of the second (vv. 18–20) so that "only lineaments of Huldah's pre-exilic oracle remains" (p. 152 n. 67). Cf. Lohfink, "Recent Discussion," 56–7 n. 87 (= *Deuteronomium*, 43 n. 87). Contrast lately Halpern, "Why Is Manasseh Blamed for the Exile?" especially 493–505.

[53] Noting the close similarities between 2 Kgs. 23:1–3 and Deut. 1–26, Long suspects that a "Dtr pattern of representing covenant making may lie in the background" (*2 Kings*, 270–1). According to Knoppers (*Two Nations Under God 2*, 130–1): "Based on the analogy of Exodus 34, the direct movement from Huldah's oracles and the covenant renewal to the Paschal feast, without any intervening reforms, is surprising. One expects that, as in Exodus 32–34, the offense has to be removed before harmony in divine-human relations can be restored." He cites for further comparison Gen. 35:2–4; Ex. 19:3–8; Josh. 24:23; Judg. 10:6–16; 1 Sam. 7:3–4; 2 Kgs. 11:17–18. See the critique by Eynikel, *King Josiah's Reform*, 343–4 n. 36.

[54] Cf. E. Talstra, "De Hervorming van Josia, of de Kunst van den Beeldenstormen,"

the Kings History are found in the regnal accounts of Asa and Hezekiah which move directly from the introductory evaluative statement that they "did right in the eyes of Yahweh" following the example of "David his father" (1 Kgs. 15:11 and 2 Kgs. 18:3; cf. 22:2) to their reform activities (1 Kgs. 15:12–15 and 2 Kgs. 18:4) without further explanation of their motivation. Although the "book"-Huldah sequence conforms to the Mesopotamian pattern of royal intervention in cultic affairs being initiated by an expression of divine displeasure in the *status quo* as confirmed by human intermediation,[55] it is the exception and not the rule for the biblical reports of such interventions.

What are we to make of all this? It seems to me that much of the scholarly discussion of this issue has been conditioned by an implicit predisposition toward the Kings account as historically and (granting the "Deuteronomic Book Hypothesis") theologically satisfying. This predisposition may be warranted, of course, but it may just as well be misleading. In my opinion, the most fruitful clue may be the Chronicler's version of Josiah's reign which testifies to the integrity of the 18th-year cluster, including the Temple renovations unit but without the reform report. If the Chronicler's siting of the burning of the bones of priests in "Judah and Jerusalem" (34:5) was inspired by a version of the Kings History which retained the original Jerusalem location of the "cemetery scene," it is not at all impossible that his version of Kings also disassociated the reform report from the 18th-year cluster. A comparison with the relevant portion of the Hezekiah's regnal account in Kings is instructive:

Hezekiah	*Josiah (K)*	*Josiah (Chr)*
A. Reign begins (18:1–2a)	A. Reign begins (22:1a)	A. Reign begins (34:1a)
B. Introduction (18:1–3)	B. Introduction (22:1b–2)	B. Introduction (34:1b–2)
		+ "Conversion" (34:3a)—8th year

Gereformeerd Theologisch Tijdschrift 88 (1988) especially 157–9 (known to me from the précis and critique given by Eynikel, *Reform of King Josiah*, 342).

[55] As outlined by L. K. Handy in "Calling the Kings to Reform: Josiah, Esarhaddon, Nabonidus" (unpublished paper presented at the annual meeting of the Society of Biblical Literature in Chicago, 22 November 1988), and "Role of Huldah in Josiah's Cult Reform," 40–53.

C. Purge (18:4)

     — Renovations (22:
      3–7)—18th year
     — "Book"/Huldah
      (22:8–20)
     — Covenant (23:1–3)
     C. Purge (23:4–20)
     — Passover (23:
      21–23)—18th year

D. Incomparability
  (18:5)
E. Consequences
  (18:6–8)

C. Purge
  (34:3b–7)—12th year
  — Renovations (34:
   8–13)—18th year
  — "Book"/Huldah
   (34:14–28)
  — Covenant (34:29–33)

  — Passover (35:1–19)—
   18th year

D. Incomparability
  (23:25)
E. Consequences
  (23:26–27)

If the KH-2 version of Josiah's reign resembled the Hezekiah account, with the reform report but without the rest of the 18th-year cluster, the KH-3 version could have resembled the Chronicler's account of Josiah, with the rest of the 18th-year cluster appended to the reform report; alternatively, the KH-2 version itself could have resembled the Chronicler's account.

A resolution of this question must take into account the likely date of the "Josianic" KH-2 edition of the Kings History. If the post-"Josianic" KH-3 edition included the material between the introduction to Jehoiakim's reign (23:36–37) and the precisely-dated notice of Jehoiachin's release (25:27–30), it cannot antedate c. 562; if that notice is secondary to KH-3, the *terminus ante quem* would be the assassination of Nebuchadrezzar's governor, Gedaliah b. Ahikam b. Shaphan, at Mizpah, dated with equal precision to c. 586 (25:22–26; cf. Jeremiah 40–41).[56] The post-Exilic KH-4 edition must have been compiled sometime thereafter, conceivably even after the Chronicler. The date of the Chronicler's work remains uncertain (the possibilities range from c. 539 to c. 200); R. W. Klein, concludes warily that "though a 4th-century date seems likely, the uncertain nature of the evidence suggests caution when tying one's interpretation to anything more historically specific than the general situation of postexilic

---

[56] See now S. L. McKenzie, "Mizpah of Benjamin and the Date of the Deuteronomistic History," *"Lasset uns Brücken bauen . . .": Collected Communications of the XVth Congress of the International Organization for the Study of the Old Testament, Cambridge 1995* (ed. by K.-D. Schunck and M. Augustin; Beiträge zur Erforschung des Alten Testaments und des Antiken Judentums 42; Frankfurt am Main/Berlin/Bern/New York/Paris/Wein: Lang, 1998) 149–155; cf. R. E. Friedman, *The Exile and Biblical Narrative* (HSM 22; Chico: Scholars, 1981) 35–6, and *idem*, "From Egypt to Egypt," 189–91.

times."[57] Dating the earlier editions of Kings is more problematic. KH-1, a historiographical work showcasing Hezekiah (who "trusted in Yahweh the god of Israel, so that there was none like him among all the kings of Judah after him nor among those who were before him" [2 Kgs. 18:5]) need not have been composed in the reign of Hezekiah; minimally, the notice that he reigned for 29 years (v. 2) could not have been written before the first years of Manasseh's reign. Similarly, the notices of Josiah's 31-year reign (22:1) and of his death at Megiddo (23:29–30) could not have been written before the heady few months of Jehoahaz's reign. If these notices were interpolated secondarily into historiographical works written during those respective reigns, the seams are invisible. The proposition that a history of Judah was composed in the course of Hezekiah's reign as a literary reinforcement of his bid for independence from Assyria, or as solace for its failure, is certainly appealing, but the latter subtext would suit as well a partisan of the *ancien régime* writing subversively under Manasseh while the wounds of defeat were still fresh (see further Chapter 7.A below).[58] The proposition that this work was revised at the apex of Josiah's reign to refocus the spotlight on him is likewise appealing, but such a revision could as well have been done immediately after his unexpected death in order to bolster the position of Jehoahaz and his supporters over the claims of his elder brother Jehoiakim and his supporters; since Jehoahaz's reign was extremely brief, and since high-placed elements of that *ancien régime*— notably members of the family of Shaphan, Josiah's influential minister and proponent of his reform—are known to have engaged in activities inimical to certain of the successor government's policies (cf. Jeremiah 36), it seems equally possible that a "Josianic" revision of a "Hezekian" Kings History was compiled by these elements in the course of Jehoiakim's reign, a subversive literary undertaking analogous in this respect to Jeremiah's scrolls which were first compiled in this same period.

---

[57] Klein, in *ABD*, 1, especially 994–5 (quotation from p. 995), and similarly Kleinig, "Recent Research in Chronicles," 46–7; cf. the commentaries.

[58] If the notice of Sennacherib's death (2 Kgs. 19:27) belongs to the "Hezekian" edition, it cannot have been produced before 681; cf. Provan, *Hezekiah*, ch. 5, concluding that it "may with confidence be assigned to a period early in the reign of Josiah" (p. 154). Eynikel hedges (*Reform of King Josiah*, 131 n. 327): "during Josiah's reign or earlier."

N. Naaman's new explanation of the relationship between the Joash and Josiah Temple renovations accounts (2 Kgs. 12:5–17 and 22:3–6) is very germane to this matter:[59]

> The two texts were written by the same author at the same time, and the detailed account of the procedure established by Joash is the background against which the account of Josiah's restoration should be read. In other words, within the sequence of the Books of Kings, Joash's regulations are considered to be in force until the time of Josiah, and the author considered it redundant to repeat them again. . . . He opened the description of . . . Josiah's temple restoration from the stage when the silver was melted and measured, assuming that his reader had the account of Joash in mind.

The author-compiler, a contemporary of Josiah, was personally familiar with the procedures used in his day, but he drew the information about the earlier procedures which Joash had changed from a "building inscription" erected in Joash's 23rd year at the dedication of the newly renovated Temple and "unearthed" in the course of Josiah's subsequent renovations of the same structure; this inscription also may have included an account of the unusual circumstances of his accession, comparable in this respect to the inscription of Bar-Rakib of Sam'al (KAI 215).[60] This source, augmented by the author-compiler's personal knowledge of conditions in his own day, provided "the main outlines of the history of Joash." Naaman suggests further that "it seems that the discovery of an old inscription gave rise to the story of the discovery of the book of the Torah in the course of the temple's restoration, which is so prominent in the account of Josiah's reform."[61] Naaman identifies the author-compiler of this material as the "Dtr historian," corresponding chronologically to my "Josianic" KH-2 author-compiler, who probably worked "a short time after the completion of the [T]emple's restoration."[62]

Naaman's propositions, while ultimately unprovable, have much to commend them. It is certainly reasonable to suppose that the earlier (i.e., pre-Exilic) author-compiler(s) of the Kings History derived some information from monumental public inscriptions to which they

---

[59] N. Naaman, "Royal Inscriptions and the Histories of Joash and Ahaz, Kings of Judah," *VT* 48 (1998) 337–44 (quotation from pp. 338–9).
[60] *Ibid.*, 340–3. Cf. M. Liverani, "L'Histoire de Joas," *VT* (1974) 452, citing similarities with the epigraphic story of Idrimi of Alalakh.
[61] Naaman, "Royal Inscriptions and the Histories of Joash and Ahaz," 343; cf. 348.
[62] *Ibid.*, 343.

had access, and the building and major renovation, or "rebuilding," of temples are demonstrable occasions for the creation and display of inscriptions commemorating that notable royal accomplishment (see Section 6.D below). Joash's "rebuilding" of the Temple is a likely candidate for such a commemoration, and the comparison of his regnal account with Bar-Rakib's epigraphic biography is both apt and suggestive.[63] Although Naaman envisions the "Josianic" Kings History (my KH-2) as the *first* edition of the work, his postulates concerning the Joash's regnal account would be consistent with the compositional history of the work endorsed in the present study if it is supposed that the earlier KH-1 version of Joash's reign lacked this information and resembled the regnal accounts of Jehoshaphat (1 Kgs. 22:41–50) and Jehoram (2 Kgs. 8:16–24) in brevity.[64] But the account of Josiah's Temple renovations remains incomplete: on the analogy with the Joash account, there should be a statement comparable to 12:6 giving Josiah's direction to "repair the House," but there is none; on the contrary, the project has already begun and the workmen are already at work "in the House of Yahweh repairing the House" (22:5b) when the narrative begins. These brief comments about Josiah's renovations do not constitute an independent narrative in their own right, in sharp contrast to the Joash account, but serve as a narratological device for getting Shaphan into the Temple to learn of Hilkiah's discovery; it is merely the prologue to the "book"/Huldah unit. The truncation might be seen as authorial license: that Josiah had initiated a major renovation of the Temple was "common knowledge" when the account was written, but the financial arrangement were not. But the financial arrangements seem a gratuitous detail, at best only tangentially relevant to plot of the "book"/Huldah unit.[65] And if that unit is essentially a fiction spun around the actual finding of Joash's inscribed monument, as Naaman proposes, it would have been recognized as such by anyone

---

[63] For text and commentary see, e.g., J. C. L. Gibson, *Textbook of Syrian Semitic Inscriptions II: Aramaic Inscriptions* (Oxford: Clarendon, 1975) 76–86; Margalit, "Studies in NW Semitic Inscriptions," 303–13.

[64] In light of these analogies, the KH-1 version might have contained no more than 12:2–5 (the introductory formulae) + 18–19 (a version of the Hazael episode) + 20–22 (closing formulae, with assassination information).

[65] The honesty of the workmen (v. 7) establishes the integrity of those who might be thought to have actually found the "book" in the course of their work, or at least to have been present when it was found.

unsympathetic with the reformers' agenda who was familiar with the facts of the matter—thus defeating the very purpose of the story.

If the nexus of the two Temple renovations accounts and Josiah's "book" discovery is an inscription of Joash discovered in the course of Josiah's reign, a pre-Exilic date for the initial composition of the narratives in question seems more likely than a date after the royal quarter in Jerusalem was destroyed and the inscription probably was lost: i.e., KH-2 rather than KH-3. Naaman imagines that they were written in Josiah's lifetime by someone personally familiar with the events in question, a virtual eye-witness: i.e., someone of Josiah's generation (he died at roughly 39 yoa in 609) or a younger contemporary. In my opinion, the factors reviewed above point not to a composition created in the reform's afterglow during Josiah's reign or even Jehoahaz's brief moment, but to a composition created after Jehoiakim's regime was in place, when many of the major players of Josiah's reign (probably including Shaphan and Hilkiah) had left the scene[66] and fading memories had begun to be embroidered by hindsight.[67] The author-compiler of this composition must have been someone in a position to know Joash's inscription and at least the basic elements of Josiah's activity in the Temple (including the identity of the major players), and who probably was not a member of Jehoiakim's regime but nonetheless had the credibility to embellish "common knowledge" with "insider information" presumed to be accurate by those who were not present and could not check his facts.[68] One documented

---

[66] Shaphan was probably a generation older than Josiah, and Hilkiah probably two: see W. B. Barrick, "Genealogical Notes on the 'House of David' and the 'House of Zadok'," *JSOT* (forthcoming).

[67] The earliest Gospels developed in similar conditions, refracting the remembered past through different prisms of hindsight. One can easily imagine that Josiah's reign engendered a variety of responses during Jehoiakim's reign, as Ahaz's undoubtedly did during Hezekiah's and Manasseh's during Josiah's. These would be reflexes of the factionalism discussed in the following chapter.

[68] Whether factual or fictional, the choice of Huldah to provide divine confirmation, rather than Zephaniah or Jeremiah (had his career begun that early) has long puzzled commentators; cf. C. T. Begg, "A Bible Mystery: The Absence of Jeremiah in the Deuteronomistic History," *IBS* 7 (1985) 139–64. The puzzlement is all the greater if the story is actually contemporary with Jeremiah's later career, or even later. The answer may lie in Huldah's comparative anonymity (*pace* Cogan-Tadmor's assertion that she was the "most prominent among the king's supporters" [*II Kings*, 295]) and reliability. That she was the wife of a (probably sympathetic) courtier surely was one basis for her credibility in the eyes of those who sought her out. The episode is depicted as a private seance with a small and select group of courtiers

individual meets these criteria perfectly: Shaphan's son "Gemariah the scribe," a younger contemporary of Josiah[69] and a supporter of Jeremiah, with a chamber in the Temple precincts under Jehoiakim, even though he is not known to have held any governmental office at the time (Jer. 36:10).[70]

If the 18th-year complex—the "book"/Huldah unit (22:8–20), with its prologue, and the Passover unit (23:21–23)—originated in the KH-2 edition of the Kings History composed in the reign of Jehoiakim, it probably was appended to the "original" reform report in the sequence preserved by the Chronicler. The KH-2 author-compiler adapted the model of Hezekiah's regnal account (see pp. 123–4 above) by inserting the 18th-year complex between the Purge Unit (C) and the Incomparability-Consequences Units (D–E). This version probably identified the content of the "book" as *habbĕrît* (possibly alluding to the "Covenant Code" [Ex. 20:23–23:19], referred to uniquely as *sēper-habĕrît* in Ex. 24:7),[71] and probably introduced the "commanded"/"sent" alternation focused on the revelation of Yahweh's will through a prophetic intermediary rather than a document:

---

hastily convened in a residential part of town—all hallmarks of secrecy, essential for a conspiracy. Neither Zephaniah nor (especially) Jeremiah seem prone to secrecy, and Jeremiah in particular might have been thought something of a "loose cannon" even by some of his courtly admirers, not a desirable commodity in a co-conspirator. Jeremiah may have been duped by the deception and used by its devisors for their own purposes. (Could his invective against the scribes whose "false pen" made "the torah of Yahweh" a lie [Jer. 8:7–12] reflect his outrage at discovering the deception?)

[69] See n. 66 above. Ahikam b. Shaphan and Gemariah b. Shaphan were of Josiah's generation, Ahikam probably being the elder since he was already an important councilor in Josiah's 18th year (2 Kgs. 22:12).

[70] The chamber of Elishama, presumably Shaphan's successor as the royal scribe, was in the adjacent palace-complex (Jer. 36:12–21). T. N. D. Mettinger's suggestion that Gemariah "was almost certainly a royal (private?) secretary since he is listed among the *śrym* (v. 12)" (*Solomonic State Officials: A Study of the Civil Government Officials of the Israelite Monarchy* [CBOT 5, Lund: Gleerup, 1971], 32) is unconvincing: even if (as seems likely) the "scribe" in the phrase *gĕmaryâhû ben-šâpân hassōpār* (v. 10) identifies Gemariah and not Shaphan, it cannot be inferred from this label that he held a governmental "office" any more than did Baruch "the scribe" (v. 32, and his seal: see N. Avigad, "Baruch the Scribe and Jerahmeel the King's Son," *IEJ* 28 [1978], 52–6), and does not account for the location of his "chamber" in the Temple precincts, rather than the palace-complex where the "royal herald"/*mazkir* (offered as a "plausible alternative" [*ibid.*]) would likely be housed.

[71] Consistent with Knoppers' suggestion that the *habbĕrît* nomenclature "reflects Dtr1's attempt to link Josiah's covenant and Passover with the Sinaitic covenant" (*Two Nations under God* 2, 131 n. 20). See further n. 77 below.

A. Introductory Formula (22:1)
   B. Evaluation (22:2)
      C.1. "The king commanded" (23:4): cult reform
         C.2. "King Josiah sent" (22:3): Temple, book, repentance
            C.3. "The king commanded" (22:12): prophetic inquiry
         C.2′. "The king sent" (23:1): covenant-making
      C.1′. "The king commanded" (23:21): Passover in Jerusalem
   B′. Evaluation (23:25–27)
A′. Concluding formula (23:28–30)

This version was subsequently modified in KH-4 (with or without an intermediate KH-3 stage) to produce the present arrangement of material, with the chiastic focus on the covenant and amplified intertextual echoes of the account of Joash's reign:

Joash	*Josiah (K)*	*Josiah (Chr)*
A. Covenant (11:17)	C. Reign begins (22:1a)	C. Reign begins (34:1a)
B. Purge (11:18–20)	D. Introduction (22:1b–2)	D. Introduction (34:1b–2) + "Conversion" (34:3a)—8th year
C. Reign begins (12:1)	E. Renovations (22:3–7)—18th year — "Book"/Huldah (22:8–20)	B. Purge (34:3b–7)—12th year
		E. Renovations (34:8–13)—18th year — "Book"/Huldah (34:14–28)
D. Introduction (12:2–4)	A. Covenant (23:1–3)	A. Covenant (34:29–33)
E. Renovations (12:5–17)	B. Purge (23:4–20)	
	— Passover (23:21–23)—18th year	— Passover (35:1–19)—18th year

Both presentations in Kings display the same basic sequence of events, but with Josiah it has a different starting-point (due to the different circumstances of Josiah's reign)[72] and adds two new elements (the "book"/Huldah unit and the Passover unit), while the sequence of

---

[72] Cf. now J. G. McConville, "Priesthood in Joshua to Kings," *VT* 49 (1999) 84–5. The sequence for Joash, with his Temple renovations (E: 12:5–17) following the covenant (A: 11:17), is a logical and historically plausible progression: Athaliah must be disposed of (11:4–16) and Joash must begin his reign (C: 12:1) before he can initiate any building activity in the Temple or anywhere else. This progression was adapted to accommodate the unique aspects of Josiah's reign—the comparatively normal beginning of his reign (i.e., apparently no political coup d'état engineered by Hilkiah) and the two units dealing with his 18th regnal year. The adjusted narrative order C-D-E-A-B for Josiah's reign with the intercalated material is neither logical nor historically plausible as noted above.

the Chronicler's presentation of Josiah bears no resemblance to it. The relevance of this template, implicit in the verbal similarity of the Temple renovations account, is further evident from the fact that both were boy-kings who came to the throne irregularly (the murder of their predecessors) with the involvement of "the people of the land," were especially interested in the Temple, and died unexpectedly under extra-ordinary circumstances.[73] Joash's "purge" (the mob action against the temple of Baal [11:18–20]) begins the moment the covenant is contracted; accordingly, Josiah's "purge" (23:4–20) had to be mentioned immediately after the covenant (vv. 1–3) and with the implication that Josiah's directive to Hilkiah and the other priests (v. 4a) was delivered while the king was still on the "standing-place" in the Temple precincts.[74] And in the course of this transformation the content of the "book" became *hattôrâ*, understood as the Book of Deuteronomy.

Was there *really* a "book" behind the story, or is it "a fiction built around the factual discovery of Joash's inscription" as Naaman would have it?[75] The stereotyped character of the "lost book" scenario noted in Chapter 1 above[76] justifies great skepticism in this matter, but the believability of the ruse that Naaman proposes requires that the contemporary audience would find it credible—that the discovery of a "lost" document really *could* have happened. If Joash's lost monumental inscription had, in fact, been discovered, other "lost" documents could have been discovered as well. Some form of the "Covenant Code" (Ex. 20:23–23:19) is one possibility,[77] some form of the "Song

---

[73] It may be significant in this regard that Joash's "purge" unit notes that "the people of the land" tore down the temple of Baal along with its altars and then "they slew Mattan the priest before the altars" (11:18). This statement resonates intertextually with the notice, added to the reform report (KH-4), that Josiah "slew all the bamoth-priests [in the cities of Samaria] upon the altars [of the bamoth-houses there]" (23:20a).

[74] This impression is facilitated by the mention of "the priests and the prophets" as participants in the covenant (23:2aβ). There is no comparable reference in 12:17, and it is often considered a gloss: e.g., Eynikel, *Reform of King Josiah*, 344.

[75] Personal communication (16 June 1999).

[76] See p. 8 and n. 26 above.

[77] Reuter concludes that Josiah's "book" was the "Book of the Covenant" (Ex. 20:22–23:33) and his reform prompted the composition of *Ur*-Deuteronomy (*Kultzentralisation*, especially 244–50); for *Urdeuteronium* as a revision of the "Book of the Covenant" which supplemented but did not replace the original see E. Otto, "The Pre-Exilic Deuteronomy as a Revision of the Covenant Code," *Kontinuum und Proprium: Studien zur Sozial- und Rechtsgeschichte des Alten Orients und des Alten Testaments* (Orientalia Biblica et Christiana 8; Wiesbaden: Harrowitz, 1996) 112–22 (with earlier literature).

of Moses" (Deuteronomy 32) another,[78] both more likely than some form of the Book of Deuteronomy. That this putative "book" motivated the reformers is almost certainly a deuteronomistic fiction.

6.C. A Possible Source for the Reform Report

The reform report was authored by a Judahite writing at a particular time, under a particular set of circumstances, and with a particular audience in mind. Unless he drew everything from his own imagination, he would have relied on sources—conceivably including his own eyewitness experience—which he represented with greater or lesser alteration. If the KH-2 edition contained both the "original" reform report and the 18th-year complex and was composed during the reign of Jehoiakim as proposed in the preceding section, the author of the report could have been (1) the same person who composed 18th-year complex, undoubtedly the KH-2 author-com-

---

For the "Book of the Covenant" as "the legal basis of Hezekiah's reform" see Albertz, *History of Israelite Religion 1*, 182–6 (quotation from p. 182) and the literature cited there. Albertz accepts the "Deuteronomic Book Hypothesis" (pp. 194–236) and thus does not consider the possibility that this was (or was thought to have been) the document in the "book"/Huldah unit and the Passover unit. In terms of content, it suits the Josianic era as well as Deuteronomy, if not better (e.g., it is hard to imagine any king—apart from W. S. Gilbert's gondoliers *cum* kings of Barataria—who would have willingly emasculated himself by promulgating the deuteronomic legislation pertaining to what are customary royal functions, to say nothing of the so-called "Law of the King" [17:14–20]), and is consistent with the "original" reform report reconstructed above; its size it more conducive to being thoughtfully read aloud twice in less than a work-day. The content is inconsistent with the "book"/Huldah-Passover story: there is nothing to warrant Huldah's interpretation or Josiah's extreme reaction, but both of these may well be fictional elements embroidering a different historical reality. Perhaps a law code first promulgated by Hezekiah and abrogated by the catastrophe of 701 was resurrected and revised by Josiah and abrogated again by Jehoiakim, whereupon the memory of it was fused with the memory of the discovery of Joash's inscription in the creation of this homiletic tale. Or perhaps this law code was first promulgated by Josiah in conjunction with the revivification of Judah initiated by Manasseh and completed by his successors, a "new Judah" requiring a new legal foundation which was abrogated by Jehoiakim, whereupon it was transformed into the threatening centerpiece of the tale woven by the partisans of the discredited *ancien régime* still convinced in the rightness of their cause. (For the historical context see Chapter 7.A below.) In either case the original promulgation undoubtedly gave it a divine imprimatur and probably an ancient (Mosaic?) pedigree as well.

[78] See especially J. R. Lundbom, "The Lawbook of the Josianic Reform," *CBQ* 38 (1976) 293–302, and *idem*, *Jeremiah 1–20*, 105–6, 109–17. Cf. also Friedman, "Deuteronomistic School," 70–80.

piler (= the scribe Gemariah b. Shaphan?) himself, or (2) a contemporary of that author, making the two works more or less contemporary; or (3) he and his work could have belonged to an earlier era, perhaps the reign of Josiah shortly after the activities it recounts. The first possibility seems unlikely for the reasons cited in the preceding section.

Handy's recent assessment of the "historical probability" of the biblical account proceeds from the observation that "in order to investigate the reliable nature of documents retelling cult narratives, it is necessary to turn to other texts from the ancient Near East which deal with cult activities."[79] For purposes of comparison he identifies four "basic types" of texts which were "produced in the name of the king regarding the cultic and religious sphere": (1) "temple inscriptions and foundation tablets"; (2) "king annal lists referring to temple activities"; (3) "apologetic documents related to temple actions"; and (4) "propaganda about temple affairs produced after the event."[80] After reviewing various Mesopotamian examples of each category, he finds that "the Josianic reform narrative" appears to align with the fourth, exemplified by Cyrus's Cylinder Inscription, and thus must be considered "non-contemporary and unreliable" as an historical source for Josiah's reform itself.[81] The apt comparison is with "the Josianic reform narrative" *en bloc*, the story about a pious king accidentally discovering the divine displeasure with the *status quo* and responding appropriately with certain actions. The issue here, however, is the reform report which Handy does not address directly.[82] In form-critical terms, the 2 Kgs. 23:4–20, whether in its "original" or expanded version, is a "report" ("*Bericht*") enumerating a series of actions by the king with what appears to be "a general reportorial sequentiality" and with some of the actions elaborated to some degree

---

[79] Handy, "Historical Probability and the Narrative of Josiah's Reform," 263.

[80] *Ibid.*

[81] *Ibid.*, 273–5, and the literature cited there (quotation from p. 275).

[82] Even "propaganda about temple affairs produced after the event" *can* contain reliable historical data—indeed, effective propaganda must have some basis in reality to be believable (as such latter-day hagiographical propagandists as Mason Weems [of George Washington] and Frederick Whittaker [of George Armstrong Custer] amply demonstrate—even if the work *in toto* (and particularly its conscious interpretation of events) is "unreliable." Consequently, he minimizes the possible relevance of his third category of documentary sources (see further below), and thus fails to capitalize on the methodological insightfulness of his inquiry.

and others not at all.[83] The relevant question is: What type of ancient Near Eastern document, which could have been available to the author-compiler(s) of the Kings History, does this report resemble?

Various commentators over the years have supposed that the reform report may have come from an archival source, assuming *ex hypothesi* that archival documents in ancient Judah would have looked like this.[84] This assumption cannot be tested because no extra-biblical Syro-Palestinian texts have yet been recovered comparable to the Mesopotamian "king annal lists referring to temple activities" judged by Handy to be "non-contemporary but reliable" sources.[85] A more promising possibility is the monumental "memorial inscription." A document of this genre "serves chiefly as a memorial of an official's career, usually a king," and typically mentions "major events, especially military victories, and building projects," sometimes pertaining to cultic matters.[86] It is distinct in form and content from a "dedicatory inscription" which "serves primarily the function of dedicating some object to a deity or cult center,"[87] analogous to the Mesopotamian foundation deposits and inscribed bricks discussed by Handy as exemplifying his first category of sources, "temple inscriptions and foundation tablets," and judged "contemporary and reliable";[88] the two genres

<hr />

[83] Long, *2 Kings*, 277, objecting to Hoffmann's use identification of the unit as an "enumeration" (*"Aufzählung": Reform und Reformen*, 218–9) because of the sequentiality and "the storylike scene at vv. 16–18."

[84] In addition to the works cited in Chapter 1 n. 2 above, see, e.g., Gray, *I–II Kings*, 714–5, and lately S. Nakanose, *Josiah's Passover* (Bible and Liberation Series; Maryknoll, NY: Orbis, 1993) 22–5. Minette de Tillesse posits a Temple archive ("Joiaquim," 354–5)

[85] Handy, "Historical Probability and the Narrative of Josiah's Reform," 267–9, stipulating (pp. 274–5): "Though formulaic passages in the book of Kings suggests that there had been annal-like records of the various rulers, Josiah included [cf. 2 Kgs. 23:28], there is no reason to assume that the story told in the book was taken carefully, or even haphazardly, from the royal annal literature; it simply makes no such claim." I am unmoved by the apparent assumption that any such extract would have been "footnoted" as in a modern dissertation, and plagiarists as a rule do not cite their sources.

[86] J. Drinkard, "The Literary Genre of the Mesha Inscription," *Studies in the Mesha Inscription and Moab* (ed. by A. Dearman; Archaeology and Biblical Studies 2; Atlanta: Scholars, 1989) 131–54 (quotation from p. 140); see also the classical presentation by [J.] M. Miller, "The Moabite Stone as a Memorial Stele," *PEQ* 106 (1974) 9–18, and further Van Seters, *In Search of History*, 188–95. K. A. D. Smelik prefers "building inscription" for Mesha's monument ("The Literary Structure of King Mesha's Inscription," *JSOT* 46 [1990] 23).

[87] Drinkard, "Literary Genre of the Mesha Inscription," 132–40 (quotation from p. 132); cf. Miller, "Memorial Inscription," 9–10.

[88] Handy, "Historical Probability and the Narrative of Josiah's Reform," 264–7

have much in common, however, and mixed examples are known.[89] The parade example of a Syro-Palestinian memorial inscription is the Mesha Inscription (KAI 181: Moabite, mid 9th century):[90] "after a lengthy prologue, the text recounts Mesha's actions in connection with the recovery of the land of Medeba and what apparently was a fairly extensive building program at Qarḥoh," including the sanctuary there. The memorial stele would belong to Handy's third category of sources, "apologetic documents related to temple actions," which he judges to be "'contemporary, but unreliable' as historical data, however useful it may be for understanding royal propaganda."[91] I would qualify this estimation to the extent that the citations of activities in a memorial such as Mesha's should be considered essentially reliable in the absence of credible evidence to the contrary,[92] even if the interpretational "spin" given to those activities, including the sequence of presentation, may not be.[93]

Although no comparable monumental inscriptions have thus far been recovered from ancient Judah, their existence can be confidently assumed (cf. 1 Sam. 15:12; 2 Sam. 18:18).[94] Two very small fragments

---

(quotation from p. 267), adding: "For all practical purposes, these texts were written to reflect accurately events taking place in as concise a manner as possible and should be taken as basically historical."

[89] Drinkard, "Literary Genre of the Mesha Inscription," 149–52, citing the Zakir inscription (KAI 202).

[90] J. M. Miller, in *ABD* (1992) 4.882–93 (quotation from p. 886); J. A. Dearman and G. L. Mattingly, in *ABD* (1992) 4.708–9. For the text and translation see K. P. Jackson and J. A. Dearman, "The Text of the Mesha Inscription," *Studies in the Mesha Inscription and Moab* (ed. by A. Dearman; Archaeology and Biblical Studies 2; Atlanta: Scholars, 1989) 93–5, and K. P. Jackson, "The Language of the Mesha Inscription," *Studies in the Mesha Inscription and Moab* (ed. by A. Dearman; Archaeology and Biblical Studies 2; Atlanta: Scholars, 1989) 96–129; cf. *ANET*, 320–1, and Gibson, *Textbook of Syrian Semitic Inscriptions I*, 71–83.

[91] Handy, "Historical Probability and the Narrative of Josiah's Reform," 269–72 (quotation from p. 272).

[92] Some of the material in such an inscription may well have been excerpted from archival sources; for examples from the Mesha Inscription (KAI 181.10–21) see E. A. Knauf, in *ZDPV* 104 (1988) 175.

[93] Dearman-Mattingly stress that the author has been "selective in arranging the sequence of events to serve his main purpose of honoring Chemosh" (in *ABD*, 4.708); similarly Drinkard, "Literary Genre of the Mesha Inscription," 140. For Hazael's propagandistic claim, in his memorial inscription found at Tel Dan, to have killed Joram b. Ahab of (North-)Israel and Ahaziah b. Joram of Judah (contrast 2 Kings 9–10) see W. M. Schniedewind, "Tel Dan Stela: New Light on Aramaic and Jehu's Revolt," *BASOR* 302 (1996) 75–90 (especially 82–5), and cf. A. Lemaire, "The Tel Dan Stela as a Piece of Royal Historiography," *JSOT* 81 (1998) 3–14.

[94] Cf. now the cautious review by S. B. Parker, "Did the Authors of the Books of Kings Make Use of Royal Inscriptions?" *VT* 50 (2000) 360–6.

of inscribed monuments (8th–7th century paleography) have been
found in the Temple-palace area,[95] and while the Siloam Tunnel
inscription (KAI 189) may not be an official, public commemoration of the digging of the tunnel, it does suggest that monumental
inscriptions documenting for posterity extra-ordinary activities sponsored
by the regime were common enough to be emulated by underlings
(in this case, perhaps the project supervisor responsible for this signal engineering feat).[96] Joash's putative "building inscription" postulated
by Naaman would be one example; if this inscription also included
an account of the unusual circumstances of his accession as Naaman
suggests, it would properly be a "memorial inscription" more comparable to Mesha's than to the recently-discovered 7th-century dedicatory inscription from neighboring Ekron.[97] It is perfectly reasonable

---

[95] Jer (7):39 and Jer (8):32. See J. Naveh, "A Fragment of an Ancient Hebrew
Inscription from the Ophel," *IEJ* 32 (1988) 195–8, M. Ben-Dov, "A Fragmentary
First Temple Period Hebrew Inscription from the Ophel," *Ancient Jerusalem Revealed*
(ed. by H. Geva; Jerusalem/Washington DC: Israel Exploration Society/Biblical
Archaeological Society, 1994) 73–5, and especially Parker, "Did the Authors of the
Books of Kings Make Use of Royal Inscriptions?" 362–4. Also of possible relevance
is a fragmentary inscribed ostracon from Arad (Arad [7]:83; paleographically late
8th century) which may be "a copy of or extract from a royal inscription": see
Parker, "Did the Authors of the Books of Kings Make Use of Royal Inscriptions?"
364–5 with earlier literature (quotation from p. 364).

[96] *ANET*, 321. See Parker, *Stories in Scripture and Inscriptions*, ch. 3. Considering its
anonymity and obscure location ("barely visible in the limited light several meters
inside a tunnel through which people did not normally pass"), the "emotional attach-
ment in the outcome and a sense of pride in the success of an exceptional technical
achievement" evident in the narrative, and the high quality of the carving, Parker
concludes that the inscription "was produced by or for the 'civil engineer' who
planned and supervised the project" and would have been the person most interested in recording these things (p. 39). The natural question is: For whom? It seems
to me that the motivation of this person would have been the same sense of earthly
immortality that motivated the a king commissioning a memorial inscription (and
those today who place bronze plaques on buildings identifying the worthies after
whom they are named and often with whose money they have been built, or those
who imbed stars bearing celebrities' names in a public sidewalk in Hollywood), and
that the means he chose to achieve it was suggested by the royal memorials with
which he was familiar and could even have had a hand in creating. According to
W. G. Dever, the inscription "certainly seems to have been executed by royal decree,
even if not erected in a very public place" ("What Did the Biblical Writers Know,
and When Did They Know It?" *Hesed ve-Emet: Studies in Honor of Ernest S. Frerichs* [ed.
by J. Magness and S. Gitin; Brown Judaic Studies 320; Atlanta: Scholars, 1998] 248).

[97] See S. Gitin, T. Dothan, and J. Naveh, "A Royal Dedicatory Inscription from
Ekron," *IEJ* 47 (1997) 1–16. Note that dedicatory inscriptions such as this typically
speak of the king's act(s) in the 3rd person (Drinkard, "Literary Genre of the Mesha
Inscription," 135), as in the Joash account. Cf. also the 1st-person "memorial inscription" of Yehaumilik of Byblos (mid 4th century) which records only temple remodeling projects (KAI 10.3–6, excerpted below).

to suppose that Josiah, like Mesha (and perhaps actually inspired by Joash's recovered example), commemorated himself and his reign in a monumental inscription, erected in some prominent place in Jerusalem, perhaps in the Temple-palace complex, in his own life-time. Even though his death at Megiddo was unexpected, and he died comparatively young, a reign of 31 years—well above the average of his predecessors since Rehoboam (roughly 23.85 years)—beginning irregularly as it did (cf. 2 Kgs. 21:23–24), was in itself a notable accomplishment, and a lengthy reign in the international *Realpolitik* maelstrom of the second half of the 7th century even moreso. If he did erect such a monument, what accomplishments might he have thought worth mentioning for posterity? The biblical record is silent about military activities or the building of cities or fortresses, but neither is beyond the realm of possibility.[98]

If Josiah did actually sponsor the sort of things credited to him in 2 Kgs. 23:4–20, they are the very sort of things likely to have been cited in such an inscription. Thus, for example, Mesha takes special note of various urban renewal projects he carried out in Qarḥoh, probably the royal quarter of Dibon, the principal city of his realm (ll. 3, 21–24):

> I made this bamah for Kemosh in Qarḥoh. . . .
> I built Qarḥoh
>   —(that is,) the walls of the parks and the walls of the acropolis.
>   And I rebuilt its gates,
>   and I rebuilt its towers.
> And I built the palace
> and I made the retaining walls of the reservoi[r for the spr]ing insi[de] the city.

Most of the actions attributed to Josiah in the "original" report, if viewed solely in terms of the activities themselves, also can be characterized as cultic urban renewal, or remodeling, projects in and around the royal quarter of Jerusalem: he removes various objects and structures—cultic equipage (v. 4), an asherah-emblem (v. 6)

---

[98] Cf. Chapter 7.A and Chapter 9.A below. Whether or not Josiah died at Megiddo as a battlefield casualty (against this possibility see now Z. Talshir, "The Three Deaths of Josiah and the Strata of Biblical Historiography [2 Kings xxiii 29–30; 2 Chronicles xxxv 20–5; 1 Esdras I 23–31]," *VT* 46 [1996] 213–36) is not germane to the matter at hand unless the "memorial inscription" was erected after his death. The quick removal of Jehoahaz (2 Kgs. 23:31–33), the most likely candidate to have done so, makes this improbable.

"houses" where weavings for the asherah-emblem were prepared
(v. 7), cultic horses and chariot(s) (v. 11), various altars (v. 12)—from
the Temple complex; he deactivates sanctuaries on the adjacent
Mount of Olives (v. 13); and he desecrates nearby tombs (vv. 16a
+ 18). Except for the "bamah" in Dibon, the functional equivalent
of the Temple in Jerusalem,[99] the projects in Mesha's enumeration
are secular in nature, but this difference bespeaks only the secular
nature of Mesha's regnal agenda as reflected in his overall com-
memorative priorities where "nation-building" activities (acquisition
of territory, resettlement of people, etc.) predominate. The memorial inscription of Yehaumilik of Byblos (mid 4th century) records
only "remodeling projects" more akin to Josiah's (KAI 10.3–6):[100]

> Now I have made for my mistress, Baalat of Byblos, this altar of bronze
> which is in this [court] and this gold engraving which is in front of
> this inscription of mine, and the birds of gold which are in the midst
> of a stone, which is upon this gold engraving and this portico and
> its pillars and the [capitals] which are upon them, and its roof, I
> made, . . .

Yehaumilik installs an altar and various architectural accouterments
in a sanctuary, while Josiah removes such things from a sanctuary:
if one king's regnal agenda saw fit to commemorate the one, another
king's regnal agenda might well have seen fit to commemorate the
other.

The events included in Mesha's memorial inscriptions are enu-
merated in a dry, list-like fashion very reminiscent of the reform
report:

KAI 181.11–13

> But I fought against the city [of Atarot] and took it,
>   and I killed the entire population of the city
>   —(that is,) a satiation for Kemosh and for Moab—
>   and I brought back from there the *ʾrʾl*-object of its *dwd*
>   and I [d]ragged it before Kemosh in Qiryat.

2 Kgs. 23:6–7

> [The king] brought out the asherah-emblem from the House of Yahweh . . .
>   and he burned it in the Wadi Kidron

---

[99] See W. B. Barrick, "The Bamoth of Moab," *MAARAV* 7 (1991) 69–78 (especially 74–6), and cf. Gleis, *Bamah*, 252.

[100] Drinkard, "Literary Genre of the Mesha Inscription," 140–2; cf. *ANET*, 656.

and he beat it to dust
and he scattered its dust. . . .
And he torn down the houses of the qadesh-personnel in the House
of Yahweh
—(that is,) the place where the women made weavings for the
asherah.

Both examples, like KAI 181.21–24 (quoted above), include statements of individual actions, statements of coordinated actions (disposition of the population and cult-object of Atarot; building the
gates and towers of Qarḥoh; the disposition of the asherah-emblem),
and statements of parenthetical clarification (pertaining to the Atarotites,
Qarḥoh, and the houses of the qadesh-personnel), presented straight-
forwardly with modest detail but no rhetorical coloration. Although
this manner of presentation seems typical of memorial inscriptions
(cf., e.g., the excerpt of Yehaumilik's inscription quoted above), their
authors were capable of embellishing their presentation with fairly
sophisticated rhetorical devices.[101] For example, rather than continue
the enumeration of Mesha's projects in Dibon by stating that he had
the people make their own cisterns, the author explains the need for
cisterns and has Mesha quote his own instructions about them, and
then simply reports the digging of the ditches for which the king
was himself responsible (ll. 24–26):

Now there was no cistern inside the city
—(that is,) in Qarḥoh—
so I said to all the people, "Make yourselves each a cistern in his
house."
I dug the ditches for Qarḥoh with Israelite captives.

Mesha's dealings with Israel are presented with considerable artistry,
including substantial background information, quotation of an absent
third-party, parenthetical asides for clarification or emphasis, and
theological causation, in what amounts to a miniature historiographical
narrative (ll. 4–9):[102]

---

[101] For the use of proverbial sayings and clever word-plays in Kilamuwa's memorial inscription (KAI 24.5–13) see F. M. Fales, "Kilamuwa and the Foreign Kings:
Propaganda vs. Power," *Welt des Orients* 10 (1979) 6–22. What follows weakens
Parker's depreciation (in "Did the Authors of the Books of Kings Make Use of
Royal Inscriptions?" 369) of Mesha's account of his building activity in Qarḥoh as
"a simple list of projects" with "no information about the construction of any one
of them."

[102] Similarly, Zakir of Hamath and Luath (North Syria, early 8th century) reca-
pitulates in some detail the cause of his war with Barhadad b. Hazael of Damascus,

Omri was king of Israel,
  and he oppressed Moab for many days because Kemosh was angry
  with his country.
And his son succeeded him,
  and he also said "I will oppress Moab"
    —in my days he said th[is]—
but I prevailed over him and over his house,
  and [North-]Israel utterly perished forever.
And Omri had taken possession of a[ll the lan]d of Mehadaba,
  and he lived in it during his days and half the days of his son(s)
    —(that is,) forty years—
but Kemosh returned it in my days.

The "cemetery scene" in the reform report (23:16a + 16b–18), although very different in content and heavily encrusted with later elaboration, nonetheless is stylistically reminiscent of these passages:

And Josiah turned and saw the tombs that were there on the hill; and he sent and took the bones out of the tombs and burned them on the altar.
  And (thus) he defiled it in fulfillment of the word of Yahweh proclaimed by the man-of-god who proclaimed these things.
He asked "What is the marker I see there?"
  And the men of the city replied: "That is the tomb of the man-of-god who came from Judah and proclaimed these things that you have done to the altar in Bethel."
"Let it be," he said. "Let no one disturb his bones."
  So they left his bones undisturbed together with the bones of the prophet who came from Samaria.

Instead of a simple statement that one particular tomb was not violated, we are given a brief narrative explaining why this was done and quoting the king's instructions to those who will implement them. As the Moabite author alludes to the historical circumstances which occasioned Mesha's war against (North-)Israel, the biblical author, through the voices of the narrator and a quoted third-party, alludes to a past episode which posits the divine causation of Josiah's desecration of the altar and relates both etiologically to the monument. In the you-are-there verisimilitude of its representation of a specific historical moment, the "cemetery scene" resembles the Siloam Tunnel inscription which memorializes the digging of the tunnel and, at least

---

and quotes his divine assurance of victory (KAI 202; *ANET*, 655–6). Cf. also Bar-Rakib's extensive rehearsal of the life and times of his father Panamuwa (KAI 215); for recent discussion see Margalit, "Studies in NW Semitic Inscriptions," 303–313.

indirectly, the monarch who ordered it and who might well have documented it in a public monument of his own.

In terms of content and style, therefore, the reform report resembles a royal memorial inscription such as Mesha's. Both also present events with "a general reportorial sequentiality" which in both cases is a literary construct and does not necessarily reflect historical reality. There are differences, to be sure, but if the "original" reform report was drawn from a royal memorial inscription, a measure of adaptation must be expected to suit the new literary context. Since the narrator in a memorial inscription typically is the king himself in the 1st-person singular,[103] the 3rd-person narrator's voice in the report would have been the most conspicuous of these.[104] Some material probably was deleted and some may have been added; the relocation and change in status of the bamoth-priests (vv. 8a + 9), topics without analogues in extant memorial or dedicatory inscriptions, are likely additions as may be portions of the unembroidered "cemetery scene" (vv. 16a + 18). The dating discrepancy between Josiah's 12th year (in Chronicles) and his 18th year (in Kings) for the beginning of the reform conceivably might derive ultimately from separate date references in the inscription to the reform activities and the erection of the monument commemorating them.[105]

The possibility that the "original" reform report derived ultimately from a royal memorial inscription (or an archival copy) accessible to the author-compiler of the "Josianic" KH-2 account of Josiah's reign is plausible, therefore, but cannot be substantiated from data now extant. There are, however, several strands of circumstantial support for this hypothesis. P. A. Bird's provocative new analysis of 23:7 offers a model of how the KH-2 author-compiler could have adapted a royal inscription to produce the "original" reform report:[106] she attributes v. 7 to "a Deuteronomistic author" who reworked a "pre-

---

[103] Drinkard, "Literary Genre of the Mesha Inscription," 142, 146.

[104] Alternatively, since dedicatory inscriptions typically speak of the king's act(s) in the 3rd person (*ibid.*, 135), one could imagine Josiah commissioning an inscription immortalizing his "negative dedication" of the Temple paraphernalia.

[105] Analogous to Mesha beginning with his construction of the sanctuary (*bmt*) in Qarhoh in the recent past "because [Kemosh] . . . let me prevail over all my enemies" (ll. 3–4) and then relating how this was accomplished in the more distant past (ll. 5–21), Josiah's inscription may have begun with a summary statement of the occasion for its installation in his 18th regnal year and then related the circumstances leading to it which began in his 12th regnal year.

[106] Bird, "End of the Male Cult Prostitute," 70–4.

Dtr source" (one "based on historical memory") in which *byt/bty qdšm* referred to the "storehouse(s) for the votive objects [*qodāšīm*], emptied by Hezekiah in payment of tribute to Sennacherib (2 Kgs [18:]15–16) and converted into workshops for the Asherah introduced by Manasseh (2 Kgs [21:]3, 7)." Second, there are other historiographical passages which resemble royal memorial inscriptions. The Joash example has already been discussed at length. Naaman also cites the account of Ahaz's Temple innovations, and in particular the new altar (16:10–16, 18), which probably derived from "a dedication inscription [either] carved on the altar itself, or on a stele/marble plate that stood near the altar, [and] known to all those who came near it."[107] Both examples contain information likely to have been found on such an inscription, and also "unusual vocabulary or irregular expressions not found elsewhere in the Dtr history in reference to building activity";[108] the reform report also meets both criteria.[109] On more stylistic grounds S. B. Parker claims an epigraphic source underlies 2 Kgs. 13:22 + 24–25 (cf. KAI 181.4–7), dealing with military campaigns and claims to territory, the dominant topic in memorial inscriptions.[110] In light of the rarity of such

---

[107] Naaman, "Royal Inscriptions and the Histories of Joash and Ahaz," 344–8 (quotation from p. 345).

[108] *Ibid.*, 336. Cf. the critique by Parker, "Did the Authors of the Books of Kings Make Use of Royal Inscriptions?" 369–70.

[109] Eynikel (*Reform of King Josiah*, ch. 4) identifies numerous unique, unusual, or un-"deuteronom(ist)ic" terms or expressions in the "original" reform report (cf. pp. 216, 231, 252, 258): priestly nomenclature (v. 4: pp. 189–92); *kēlîm* in the sense of "cultic vessels/equipage" (v. 4: p. 195); *šadēmôt* (v. 6: p. 224); *NS*' + *'pr* (v. 6: pp. 215–6); the work of Asherah's functionaries (v. 7: pp. 230–1); "new usage" of *TM*' (vv. 8a, 10, 13: pp. 233–4); "Geba to Beer-sheba" (v. 8a: pp. 234–5); the "parwarim" (v. 11: p. 250); *ŠPR* + *bā'eš* with a place-name (v. 11: pp. 250–2); two Temple courts (v. 12: pp. 256–7); *RSS* (v. 12: pp. 257–8); *har-hamašḥît* (v. 13: pp. 258–9); *mîmîn* + *L* (v. 13: p. 259); "filling their places with human bones" (v. 14b: pp. 271–2 ["little in common with other verses in the dtr history"]); "rather unique" vocabulary in most of v. 16 (pp. 279–80); *ṣîyûn* (v. 17a: p. 280); *'ŠH* + *'L* as "do in relation to" (v. 17b: p. 280). Eynikel's own analysis seemingly undermines his conclusion that "numerous links with the preceding chapters of 1 and 2 Kings" justify attributing the report to a "deuteronomistic" hand (p. 353). Jones cites "the exceptional use of the term 'temple of Yahweh' (instead of the more usual 'house of Yahweh')" as evidence of a "pre-Deuteronomistic" source (*1–2 Kings*, 616), but this could as well be a reference to the temple-building distinct from the temple-complex as a whole (and surely "house of Yahweh" cannot be considered a distinctively "deuteronomistic" phrase); cf. Hoffmann, *Reform und Reformen*, 246.

[110] Parker, *Stories in Scripture and Inscriptions*, 61–3, 74. More distant examples include 2 Kgs. 13:2–5 (+ 7?) (pp. 63–5) and 2 Sam. 8:3–6, 13–15 (pp. 68–73, 75); cf. Josh. 10:28–29 (pp. 66–8). Parker now considers 2 Kgs. 13:22 + 24–25 "exceptional"

comparable material Parker opines that "the most we may safely conclude is that [the Judahite historians] may have been generally aware of such royal inscriptions and occasionally disclosed that familiarity when the subject of their narrative evoked it."[111] I submit that the "original" reform report is another narrative dealing with a very different subject which nonetheless also discloses this familiarity.

and "perhaps best explained, like [13:]3, as influenced by common court ideology and language" ("Did the Authors of the Books of Kings Make Use of Royal Inscriptions?" 366–8 [quotation from p. 368]). Cf. also, e.g., Montgomery, *Kings*, 35–6; Van Seters, *In Search of History*, 300–1.

[111] Parker, *Stories in Scripture and Inscriptions*, 75, adding (p. 133) that "the exiguity of similar material in the Deuteronomistic History strongly suggests that the historian did not in general use royal inscriptions as a source." His assessment is more negative in "Did the Authors of the Books of Kings Make Use of Royal Inscriptions?" 374–6, concluding that "commentators on Kings are not justified in referring to its use of such inscriptions" (pp. 375–6); I disagree.

CHAPTER SEVEN

SOME HISTORICAL ASPECTS OF JOSIAH'S REFORM (I): JOSIAH'S JUDAH

Insofar as 2 Kgs. 23:4–20 might reflect actions actually undertaken by Josiah b. Amon—and no convincing argument has yet been advanced to deny this possibility[1]—they would have grown out of the complex environment of 7th-century Judah and would have been in large measure responses to that environment. As noted in Chapter 1 above, the Kings History represents Josiah's reform taking place in a fictive world devoid of the geo-political and socio-religious realities arising from the multifaceted "Assyria factor," both internationally and domestically, in Josiah's world. While the Kings account clearly does not depict "what really happened," it may nonetheless contain information deriving ultimately from Josiah's world which is retrievable, if only in part and with considerable circumspection. To do so, it is necessary to begin with a sketch of Josiah's Judah.

7.A. Judah from Hezekiah to Josiah

If the 8th was "the greatest of centuries,"[2] a Judahite living at the end of that century would have missed the greatness for the misery: the southern hinterland of Judah devastated by Assyrian troops and the greater part of its population killed (possibly including Hezekiah's heir-apparent)[3] or uprooted in the course of Hezekiah's unsuccessful bid for independence from Assyria.[4] Sennacherib boasts:[5]

---

[1] Of the numerous methodological discussions published of late see in particular E. A. Knauf, "From History to Interpretation," *The Fabric of History: Text, Artifact and Israel's Past* (ed. by D. V. Edelman; JSOTSup 127; Sheffield: JSOT, 1991) 26–64; Nieher, "Reform des Joschija," especially 34–41; Uehlinger, "Gab es eine joschijanische Kultreform?" especially 59–70.

[2] P. J. King, "The Eighth, the Greatest of Centuries?" *JBL* 108 (1989) 3–15.

[3] For this possibility see Barrick, "Dynastic Politics," 577, and *idem*, "Genealogical Notes" (forthcoming).

[4] For the period in general cf. the standard histories and H. H. Rowley's classic "Hezekiah's Reform and Rebellion," *Men of God: Studies in Old Testament History and Prophecy* (London: Nelson, 1963) 98–132 (= *BJRL* 44 [1961–1962] 395–461), with earlier literature. The current archaeological record indicates that the region north

I laid siege to 46 of his strong cities, walled forts and to the countless small villages in their vicinity, and I conquered (them). . . . I drove
out (of them) 200,150 people,[6] young and old, male and female, horses,
mules, donkeys, camels, big and small cattle beyond counting, and
considered (them) booty. . . . His towns [in the Shephelah] which I had
plundered, I took away from his country and gave them (over) to
Mitinti, King of Ashdod, Padi, King of Ekron, and Sillibel, King of
Gaza. Thus I reduced his country, but I still increased the tribute and
the *katrû*-presents (due) to me (as his) overlord which I imposed (later)
upon him beyond the former tribute, to be delivered annually. . . .

The pitifully wasted and depopulated countryside is depicted by Isaiah,
presumably an eye-witness (Isa. 1:7–9;[7] cf. also, e.g., 2:12–20; 3:2–4;
5:5–17; 6:9–12; Mic. 1:10–16; 5:10–14):

Your land is desolation,
    Your towns are burnt with fire.
Your soil, before you, aliens eat her,
    And she is desolation like the overthrowing of aliens.
There remains the daughter of Zion,
    Like a booth in a vineyard,
    Like a lodge in a cucumber-patch,
    Like a town preserved.
Had Yahweh Sabaoth not left us a tiny remnant,
    Like Sodom would we be,
    Gomorrah we would resemble.

The archaeological record suggests that Judah in the 8th century
had supported a population of c. 120,000, but in the first half of
the 7th century only c. 65,000 people (without the ruined Shephelah,
lost to Philistia in 701), more than a quarter of them in a much
enlarged Jerusalem and most of the remainder in the hill country.[8]

---

of Jerusalem was not harmed spared by Assyrian military campaigns during this
period; for references see n. 8 below.

[5] *ANET*, 288.

[6] This is nearly twice the estimated population of Judah (see below). If the figure
is more-or-less accurate, it must include a huge number of displaced persons from
the north and elsewhere; even if the number is inflated (see, e.g., S. Stohlmann,
"The Judaean Exile after 701 BCE," *Scripture in Context II: More Essays on the Comparative
Method* [ed. by W. W. Hallo *et al.*; Winona Lake: Eisenbrauns, 1983] especially
152–61, and cf. Chapter 3 n. 39 above), a substantial depopulation and the reality of exile in Judah are certain.

[7] On Isa. 1:7–9 cf. the reservations of E. Ben Zvi, "Isaiah 1,4–9, Isaiah, and the
Events of 701 BCE in Judah," *SJOT* 5/1 (1991) 95–111.

[8] For the archaeological record see I. Finkelstein, "The Archaeology of the Days
of Manasseh," *Scripture and Other Artifacts: Essays on the Bible and Archaeology in Honor*

The economic decline following the loss of the Shephelah, Judah's "breadbasket,"[9] and the heavy reparations imposed by Sennacherib (cf. 2 Kgs. 18:14–16) are evident in Judah's annual tribute somewhat later of only ten minas of silver, substantially less than Moab and Ammon for the year in question.[10] Hezekiah's disastrous gamble was, in every sense, a defining moment in the history of Judah. As E. Ben Zvi summarizes,[11] "the 'break' between the 'old' Judah of the eighth century and the 'new' Judah of the seventh century was even sharper than what might have been, because much of the former did not evolve into the latter, but was violently destroyed in 701 BCE."

The physical expansion of residential Jerusalem in the century between Hezekiah and Josiah, documented in the archaeological record,[12] testifies to an extraordinary population shift—from c. 7,500/

---

of Philip J. King (ed. by M. D. Coogan et al.; Louisville: Westminster John Knox, 1994) 176–7, and A. G. Vaughn, Theology, History, and Archaeology in the Chronicler's Account of Hezekiah (Archaeology and Biblical Studies 4; Atlanta: Scholars, 1999) ch. 2. Cf. M. Broshi and I. Finkelstein, "The Population of Palestine in Iron Age II," BASOR 287 (1992) 51–2 (estimating a population of c. 110,000). See also n. 6 above.

[9] A. F. Rainey claims that "there is no solid indication . . . of how far into the Shephelah the Philistine control extended" ("The Biblical Shephelah of Judah," BASOR 251 [1983] 16), but the archaeological record evinces no differentiation in this regard, and the Assyrian presence at Gezer (see R. Reich and B. Brandi, "Gezer under Assyrian Rule," PEQ 117 [1985] 41–54) and the extraordinary commercial dominance of contemporary Ekron IIC (see S. Gitin, "Urban Growth and Decline at Ekron in the Iron II Period," BA 50 [1987] 206–22, and idem, "Tel Miqne-Ekron: A Type-Site for the Inner Coastal Plain in the Iron Age II Period," Recent Excavations in Israel: Studies in Iron Age Archaeology [ed. by S. Gitin and W. G. Dever; AASOR 49; Winona Lake: Eisenbrauns, 1989] 23–58; Halpern, "Jerusalem and the Lineages," 45–7, and idem, "Sybil, or the Two Nations? Archaism, Kinship, Alienation, and the Elite Redefinition of Traditional Culture in Judah in the 8th–7th Centuries BCE," The Study of the Ancient Near East in the Twenty-First Century: The William Foxwell Albright Centennial Conference [ed. by J. S. Cooper and G. N. Schwartz; Winona Lake: Eisenbrauns, 1996] 320–1) further indicate that Jerusalem had no independent control over the entire region.

[10] ANET, 301: see R. H. Pfeiffer, "Three Assyriological Footnotes to the Old Testament," JBL 47 (1928) 185, and cf. Gane, "Role of Assyria," 28–30; the unnamed Assyrian king is probably Esarhaddon or Assurbanipal. For Assyrian despoliation in general see M. Elath, "The Impact of Tribute and Booty on Countries and People within the Assyrian Empire," AfO 9 (1982) 244–51.

[11] Ben Zvi, "Prelude to a Reconstruction," 33.

[12] For the expansion westward see M. Broshi, "The Expansion of Jerusalem in the Reigns of Hezekiah and Manasseh," IEJ 24 (1974) 21–6, and Broshi-Finkelstein, "Population of Palestine in Iron Age II," 51–2; Y. Shiloh, "Judah and Jerusalem in the Eighth-Sixth Centuries BCE," Recent Excavations in Israel: Studies in Iron Age Archaeology (ed. by S. Gitin and W. G. Dever; AASOR 49; Winona Lake: Eisenbrauns, 1989) 97–105; Mazar, Archaeology of the Land of the Bible, 417–24; Ahlström, History

c. 6.25% of the total population of Judah to c. 25,000/c. 38.46% of the total population[13]—caused largely by an influx of new peoples. Many probably were refugees from the north following the fall of (North-)Israel, bringing with them ideas, traditions, and practices more at home in the north than in Judah or Jerusalem; merchants and refugees (political and otherwise [cf. 2 Kgs. 18:8]) from Philistia also may have found their way to Jerusalem in Assyria's wake,[14] with ideas and practices of their own (cf. Zeph. 1:9).[15] We also must include resident aliens servicing the flourishing international commerce (cf. 1 Kgs. 20:34)[16] which itself generated cosmopolitan cul-

---

of Ancient Palestine, 681. Cf. also A. D. Tushingham, "The Western Hill under the Monarchy," *ZDPV* 95 (1979) 39–55; H. Geva, "The Western Boundary of Jerusalem at the End of the Monarchy," *IEJ* 29 (1979) 84–91; J. Rogerson and P. R. Davies, "Was the Siloam Tunnel Built by Hezekiah?" *BA* 59 (1996) 138–49. The most recent sifting of the evidence by Vaughn (*Theology, History, and Archaeology*, 59–71) concludes that the westward expansion began before the fall of (North-)Israel; nonetheless, it is reasonable to suppose that it accelerated with the events of the last quarter of the century. For the expansion down the eastern slope (unknown to Vaughn *et al.* when their studies were made) see Shanks, "Everything You Ever Knew about Jerusalem Is Wrong," 20–9.

[13] See n. 8 above. These figures do not take into account the population housed between the walls on the eastern slope.

[14] Relations between Ekron and Jerusalem were close enough for the anti-Assyrian faction in the former to entrust their deposed king Padi to Hezekiah's care; note the two *lmlk*-stamped jar handles, one reading *lmlk hbrn*, found in the fill covering the debris of Ekron IIA, contemporary with Lachish III (see Gitin, "Tel Miqne-Ekron: A Type-Site," 26). It may well be that Hezekiah had a hand in the coup which certainly favored his own anti-Assyrian agenda. Sennacherib reports that he restored Padi to his throne, executed "the officials and patricians who had committed the crime," took as prisoners-of-war "(common) citizens who were guilty of minor crimes," and "the rest of them, those who were not accused of crimes and misbehavior, I released" (*ANET*, 287–8). The surviving disaffected elements surely would have seen Jerusalem as a comparatively safe haven. For the commercial aspects, especially relevant for Ekron IIC slightly later, see nn. 9 above and 16 below.

[15] "Leaping over the threshold" is a ritualistic or symbolic act of some sort, the significance of which is uncertain (cf. the familiar childhood superstition of stepping over cracks in the sidewalk so as not to "break your mother's back"). Most commentators see a connection with the equally puzzling Philistine practice mentioned in 1 Sam. 5:5, but this too is uncertain: cf., e.g., Roberts, *Nahum, Habakkuk, and Zephaniah*, 175, 179; Ben Zvi, *Zephaniah*, 95–102, 278–82; Berlin, *Zephaniah*, 79–80. Of potential relevance to both passages are the meter-long "divine" footprints carved into the thresholds leading into the cella of the IA Ishtar temple at Ain Dara in north Syria: see A. Abu Assaf, *Der Tempel von 'Ain Dara* (Damaszener Forschungen 3; Mainz am Rhein: Zabern, 1990) 15–6.

[16] On *ḥûṣôt*, "foreign bazaars," and comparable institutions in the ancient Near East see M. Elat, "The Monarchy and the Development of Trade in Ancient Israel," *State and Temple Economy in the Ancient Near East* (ed. by E. Lipiński; Orientalia Lovaniensia Analecta 6; Leuven: Department Orientalistiek, 1979) 2.543–5, and

tural undercurrents. Most of the newcomers, however, probably came from Judah itself.

In Hezekiah's mobilization for rebellion,[17] a limited number of fortified and specially provisioned[18] cities, notably Jerusalem[19] and Lachish, served as defensive keeps sheltering the populace—established residents and the many more who fled or were removed there for safety—against the Assyrian invader. This was one component of a comprehensive reorganization of the realm orchestrated by the king and a burgeoning administrative apparatus centered on the palace and the Temple.[20] Provisioning the bulging capital (not to mention the other fortified cities) necessitated a larger and more top-heavy bureaucracy than the system attributed to Solomon (1 Kgs. 4:7–19, 22–23)[21]—e.g., at least 18 different names of Hezekian

---

S. Yeivin, "The Divided Kingdom: Rehoboam-Ahaz/Jeroboam-Pekah," *The Age of the Monarchies: Political History* (ed. by A. Malamat; World History of the Jewish People 4:1; Jerusalem: Massada, 1979) 138. For evidence of "an Egyptian [commercial] enclave with its own sanctuary" at 7th-century Ashkelon see L. E. Stager, "Ashkelon and the Archaeology of Destruction; Kislev 604 BCE," *I-E* 25 (1996) 68*–9*.

[17] For this paragraph see Halpern, "Jerusalem and the Lineages," especially 18–27, and *idem*, "Sybil, or the Two Nations?" especially 312–21. Cf. now W. Zwickel, "Die Wirtschaftsreform des Hiskia und die Sozialkritik der Propheten des 8. Jahrhunderts," *EvT* 59 (1999) 356–77.

[18] For the function of the *lmlk*-stamped jars in the government-supervised distribution of wine and/or oil in Hezekiah's Judah (cf. 2 Chron. 32:27–29) see now Vaughn, *Theology, History, and Archaeology*, ch. 3. Earlier treatments emphasizing their function in siege preparations include N. Naaman, "Sennacherib's Campaign to Judah and the Date of the *lmlk* Stamps," *VT* 29 (1979) 61–86, and Mazar, *Archaeology of the Land of the Bible*, 455–8.

[19] Against denying "Hezekiah's Tunnel" in Jerusalem to Hezekiah (with Rogerson-Davies, "Was the Siloam Tunnel Built by Hezekiah?" 138–49) see R. Hendel, "The Date of the Siloam Inscription: A Rejoinder to Rogerson and Davies," *BA* 59 (1996) 233–7, and S. Norin, "The Age of Siloam Inscription and Hezekiah's Tunnel," *VT* 48 (1998) 37–48. Sennacherib mentions "irregular and elite troops" which Hezekiah "brought into Jerusalem, his royal residence, in order to strengthen (it)" (*ANET*, 288), necessitating special billeting and provisioning arrangements.

[20] For the antecedent situation, with special attention to the archaeological record, see J. S. Holladay, Jr., "The Kingdoms of Israel and Judah: Political and Economic Centralization in the Iron IIA-B (ca. 1000–750 BCE)," *The Archaeology of Society in the Holy Land* (ed. by T. E. Levy; New York: Facts on File, 1995) 368–98; cf. Dever, "Social Structure in Palestine," 417–31.

[21] For the issues involved see R. C. Hunt, "The Role of Bureaucracy in the Provisioning of Cities: A Framework for Analysis of the Ancient Near East," *The Organization of Power: Aspects of Bureaucracy in the Ancient Near East* (2nd edn.; ed. by McG. Gibson and R. D. Biggs; Studies in Ancient Civilization 46; Chicago: Oriental Institute, 1991) 141–68. For parallels to Solomon's system see R. P. Dougherty, "Cuneiform Parallels to Solomon's Provisioning System," *AASOR* 5 (1923–1924)

governmental personnel are known from 73 official seal impressions from Lachish alone[22]—at the expense of the peasantry actually providing the foodstuffs.[23] These measures would have been implemented quickly and under duress and very likely without the administrative finesse needed to "sell" such revolutionary innovations to a populace unaccustomed to change: whether Hezekiah came to the throne in 727/6 or 715/4,[24] it seems likely that a preemptive strike by Sargon II in the course of his 712 campaign to quell Ashdod's rebellion (in which Judah could have been implicated)[25] had revealed the need for an extra-ordinary mobilization effort which he initiated a few years later, perhaps stimulated by Manasseh's birth and the revolutionary stirrings of Sidon, both c. 709, but in any event sometime before Sargon's death in 705.[26] Adding insult to injury, Hezekiah's "removal" of the bamoth (2 Kgs. 18:4a, 22) could hardly have endeared him to the countless Judahites accustomed to worshipping there and dependent on them for their socio-religious needs (cf. the outcry which invariably greets the announcement that the local parish church or neighborhood school—or post office, for that matter—is

---

23–65, and D. B. Redford, "Studies in Relations between Palestine and Egypt during the First Millennium BC: The Taxation System of Solomon," *Studies on the Ancient Palestinian World Presented to Professor F. V. Winnett* (ed. by J. W. Wevers and D. B. Redford; Toronto Semitic Texts and Studies 2; Toronto: University of Toronto, 1972) 141–56.

[22] G. Barkay and A. G. Vaughn, "*lmlk* and Official Seal Impressions from Tel Lachish," *TA* 23 (1996) 61–74. For such Hezekian seals in general cf. *idem*, "New Readings of Hezekian Official Seal Impressions," *BASOR* 304 (1996) 29–54, and Vaughn, *Theology, History, and Archaeology*, 110–35.

[23] For one aspect see M. L. Chaney, "Debt Easement in Israelite History and Tradition," *The Bible and the Politics of Exegesis: Essays in Honor of Norman K. Gottwald on his Sixty-Fifth Birthday* (ed. by D. Jobling *et al.*; Cleveland: Pilgrim, 1991) 127–39 and accompanying notes (with earlier literature).

[24] Recently, e.g., N. Naaman, "Hezekiah and the Kings of Assyria," *TA* 21 (1994) 235–54, and Vaughn, *Theology, History, and Archaeology*, 7–14.

[25] A convincing case is presented by J. Goldberg, "Two Assyrian Campaigns against Hezekiah and Later Eighth Century Biblical Chronology," *Bib* 80 (1999) 360–90 dating Hezekiah's ascension to 726/5. For an attack in 720 see M. A. Sweeney, "Sargon's Threat against Jerusalem and Isaiah 10,27–32," *Bib* 75 (1994) 457–70, and K. L. Younger, Jr., "Sargon's Campaign against Jerusalem—A Further Note," *Bib* 77 (1996) 108–10.

[26] If Manasseh came to the throne in 697 at 12 yoa, he would have been born about 709—an auspicious time for Assyrian power, Babylon having been retaken from Merodach-Baladan II in 710. It is hard to see how the destruction of Ashdod by Sargon II shortly after 712 would have caused Hezekiah to flirt with the idea of rebellion (so Halpern, "Sybil, or the Two Nations?" 312), but Sidon's revolt beginning about 709 would have been a different matter, especially now that the succession seemed assured for two generations.

being closed for reasons of economy).[27] The enlarged governmental bureaucracy, in turn, spawned new political and social urban elites independent of traditional kinship and ancestral systems of status and support,[28] along with new ideological and theological underpinnings for their existence. The power of the central government grew at the expense of more traditional, decentralized, kinship-based authority structures.[29]

Hezekiah's compliant grandson Manasseh,[30] who came to the throne at 12 yoa (c. 697) certainly with Assyrian backing, inherited this administrative infrastructure and tailored it to his agenda. Judah's recovery and Manasseh's unprecedented 55-year reign (2 Kgs. 21:1) are twin testaments of the new regime's successful exploitation of Judah's commercial value to the Assyrian empire, the material consequence of the king's fealty to his Assyrian overlord. Ben Zvi identifies the

---

[27] Hezekiah's religious "reform" must be understood as part of this process, either by design or by coincidence. Halpern's high estimation of the "reform" in this enterprise is possible but not essential to his political reconstruction, nor is it well-grounded in the biblical evidence; cf. the minimal positions advanced by L. K. Handy, "Hezekiah's Unlikely Reform," *ZAW* 100 (1988) 111–5, and N. Naaman, "The Debated Historicity of Hezekiah's Reform," *ZAW* 107 (1995) 105–17. In particular, Halpern's contention that "Hezekiah suppressed rural worship, but not worship at state centers" ("Sybil, or the Two Nations?" 317; cf. also *idem*, "Yhwh's Retainers Retired," 143) is without evidential support of any kind and seems contrary to 2 Kgs. 18:4a, 22, and to much of the archaeological data he cites (notably the "recycled" Beer-sheba altar); on the bamoth see Chapter 9 below. The Chronicler's version of Hezekiah's reign cannot be accepted at face-value (with, e.g., O. Borowski, "Hezekiah's Reforms and the Revolt against Assyria," *BA* 58 [1995] 148–55) any more than can his accounts of Manasseh or Josiah.

[28] See J. Blenkinsopp, *Sage, Priest, Prophet: Religious and Intellectual Leadership in Ancient Israel* (Library of Ancient Israel; Louisville: Westminster John Knox, 1995) especially 32–7 and accompanying notes. For the emergence of "an elitist class of political significance within the city" of Babylon in this period see J. A. Brinkman, "Babylonia under the Assyrian Empire," *Power and Propaganda: A Symposium on Ancient Empires* (ed. by M. T. Larsen; Mesopotamia 7; Copenhagen: Akademisk, 1979) 238.

[29] For the family laws of Deut. 19:1–25:19 from this perspective see N. Steinberg, "The Deuteronomic Law Code and the Politics of State Centralization," *The Bible and the Politics of Exegesis: Essays in Honor of Norman K. Gottwald on His Sixty-Fifth Birthday* (ed. by D. Jobling *et al.*; Cleveland: Pilgrim, 1991) 161–70 and accompanying notes. Steinberg identifies "the inception of the monarchy as the beginning locus for the gradual promulgation of legislation emphasizing the nuclear family" at the expense of the clan or tribe (p. 169); while this is surely correct, her sociological analysis of this material suits the era of Hezekiah excellently. Cf. also Y. Suzuki, "Deuteronomic Reformation in View of the Centralization of the Administration of Justice," *Annual of the Japanese Biblical Institute* 13 (1987) 22–58.

[30] On Manasseh's genealogical relationship to Hezekiah see n. 3 above.

hallmarks of this "economic and political integration into the general area under neo-Assyrian hegemony":[31]

(1) a flourishing trade together with intensive crops designed to support it;
(2) local centers channeling humanpower, production, and military resources, including the building and strengthening of fortresses and walled urban centers to meet the needs of this trade; and
(3) a correlated development of the service-sector in society, together with an increasing tendency to centralization and urbanization, which is well attested in Jerusalem.

This integration also led to a greater variety in the attested material culture and to an increased contact between Judahites and non-Judahites [including Assyrians, Aramean-Assyrians, Philistines, Edomites, Phoenicians, Arabians, and Egyptians], in which not only the Judahite elites took part.

A government-sponsored reurbanization program began, probably first into the arid zones to the east and south of the Judean hills to exploit their agricultural potential (necessitated by the loss of the Shephelah) and logistical advantages for the Arabian trade,[32] and by mid-century (perhaps coincident with the restoration of the lost territory, probably at mid-century)[33] in the Judean hills and the Shephelah. This program did not replicate antebellum conditions:[34]

---

[31] Ben Zvi, "Prelude to a Reconstruction," 32–3 (quotations from p. 32 and n. 7). Cf. also R. Nelson, "*Realpolitik* in Judah (687–609 BCE)," *Scripture in Context II: More Essays on the Comparative Method* (ed. by W. W. Hallo *et al.*; Winona Lake: Eisenbrauns, 1983) 177–89; Halpern, "Sybil, or the Two Nations?" 322–7. For the Arabian trade see now L. Singer-Avitz, "Beersheba—A Gateway Community in Southern Arabian Long-Distance Trade in the Eighth Century BCE," *TA* 26 (1999) 3–74. Halpern's claim that the resurgence of the west generally and of Judah in particular "made Manasseh a junior partner, in effect, in the administration of the empire" ("Sybil, or the Two Nations?" 323) seems a bit extreme; cf. Gitin, "Neo-Assyrian Empire and its Western Periphery," 77–103. On the dominant role of contemporary Ekron see also n. 33 below.

[32] Finkelstein, "Archaeology of the Days of Manasseh," 177–9.

[33] The return of this territory is undocumented, but the marriage of Amon to Jedidah of Bozkath in the Shephelah, contracted sometime before c. 647 when Josiah was born (2 Kgs. 21:1, 19; 22:1), would support the surmise that the transfer of the region back to Judah occurred at mid-century; any northern territory ceded to Judah (see Chapter 3 n. 39 above) could have occurred at this time as well. It was in 648 that Ashurbanipal concluded the rebellion of Babylon, disposed of Shamash-shum-ukin, and began to return order to his empire; this would have been the occasion for Manasseh to have formally renewed his fealty, the historical episode which could underlie 2 Chron. 33:11–17 (with certainty, e.g., Rainey, "Biblical Shephelah of Judah," 16, and *idem*, "Manasseh, King of Judah," 160–1, and more

[A]pparently to avoid having to deal with the traditional leadership of the old urban centers, new centers were established on new sites. Despite a massive building program, the old cities were left largely in ruins [Lachish II is an exception]. In addition, there was a major program of building royal fortresses throughout the nation, fortresses that were strictly subject to Jerusalem and were often manned by non-Judaean mercenaries. The best evidence indicates that the centralization began in the closing years of Manasseh's reign.

Most of the settlers probably were transplantees from Jerusalem, "the only human capital for Manasseh's paramilitary hinterland."[35] Plainly, "in the latter days of Hezekiah and in the reign of Manasseh, Judah went through a painful transformation from a relatively large state with a varied economic system to a small community, in fact not much more than a city-state, with a large capital and a small but densely settled countryside."[36] This transformation, like the building projects, continued into the reigns of his successors.[37]

These developments encouraged factionalism and dissent of all sorts throughout society, exacerbating the fissures opened by the Syro-Ephraimitic War[38] and the dynastic crisis in the course of Ahaz's

---

cautiously, e.g., Ahlström, *History of Ancient Palestine*, 730–9 ["may not be a complete invention" (p. 733)]; rejecting the possibility, e.g., Ben Zvi, "Prelude to a Reconstruction," 39–41), and conceivably was rewarded for his faithfulness by return of the Shephelah, analogous to the treatment earlier accorded Necho I (see *ANET*, 295). Assyrian sources are silent on this matter, but the coincidence of dates is remarkable nonetheless.

[34] L. Tatum, "King Manasseh and the Royal Fortress at Horvat Usa," *BA* 54 (1991) 136–45 (quotation from p. 144). Cf. also Mazar, *Archaeology of the Land of the Bible*, 416–55; Halpern, "Lineages," 59–77; Finkelstein, "Archaeology of the Days of Manasseh," 169–87.

[35] Halpern, "Sybil, or the Two Nations?" 322–5 (quotation from p. 323); see also *idem*, "Lineages," 59–77.

[36] Finkelstein, "Archaeology of the Days of Manasseh," 181.

[37] Even if, with Finkelstein, the archaeological record suggests that "the partial recovery of the Shephelah took place in the 'Lachish II' period, that is, the late seventh century BCE" ("Archaeology of the Days of Manasseh," 169–187 [quotation from p. 181]), that record cannot reflect the diplomatic and organizational lead-time which preceded these building activities and undoubtedly were accomplished by Manasseh (cf. n. 33 above).

[38] In addition to the standard histories cf. lately Y. Gitay, "Isaiah and the Syro-Ephraimite War," *The Book of Isaiah/Le Livre d'Isaïe: Les Oracles et leurs Reflectures Unité et Complexité de l'Ouvrage* (ed. by J. Vermeylen; BETL 81; Leuven: University, 1989) 217–30; C. S. Ehrlich, "Coalition Politics in Eighth Century BCE Palestine: The Philistines and the Syro-ephraimite War," *ZDPV* 107 (1991) 48–58; Irvine, *Isaiah, Ahaz, and the Syro-Ephraimitic War*; R. Tomes, "The Reason for the Syro-Ephraimite War," *JSOT* 59 (1993) 55–71.

reign.[39] A conspicuous example is Isaiah b. Amoz,[40] a royal councilor of *l'ancien régime* but less effective with Hezekiah: he opposed the new king's anti-Assyrian foreign policy and much that it entailed, even criticizing the urban renewal measures concomitant with the enlargement of Jerusalem and strengthening of its fortifications: "you counted the buildings in Jerusalem, and tore down houses to strengthen the wall" (Isa. 22:10).[41] Many of the owners/occupants of those houses may not have been very enthusiastic either. The westward expansion of the city brought about changes in older burial patterns, including the clearing of some tombs (such as the 9th-century burial caves on the eastern slope of the Western hill)[42] which cannot have endeared the living descendants of the occupants to those responsible for this unconscionable action (see further Section 7.B below). A generation or two later some disgruntled courtiers (their agenda is unknown), not content with talk, assassinated the new king Amon and, in turn, were killed by the so-called "people of the land" who installed 8-year-old Josiah on the throne (2 Kgs. 21:23–24)[43]—an

[39] For the identity of the "Son of Tabeel" see now J. A. Dearman, "The Son of Tabeel (Isaiah 7.6)," *Prophets and Paradigms: Essays in Honor of Gene M. Tucker* (ed. by S. B. Reid; JSOTSup 229; Sheffield: JSOT Academic, 1991) 33–47, tentatively favoring a Phoenician prince over an Aramean (perhaps Rezin himself).

[40] For Micah's rather different dissent, from a different socio-political locus, in this context see G. V. Pixley, "Micah: A Revolutionary," *The Bible and the Politics of Exegesis: Essays in Honor of Norman K. Gottwald on His Sixty-Fifth Birthday* (ed. by D. Jobling *et al.*; Cleveland: Pilgrim, 1991) 53–60 and accompanying notes.

[41] Cf. also, e.g., Isa. 2:6–22; 8:11–15; 22:8b–11; 30:1–5, 6–7; 31:1–3: for discussion see, e.g., W. A. Irwin, "The Attitude of Isaiah in the Crisis of 701," *JR* 16 (1936) 406–418; J. Høgenhaven, "Prophecy and Propaganda: Aspects of Political and Religious Reasoning in Israel and the Ancient Near East," *SJOT* 3/1 (1989) 125–41, and *idem*, "The Prophet Isaiah and Judaean Foreign Policy under Ahaz and Hezekiah," *JNES* 49 (1990) 351–4; F. J. Gonçalves, "Isaie, Jérémie et la Politique internationale de Juda," *Bib* 76 (1998) especially 283–91, 296–8. In terms of historical reality, Hezekiah and Isaiah were hardly "the ideal complementary leaders in all the history of prophecy and kingship" (H. Gevaryahu, "Isaiah and Hezekiah: Prophet and King," *Dor le-Dor* 16 [1987–1988] 79) represented in the final form of the biblical record and later tradition.

[42] See conveniently Mazar, *Archaeology*, 419–20, 525; cf. the other works cited in Chapter 3 n. 21 above. See also n. 102 below.

[43] The Amon episode may be the key to understanding the political dynamics of Josiah's reign, but it is exasperatingly opaque. The possible motives of the participants are catalogued by Miller-Hayes (*History of Ancient Israel and Judah*, 376): "Were these events inspired by groups who sought to change the cultic and religious life of Judah? Or was it an effort to stifle anti-Assyrian sentiments and preserve the status quo? Or was there some attempted palace coup by other and older sons of Manasseh who would have been forty-five years old when Amon was born?

ominous beginning for a reign destined to be engulfed in controversy. In this fluid context, the most fundamental verities of Judahite life no longer could be taken for granted. Current events challenged antebellum ideology and theology. M. Cogan catches the mood:[44]

> A feeling of disillusionment in YHWH'S ability to change the fortunes of his people was abroad. Isaiah's promises of ultimate victory over the Assyrian army notwithstanding (e.g., Isa. 10.12–19), Judah's observable situation for close to a century was subservience to the will of Assyria. Owing to this political decline, Judahites succumbed to the lure of new gods.

This disconnect between geo-political reality and ideological (or theological) theory contributed to a disconnect between the generations—a "generation gap," to use the term coined in the tumultuous 1960s to describe "the difference in social values, behavioral attitudes, and personal aspirations of one generation and that of the next generation, especially the generation of adolescents and young adults and that of their parents."[45]

The solidarity of the generations in monarchic Judah is evident in the tombs and attendant burial practices of the period. The entombed ancestors represented continuity, the underpinning of traditional Israelite society. Halpern puts it succinctly:[46] "The Israelite inherited the house of his ancestors, the fields of his ancestors, the tools of his ancestors, the gods of his ancestors, and, in the end, the place of his ancestors in the tomb." This statement also describes what anthropologist M. Mead terms "postfigurative" cultures or societies, characterized by "the assumption expressed by the older generation in their every act, that their way of life (however many

---

Or were the assassins inspired by a nationalistic surge which thought the time had come to de done with submission?" For the last option see the classic treatment by A. Malamat, "The Historical Background of the Assassination of Amon, King of Judah," *IEJ* 3 (1953) 26–9. For the "people of the land" see J. P. Healey, in *ABD* (1992) 1.168–9 and the literature cited there.

[44] Cogan, *Imperialism and Religion*, 95.

[45] C. L. Barnhart *et al.* (eds.), *The Barnhart Dictionary of New English since 1963* (Bronxville/New York/San Francisco/London: Barnhart/Harper & Row, 1973) 184. For the era see, e.g., R. V. Daniels, *Year of the Heroic Guerrilla: World Revolution and Counterrevolution in 1968* (New York: Basic Books, 1989), and J. C. McWilliams, *The 1960s Cultural Revolution* (Guides to Historic Events of the Twentieth Century (London/Westport, Conn.: Greenwood, 2000).

[46] Halpern, "Jerusalem and the Lineages, 49–59 (quotation from p. 59); see also *idem*, "Sybil, or the Two Nations?" 295–303.

changes may, in fact, be embodied in it) is unchanging, eternally the same."[47] In monarchic Judah this intermeshing of the generations found tangible expression in the jumble of accumulated bones in the charnel repository of bench-style tombs (the dominant style in Judah by the 8th century) comprising as many as 100 individuals or more in a century of use.[48] The living link with the ancestors was the grandparents, "those who embodied the longest stretch of the culture, who were the models for those younger than themselves, in whose slightest tone or gesture acceptance of the whole way of life was contained."[49] This continuum with the grandparents and the entombed ancestors was ruptured by the massive dislocations at the end of the 8th century.

A "postfigurative culture," according to Mead, is "one in which much of the unchanging culture remains unanalyzed and which must be exemplified by three generations in continuing contact."[50] The generation which supplied the soldiers who fought Sennacherib's army was decimated by death and deportation. The debacle depleted substantially the number of living grandparents, and especially grandfathers, for the generations which came of age in its wake[51]—the generations of Shaphan and Hilkiah, the boy-king Josiah's principal

---

[47] M. Mead, *Culture and Commitment: A Study of the Generation Gap* (Garden City: Natural History/Doubleday, 1970) 2–3.

[48] Bloch-Smith, *Judahite Burial Practices*, 48, 51–2; cf. now Yezerski, "Burial-Cave Distribution," 253–270.

[49] Mead, *Culture and Commitment*, 3. The grandparents probably remained potent among one's deceased ancestors for this reason: e.g., in the Assyrian prescriptions for dealing with ghosts "the generation of the grandparents is normally the limit of genealogical depth resorted to" (W. W. Hallo, "Royal Ancestor Worship in the Biblical World," *Sha'arei Talmon: Studies in the Bible, Qumran, and the Ancient Near East presented to Shemaryahu Talmon* [ed. by M. Fishbane *et al.*; Winona Lake: Eisenbrauns, 1992] 398, referencing J. Scurlock, *Magical Means of Dealing with Ghosts in Ancient Mesopotamia* [unpublished dissertation, University of Chicago, 1988] 353, 356). Shaphan's genealogy spans three generations (2 Kgs. 22:3). Truly exceptional is a Hebrew bulla of a seal (c. 600) identifying *four* generations: "Belonging to Hoshea (b.) Achbor (b.) Elishama (b.) Hoshea" (R. Deutsch and M. Heltzer, *Windows to the Past* [Tel Aviv-Jaffa: Archaeological Center, 1997] 38–40 [#96 (31)]).

[50] Mead, *Culture and Commitment*, 60, further elaborated in ch. 1.

[51] Documented in the mass burials at Lachish, presumably causalities of the siege in 701. The 695 retained crania of the estimated 1500 hastily-buried bodies unearthed there consist of 360 adult males, 274 adult females, and 61 immature individuals; the adults "were younger, on the average, than cemetery populations are expected to be," and included "very few aged individuals": see D. L. Risdon, "A Study of the Cranial and other Human Remains from Palestine Excavated at Tell Duweir (Lachish) by the Wellcome-Marston Archaeological Research Expedition," *Biometrika* 31 (1939) especially 102–28 (quotations from p. 161).

handlers and architects of the reform[52]—and also compromised their credibility, a situation resembling Mead's "cofigurative" culture/society in which "the prevailing model for members of the society is the behavior of their contemporaries."[53] According to Mead:[54]

> With the removal of the grandparents physically from the world in which the child is reared, the child's experience of his future is short-ened by a generation and his links to the past are weakened. . . . The past, once represented by living people, becomes shadowy, easier to abandon and to falsify in retrospect. . . . Where grandparents are absent or lose their power to control, the young may ostentatiously ignore adult standards or assume a mien of indifference to them. The ado-lescent enacts his limited and labeled role with the next younger group as his audience, and full cofiguration is established in which those who provide his models are only a few years older than those who are learning.

The influx of new peoples into Jerusalem, most having fled or been removed there from the hinterlands of Judah and cut off from their traditional support networks and the tombs of their ancestors, cre-ated a situation not unlike the immigrant or refugee experience in which

> the locus of power is not the elders, who are disregarded, but a younger age group, and the first generation of adapted children set a style that may perpetuate a thinner version of the older culture. In this kind of cofiguration, the loss of the grandparents is not compensated for. When the adults who made the transition reach grandparental age, they do not reconstitute, except in isolated cult groups or aristocracies, the lost three-generation organization.[55]

Further, according to Mead:[56] "The absence of grandparents usually also means the absence of a closed, narrow ethnic community. In contrast, when grandparents are part of a group immigrating into an alien society, the close ties within a village community may serve

---

[52] For the generations of Shaphan and Hilkiah see Barrick, "Dynastic Politics," especially 570–82, and *idem*, "Genealogical Notes" (forthcoming).

[53] Mead, *Culture and Commitment*, 32, further elaborated in ch. 2.

[54] *Ibid.*, 44–5

[55] *Ibid.*, 50, adding (p. 44): "The transition to a new way of life, in which new skills and modes of behavior must be acquired, appears to be much easier when there are no grandparents present who remember the past, shape the experience of the growing child and reinforce, inarticulately, all the unverbalized values of the old culture."

[56] *Ibid.*, 44.

to keep the immigrant community intact." These conditions now obtained in Jerusalem where the transplantees, to quote Halpern,[57]

> were concentrated to an extent that forbade village patterns of residence, and this deprived them of the institutions of shared fields, tombs, and compounds. The newcomers were in no position to articulate their kinship in the circumscribed capital as they had in the village. They were virtual refugees, displaced persons, deprived of a history of kinship relations because of the nature of the urban setting.

The resettlement of the hinterland perpetuated this dislocation by redistributing this population in the interests of the state, apparently without regard to antebellum geographic connections; there is no indication that people were returned to their ancestral neighborhoods.[58]

The archaeological record reveals traces of this transformation in Judah. Thus, e.g., there seems to be a reduction in the average size of cooking pots and ovens, indicating a reduction of the size of the family unit being fed.[59] The layout and location of the new settlements, mostly smallish forts rather than traditional towns, seem to "reflect a new economic order, geared mainly to state trade . . . hierarchical in nature, military in organization."[60] And while tomb-architecture in Palestine is very conservative, evincing little basic change over centuries,[61] Halpern detects "a marked shift . . . toward single-chambered rock-hewn tombs in the countryside in this era," including in the 7th century, "for the first time, examples of single burials," indicating that "the ancestral community, the kin corporation, had moved decidedly in the direction of smaller units, probably centered on the nuclear family."[62] Most notable are the tombs of the Silwan

---

[57] Halpern, "Sybil, or the Two Nations?" 328.

[58] Cf. *ibid.*, 324 and n. 86.

[59] Halpern, "Jerusalem and the Lineages," 71, and *idem*, 'Sybil, or the Two Nations?" 327.

[60] Halpern, "Jerusalem and the Lineages," 70, with T. L. McClellan, "Towns to Fortresses: The Transformation of Urban Life from the 8th to 7th Century BC," *Society of Biblical Literature Seminar Papers 1978* (ed. by P. J. Achtemeier; Missoula: Scholars, 1978) 277–86. Cf. Finkelstein, "Archaeology of the Days of Manasseh," 172–6.

[61] Cf. Bloch-Smith, *Judahite Burial Practices*, ch. 1.

[62] Halpern, "Jerusalem and the Lineages," 71–2; cf. *idem*, "Sybil, or the Two Nations?" 326–7 ("the old clan sections were breaking down as tomb groups; the extended family now cared, individually, for its own dead"). But cf. Bloch-Smith, *Judahite Burial Practices*, 147–8: "Mortuary remains, both from Jerusalem and throughout the kingdom, demonstrate that the Judahite conception of the tomb and the

necropolis overlooking the Wadi Kidron opposite Jerusalem: they are distinctive in location (high up on a cliff, making access to the tomb entrances difficult) and style,[63] and—most important for the present discussion—by "the total absence of [rock-cut] bone repositories" otherwise "highly characteristic" of Judahite tombs, and "a typical feature of family tombs," in this period;[64] they are, in fact, the tombs of the Jerusalem elites—chief among them the courtly families—produced by the administrative needs and cultural currents of Hezekiah's Judah and perpetuated, and augmented, into Josiah's Judah.[65] Tomb #35 is especially noteworthy:[66] an inscription over the entrance identifies the occupant as "—yahu who is Over-the-House," probably Hezekiah's majordomo Shebna whose ostentatious tomb "in the rock" was scorned by Isaiah (22:15–25); Shebna's father is not identified in either source (unlike his rival Eliakim b. Hilkiah), suggesting that he was perhaps "an upstart, a parvenu, an individual of ignoble birth."[67] Although the evidence is largely inferential, a "generation gap" within those elites very likely was a contributing psychological dynamic driving Shaphan's affinity and informing its "reform" agenda.

Disillusionment and disorientation, compounded by a psychic break with the past, expanded the gradations of Yahwism in 7th-century Judah (see further Section 7.B below). Josiah, like Oliver Cromwell and the Counter-Reformationists, sought to radically narrow this spectrum.[68] His "reform" was no doubt informed to some degree by the international scene—the coincidence of Josiah's 8th regnal year (2 Chron. 34:3a), about 633/2 by most chronologies, with the

---

fate of the deceased remained consistent throughout the Iron Age. . . . The only deviations reflected in burial were relative wealth and status for kings and civic and religious functionaries."

[63] See especially the works by Ussishkin cited in Chapter 3 n. 21 above.

[64] Ussishkin, *Village of Silwan*, 303.

[65] Cf. Halpern, "Sybil, or the Two Nations?" 324–5, and the literature cited there. The documented tax-collecting system during Josiah's reign (see Heltzer, "Some Questions Concerning the Economic Policy of Josiah," 105–8), functioning as early as his 3rd year when he was 11 years old and still under the regency of courtiers sympathetic with the policies of Manasseh and Amon (cf. Barrick, "Dynastic Politics," 565–70), presumably was not a Josianic innovation.

[66] Ussishkin, *Village of Silwan*, 188–202.

[67] J. T. Willis, "Historical Issues in Isaiah 22,15–25," *Bib* 74 (1993) 60–70 (quotation from p. 63), with earlier literature; for the pericope see also *idem*, "Textual and Linguistic Issues in Isaiah 22,15–25," *ZAW* 105 (1993) 377–99. Willis does not discuss the archaeological data or the issues considered here.

[68] Cf. Halpern, "Jerusalem and the Lineages," 77–9, 81–91.

resumption of the Egypto-Assyrian alliance following a decade or so of independence during which Egyptian self-interest spread up the Philistine coast,[69] was a demonstration of relative Assyrian weakness and Egyptian strength which may well have emboldened various nationalistic elements in Judahite society.[70] But the reactionary pogrom engineered by Shaphan and Hilkiah on behalf of the boy-king is explicable primarily in terms of these internal factors without positing an overriding external political agenda.

7.B. THE WORLD ABOVE AND THE WORLD BELOW

Astral deities/worship praxis figure prominently in the reconstructed "original" version of the reform report: Josiah destroys the equipage for Baal, Asherah, and the Host of Heaven from the "temple(-room?) of Yahweh" (v. 4a–bβ: *hêkāl yhwh* [cf. 1 Sam. 3:3]), removes the horses "which the kings of Judah had given/dedicated to the sun" from the entrance to the Temple (v. 11a: *mibbōʾ/měbōʾ bêt-yhwh*)[71] and burns the chariot(s)[72] of the sun associated with them (v. 11b), and destroys the roof-top altars "which the kings of Judah had made" and the altars "which Manasseh had made" in the two courts of the Temple (v. 12).[73] Of these, only the horses can be connected to "for-

---

[69] See A. Spalinger, "Psammetichus, King of Egypt: I," *JARCE* 13 (1976) 133–47, *idem*, "Psammetichus, King of Egypt: II," *JARCE* 15 (1978) 49–57, and *idem*, "The Concept of the Monarchy during the Saite Epoch—An Essay of Synthesis," *Or* 47 (1978) 12–36; cf. Naaman, "Kingdom of Judah under Josiah," especially 39–41, 57–8 (dating the alliance to "the late 620s" [p. 39]).

[70] Very likely Shaphan and his affinity were so disposed, as apparently were Zephaniah (as well-argued by Haak, "Zephaniah's Oracles against the Nations") and Jeremiah (cf. Chapter 3 nn. 36–37 above).

[71] For the text-critical problem see the commentaries and now T. Giancarlo, "La Locuzione *měbōʾ bêt-JHWH* (2 Re 23,11aβ) nelle Versioni antiche," *RivB* (1997) 387–407. The treatment of the horses and the location and function of "the chamber of the official Nathan-melek" and "the parwarim" are unclear. For a possibly relevant artifact see P. Kyle McCarter, "The Bulla of Nathan-Melech, the Servant of the King," *Realia Dei: Essays in Archaeology and Biblical Interpretation in Honor of Edward F. Campbell, Jr., at his Retirement* (ed. by P. H. Williams, Jr., and T. Hiebert; Scholars Press Homage Series 23; Atlanta: Scholars, 1999) 142–53.

[72] See Chapter 1 n. 7 above.

[73] The function of the roof-top altars is not given (cf. Josh. 2:6; Judg. 16:271 Sam. 9:25–26; 2 Sam. 11:2; 16:2; Isa. 15:3; 22:1, 13; Jer. 48:38; Neh. 8:16]; astral praxis seems a reasonable inference (especially if the association with Ahaz is authentic), although there are other possibilities. The function of Manasseh's altars is not given in 23:12 (or 21:4), but 21:5 connects them with "all the Host of Heaven."

eign" (Phoenician, Aramean, Assyrian) praxis with any degree of confidence,[74] but even this is open to question.[75]

The extent to which Assyria imposed religious obligations on its vassals is much disputed.[76] A religious dimension of vassal status is implicit in the surviving treaties between Assyria and its clients, and some sort of cultic demonstration of loyalty seems likely as diplomatic prudence if nothing else. And the long and lingering shadow of Assyria surely would have heightened the appeal of "things eastern" (i.e., Aramean)[77]—a "natural process of assimilation"—from at

---

[74] Classically Oestreicher, *Grundgesetz*, 53–5; cf. E. Weidner, "Weise Pferde im Alten Orient," *BiOr* 9 (1952) 157–9, and, more recently, e.g., Cogan-Tadmor, *II Kings*, 288, and Laato, *Josiah and David Redivivus*, 44. A connection with "typically Assyrian divination practices" is advanced by O. Keel and C. Uehlinger, *Gods, Goddesses, and Images of God in Ancient Israel* (trans. by T. H. Trapp; Minneapolis: Augsburg Fortress, 1998) 343–4, 371 (quotation from p. 371), with Spiekermann, *Juda unter Assur*, 245–56; but now modified: cf. O. Keel and C. Uehlinger, "Jahwe und die Sonnengottheit von Jerusalem," *Ein Gott allein? JHWH-Verehrung und biblischer Monotheismus im Kontext der israelitischen und altorientalischen Religionsgeschichte: 13. Kolloquium der Schweizerischen Akademieder Geistes- und Sozialwissenschaften 1993* (ed. by W. Dietrich and M. A. Klopfenstein; Freiburg: Universitäts, 1994) 301 and n. 60, and Uehlinger, "Gab es eine joschijanische Kultreform?" 74–7. On the c. 600+ clay figurines, some of horses with sun-disks (?) on their heads, see T. A. Holland, "A Study of Palestinian Iron Age Baked Clay Figurines, with Special Reference to Jerusalem: Cave I," in Eshel-Prag, *Excavations by K. M. Kenyon in Jerusalem 1961–1967, 4*, 159–89 (= *Levant* 9 [1977] 121–55); cf. Ahlström, *History of Ancient Palestine*, 735–6, and Keel-Uehlinger, *Gods, Goddesses, and Images of God*, 342–4. The proposition that Baal and Asherah are Assyrian deities masquerading behind West Semitic names (cf. Spiekermann, *Juda unter Assur*, 200–25, followed by, e.g., Schmidt, *Israel's Beneficent Dead*, 237–51) must be read into the text.

[75] For an indigenous explanation of the horses, and also the Temple equipage for "the host of heaven" in v. 4 and the worship of celestial bodies in the supplementary notice in v. 5, see J. G. Taylor, *Yahweh and the Sun: Biblical and Archaeological Evidence for Sun Worship in Ancient Israel* (JSOTSup 111; Sheffield: JSOT, 1993) *passim* (and for 23:11 pp. 176–82). See further n. 86 below.

[76] The case against imposition is presented by McKay, *Religion in Judah*, and Cogan, *Imperialism and Religion*, while a more positive position is advocated by Spiekermann, *Juda unter Assur*. On the important difference in this regard between provinces and client states see also J. N. Postgate, "The Land of Assur and the Yoke of Assur," *World Archaeology* 23 (1992) 247–63. For recent reviews of the state of the question see Lowery, *Reforming Kings*, 134–41, and M. Cogan, "Judah under Assyrian Hegemony: A Re-Examination of Imperialism and Religion," *JBL* 112 (1993) 403–14.

[77] As Keel-Uehlinger observe (*Gods, Goddesses, and Images of God*, 287): "By the end of the eighth century, the Assyrian government apparatus had taken on a significantly Aramaic character. The Aramean language itself achieved an increasingly greater significance, along with the Assyrian language, as a governmental language in the Trans-Euphrates region (see 2 Kgs 18:26). One must thus consider an impact on Palestine that came not only from the Assyrians but, even more, one that originated with the Arameans."

least the reign of Ahaz (cf. 2 Kgs. 16:10–16) onward;[78] this would
have been especially true, but not exclusively so, among the elites
(cf. Zeph. 1:8)[79] and is, in fact, evidenced in their surviving furnish-
ings[80] and personal effects (including impressions of the signet of a
"governor of the city [of Jerusalem?]" [*śr h'r*: cf. 2 Kgs. 23:8b; 2
Chron. 29:20; 34:8] depicting his investiture by the king of Judah),[81]
reminiscent of the appeal of "things Egyptian" among the local elites
of late LB Canaan.[82] Hezekiah's own seal bears a 2-winged beetle
pushing a ball of dung, symbolizing the rising sun (cf. Mal. 4:2),
familiar from Egypt and Phoenicia and consistent with the iconography of the contemporary *lmlk* sealings[83] (Ahaz's extant seal, by

---

[78] See Cogan, *Imperialism and Religion*, 88–96 (quotation from p. 95), adding: "[T]he
diminutive Judahite state was buffered on all sides by the cultural patterns dominant in the Assyrian empire. Although Assyria made no formal demands for cultural uniformity among its subjects, one of the by-products of political and economic
subjugation was a tendency toward cultural homogeneity. Involved as it was in
imperial affairs, Judah was faced with the problem of assimilation of foreign norms,
on a national scale, for the first time in its history." Cf. also Postgate, "Land of
Assur," 257–61 (quotation from p. 260): "we should not see the client rulers as
cowering in their citadels waiting to be irradiated with Assyrian influence, but
absorbing the scene in Nineveh, fingering the tapestries and envying the silverware."

[79] On Zeph. 1:8, in addition to the commentaries, cf. Ben Zvi, *Zephaniah*, especially 278–82.

[80] E.g., the burned remains of decorated boxwood furniture, presumably imported
from North Syria (where this tree is native) in the 7th century, recovered from the
"Burnt Room" in Jerusalem (see Y. Shiloh, "The Material Culture of Judah and
Jerusalem in Iron Age II: Origins and Influences," *The Land of Israel: Cross-Roads of
Civilizations* [ed. by E. Lipiński; Orientalia Loveniensia Analecta 19; Leuven: Peeters,
1985] 139–40).

[81] N. Avigad, "The Governor of the City," *IEJ* 26 (1976) 178–82; *idem*, "The
'Governor of the City' Bulla," *Ancient Jerusalem Revealed* (ed. by H. Geva; Jerusalem/
Washington DC: Israel Exploration Society/Biblical Archaeological Society, 1994)
138–40; G. Barkay, "A Second 'Governor of the City' Bulla," *Ancient Jerusalem
Revealed* (ed. by H. Geva) 141–4. For a "representative collection of personal adorn-
ment worn by the women [and men?] of Jerusalem during the [late] monarchy,"
evincing Assyrian, Egyptian, and other foreign stylistic affinities, see Barkay,
"Excavations at Ketef Hinnom," 99–101 (quotation from p. 99). Cf. the three hoards
of contemporary jewelry with Phoenician and Assyrian affinities from Ekron reported
by Golani-Sass, "Three Seventh-Century BCE Hoards," 57–81.

[82] Cf. C. R. Higginbotham, "Elite Emulation and Egyptian Governance in
Ramesside Canaan," *TA* 23 (1996) 154–69, and *idem*, "The Egyptianizing of Canaan,"
BARev 24/3 (1998) 36–43, 69.

[83] F. M. Cross, "King Hezekiah's Seal Bears Phoenician Imagery," *BARev* 25/2
(1999) 42–5, 60, and *idem*, "A Bulla of Hezekiah, King of Judah," *Realia Dei: Essays
in Archaeology and Biblical Interpretation in Honor of Edward F. Campbell, Jr., at his Retirement*
(ed. by P. H. Williams, Jr., and T. Hiebert; Scholars Press Homage Series 23;
Atlanta: Scholars, 1999) 62–6. Cf. B. Sass, "The Pre-Exilic Hebrew Seals: Iconism vs.

contrast, is aniconic).[84] But the solar praxis which the horses betoken "is equally likely to have had a continuous local ancestry going back to Canaanite origins in the Late Bronze Age."[85] J. G. Taylor's recent study finds that "in at least the vast majority of cases, biblical passages which refer to sun worship in Israel do not refer to a foreign phenomenon borrowed by idolatrous Israelites, but to a Yahwistic phenomenon which Deuteronomistic theology came to look upon as idolatrous."[86] Nonetheless, the decorated artifacts of this period display a "general tendency toward *the astralization* of the religious symbol system . . ., noticeable not only on imported glyptic art but also on what was produced locally in many different formats," different from the preceding periods:[87] "during the seventh century, preference was given to the divine powers being accepted and worshiped in their astral form, with emphasis on their *nocturnal* appearance in the starry heavens." The indigenous solar dimension of Yahwism (cf. the nomenclature "Yahweh-of-Hosts")[88] would have facilitated the assimila-

---

Aniconism," *Studies in the Iconography of Northwest Semitic Inscribed Seals* (ed. by B. Sass and C. Uehlinger; Fribourg/Göttingen: University/Vandenhoeck & Ruprecht, 1992) 214–9; it is worth noting in this connection "the unprovenanced seal of Manasseh, the King's Son . . ., has a straight-winged beetle in the top register, either suspect or an iconographic 'first'" (p. 214).

[84] R. Deutsch, "First Impression: What We Learn from King Ahaz's Seal," *BARev* 24/3 (1998) 54–6, 62. This would be consistent with Halpern's contention that a theological iconoclasm undergirded Ahaz's removal of "all plastic art from the temple nave" ("Sybil, or the Two Nations?" 310–1, citing 2 Kgs. 16:8, 17). The congruence of Hezekiah's seal with the *lmlk* sealings makes it difficult to attribute the motif to Assyrian imposition. It cannot be assumed, however, that these were the *only* seals used by these individuals.

[85] Dever, "Silence of the Text," 152–3 (quotation from p. 152); similarly Smith, *Early History of God*, ch. 4, and *idem*, "The Near Eastern Background of Solar Language for Yahweh," *JBL* 109 (1990) 29–39 ("while possibly due in some measure to external influence, the solar cult in the Jerusalem temple seems to have been primarily an indigenous development" [p. 39]), and Ackerman, *Under Every Green Tree*, 93–9 ("it is impossible to decide whether solar worship in seventh and sixth-century Judah is a Mesopotamian or a west Semitic cult, or whether, perhaps, the Jerusalem cult incorporates elements from both Mesopotamia and the West" [p. 98]). Astral references are of little value for dating purposes: cf. J. B. Curtis, "Astral Worship and the Date of Deuteronomy," *PEGLMBS* 14 (1994) 87–93.

[86] Taylor, *Yahweh and the Sun*, 257; see also *idem*, "Was Yahweh Worshipped as the Sun?" *BARev* 20/3 (1994) 52–61, 90–91. Cf. the critique by S. A. Wiggins, "Yahweh: The God of the Sun?," *JSOT* 71 (1996) 89–106, and the rebuttal by J. G. Taylor, "A Response to Steve A. Wiggins, 'Yahweh: The God of the Sun?'" *JSOT* 71 (1996) 107–19. See further Keel-Uehlinger, "Jahwe und die Sonnengottheit von Jerusalem," 269–306, and *idem*, *Gods, Goddesses, and Images of God*, ch. 7.

[87] Keel-Uehlinger, *Gods, Goddesses, and Images of God*, ch. 8 (quotations from p. 369).

[88] Cf. T. N. D. Mettinger, "YHWH SABAOTH—The Heavenly King on the

tion of "foreign" astral elements.[89] The great popularity of astral deities reflected in these biblical notices[90] is further demonstrated by the references to roof-top worship among the populace at large in this period (Jer. 19:13; 32:29; Zeph. 1:5)[91] and the persistent devotion paid to the "Queen of Heaven" (perhaps a native hybrid of Astarte and Ishtar which had begun evolving "sometime during the last centuries of the second millennium") especially by Judahite women in the late monarchic era and later (Jer. 7:16–20; 44:15–19, 25).[92]

Cherub Throne," *Studies in the Period of David and Solomon and Other Essays* (ed. by T. Ishida; Winona Lake: Eisenbrauns, 1982) 109–138; Taylor, *Yahweh and the Sun*, 99–105, *et passim*.

[89] For the potential of Phoenician influence (consistent with much of the iconography [cf. n. 83 above]) see most recently H. Niehr, "JHWH in der Rolle des Baalšamem," *Ein Gott allein? JHWH-Verehrung und biblischer Monotheismus im Kontext der israelitischen und altorientalischen Religionsgeschichte: 13. Kolloquium der Schweizerischen Akademie der Geistes- und Sozialwissenschaften 1993* (ed. by W. Dietrich and M. A. Klopfenstein; Freiburg: Universitäts, 1994) 307–26; cf. also E. Gubel, "The Iconography of Inscribed Phoenician Glyptic," *Studies in the Iconography of Northwest Semitic Inscribed Seals* (ed. by B. Sass and C. Uehlinger; Fribourg/Göttingen: University/Vandenhoeck & Ruprecht, 1992) 101–29.

[90] Virtually all commentators see Ezek. 8:16—the men standing between the Temple-building and the altar "with their backs to the Temple and their faces toward the east, bowing down toward the east *laššāmeš*"—as sure confirmation that sun-worship was part of the official Temple cultus as the close of the monarchy ("the trump card in the hand of those wagering for a solar connection with Yahweh" [Wiggins, "Yahweh: The God of the Sun?" 103]), Nonetheless, it could well be prophetic hyperbole misrepresenting a practice of offering homage while facing in the direction of the distant suzerain—such as the apparently well-established practice at Erech (during the reign of Ashurbanipal?) of "turn[ing] our faces to Assyria in our prayers to the gods/deity of the king" (ABL 1387 rev. 8–11: see Pfeiffer, "Three Assyriological Footnotes," 186–7). Such a religio-political practice, rather than actual (and repudiated) sun-worship, seems a more likely ancestor for the later practice of diasporic Yahwists of facing Jerusalem in their worship (cf., e.g., 1 Kgs. 8:44, 48; Ps. 5:8; 28:2; Dan. 6:11; Tobit 3:11; 3 Ezra 4:58).

[91] Note the "small incense altar (without horns) made of sandstone" found "sitting on top of the roof debris [of the Counting House/Building 234]" at contemporary Ashkelon: L. E. Stager, "Ashkelon and the Archaeology of Destruction; Kislev 604 BCE," *I-E* 25 (1996) 66*.

[92] See S. Ackerman, "'And the Women Knead Dough': The Worship of the Queen of Heaven in Sixth-Century Judah," *Gender and Difference in Ancient Israel* (ed. by P. L. Day; Philadelphia: Fortress, 1989) 109–124 (quotation from p. 117), and *idem*, *Under Every Green Tree*, ch. 1, with earlier literature (including noteably M. Delcor, "Le culte de la 'Reine du Ciel' selon Jer 7,18; 44,17–19, 25, et ses survivances: Aspects de la religion populaire féminine aux alentours de l'Exil en Juda et dans les communautés juives d'Egypte, *Environnement et Tradition de l'Ancien Testament* [AOAT 228; Kevelaer/Neukirchen-Vluyn: Butzon & Bercker/Neukirchener, 1990] 138–59 [= *AOAT* 211 (1982) 101–22]). Cf. more recently C. Houtman, in *DDD*

The references to the removal of astral paraphernalia from the Temple in the "original" reform report are consistent with this historical milieu:[93] it is not at all implausible that certain influential Judahites, grandsons of those who experienced the debacle of 701 and its aftermath, came to view this accelerating astral fascination with disapproval and took steps to repress it in the course of Josiah's reign. Jer. 8:1–2 may be the most visceral rhetorical attack on the astral partisans in the biblical record:

> At that time, says Yahweh, the bones of the kings of Judah, the bones of its princes, the bones of the priests, the bones of the prophets, the bones of the inhabitants of Jerusalem will be brought out of their tombs; and they will be spread before the sun and the moon and all the host of heaven which they loved and served and went after, and which they sought and worshipped; and they will not be gathered or buried, but will be like dung on the surface of the ground.

This is a prophetic analogy "pictur[ing] YHWH's punishment of Jerusalem in terms of an earthly overlord punishing his loyal subjects by carrying out, to the letter, the sanctions of their broken oaths"[94] (cf. the refraction in Deuteronomy 13 of Assyrian provisions concerning the suppression of political subversion, notably in the vassal treaties of Esarhaddon).[95] But it is not impossible that it also alludes to an event of this sort which had actually occurred closer to home in the lifetime or recent memory of Jeremiah's original audience. The "cemetery scene" in 2 Kgs. 23:16a depicts just such an event (see further Chapter 8 below).

(1995) 1278–83; K. J. H. Vriezen, "Cakes and Figurines: Related Women's Cultic Offerings in Ancient Israel," *On Reading Prophetic Texts: Gender-Specific and Related Studies in Memory of Fokkelien van Dijk-Hemmes* (ed. by B. Becking and M. Dijkstra; Leiden/New York/Köln: Brill, 1996) 251–63; Keel-Uehlinger, *Gods, Goddesses, and Images of God*, 292–4, 370.

[93] Cf. Keel-Uehlinger, *Gods, Goddesses, and Images of God*, 369, 372.

[94] M. Cogan, "A Note on Disinterment in Jeremiah," *Gratz College Anniversary Volume on the Occasion of the Seventy-fifth Anniversary of the Founding of the College 1895–1970* (ed. by I. D. Passow and S. T. Lachs; Philadelphia: Gratz College, 1971) 32. The view of some commentators, on the basis of Jer. 22:19 and 36:30, that at least Jehoiakim did suffer this fate cannot be sustained (cf. Josephus, *Ant.* 10.6.3): see *ibid.*, 32–4; cf., e.g., Holladay, *Jeremiah 1*, 598, and Carroll, *Jeremiah*, 431–4, and see further J. M. Berridge, in *ABD* (1992) 3.665. For the imagery see W. G. E. Watson, *Classical Hebrew Poetry: A Guide to Its Techniques* (JSOTSup 26; Sheffield: JSOT, 1984) 312–3.

[95] See P. E. Dion, "Deuteronomy 13: The Suppression of Alien Religious Propaganda in Israel during the Late Monarchical Era," *Law and Ideology in Monarchic Israel* (ed. by B. Halpern and D. W. Hobson; JSOTSup 124; Sheffield: JSOT, 1991) 147–216, arguing for a Josianic date.

The nether-world held an even greater fascination. This is evident in the persistence of tombs and attendant burial practices throughout the biblical period. As already noted, the continuity personified by the jumble of accumulated bones in the charnel repository of the ancestral tomb, foundational for traditional Israelite society, was shattered by the massive physical dislocations at the end of the 8th century and the psychic dislocations which accompanied them. E. Bloch-Smith summarizes:[96]

> In Judahite culture, the dead were an integral part of the social organization. Individuals believed that their descendants would nourish and care for them following death, just as they provided for their predecessors. Moreover, the legitimacy of land holdings was validated by the ancestral tomb, and the prosperity of the land may have been thought to be insured or blessed by the benevolent ancestors. Disrupting the mortuary cult represented a radical move.

Hezekiah and Sennacherib, by design and by coincidence, did exactly that.

Care of the ancestors and their resting places was a profound obligation falling to their descendants, and seeking the ancestors' advice and guidance was its natural corollary. The cult of the dead, "defined as the belief in the empowered dead with the attendant practices stemming from that belief, was a feature of Israelite praxis throughout the Iron Age."[97] Deut. 18:10–11 lists eight different forms of "mediation with the other world"[98] which Israelites are not to

---

[96] Bloch-Smith, *Judahite Burial Practices*, 132.

[97] *Ibid.*, 150. Recent discussions of necromancy and the "cult of the dead" along the lines followed here include K. Spronk, *Beatific Afterlife in Ancient Israel and in the Ancient Near East* (AOAT 219; Kevelaer/Neukirchen-Vluyn: Butzon & Bercker/Neukirchener, 1986); M. S. Smith and E. Bloch-Smith, "Death and Afterlife at Ugarit and Ancient Israel," *JAOS* 108 (1988) 277–84; Lewis, *Cults of the Dead*; Smith, *Early History of God*, 126–32; Bloch-Smith, "Cult of the Dead in Judah," 213–24, and *idem*, *Judahite Burial Practices*, especially ch. 3; K. van der Toorn, *Family Religion in Babylonia, Syria and Israel: Continuity and Change in the Forms of Religious Life* (Studies in the History and Culture of the Ancient Near East 7; Leiden/New York/Köln: Brill, 1996) especially pt. 3. For Ugarit see M. H. Pope, "The Cult of the Dead at Ugarit," *Probative Pontificating in Ugaritic and Biblical Literature: Collected Essays* (ed. by M. S. Smith; UBL 10; Münster: Ugarit, 1994) 225–50 (= *Ugarit in Retrospect: Fifty Years of Ugarit and Ugaritic* [ed. by G. D. Young; Winona Lake: Eisenbrauns, 1981] 159–79); Schmidt, *Israel's Beneficent Dead*, ch. 3; D. Pardee, "*Marziḫu, Kispu*, and the Ugaritic Funerary Cult: A Minimalist View," *Ugarit, Religion and Culture (Proceedings of the International Colloquium on Ugarit, Religion and Culture; Edinburgh, July 1994): Essays Presented in Honour of Professor John C. L. Gibson* (ed. by N. Wyatt *et al.*; UBL 12; Münster: Ugarit, 1996) 273–87, with earlier literature.

[98] Blenkinsopp, "Deuteronomy and the Politics of Post-Mortem Existence," 11.

practice,[99] testifying to the popularity and professional sophistication of the necromantic enterprise;[100] the terminology is "almost entirely domestic," implying "an almost entirely domestic praxis."[101] Isaiah's is the first negative voice among the prophets.[102] The biblical picture suggests that[103]

> prior to the seventh century, feeding the dead and other practices of care and veneration of the dead flourished in various social strata and quarters of Israelite society.... Prior to ca. 750, the people engaged in both necromancy and other practices (Isaiah 8:18; Deuteronomy 26:14 . . .). The kings had their own elaborate death cult (2 Samuel 18:18; 2 Kings 9:34–37 and 21; cf. 1 Samuel 20) which at least some priests tolerated (see Ezekiel 43:7–9). The prophets in the early periods did not object to necromancy. Here the criticism against the marzeah feast in Amos 6:1–6 compared with Jeremiah 16:5–9 is illustrative. Amos deplores the marzeah not because of any funerary association as in Jeremiah 16, but because of the exploitation of the poor symbolized in the lavish luxuries enjoyed at the feast.... After necromancy fell under prophetic and legal indictment ca. 750, other practices pertaining to the dead which had not been criticized previously likewise fell under condemnation.

---

[99] For the terminology cf. (all with earlier literature), e.g., J. Lust, "On Wizards and Prophets," *VTSup* 26 (1974) 133–42; H. A. Hoffner, "Second Millennium Antecedents to the Hebrew *'ôb*," *JBL* 86 (1967) 385–401, and *idem*, in *TDOT* (revised, 1977) 1.130–4; J. Ebach and U. Rüterswörden, "Unterweltbeschwörung im Alten Testament: Untersuchhungen zur Begriffs- und Religionsgeschichte des *'ob*," *UF* 9 (1977) 57–70, 12 (1980) 205–20; J. K. Kuemmerlin-McLean, in *ABD* (1992) 4.468–9; H. L. Bosman, "Redefined Prophecy as Deuteronomic Alternative to Divination in Deut. 18:9–22," *Acta Theologia* 16 (1996) 3–5. Among the commentaries see, e.g., Cogan-Tadmor, *II Kings*, 267. See further n. 101 below.

[100] Against this scholarly consensus cf. Schmidt, *Israel's Beneficent Dead*, especially ch. 4.

[101] F. H. Cryer, *Divination in Ancient Israel and its Near Eastern Environment* (JSOTSup 142; Sheffield: JSOT, 1994) 256–62 (quotation from p. 261).

[102] Kenyon's Cave 1 (see the references cited in Chapter 5 n. 47 above), halfway down the slope of the south-eastern hill in Jerusalem, above the Gihon spring, may be germane. It appears to have been a tomb "recycled" for some other function which came to an end with the erection of the new inner city-wall and adjacent street c. 700. Although its new function is disputed, it possibly served as the "shop" for an intermediary of some sort, "where [poorer] people came to make offerings to enhance fertility, or to have their fortunes told" (see now Steine, "Two Popular Cult Sites," 16–28 [quotation from p. 25]; cf. K. Prag, "Summary of the Reports on Caves I, II and III and Deposit IV," in Eshel-Prag, *Excavations by K. M. Kenyon in Jerusalem 1961–1967*, 4, 209–16); a necromantic association is suggested only by its location in a tomb which people would have passed *en route* to the spring below and the functional tombs beyond.

[103] Smith-Bloch-Smith, "Death and Afterlife," 282; see also Bloch-Smith, *Judahite Burial Practices*, 126–32. Cf. also F. Stolz, "Der Streit um die Wirklichkeit in der Sudreichsprophetie des 8. Jahrhunderts," *Wort und Dienst* 12 (1973) 9–30.

If the negative criticism began as a "respon[se] to necromancy as a form of competition to prophecy,"[104] the underlying cause must have been the inadequacy of that form of intermediation to satisfy those elements within Judahite society who came to rely more on necromantic alternatives.[105] The several crises of the 8th century and the ensuing disillusionment and disorientation of the 7th century would have severely compromised the credibility of those intermediaries whose "prophecies" were debunked by current events and whose methodology, lacking the "eastern" cachet, had become unfashionable.[106] A contributing factor could have been a theological and functional nexus between necromancy and astral phenomena, especially the sun, which may well have existed in the west as in the east, as a Neo-Babylonian necromantic incantation illustrates:[107]

> O Šamaš, judge of heaven and Underworld, Foremost One of the Anunnaki! O Šamaš, Judge of all the Lands, Šamaš, Foremost and Resplendent One! You keep them [i.e., ghosts] in check, O Šamaš, the Judge. You carry those from Above down to Below, those from Below to Above.

---

[104] Smith-Bloch-Smith, "Death and Afterlife," 282; cf. Bloch-Smith, *Judahite Burial Practices*, 131–2.

[105] For the counter-argument of one segment of the competition in Deut. 18:9–22 see now Bosman, "Redefined Prophecy," 1–23, hypothesizing (p. 14) a "blurring of the religious functions of diviners and prophets in Israel and that the priestly community coopted the prophets to enhance their own power base by using Moses as a model to link prophets and priests—thereby eliminating diviners"; cf. L. L. Grabbe, *Priests, Prophets, Diviners, Sages: A Socio-Historical Study of Religious Specialists in Ancient Israel* (Valley Forge, PA: Trinity International, 1995) chs. 4–5 (especially pp. 139–51).

[106] I. L. Finkel, "Necromancy in Ancient Mesopotamia," *AfO* 29–30 (1983–1984) 2–17. Schmidt (*Israel's Beneficent Dead*, 220–45, 276–7, 281–5, *et passim*) overestimates the prevalence of Neo-Assyrian necromancy; Finkel, by contrast, is extremely guarded and summarizes that "there are scattered if sketchy indications from certain texts that necromancy was practised on occasion in Mesopotamian society ("Necromancy," 2), and S. L. Holloway concludes similarly that "necromancy was rarely practiced in Mesopotamia" (personal communication, 7 January 2000).

[107] K 2779 12–14 (after Finkel, "Necromancy in Ancient Mesopotamia," 11). Such necromantic incantation texts suggest that it is, "quite appropriately, Šamaš who has the power and authority to bring up (*šūlû*) a ghost from the under-world and the whole operation is put under his auspices (p. 5 in reference to BM 36703 ii 1¹–23¹; cf. also K 2779 1–22]); cf. Reiner, *Astral Magic in Babylonia*, chs. 6 and 8. For Ugaritic evidence see D. Pardee, "RS 1.005 and the Identification of the *GTRM*," *Ritual and Sacrifice in the Ancient Near East: Proceedings of the International Conference Organized by the Katholieke Universiteit Leuven from the 17th to the 20th of April 1991* (ed. by J. Quaegebeur; OLA 55; Leuven: Peeters, 1993) 303–17. Note the juxtaposition of astral praxis and the desecration of corpses in Jer. 8:1–2.

Bloch-Smith's correlation of this prophetic criticism with the archaeological record is instructive:[108]

> [T]he promulgators of the Holiness and Deuteronomic Law Codes,
> the Deuteronomist and the prophets (notably Isaiah), attempted to
> purify the Jerusalem Temple cult and the people and to safeguard
> their own prerogatives. These moves to discredit the dead and those
> who attained their knowledge from the dead was the "official" policy
> beginning late in the eighth century BCE. The injunctions appear to
> have been aimed at intermediaries, priests and prophets who consulted
> the dead, that is, at individuals who challenged the authority and
> usurped some of the roles of self-styled "legitimate" priests and prophets
> by claiming access to transmundane knowledge. Judahite citizenry was
> enjoined not to offer tithed food to the dead and forbidden to con-
> sult the dead through intermediaries, but they were neither forbidden
> to provide for the needs of the dead nor to consult them personally.
> The fact that officialdom attempted to curtail but not suppress or halt
> death cult activities testifies to the degree that the cult was integrated
> into Judahite social, religious and economic fabric.

Isaiah's stance against the cult of the dead[109] dovetails with his stance
against the high official Shebna and his ostentatious tomb (Isa.
22:15–25) as the protestations of "a self-styled 'legitimate' prophet"
and royal councilor whose status at court had become endangered
by the new elites (cf. 1 Kgs. 12:6–17) and the altered circumstances.
Indeed, his prophetic credentials would have been seriously compromised if Hezekiah was, in fact, not Ahaz's promised son (Isa.
7:1–9:6),[110] but his younger brother, Ahaz having died without a
male heir[111]—and since Hezekiah would not have been king had
these prophecies been fulfilled, one wonders how sympathetic he and
his partisans at court would have been toward the prophet in the
first place. That Shebna remained in government service despite having become, in Isaiah's eyes, "the shame of his master's house" (Isa.
22:20; cf. 2 Kgs. 18:13–19:7) and completed his tomb (if the "Tomb

---

[108] Bloch-Smith, *Judahite Burial Practices*, 150–1; cf. 130–2.

[109] See Chapter 5 n. 116 above.

[110] Cf. J. Jensen, in *ABD* (1992) 3.392–5, and the literature cited there.

[111] The case recently advanced by D. V. Etz for making Ahaz and Hezekiah
half-brothers ("The Genealogical Relationships of Jehoram and Ahaziah, and of
Ahaz and Hezekiah, Kings of Judah," *JSOT* 71 [1996] especially 50–3; cf. further
Barrick, "Genealogical Notes" [forthcoming]) is appealing and, if correct, demonstrates the seriousness of the succession crisis under Ahaz (childless or predeceased
by his heir-apparent), underscores the threat posed by the partisans of the "Son of
Tabeel," and certainly casts doubt on Isaiah's standing vis-à-vis the new regime.

of the Royal Steward" [#35] at Silwan is indeed his)[112] suggests that Isaiah had reason to worry.[113] It is noteworthy that his attack on Shebna is said to have been delivered in the "Valley of Vision" (Isa. 22:1: *gê' ḥizzāyôn*), plausibly identified as the Ben-Hinnom Valley[114] and thus in the near vicinity—perhaps even in sight of—the Silwan necropolis and the construction site of the tomb itself.

It is impossible to imagine that Josiah's reform did not include measures against the cult of the dead. Even without reference to Deuteronomy or the Holiness Code, a faction at court holding such views on the subject can be safely posited. Josiah's scribe Shaphan (2 Kgs. 22:3–10), his sons Ahikam[115] and Gemariah and their descendants were major players in this faction for several reigns.[116] Another allied group was the influential but enigmatic "people of the land" (*'ām-hā'āreṣ*), credited with having secured the succession for Josiah (21:24)[117] and later for his younger son Jehoahaz (23:30), and sorely penalized for the latter when Necho installed Jehoiakim instead (23:35); this group inclined toward reactionary, nativistic views and

---

[112] See further Section 7.A and nn. 66 and 67 above and Chapter 8 below.

[113] T. R. Hobbs doubts that the tomb is his because of Isaiah's accusation (in *ABD* [1992] 5.1172–3), but he ignores the hyperbolic nature of Isaiah's attack, overestimates the prophet's influence at this point in his career (see n. 111 above), and minimizes the fact that despite having to "suffer a public humiliation" in return for his "public misdeed," he was given the only "slightly diminished" position of "scribe" (2 Kgs. 18:18[Isa. 36:3], 37[Isa. 36:22]; 19:2[Isa. 37:2]; cf. 15:5). If it is Shebna's tomb, the fact that he is still identified by the older title in its inscription might indicate that his demotion was only temporary, a further embarrassment to Isaiah's credibility. S. C. Layton considers the common theophore -*yāhû* insufficient for the identification ("The Steward in Ancient Israel: A Study of Hebrew (*'ăšer*) *'al-habbayit* in its Near Eastern Setting," *JBL* 109 [1990] especially 637–9, with earlier literature).

[114] See Chapter 5 n. 85 above.

[115] *Pace* Cogan-Tadmor who argue that the two were not related (*II Kings*, 282), Ahikam may have outranked his father, especially if he was of Josiah's generation (22:12[2 Chron. 34:20]). Wilcoxen speculates ("Political Background of Jeremiah's Temple Sermon," 158–62) that Shaphan "was old enough to have been one of those advisers or regents responsible for the political decisions that led to Josiah's second marriage and the beginning of the reform program." See further Barrick, "Dynastic Politics," 564–82, and *idem*, "Genealogical Notes" (forthcoming).

[116] Cf. 2 Kgs. 25:22; Jer. 26:24; 29:3; 36:10–19; 39:14; 40:5, 9, 11; 41:2; 43:6. M. Smith sees the families of Shaphan, Hilkiah, Achbor, and perhaps others as "the backbone of the Yahweh-alone party, much as the great Whig families of England were the backbone of that unorganized but definite party" (*Palestinian Parties and Politics that Shaped the Old Testament* [ACLS Lectures on the History of Religions 9; New York/London: Columbia University, 1971] 46); cf. N. Fox, "Royal Officials and Court Families: A New Look at *yldym* (*yĕlādîm*) in 1 Kings 12," *BA* 59 (1996) 225–32 (including relevant epigraphic data and bibliography).

[117] See n. 43 above.

riotous behavior for a "higher good" (cf. 11:18). Now in power, this affinity (or faction)[118] could replace Isaiah's rhetoric with action—and the tombs lining the Wadi Kidron, some undoubtedly containing the remains of deceased members (and certainly parents of members) of opposing affinities,[119] within sight of the Temple and palace-complex, would have been an irresistible target.

It is very surprising, therefore, that the final form of the reform report should include a desecration of tombs at Bethel (23:16–18) but not in Jerusalem. The omission, I submit, is the result of the compositional history of this material which moved the "cemetery scene" to Bethel. In the "original" version of the reform report, vv. 16a (+ 16b–18?) referred to a ransacking of tombs in Jerusalem, specifically those lining the Kidron. The osteal occupants of these tombs, and their living descendants who carefully cared for them, were "the opposition" religiously and politically, Shebna's Cavaliers to Josiah's Roundheads. The deceased were "recycled" to serve the new interests of the state as pollutants (v. 16a);[120] some of the living may also have been "recycled" analogously (see Chapter 9.B below) while others presumably fared less well (cf. the fate of the prophet Uriah b. Shemaiah when "the opposition" returned to power [Jer. 26:20–24]). The outrage would have festered in the common consciousness, fueling the antagonism of both sides through the Babylonian

---

[118] Neither "affinity" nor "faction" implies a monolithic group, like-minded on all the issues of the day. "Politics makes strange bedfellows" then as now, and it cannot be assumed that the varied interests of the various elements were all and always congruent, as recognized in R. D. Haak's insightful discussion of the place of the prophet Habakkuk vis-à-vis these elements (*Habakkuk* [VTSup 44; Leiden/New York/København/Köln: Brill, 1992] 141–9).

[119] Perhaps including Immer (or his father), whose son Pashur and grandson Gedaliah would oppose Jeremiah and the family of Shaphan (Jeremiah 20; 38). The priestly family of Immer remained prominent after the Exile (cf. Ezra 2:1–2, 37[Neh. 7:6–7, 40]; 10:19–20; Neh. 11:13.

[120] See further Chapters 8 and 9 below. Cf. the public hanging and decapitation of the deceased Regicides (Cromwell, his son-in-law and intimate Major-General Henry Ireton, and President of the Court John Bradshaw, all having been prominently interred in Westminster Abbey) in January 1661 following the Restoration of Charles II, their severed heads displayed on poles atop the façade of Westminster Hall "to awe, impress, horrify and perhaps even sadden the public gaze" until at least 1684: see A. Fraser, *Cromwell: The Lord Protector* (New York: Knopf, 1974) 691–8 (quotation from p. 693), and especially L. Clymer, "Cromwell's Head and Milton's Hair: Corpse Theory in Spectacular Bodies of the Interregnum," *Eighteenth Century: Theory and Interpretation* 40 (1999) 91–112 (my thanks to Dr. T. K. Meier for this reference).

crisis and beyond,[121] and providing a powerful subtext for Jeremiah's projections of the Ben-Hinnom Valley filled with corpses (7:32–33) and of disinterred bones left to the elements (8:1–2) and for Ezekiel's vision of a valley full of bones (37:1–14).

While governmental actions inevitably impact the lives of the populace—those who produce the food, make the pottery, pay the tithes, construct the tombs, and fight the battles—nothing in the reform report, except the closing of the bamoth, suggests that Josiah's pogrom concerned them directly, and there is little evidence elsewhere of an appreciable "trickle-down" effect: the astral world continued to fascinate (cf., e.g., Jeremiah 44), and the archaeological record suggests that traditional burial customs continued unfazed. It might best be characterized as a court putsch orchestrated by a relatively small disaffected group within the upper echelons of Judahite society whose views on religious (and political) matters were not widely shared or particularly popular within that society as a whole[122] (analogous in this respect to the "Akhenaten revolution").[123] That this group constituted a minority among the ruling elites (not to mention the populace at large) is indicated by the reversal in religious and foreign policies following Josiah's untimely death at Megiddo.[124] But silence

---

[121] The citation of the treatment Micah by Hezekiah in Jeremiah's defense against the charge of anti-governmental rabble-rousing in the Temple (Jer. 26:7–19), if credible, points to the long memories of the participants in this struggle.

[122] Cf. the discussion by B. O. Long, "Social Dimension of Prophetic Conflict," *Semeia* 21 (1982) 31–53, and P. Dutcher-Wells, "The Social Location of the Deuteronomists: A Sociological Study of Factional Politics in Late Pre-Exilic Judah," *JSOT* 52 (1991) 77–94. Albertz's claim that the reform movement "could rely on a broad range of support in Judahite society" (*History of Israelite Religion I*, 201–6, quotation from p. 203) seems overly generous.

[123] On the "Akhenaten revolution" see D. B. Redford, *Akhenaten: The Heretic King* (Princeton: Princeton University, 1984), and *idem*, in *ABD* (1992) 1.135–7.

[124] One illustration is provided by J. M. Cahill's recent study of the IAII vessels bearing rosette seal impressions, sometimes attributed to Josiah ("Rosette Stamp Seal Impressions from Ancient Judah," *IEJ* 45 [1995] 230–52): "the vessels circulated during the late seventh and early sixth centuries BCE and . . . their production may have been initiated by *Jehoiakim* in response to the threat of Babylonian invasion that followed the Egyptian defeat at the Battle of Carchemish in 605 BCE. The significance of the rosette motif indicates that the vessels . . . were intended for royal or official use and . . . demonstrates both the Assyrian impact on and the continuity of Judaean culture from the eighth to the seventh centuries BCE" (p. 252 [emphasis supplied]). That the rosette motif reflects "Assyrian influence" (*ibid.*) seems likely, but it too is part of the cultural predisposition for "things eastern" (cf. *ibid.*, 252 and n. 33).

shrouds the failure of Josiah's religious reform in the Kings History, as impenetrable as that obscuring the failure of Hezekiah's anti-Assyrian program. Their failure, however, does not imply that they are fictional creations of later generations.[125]

---

[125] *Pace*, e.g., Handy, "Historical Probability and Josiah's Reform," 275.

CHAPTER EIGHT

SOME HISTORICAL ASPECTS OF JOSIAH'S REFORM (II): TOMB-ROBBING AND BONE-BURNING (2 KINGS 23:16A)

The unusual episode in Josiah's reform pogrom reported in 2 Kgs. 23:16a requires special comment:[1] the king himself "turns" from doing something else,[2] espies "the tombs there on the mountain," whereupon: *wayyišlaḥ wayyiqqaḥ ʾet-haʿăṣāmôt min-haqqĕbārîm wayyiśrop ʿal-hammizbēaḥ wayĕṭamēʾēhû*; "and he sent and took the bones out of the tombs and burned them upon the altar and defiled it." *In situ*, this is the fulfillment of the Judahite man-of-god's prediction recorded in 1 Kgs. 13:2: *wĕzābaḥ ʿāleyka ʾet-kōhănê habbāmôt hammaqṭirîm ʿāleykā wĕʿaṣmôt ʾādām yiśrĕpû ʿāleykā*. As the original prediction in its immediate context does not identify the origin of the "human bones" to be burned,[3] it also gives no clue as to the motivation of the burning. It is on this point that 23:16a is ambiguous: is the burning done just to "defile" the altar or (also) for some other purpose?

Physical contact with the remains of deceased persons defiles (Lev. 21:1–4, 10–12; 22:4–7; Num. 5:2–4; 6:6–12; 9:6–14; 19:11–21; 31:19–24; cf. Ezek. 44:25–27), and with extraordinary virulence; indeed, "within the levitical scheme of impurity, . . . [t]he corpse is the most powerful impurity, being the only source that can pollute persons and objects for seven days."[4] Deliberate defilement by means of contact with human remains is presumably the intent of the action noted in 23:14b: *wayĕmallēʾ ʾet-mĕqômām ʿaṣmôt ʾādām*; "and he filled

---

[1] An earlier version appears as "Burning Bones at Bethel: A Closer Look at 2 Kings 23:6a," *SJOT* 14/1 (2000) 3–15.

[2] On the discontinuity of v. 15 and vv. 16a (+ 16b–18) see Chapter 3.D above.

[3] Certainly before the addition of the slaughter of the priests and arguably thereafter: see Chapter 3.B–C above.

[4] See Wright, *Disposal of Impurity*, ch. 5 and pp. 196–9 (quotation from p. 115), and *idem*, in *ABD* (1992) 6.729–41 (especially pp. 730–31); cf. also T. Frymer-Kensky, "Pollution, Purification, and Purgation in Biblical Israel," *The Word of the Lord Shall Go Forth: Essays in Honor of David Noel Freedman in Celebration of his Sixtieth Birthday* (ed. by C. L. Meyers and M. O'Connor; Winona Lake: Eisenbrauns, 1983) 399–414 (especially pp. 399–404), and J. Milgrom, "The Rationale for Biblical Impurity," *JANES* 22 (1993) 107–11.

their places with human bones." According to Num. 19:11–21 and
31:19–24, it is possible to remove such defilement (except of the
High Priest [Lev. 21:10–12]);[5] presumably this happened after the
Temple itself was defiled, during the tenure of the Roman governor
Coponius (6–9), when some Samaritans gained access during Passover
and "threw about dead men's bones in the porticoes."[6] But burning
human bones in order to defile that which they are burned upon is
not attested in biblical law or literature.[7] Despite this absence of evidence, the existence of the practice in the biblical world is presup-
posed in order to explain the bone-burning in 23:16a in this way.

Most commentators have little to say about this passage, perhaps
assuming that the burning would have been thought to have intensified
the intrinsic contagion of human bones.[8] This is a logical enough
deduction, although with no evidential basis. M. Haran goes further,
claiming that burning the bones upon the altar made the defilement
irreversible because "the ashes penetrated into the ruins."[9] He does

---

[5] See D. P. Wright, "Purification from Corpse-Contamination in Numbers xxxi
19–24," *VT* 35 (1985) 213–23, *idem, Disposal of Impurity*, 196–200 and accompanying notes, and *idem*, in *ABD*, 6.730–1.

[6] Josephus, *Ant.* 18.2.2. Lam. 2:20 implies that the Temple suffered corpse-
contamination at the hands of the Babylonians in the course of its destruction,
exceptional circumstances which (ultimately) resulted in a complete rebuilding. Much
later, according to 1 Mac. 4:36–52, the "blameless priests devoted to the law," after
some deliberation, opted to replace the Temple altar "profaned" by Antiochus IV,
its stones being stored "in a convenient place on the Temple hill until there
should come a prophet to tell what to do with them," but 1:20–28 gives no indication of the means of profanation employed (although v. 24b does mention "deeds
of murder").

[7] 1 Sam. 31:11–13 reports that the people of Jabesh-Gilead rescued the bodies
of Saul and his sons and then burned them, apparently an *ad hoc* undertaking probably to protect them from further profanation; the corpses were not completely
incinerated, for after the burning "they took their bones and buried them" (v. 13).
W. Zwickel uses the Amman Airport installation (see n. 15 below) to illuminate this
episode ("I Sam 31, 12f. und der Quadratbau auf dem Flughafengelände bei
Amman," *ZAW* 105 [1993] 165–74), but his case is too circumstantial to be convincing. 1 Chron. 10:12b omits the burning which may be a secondary embellishment (cf. 2 Sam. 21:12–14): see, e.g., P. K. McCarter, *I Samuel* (AB 8; Garden
City: Doubleday 1980) 442. The incineration of Zimri (1 Kgs. 16:18) was a sui-
cide. The burning for Asa (2 Chron. 16:14; cf. 21:19–20) refers to certain funerary customs, not cremation. For Amos 2:1 see n. 19 below.

[8] Thus, e.g., Jones says only that "burning 'men's bones' on the altar was a
means of rendering it cultically impure" (*1–2 Kings*, 264), while most of Long's discussion (*2 Kings*, 276) is devoted to the narratological relationship with 1 Kings 13.
There is virtually no discussion of this verse in the standard commentaries (e.g.,
Montgomery, Gray, De Vries, Cogan-Tadmor, Hobbs, Wiseman, and Provan).

[9] Haran, *Temple and Temple Service*, 138. Concerning 2 Chron. 34:4b–5a Japhet

not substantiate his claim, however, and although interesting, it will not bear closer scrutiny.

Since 60% of bone is inorganic and non-burnable, the "ashes" of a cremated body (properly "cremains," and averaging 3–9 pounds depending on the size of the corpse) consist principally of boney residua.[10] Burning bodies completely to ashes was technologically difficult in antiquity, as witnessed, e.g., by the burnt content of the burial jars of very young children (whose bones, without the calcium content of older bones, would have been most easily incinerated) recovered from Carthage and elsewhere.[11] The scene in 2 Kgs. 23:16 evidently envisions incineration by a wood fire in the open air, analogous to the "open" (or "mixed") technique of pottery firing. The core of a wood fire (the bottom center, at its largest roughly half the height and half the diameter of the pyre), regardless of type of wood or size, reaches a constant 1000° C before ashes have accumulated, while from the edges of the core to the sides and top of the pyre the temperature range drops to 700–800°;[12] ethnographic data on "open" pottery firing suggest a typical temperature range of c. 500–800° C.[13] The very fragmentary osteal remains of open-air cremations from the LBII Amman Airport installation (comprising at least two adults, a woman over 40 years of age and a man in

observes (*I–II Chronicles*, 1023): "Since the 'pollution of the dead' was regarded as the utmost form of defilement, this treatment of the cultic objects represents the greatest degradation possible; it desecrated them for ever."

[10] For a thorough presentation of the scientific and technological aspects of cremation see K. V. Iserson, *Death to Dust: What Happens to Dead Bodies?* (Tucson: Galen, 1994) especially 261–4, and the literature cited there. My thanks to David Marquis of Michelotti, Sawyers, and Nordquist Mortuary and Crematory, Billings MT, for sharing with me his expertise in this area.

[11] For the Carthage material see Brown, *Late Carthaginian Child Sacrifice*, 16, 52–4, with earlier literature (especially the analyses of J. H. Schwartz, unavailable to me); the identifiable human bones range from premature and new-born infants to children of four years old; for examples from elsewhere see also P. A. Bieńkowski, "Some Remarks on the Practice of Cremation in the Levant," *Levant* 14 (1982) 80–9, and the comprehensive inventories assembled by Bloch-Smith, *Judahite Burial Practices*, 52–5 (introduced into the region by the Phoenicians), 178–9, 210–4, 244–5 (with literature).

[12] Reported by N. H. Gadegaard, "On the So-Called Burnt Offering Altar in the Old Testament," *PEQ* 110 (1978) 37–8.

[13] See O. S. Rye, *Pottery Technology: Principles and Reconstruction* (Manuals on Archaeology 4; Washington, DC: Taraxacum, 1981) 96–8 and 102–3 Table 3, with literature. My very special thanks to Prof. emer. Marcia L. Selsor (late of Montana State University-Billings and the technical staff of *Ceramics Monthly*), an authority on the subject, for introducing me to the history, technology, and artistry, of pottery firing and kiln design and construction.

his late teens) display a "tendency for the bones of the upper trunk and head to show heavier signs of burning than the ones from the rest of the body, especially the extremities[,] . . . indicat[ing] a relatively small fire, incapable of consuming the whole body equally";[14] the remains "imply that the bones were articulated when burned from which the conclusion may be inferred that the burning took place relatively soon after death, at least prior to the complete decay of the flesh."[15] (The fact that any identifiable bone fragments at all survived exposure to the elements to be recovered is itself noteworthy.) Some of the few identifiable human bone fragments from one of the recently-discovered IAII cinerary urns from Tyre (from a wrist and finger of an individual perhaps 14+ years of age) appear to have been "exposed to a high temperature (probably over 800 degrees C) for a prolonged period[,] . . . indicat[ing] that they were cremated very efficiently as it is difficult to maintain such a high temperature for a long time."[16] The modern cremation "tophet" (cf. 23:10) is a brick-lined chamber, analogous to a pottery kiln; modern kilns, more efficient than their ancient counterparts, can achieve a temperature range of 1000–1300° C (depending on design).[17] But even with current cremation technology, which allows chamber temperatures to reach that of a modern kiln (the heat generated by the burning corpse and container as well as the fuel), sizable bone fragments

---

[14] R. M. Little, "Human Bone Fragment Analysis," *The Amman Airport Excavations, 1976* (ed. by L. G. Herr; AASOR 48; Winona Lake: ASOR, 1983) 47–55 (quotation from p. 50).

[15] Herr, "Stratigraphy," 23. He reports the observation of W. H. Shea that "for the upper vertebrae to be burned to the extent that some seem to have been, some preparation of the corpse for burning may have been done," but he does not elaborate. J. B. Hennessy suggests that the blood may have been drained from (some of) the bodies before burning ("Thirteenth Century BC Temple of Human Sacrifice," 100; cf. Y. Sakellarakis and E. Sapouna-Sakellaraki, "Drama of Death in a Minoan Temple," *National Geographic* 159/2 (1981) 205–22 (especially 219).

[16] J. Conheeney and A. Pipe, "Notes on Some Cremated Bone from Tyrian Cinerary Urns (AUB Rescue Action 'Tyre 1991')," in Seeden, "*Tophet* in Tyre?" 83–5 (quotation from p. 85). The intact urn (cinerary urn 2/TT 91.2: figs. 3–4 and 67–68 [pp. 53–4, 79–82]) has 7th-century parallels.

[17] Rye, *Pottery Technology*, 98–100 and 102–3 Table 3. For ancient kilns see L. Scott, "Pottery," *A History of Technology* (ed. by C. Singer *et al.*; New York/London: Oxford University, 1965) 1.376–412 (especially 391–7); for ancient Palestine cf. B. G. Wood, in *ABD* (1992) 4.38–9 with literature. The only ancient tophet installation (?) known archaeologically is at Akhziv and is described by the principal excavator, E. Mazar (*apud* S. R. Wolff, "Archaeology in Israel," *AJA* 98 [1994] 495) as "a tall, round structure . . . built of unhewn stones and plastered inside, and . . . preserved to a height of 2.30 m."

remain in the ashes and they may not completely disappear even after pulverizing (usually the second step of the process in the USA, especially if the ashes are to be scattered).[18] Thus if even nearly complete incineration was possible at all in ancient Israel (cf. 1 Sam. 31:12–13), it would have been extra-ordinary, particularly horrific (cf. Isa. 33:11–12), and subject to criticism (cf. Amos 2:1),[19] especially when done intentionally as Haran would have it here. One could argue, of course, that the intentional defilement of a locus of cultic purity such as an altar would have been extra-ordinary enough to risk such revulsion and perhaps even to justify the practice.

But ashes (osteal or otherwise) do not "penetrate" stone. Burning a corpse at a relatively low temperature is likely to produce some fatty residue which could penetrate the surface of porous brick or stone; the more desiccated the body, the less residue is produced and bones alone produce none. (Cremation today normally leaves no fatty residue.) It is certainly reasonable to assume that the great majority of bodies removed from the tombs in this episode were partially or completely desiccated and that few (if any) were as "fresh" as those at the Amman Airport installation. No evidence of such residue on the stones of the pyre there (the "structured stone pile" north of the building) is reported, but the likelihood of survival is nil.[20] Ashes might well infiltrate *between* stones or bricks (regardless of the presence of mortar), of course, but they would dissipate once the object constructed of such materials was broken up, as an altar deliberately defiled in this way surely would have been (cf. the

---

[18] See n. 10 above.

[19] Burning a body "to lime" (*laśśîd*) is indicative of complete incineration (cf. Isa. 33:11–2), and the implication is that this was extraordinarily harsh treatment of which Amos (and presumably others) disapproved. Among the commentators, e.g., E. Hammershaimb thinks that Amos's complaint is that the Moabites treated the king of Edom "as one would treat a dangerous criminal" (cf. Gen. 38:24; Lev. 20:14; 21:9; Josh. 7:15, 25: *The Book of Amos: A Commentary* [trans. by J. Sturdy; New York: Schocken, 1970] 41–2), while H. W. Wolff supposes that *laśśîd* implies that "the Moabites had manufactured from these royal ashes some substance which could be used to whitewash stones (Dtn 27:2, 4) and houses" of which Amos disapproved (cf. Targ.): *Joel and Amos* [trans. by W. Janzen *et al.*; ed. by S. D. McBride; Hermeneia; Philadelphia: Fortress, 1977] 162–3; cf. Paul, *Amos*, 72). R. S. Cripps thinks that the king's remains may have been burned after his tomb had been vandalized (*A Critical and Exegetical Commentary on the Book of Amos* [2nd edn.; London: SPCK, 1955 (originally 1929)] 136); so too F. I. Andersen and D. N. Freedman, *Amos* (AB 24A; New York: Doubleday, 1989) 287–8, and Paul (*Amos*, 72 and n. 270), noting the Assyrian practice.

[20] Herr speaks only of discoloration resulting from burning ("Stratigraphy," 13–5).

displaced stones of the horned altar at Beer-sheba).[21] In short, Haran's explanation does not suit the circumstances of the bone-burning reported in 2 Kgs. 23:16a.

Want of a satisfactory rationale,[22] absence of relevant levitical legislation, and the fact that no burning at all is mentioned in 2 Kgs. 23:14a, could imply that the burning in 23:16 was more to disgrace the persons whose bones they were (again, cf. Amos 2:1) than the altar on which they were burned and which, in any event, would have been defiled by contact alone. Tomb-robbing is amply attested in antiquity. The desecration of tombs was a dreadful prospect for ancient Near Eastern peoples. The occupant of Silwan tomb #35, probably Hezekiah's majordomo Shebna (see Chapter 7.B above), warns passersby:[23]

> This is—yahu who is Over-the-House. There is no silver and no gold here, but [only his bones] and the bones of his maidservant with him. Cursed be the man who will open this.

Eshmunazar of Sidon (5th century) worries that his bones might be moved (KAI 14):[24]

---

[21] Y. Aharoni, "The Horned Altar at Beer-sheba," *BA* 37 (1974) 2–6, and Z. Herzog, A. F. Rainey, and S. Moshkovitz, "The Stratigraphy at Beer-sheba and the Location of the Sanctuary," *BASOR* 22 (1977) 57 Fig. 4. A. F. Rainey considers that "at least some of its stones [had been] disposed of *carefully*: built into a repaired store-house wall or buried under the rampart outside the gate" ("Hezekiah's Reform and the Altars at Beer-sheba and Arad," *Scripture and Other Artifacts: Essays on the Bible and Archaeology in Honor of Philip J. King* [ed. by M. D. Coogan *et al.*; Louisville: Westminster John Knox, 1994] 339 [emphasis mine]). Note the "black stain marks" on the surface of the upper stones, indicating use of a metal grill in the burning operation. 1 Kgs. 13:3 + 5 (cf. Amos 9:1) suggests that the Bethel altar may have been (or was remembered as having been) similarly constructed. 2 Kgs. 23:15 also may point in this direction, but it is too text-critically unstable to bear much weight (cf. RSV with NJPSV); see Chapter 3 nn. 62–63 and 66 above. The altar of the Arad temple was constructed differently: see Z. Herzog, M. Aharoni, A. F. Rainey, and S. Moshkovitz, "The Israelite Fortress at Arad," *BASOR* 254 (1984) 11 and Fig. 11; Z. Herzog, M. Aharoni, and A. F. Rainey, "Arad: An Ancient Israelite Fortress with a Temple to Yahweh," *BARev* 13/2 (1987) 29–34.

[22] Notwithstanding the element of parody in offering "a sacrilege of a sacrifice" (Long, *2 Kings*, 276) which reverses the expected ritual experience and effect(s) much as does a so-called "Black Mass."

[23] For the text and discussion see N. Avigad, "The Epitaph of a Royal Steward from Siloam Village," *IEJ* 3 (1953) 137–52; Gibson, *Textbook of Syrian Semitic Inscriptions 1*, 23–4; Ussishkin, *Village of Silwan*, 247–50.

[24] *ANET*, 662. For this and other Phoenician mortuary inscriptions see J. C. Greenfield, "Scripture and Inscription: The Literary and Rhetorical Element in Some Early Phoenician Inscriptions," *Near Eastern Studies in Honor of W. F. Albright* (ed. by H. Goedicke; Baltimore: Johns Hopkins University, 1971) especially 259–65,

I am lying in this casket and this grave, in a place which I (myself) built. Whoever you are, ruler and (ordinary man), may he not open this resting-place and may he not . . . take the casket in which I am resting, and may he not carry me away from this resting-place to another resting-place! Even if people goad you, do not listen to their talk, for any ruler and any man who shall open this resting-place or who shall take up this the casket in which I am resting or who shall carry me away from this resting-place—may they not have a resting-place with the shades, may they not be buried in a grave, and may they not have a son and seed to take their place.

The curse of non-burial has numerous biblical parallels.[25] The purposeful desecration of tombs is attested as an extreme neo-Assyrian punishment for political and religious disloyalty. Thus, concerning the Elamites, Assurbanipal records:[26]

The tombs of their former and later kings, (who had) not revered Ashur and Ishtar, my lords, (who had) harassed my royal ancestors, I ravaged, tore down, and laid open to the sun. Their bones I carried off to Assyria, thus imposing restlessness upon their spirits, and depriving them of food offerings and libations.

As with Eshmunazar's fear, the removal of the Elamites' bones from Susa to Assyria was understood to be an act offensive to the bones[27] and only secondarily (if at all) to their destination.[28]

---

and B. Peckham, "Phoenicia and the Religion of Israel: The Epigraphic Evidence," *Ancient Israelite Religion: Essays in Honor of Frank Moore Cross* (ed. by P. D. Miller *et al.*; Philadelphia: Fortress, 1987) especially 81–3, and the literature cited there.

[25] See, e.g., Deut. 28:26; 1 Sam. 17:46; 1 Kgs. 14:11; 16:4; 21:19, 23–24; 2 Kgs. 9:10; Isa. 5:25; Jer. 7:33; 9:21; 14:16; 15:3; 16:4; 19:7; 22:18–19; 25:33; 26:22–23; 34:20; 36:30; Amos 8:3; Ps. 79:2–3. This curse also figures in international statecraft: for discussion see classically D. R. Hillers, *Treaty-Curse and the Old Testament Prophets* (Biblica et Orientalia 16; Rome: Pontifical Biblical Institute, 1964) ch. 4 (especially pp. 68–9), and M. Weinfeld, *Deuteronomy and the Deuteronomic School* (Oxford: Clarendon: 1972) 116–46.

[26] For the text and discussion see Cogan, "Note on Disinterment in Jeremiah," 29–34; cf. also Weinfeld, *Deuteronomy and the Deuteronomic School*, 140–1. For the Mesopotamian perspective on such matters see now W. W. Hallo, "Disturbing the Dead," *"minhah le-nahum": Biblical and Other Studies Presented to Nahum M. Sarna in Honour of his 70th Birthday* (ed. by M. Brettler and M. Fishbane; JSOTSup 154: Sheffield: JSOT, 1993) 183–92, and the literature cited there.

[27] This is graphically illustrated by the Assyrian treaty-curse: "may the grain for grinding disappear from you; instead of grain may your sons and daughters grind your bones . . ." (S. Parpola and K. Watanabe, *Neo-Assyrian Treaties and Loyalty Oaths* [SAA 2; Helsinki: University of Helsinki, 1988] no. 6, p. 46) probably depicted in an Assurbanipal relief (BM 124801 [p. 47 Fig. 14]). My thanks to Dr. S. W. Holloway for the reference.

[28] Probably related to this *post mortem* punishment is Assurbanipal's prayer concerning

This practice plainly underlies Jer. 8:1–2 (quoted in Chapter 7.B [p. 164] above) which envisions the desecration of Jerusalem tombs as a *post mortem* punishment of those who had engaged in the worship of astral deities.[29] As a practical matter, such an action would have been devastating to the living descendants of the deceased who were still worshipping the same astral deities and tending the tombs.

Finally, the story of Korah's rebellion (Numbers 16) provides an etiological warrant for seeing cremation as a punishment for individuals judged to have "despised Yahweh" (vv. 30, 35) in Israelite experience.[30] At issue in the story is priestly status: the victims in this complex pericope had vied unsuccessfully for full priestly status, and it concludes with the Levites established as guardians of the sacred realm centered on the altar at which they do not officiate, indeed cannot even touch, altar service being limited to the Aaronites (Num. 18:1–7; cf. 3:7).[31] This is consistent (although not necessarily identical) with the status of the transplanted bamoth-priests in 2 Kgs. 23:8a + 9 (however one understands the *kî 'im* conjunction; see Chapter 9.B below), but not with the status of the Levites in Deut. 18:6–8 and even less 33:10b.[32]

All of this is consistent with the treatment of the tombs, personally supervised by Josiah (remarkable in itself), reported in 2 Kgs. 23:16a. 2 Kings 23 has Josiah, through his agents, vigorously attack astral worship (23:4b, 5b, 11, 12aα, 12aβ [cf. 21:5]) and also dishonor Jerusalem cemeteries (23:6 [cf. Jer. 26:22–23]; cf. 4bα, 12b).

Gyges of Lydia who "had become unfaithful to the word of Ashur": "I prayed to Ashur and Ishtar: 'Let his corpse be cast before his enemy; his bones carried off (i.e., scattered about).' That which I implored of Ashur, came about. Before his enemies his corpse was cast; his bones were carried off. The Cimmerians, whom he had defeated by invoking my name, rose up and swept over his entire land" (Prism A II 111–125: see M. Cogan and H. Tadmor, "Gyges and Ashurbanipal: A Study in Literary Transmission," *Or* 46 [1977] 79).

[29] Among recent commentaries see, e.g., Carroll, *Jeremiah*, 224–6; Holladay, *Jeremiah 1*, 271–2; McKane, *Jeremiah*, 1.181–2; Craigie, *Jeremiah 1–25*, 126–7.

[30] See J. Milgrom, "Korah's Rebellion: A Study in Redaction," *De la Tôrah au Messie: Mélange Henri Cazelles* (ed. by M. Carrez *et al.*; Paris: Desclée, 1981) 135–46; *idem.*, "The Rebellion of Korah, Numbers 16–18: A Study in Tradition History," *Society of Biblical Literature 1988 Seminar Papers* (ed. by D. J. Lull; SBLSP 27; Atlanta: Scholars 1988) 570–3; *idem*, *Numbers* (JPSTC 4; New York/Philadelphia: Jewish Publication Society, 1990) 129–39, 414–23, and accompanying notes. For burning as a punishment of certain sexual crimes see Gen. 38:24; Lev. 20:14; 21:9.

[31] Cf. Milgrom, *Numbers*, 16–7, 146–9, 423–4.

[32] For a possible Josianic connection for the final recension of the Korah story see Milgrom, "Rebellion of Korah," 572–3.

It is not at all implausible, in this context, that burning the bones of the ancestors of his religious adversaries—whom his supporters certainly would have considered to have "despised Yahweh"—was part of his pogrom (see further Chapter 7.B above). It seems more reasonable, therefore, to suppose that the burning of the anonymous osteal contents of those tombs was a further affront of this sort,[33] which had the additional effect of defiling the altar in terms of the levitical law of contact, than to hypothesize a special defilement-by-bone-burning operation just to explain this passage. This is consistent with the compositional analysis of 23:16–18 (see Chapter 3.F above) which found reason to consider *wayĕṭamě'ēhû* in v. 16a part of a secondary expansion reconciling the bone-burning notice with the evolving story of the man-of-god at Bethel.

---

[33] Thus Dever, "Silence of the Text," 158: "Perhaps this can be seen simply as an instance of Josiah's attempt to blot out the very memory of noble families who had supported Manasseh. . . ."

CHAPTER NINE

SOME HISTORICAL ASPECTS OF JOSIAH'S
REFORM (III) JOSIAH AND THE BAMOTH

The likelihood that v. 14b—*wayĕmallē' 'et-mĕqômām 'aṣmôt 'ādām*—"contains eye-witness history"[1] makes identifying the antecedent of *mĕqômām* especially important. *In situ*, it would appear to be "the masseboth and the asherim" of v. 14a,[2] but this only defers the problem, for where were these objects located?[3] That question is mooted, however, by the compositional history of this material which disassociates v. 14b from v. 14a (see Chapter 5.F above). The action in v. 14a presumably was purposeful, and it is probable that the purpose devolved from the contaminatory properties of human bones (see Chapter 8 above). In the reconstructed "original" version of the reform report Josiah is said to have "defiled" (*ṬMʾ*) the bamoth "in the cities of Judah" (v. 8a), the Solomonic bamoth on the Mount of Olives (v. 13), and an altar near a cemetery in the Jerusalem vicinity (v. 16a).[4] Since the altar was defiled by contact with bones, it is a reasonable inference that bones were the agent used in the other defilements as well.[5]

---

[1] Eynikel, *Reform of King Josiah*, 272.

[2] E.g., R. J. Petty, *Asherah: Goddess of Israel* (American University Studies 7.74; New York/Bern/Frankfort am Main/Paris: Peter Lang, 1990) 140, imagining that the sockets into which the asherim had been fitted were filled with bones.

[3] Some commentators (e.g., Long, *2 Kings*, 275) see this as a general reference to Judah as a whole.

[4] There is no biblical justification for attributing to Josiah's pogrom the desecration of the 7th–6th-century Edomite shrine (by crushing cultic objects) at En Hatzeva, c. 20 miles southwest of the Dead Sea, as do Cohen-Yisrael, "Smashing the Idols," 41–51, 65. It could as well be the result of Judah's southward expansion (on which see Finkelstein, "Archaeology of the Days of Manasseh," 175–7, 180–1, and cf. I. Beit Arieh, "The Edomites in Cisjordan," *You Shall Not Abhor an Edomite for He Is your Brother: Edom and Seir in History and Tradition* [ed. by D. V. Edelman; Archaeology and Biblical Studies 3; Atlanta: Scholars, 1995] 33–40 [especially pp. 35–6]) or even Babylonian military movements during this period.

[5] As recognized by Haran, *Temples and Temple Service*, 138 and n. 8.

9.A. THE BAMOTH IN THE CITIES OF JUDAH

The issue of cultic centralization (2 Kgs. 23:8a + 9)—the elimination of alternative loci of state-sanctioned (or -sponsored) public worship of Yahweh, the patron god of the state—is the centerpiece of the final version of reform report and also stands out in the "original" version. Presumably it has some basis in fact, but while its theological significance seems clear enough, its exact nature and practical significance as an official governmental action in Josiah's Judah are not.

If the report of Manasseh's "rebuilding" of the bamoth which Hezekiah had "destroyed" in "the cities of Judah" (18:4a and 21:3a; cf. 23:5a, 8a) is credible,[6] this endeavor must be understood in the context of the building program and the royal administrative system of which it was a part (see Section 7.A above). The building program probably extended into Josiah's reign, and the administrative system certainly did. The narrative itself thus defines these installations as "the national shrines of the country,"[7] part of the deliberate "official" machinery of state rather than spontaneous expressions of "popular" religiosity;[8] this probably reflects historical reality and is not a rhetorical representation.[9] Even if *ʿîr* is construed generously,[10] the archaeological record suggests that there would have been a limited number of these bamoth for Josiah to "defile" (v. 8a) once official governmental policy toward them had changed, probably in Josiah's 12th or 18th regnal year.

There is no biblical evidence (discounting 2 Chron. 34:3–8 which is interpretative) that these bamoth were physically destroyed as commentators and historians generally assume: thus e.g., Lohfink claims that "we can differentiate between an abolition of sacrifices outside

---

[6] This report need not mean (and in view of the archaeological record of the reurbanization of Judah, probably does not mean) that the very same installations were rebuilt in the very same "cities."

[7] Ahlström, *Royal Administration*, 66.

[8] For the concept of "official" Judahite religion see the considerations raised by J. Berlinerblau, "Preliminary of the Sociological Study of Israelite 'Official Religion'," *Ki Baruch Hu: Ancient Near Eastern, Biblical, and Judaic Studies in Honor of Baruch A. Levine* (ed. by R. Chazan *et al.*; Winona Lake: Eisenbrauns, 1999) 153–69, with earlier literature.

[9] For the bamah phenomenon in general see the works cited in Chapter 5 n. 136 above.

[10] Cf. E. Fry, "Cities, Towns and Villages in the Old Testament," *BT* 30 (1979) 434–8.

Jerusalem under Hezekiah and a destruction of the sanctuaries themselves under Josiah.[11] The biblical evidence, such as it is, suggests the opposite: "removal" (2 Kgs. 18:4a: *SWR*) may well imply destruction (and interpreted as such by *'BD* in 21:3a), but what is "defiled," even by contact with human bones, can be decontaminated (in principle) through some ritualistic procedure (cf. Josephus, *Ant.* 18.2.2). Refracted through the prism of the "Deuteronomic Book Hypothesis," defilement must mean "destruction" (Deut. 12:2: *'BD*), but without this refraction it is not clear from the report itself whether the decommissioning of these bamoth was meant to be temporary[12] or permanent.

The treatment of the temple-complex in the IAII Arad fortress may be relevant to this question, but its value is seriously compromised by the controversies surrounding the archaeological record there. According to the excavation/publication team,[13] the Stratum IX fortress with its temple-complex and courtyard altar was destroyed by Tiglath-Pileser III or by Edomites/Philistines (cf. 2 Chron. 28:17–18); by the end of its Stratum VIII successor (|| Lachish III: late-8th century), the altar had been buried in a 1-m. fill, the courtyard becoming a level open area in front of the remodeled temple.[14] The treatment of the altar could be evidence of Hezekiah's reputed attack on the bamoth (cf. the use of the *ZBH* + *QTR* couplet with bamoth in "Hezekiah" KH-1, but *QTR* alone in "Josianic" KH-2). If the altar was covered over when the Stratum VIII temple-complex was built, the disposition of the altar is potentially relevant only if the Stratum VIII fortress was built by Hezekiah, his "removal" of this bamoth being an act of omission, by not restoring the courtyard altar, sometime before 701; if the altar was covered over at some subsequent point prior to the destruction of Stratum VIII, his "removal"

---

[11] N. Lohfink, in *IDBSup* (1976) 231.

[12] Cf., e.g., Oestreicher, *Grundgesetz*, 48–9; Hollenstein, "Literarkritische Erwägungen," 332.

[13] Herzog-Aharoni-Rainey-Moshkovitz, "Israelite Fortress at Arad," 19–26, and Herzog-Aharoni-Rainey, "Arad," 30–5.

[14] Reassessments by O. Zimboni ("The Iron Age Pottery of Tel Eton and its Relation to the Lachish, Tell Beit Mirsim and Arad Assemblages," *TA* 12 [1985] 63–90) and A. Mazar and E. Netzer ("On the Israelite Fortress at Arad, *BASOR* 263 [1986] 87–91; cf. Z. Herzog, "The Stratigraphy of Israelite Arad: A Rejoinder," *BASOR* 267 [1987] 77–9) suggest a much shorter period (c. 50 years) between Strata X–VIII. D. Ussishkin ("The Date of the Judaean Shrine at Arad," *IEJ* 38 [1988] 142–57 [especially pp. 151–2, 154]) prefers an early-7th century date for the founding of the temple-complex. Cf. D. W. Manor and G. A. Herion, in *ABD* (1992) 1.331–6.

of this bamoth was the permanent decommissioning of the altar but apparently not of the temple-building and its cult niche.[15] In the Stratum VII fortress (|| Lachish II: late-7th century) the temple is not rebuilt. If Josiah built the Stratum VII fortress,[16] his "defiling" of this bamah also was an act of omission by not restoring the temple-complex—but 2 Kgs. 23:8a implies that Josiah actually did something to decommission an existing cultic installation. There may be some evidence of this at Arad: two incense altars found on one of the steps of the entrance to the cella "had been carefully laid on their sides and 'buried', after having been removed from their original position in the cella"[17] and the interior of the cella was "affected by a fierce fire" which did not affect "[its] front part" or the steps.[18] Postulating a deliberate act of desecration analogous to that reflected in 23:16a permits the suggestion that Josiah "defiled" the Stratum VIII temple by burying the incense altars and burning the cella. The stratigraphy is very uncertain, however, and until the archaeological record is clarified the site presents only tantalizing possibilities.

As "national shrines" (cf. *miqdaš-melek* and *bêt mamlākâ* [Amos 7:13]), these bamoth probably replicated certain aspects of the Jerusalem Temple of which they were, in some sense, extensions.[19] That Yahweh

---

[15] It is not clear from the published accounts which option correlates best with the archaeological record; Vaughn's recent assessment (*Theology, History, and Archaeology*, 48–9) favors the second.

[16] The only Judahite candidates are Manasseh/Amon and Josiah; a role for the Edomites in is advocated by Ahlström, *History of Ancient Palestine*, 723–4.

[17] Ussishkin, "Date of the Judaean Shrine at Arad," 154 and n. 35, adding that "it is now difficult to ascertain whether the removal of the altars was carried out before the destruction . . . or immediately afterward." Herzog-Aharoni-Rainey-Moshkovitz imply (erroneously, according to Ussishkin) that the altars originally stood on the step and claim that they were "covered with a thick layer of plaster to protect them from damage" ("Israelite Fortress at Arad," 22).

[18] Ussishkin, "Date of the Judaean Shrine at Arad," 154, concluding that "the final destruction of the shrine by fire occurred at the same time as the final destruction of the Judaean fort, at the end of Stratum VI."

[19] Cf. the standard "government-issue" tripartite gates of the period. Analogously, the distinctive IA terracotta model shrines, "probably used in houses or small sanctuaries" for more private worship (of Astarte?), were deliberately fabricated to be "a modest reflection of a [particular] temple type generally thought of as 'Phoenician,' but which has prototypes in the Canaanite temples of the Late Bronze Age" (S. S. Weinberg, "A Moabite Shrine Group," *Muse* 12 [1978] 30–48 [quotations from pp. 46 and 44]). According to H. Niehr, the staff of the temple at Elephantine saw themselves as "a branch of the Jerusalem temple" ("Religio-Historical Aspects of the 'Early Post-Exilic' Period," *The Crisis of Israelite Religion: Transformation of Religious Tradition in Exilic and Post-Exilic Times* [ed. by B. Becking and M. C. A. Korpel; OTS 42; Leiden/Boston/Köln: Brill, 1999] 240). And E. Stern reports that the

was worshipped at the bamoth as at the Temple is evident from the fact that priests who had officiated there were incorporated into the priestly staff of the Temple by Josiah (2 Kgs. 23:9); their previous relationship with the Temple is not given and must be conjectured. Deities other than Yahweh were recognized in the Temple, but while it contained cultic equipage for them (v. 4a) and utilitarian functionaries associated with its Asherah-object (vv. 6–7),[20] the narrative does not mention a priesthood dedicated to the service of these deities. If the Temple did possess such a priesthood, it is hard to imagine that its disposition could have been passed over in silence while the destruction of the paraphernalia is described at some length.[21] It may have been the case that the *same* priesthood serviced both Yahweh and the other deities worshipped at the Temple and, analogously, at the bamoth.[22] If the Yahwistic priests resident at the Temple also officiated in the cultus of these other deities there, either (1) they were different personnel than those deployed with the high-priest Hilkiah in the removal of the paraphernalia of that cultus and their fate is not recorded, or (2) they were the same personnel, their religious allegiance having the flexibility of the proverbial Vicar of Bray's. Since the cultic credentials of the resident Yahweh priest-hood, no less than those of the bamoth-priests, would have been rendered suspect by the presence in the Temple of the parapher-nalia used in their cultus (even if they had not actually participated in the rites directed to these deities),[23] they would have required "purification" of some sort. This may be intimated in v. 9.

---

plan of the Samaritan temple-complex on Mt. Gerizim "highly resembles that of the temple in Jerusalem as it is described by Ezekiel" ("Religion in Palestine in the Assyrian and Persian Periods," *The Crisis of Israelite Religion: Transformation of Religious Tradition in Exilic and Post-Exilic Times* [ed. by B. Becking and M. C. A. Korpel; OTS 42; Leiden/Boston/Köln: Brill, 1999] 255).

[20] See Bird, "End of the Male Cult Prostitute," 64–75, stressing that *qdšm* (what-ever it may signify) refers not to the female weavers, but to the "house(s)" in which they performed this activity. The status (priestly, levitical, or utilitarian) and place-of-residence (in "chambers" within the Temple precincts or the acropolis generally, or elsewhere in Jerusalem), of these weavers are unknown.

[21] Moreso if v. 5 actually does refer to priests of deities other than Yahweh at the bamoth as most commentators maintain (see Chapter 5.A above).

[22] Traditional scholarly monotheistic bias has tended to view the "other" deities as interlopers or at best, as invited "guests" in the Temple. It is more likely that we must consider a more integrated model; for one example cf. L. K. Handy, *Among the Host of Heaven: The Syro-Palestinian Pantheon As Bureaucracy* (Winona Lake: Eisenbrauns, 1994).

[23] Scholars often minimize or ignore this question: e.g., Stern goes so far as to distinguish between "the monotheistic, central cult practiced in the temple of Jerusalem

9.B. The Fate of the Bamoth-Priests

V. 9 describes the disposition of the bamoth-priests:

> ʾak lōʾ yaʿălû kōhănê habbāmôt ʾel-mizbēaḥ yhwh bîrûšālāim,
> kî ʾim-ʾākĕlû maṣṣôt bĕtôk ʾăhêhem.

The long-accepted interpretation of this verse holds that the bamoth-priests[24] were absorbed into the staff of the Jerusalem Temple in a subordinate capacity without altar privileges, in contravention of the provisions of Deut. 18:6–8: the bamoth-priests "did not come up to the altar of the Lord in Jerusalem, but they ate unleavened bread among their brethren" (RSV).[25] The discrepancy with Deut. 18:6–8[26] is attributed typically to the presumed reluctance of the resident Jerusalem priesthood to grant the dispossessed bamoth-priests a status equal to their own,[27] or to the presumed cultic contamination

---

by its priests" and "Yahwistic paganism," evident in the material culture of Judah in this period, practiced everywhere else ("Religion in Palestine," 252–3).

[24] According to some commentators, the non-resident priests brought to Jerusalem (v. 8aα) included some who had served at the bamoth (v. 8aβ + 9) and some who had not: see especially R. D. Nelson, "The Role of the Priesthood in the Deuteronomistic History," *VTSup* 43 (1991) 142–3, and cf., e.g., J. G. McConville, *Law and Theology in Deuteronomy* (JSOTSup 33; Sheffield: JSOT, 1984) 133.

[25] Similarly, e.g.: "The priests of the high places, however, could not go up to the altar of Yahweh in Jerusalem, but they ate unleavened bread in the company of their brother priests" (JB); "These priests, however, never came up to the altar of the Lord in Jerusalem but used to eat unleavened bread with the priests of their clan" (NEB); "Although the priests of the high places did not serve at the altar of the Lord in Jerusalem, they ate unleavened bread with their fellow priests" (NIV); "The priests of the high places could not function at the altar of the Lord in Jerusalem; but they, along with their relatives, ate the unleavened bread" (NAB); "The priests of the shrines, however, did not ascend the altar of the Lord in Jerusalem, but they ate unleavened along with their kinsmen" (NJPSV); "But the priests of the high places did not ascend the altar of YHWH in Jerusalem, though they ate unleavened bread together with their fellow (priests)" (Cogan-Tadmor, *II Kings*, 279).

[26] Lowery claims, contradictorily, that vv. 8a + 9 "imply ... that Josiah called all the high place priests in to Jerusalem, presumably to serve at the central shrine, in accordance with the terms of Deut. 18.6–7," but "the high place priests of vv. 8–9 do not go up to serve at the central sanctuary" (*Reforming Kings*, 206–7).

[27] Cf., e.g., Burney, *Notes*, 359; Noth, *History of Israel*, 277; de Vaux, *Ancient Israel*, 363; M. Weinfeld, "Cult Centralization in Israel in Light of a Neo-Babylonian Analogy," *JNES* 23 (1964) 211 n. 46; Smith, *Palestinian Parties*, 49–50, 225–6 nn. 248–249; A. Phillips, *Deuteronomy* (CBC; Cambridge: Cambridge University, 1973) 123; Hermann, *History*, 268. So also Bright, but adding (*History of Israel*, 323): "The clergy of the abolished Yahwistic shrines were naturally not eager to surrender their ancient prerogatives and meekly integrate themselves with the priesthood of Jerusalem,

adhering to the bamoth-priests from their former service which rendered them unfit to officiate at the Temple.[28] The eating of unleavened bread is seen typically as an elliptical reference to the priestly
portions of sacrificial foods which the resident priesthood now shared
with the newcomers whom Josiah had deprived of their livelihood.[29]

This scenario is doubtful on its face. Notwithstanding the king's
personal involvement, the architects of Josiah's religious reform evidently were the royal scribe Shaphan b. Azaliah b. Meshullam (cf.
2 Kgs. 22:3) and the high-priest Hilkiah b. Shallum/Meshullam (cf.
1 Chron. 5:39; 9:11; Ezra 7:1–2; Neh. 11:11). Shaphan was the
king's liaison with the Temple (22:3–7, 9–10) over which Hilkiah,
possibly his uncle,[30] had jurisdiction. It is Hilkiah who reportedly
found the "book" (22:8, 10) which, according to the story in Kings,
was the stimulus for the covenant and reform once Shaphan had
read it to the king (vv. 10–11) and it's contents had been verified
by Yahweh through the wife of another court official who happened
to be a prophetess, contacted (and presumably selected) by a dele-
gation headed by Hilkiah and including Shaphan and his son Ahikam
(vv. 12–20).[31] Some skeptics, reasonably enough, even credit Hilkiah
with having created the document.[32] Be that as it may, Hilkiah, by
virtue of his position as high-priest, had to have been a key player
in any enterprise pertaining to the Temple. That Josiah's pogrom
pertained *primarily* to the Temple is plain enough from the content
and structure of the report of it in Kings. Hilkiah's full support of

---

and many of them refused to do so (II Kings 23:9)." The inference is logical enough,
but is beyond the reach of the evidence cited.

[28] Cf., e.g., Mayes, *Deuteronomy*, 278–9; Nelson "Role of the Priesthood," 142–3;
Washburn, "Perspective and Purpose," 70; Laato, *Josiah and David Redivivus*, 57.
Cogan-Tadmor (*II Kings*, 287) follow Friedman (*Exile and Biblical Narrative*, 65–6) and
consider this restriction analogous to that placed on blemished priests in Lev.
21:16–23; cf. also Wiseman, *1–2 Kings*, 302.

[29] Cf., e.g., Montgomery, *Kings*, 532; Jones, *1–2 Kings*, 621; Cogan-Tadmor, *II
Kings*, 287. Nelson ("Role of the Priesthood," 143, citing Gen. 19:3 and 1 Sam.
18:24) thinks in terms of the "bread of hospitality." There is no text-critical warrant for emending the text as does Gray, *I–II Kings*, 730 n. 1, 735, reading
miṣwat/miṣwôt ("statuary perquisites"; cf. Neh. 13:5) or *mĕnāyôt* ("portions").

[30] On the possible genealogical relationship between Shaphan and Hilkiah (identifying Shaphan's grandfather Meshullam as Hilkiah's father and predecessor as
high-priest Shallum/Meshullam) see my "Genealogical Notes" (forthcoming), and
"Dynastic Politics," 576, 578.

[31] See Chapter 7 n. 115 above.

[32] As in the eye-catching title of J. Elayi's essay, "Name of Deuteronomy's Author
Found on Seal Ring," *BARev* 13/5 (1987) 54–6. See Chapter 1 n. 24 above.

the reform which "cleaned up the mess" in the Temple over which he had charge suggests that he had assumed the position only recently—perhaps as part of the shifting court politics in Josiah's 8th regnal year, occasioned by the death or removal of the high-priest who had served in the latter part of Manasseh's reign and also under Amon.[33] These factors make it very difficult to imagine that the disposition of the bamoth-priests reported in v. 9 was an afterthought foisted upon the king and his councilors, including Hilkiah, by a recalcitrant Jerusalem priesthood headed by Hilkiah. It is much more likely that v. 9 describes an intended action no less consistent with the reformers' agenda than the other actions described in 23:4–20—there is nothing in the pericope itself or elsewhere in the biblical record to suggest otherwise.[34]

That the traditional understanding of 2 Kgs. 23:9 cannot be taken for granted is evident from D. L. Washburn's labored defense of it:[35]

> [V. 9] begins with . . . an imperfect form that, according to traditional grammars, signifies either present/future tense or linear action. The linear aspect is possible, but the next clause . . . has a perfect, which should represent "completed" action if the imperfect represents "incomplete" action. Actually, both [verbs] in context must be past tense, and both must be linear in aspect. It is *unreasonable* to think that these priests "continually" did not go up to the altar, but "one time" ate unleavened bread with their fellow priests. *Clearly*, they were forbidden ever to minister at the altar, but were treated as priests of Yahweh in other respects for the rest of their days. This overlapping of the verbal system should caution expositors against reading too much into the tense of a Hebrew verb, especially in later writings. It illustrates the linguistic "sloppiness" that infects any language over the course of time.

But what evidence is there, other than this text, that these priests on this occasion "were forbidden ever to minister at the altar"? I

---

[33] See especially Barrick, "Dynastic Politics" 564–82 (especially 579–82), and cf. *idem*, "Genealogical Notes" (forthcoming). Hilkiah evidently was succeeded, sequentially, by his son Azariah and grandson Seraiah (2 Kgs. 25:18; 1 Chron. 5:39–41; 9:10–11; Ezra 7:1), but their allegiances vis-à-vis the reform program are unknown; the example of Jaazaniah b. Shaphan (Ezek. 8:11: see Chapter 7 n. 90 above) indicates that their loyalties might well have been different.

[34] Ezek. 44:6–16 is probably irrelevant to this question: see J. G. McConville, "Priests and Levites in Ezekiel: A Crux in the Interpretation of Israel's History," *TynBul* 34 (1983) 4–9, and cf. *idem, Law and Theology in Deuteronomy*, 124–35, 142–7; R. K. Duke, "Punishment or Restoration? Another Look at the Levites of Ezekiel 44.6–16," *JSOT* 40 (1988) 61–81.

[35] "Perspective and Purpose," 70 n. 38 (emphasis supplied).

know of nothing beyond the sheer weight of exegetical convention
buttressed by historical/theological presupposition. On grammatical
grounds alone, the combination of verbal tenses with *kî 'im* points
to a very different understanding of the passage. A systematic analysis of the 134 occurrences of the *kî 'im* + Verb idiom in Biblical
Hebrew[36] finds that the accepted interpretation of v. 9 would require
both *'LH* and *'KL* to be in the same tense.[37] In 23:9, however, *'LH*
is in Imperfect and *'KL* is in Perfect, favoring—if not requiring—a
sense comparable to the other biblical attestations of the conjunction with this verbal sequence:[38]

Gen. 32:27b
. . . *lō' 'ăšallēhăkā kî 'im-bēraktānî*,

. . . I will not let you go *until/unless* you have blessed me.

---

[36] Such as the unpublished studies by J. A. Wilcoxen (which prompted my first
inquiry into the matter) and D. A. Snyder (provided me by D. G. Pardee of the
University of Chicago, who also critiqued an earlier version of what follows) for
which I am indebted. Hebrew lexica and grammars customarily give a variety of
contradictory translational equivalents with no means to choose among them in a
given passage; cf., recently, S.-M. Kang, "The Authentic Sermon of Jeremiah in
Jeremiah 7:1–20," *Texts, Temples, and Traditions: A Tribute to Menahem Haran* (ed. by
M. V. Fox *et al.*; Winona Lake: Eisenbrauns, 1996) 156: "As a single conjunction,
it can mean 'but'; as an opening for conditional clauses, it can mean 'surely if'.
After a negative clause, *kî 'im-* means 'except'; in the emphatic context it can be
translated 'unless'. . . . Usually, however, its meaning is adversative. . . ." See also
C. Van Leewen, "Die Partikel *'im*," *OTS* 18 (1973) especially 42–7; A. Schoors,
"The Particle *kî*," *OTS* 21 (1981) 240–76; W. T. Classen, "Speaker-Oriented Functions
of *kî* in Biblical Hebrew," *JNSL* 11 (1983) 29–46; J. Muilenburg, "The Linguistic
and Rhetorical Usages of the Particle *kî* in the Old Testament," *Hearing and Speaking
the Word: Selections from the Work of James Muilenburg* (ed. by T. F. Best; Chico: Scholars,
1984) especially 213–5 (= *HUCA* 32 [1961] 140–2); A. Aejmelaeus, "Function and
Interpretation of *kî* in Biblical Hebrew," *JBL* 105 (1986) 193–209.

[37] Cf. Waltke-O'Connor, *Introduction to Biblical Hebrew Syntax*, 642–3. MT contains
roughly 100 clear instances of this combination: e.g., Gen. 35:10b (*lō'-yiqqārē' šimkē
'ôd ya'ăqōb kî 'im-yiśrā'ēl yihyeh šēmekā* . . .; "No longer will your name be called "Jacob,"
but instead "Israel" will be your name . . ."); 1 Kgs. 8:19 (*raq 'attâ lō' tibneh habbāyit,
kî 'im-binēkā . . . hû'-yibneh habbayit lišmî*; "But you will not build the House, *but instead*
your son . . . he will build the House for my name."); 2 Kgs. 17:35aβ–36a (. . . *lō'
tîrē'û 'ĕlōhîm 'ăhērîm*, . . . *kî 'im-'et yhwh* . . . *'ōtô tîrā'û*; "You will not fear other gods . . .
but instead Yahweh . . . him you will fear."); 2 Kgs. 23:22–23 (*kî lō' na'ăśâ kappesah
hazzeh mîmê haššōpĕtîm 'ăšer šāpĕtû 'et yiśrā'ēl*, . . . *kî 'im-bišmōneh 'eśreh šānâ lammelek
yō'šîyāhû, na'ăśâ happeseḥ hazzeh* . . .; "For such a Passover was not observed from the
days of the judges who judged Israel . . . *but instead* in the eighteenth year of King
Josiah this Passover was observed. . . .").

[38] For analogous combinations having the same meaning: Gen. 42:15; 2 Sam.
3:13; 5:6; 1 Kgs. 17:1; 2 Kgs. 4:24; Lam. 5:21–22. Cf. C. Brokelmann, *Hebräische
Syntax* (Neukirchen: Erziehungsvereins, 1956) 159–60.

Lev. 22:6b

wĕlōʾ yōʾkal min-haqqŏdāŝîm kî ʾim-rāḥaṣ bĕŝārô bammāyim;

[the unclean person] shall not eat from the holy things *until/unless* he has washed his flesh in water.

Isa. 55:10–11

kî kaʾăŝer yērēd haggeŝem wĕhaŝŝeleg min-haŝŝāmayim wĕŝām-mâ lōʾ yāŝûb kî ʾim-hirwâ ʾet-hāʾāreṣ . . . kēn yihyeh dĕbārî ʾăŝer yēṣēʾ mippî lōʾ-yāŝûb ʾēlay rêkām kî ʾim-ʿāŝâ ʾet-ʾăŝer ḥāpaṣtî . . .;

For as the rain and snow fall from the heavens and do not return there *unless/until* they have watered the earth, . . . so will be my word which goes out of my mouth—it will not return to me empty *until/unless* it has done what I intended. . . .[39]

Isa. 65:6b

lōʾ ʾeḥĕŝeh kî ʾim-ŝillamtî . . .;

I will not keep silent *until/unless* I have repaid. . . .[40]

Amos 3:7

kî lōʾ yaʿăŝeh ʾădōnay yhwh dābār, kî ʾim-gālâ sôdô ʾel-ʿăbādāyw hannĕbîʾîm;

For the Lord Yahweh will not do something *until/unless* he has revealed his secret to his servants the prophets.

Ruth 3:18b

kî lōʾ yiŝqōṭ hāʾîŝ kî ʾim-killâ haddābār hayyôm;

For the man will not rest *until/unless* he has settled the matter today.[41]

Esther 2:14b

lōʾ-tābôʾ ʿôd ʾel-hammelek kî ʾim-hāpēṣ bāh hammelek wĕniqrĕʾâ bĕŝem;

She would not go to the king again *until/unless* the king desired her and she was summoned by name.

---

[39] Cf. LXX (with *eōs*) against RSV, NJPSV, etc. J. L. McKenzie likens Yahweh's "word" to "a messenger or an agent vested with power [who] never returns with [his] mission unaccomplished" (*Second Isaiah* [AB 20; Garden City: Doubleday, 1968] 144, translating ". . . it shall not return to me unfulfilled; No, it will accomplish all that I wish . . ." [p. 142]); the analogy has merit, but to a slightly different end: the reliable messenger will not return empty-handed (literally) unless he has delivered the message he was carrying to the intended recipient, and did not throw it away, let it fall into unfriendly hands, etc. Isa. 65:6b is comparable.

[40] Cf. LXX (with *eōs*) against RSV, NJPSV, etc.

[41] Cf. LXX (with *eōs*) against RSV, NJPV, etc. The desirable state of "rest" will be achieved only when business is concluded; Isa. 65:6b is comparable.

Consistent with this pattern, the sense of 2 Kgs. 23:9 should be: "But the bamoth-priests would/could not go up to the altar of Yahweh in Jerusalem *unless/until* they had eaten unleavened bread with their brothers."[42] To paraphrase Washburn, "these priests 'continually' did not go up to the altar, unless they 'one time' had eaten unleavened bread with their fellow priests."

V. 9 asserts, therefore, that the relocation of the bamoth-priests to Jerusalem (v. 8a) was accompanied by a change in their access to the altar of the Temple: either (1) the bamoth-priests now, for the first time, were permitted to officiate at the altar like the resident priesthood provided that they had qualified to do so by having eaten unleavened bread with them, or (2) their former access to that altar now was limited by the requirement of having eaten unleavened bread with the resident priesthood. In either case, "eating unleavened bread with their brothers" would have functioned as a (re)ordination ritual of some sort (as in Ex. 29:1–37 or Lev. 8:22–28, 31–35),[43] conceivably in conjunction with the special Passover (23:21–23),[44] rendering both the dispossessed bamoth-priests *and* the resident priests ritually fit to serve at the altar. If the "defiling" of the Judahite bamoth was intended to decommission them permanently, this (re)ordination would have been a one-time-only measure applicable only to the generation of bamoth-priests affected by Josiah's actions, no new bamoth-priests being anticipated in the future. Alternatively, if "eating unleavened bread with their brothers" refers to the receipt of priestly portions (cf. Lev. 2:3–10; 6:9–12, 22; 7:6–10; 21:22–23; etc.),[45] this would mean that altar privileges were granted

---

[42] So Ahlström, *Royal Administration*, 68–9; cf. H. Guthe, "Das Passahfest nach Dtn. 16," *Abhandlungen zur semitischen Religionskunde und Sprachwissenschaft Wolf Wilhelm Grafen von Baudissin . . . überreicht . . .* (ed. by W. Frankenberg and F. Küchler; BZAW 33; Giessen; Töpelmann, 1918) 228–9.

[43] The biblical record gives only hints of the normal priestly ordination operation, and nothing at all about extra-ordinary procedures: the provisions in Ex. 29:1–37 and Lev. 8:22–28, 31–35 include the eating of unleavened bread (vv. 2, 23); those in Num. 8:5–22 (concerning Levites) do not. For the anointing provision see now D. Fleming, "The Biblical Tradition of Anointing Priests," *JBL* 117 (1998) 401–14 (with earlier literature). For one type of ordination ceremony, which includes the anointing and shaving of the female candidate and the eating of breads and other foodstuffs, see *idem*, *The Installation of Baal's High Priestess at Emar* (HSS; Atlanta: Scholars, 1992).

[44] According to J. B. Segal, however, "the test of ritual cleanness was not in connexion with the eating of *massoth* but the eating of the Pesah victim; and it was in no way confined to the priests" (*The Hebrew Passover from the Earliest Times to AD 70* [London Oriental Series 12; London: Oxford University, 1963] 216–7 n. 8).

[45] For discussion see recently J. Milgrom, *Leviticus 1–16* (AB 3; New York:

only to those bamoth-priests who had served at the Temple and received priestly portions there in the past. In either case, only the bamoth-priests who failed the unleavened bread test would have been denied altar privileges at the Temple, and of their fate the pericope gives no information. Both possibilities correlate well with the notion of a court putsch aimed at "purifying," in this instance, the Yahweh priesthood and placing it more firmly under the control of the faction now in power, which included the (newly appointed?) high-priest Hilkiah. And with the exclusivity resulting from this new doctrinal "purity" came baser political and economic benefits, also potent motivational factors.[46]

Among the many implications of this new understanding of 2 Kgs. 23:8a + 9 is the institutional relationship of the bamoth and their priestly staffs with the Jerusalem Temple and its priestly staff. If these bamoth were, in fact, created by Manasseh as part of his rehabilitation of the Judahite hinterland, they must have had an official status of some sort and would have functioned in some fashion within the governmental infrastructure. The natural point of linkage would have been not the palace, but the Temple of which these state-sponsored were satellites of a sort.[47] The priests of these sanctuaries would have been provided by the Temple from its own priestly staff (their "brothers") or from regional priests (or priestly families) disenfranchised by Hezekiah and Sennacherib. In this context, these priests may well have had altar privileges in Jerusalem before their appointment to the new satellite sanctuaries, and which they retained after their appointment; if so, the provisions of 23:9 would have perpetuated those privileges, but limited them only to those priests who had met the unleavened bread requirement, whether construed as a (re)ordination ritual or as the receipt of priestly portions for past Temple service. That this system of satellite sanctuaries was not a

---

Doubleday, 1991) 182–8, 202, 392–6, 407, 411–4. The IA bowls inscribed with the word *QDŠ* may have been used for the collection/distribution of the priestly portions: see G. Barkay, "A Bowl with the Hebrew Inscription *QDŠ*," *IEJ* 40 (1990) 124–9; cf. *idem*, "'Your Poor Brother': A Note on an Inscribed Bowl from Beth Shemesh," *IEJ* 41 (1991) 239–41.

[46] Cf. W. E. Claburn, "The Fiscal Basis of Josiah's Reform," *JBL* 92 (1973) 11–22, and now S. Nakanose, *Josiah's Passover: Sociology and the Liberating Bible* (Bible and Liberation Series; Maryknoll, NY: Orbis, 1993) 91–2 *et passim* (cf. M. Delcor, "Réflexions sur la Pâque du temps de Josias d'aprés 2 Rois 23, 21–23," *Environnement et Tradition de l'Ancien Testament* [AOAT 228; Kevelaer/Neukirchen-Vluyn: Butzon & Bercker/Neukirchener, 1990] 90–104 [= *Hénoch* 4 (1982) 205–19]).

[47] Or (to use an analogy from academe) regional or branch campuses.

Manassaic innovation is suggested by the temple-like sanctuary in
the royal fortress at Arad, of uncertain date but at least pre-Hezekian
and possibly Solomonic (see Section 9.A above). The administrative
system attributed to Solomon, and probably having some factual
basis (whether Solomonic or later),[48] provides useful models: the
appointment of district governors (1 Kgs. 4:7–19), some (such as his
sons-in-law) sent out from the capital and others probably chosen
from the local dignitaries in the region to be governed, constituting
"a network of representatives for [Solomon's] expansive plans and
aims" beyond his base in Jerusalem and Judah;[49] and their monthly
rotation of provisioning of the king's household. The ecclesiastical
corollary to this arrangement would be certain Temple priests serving in rotation also at certain sanctuaries in the districts, and *vice
versa*. A literary parallel, of disputed historicity, is Jehoshaphat's dis-
patch of five princes, two priests, and nine Levites who "went about
through all the cities of Judah and taught among the people" (2
Chron. 17:7–9).[50]

This understanding of 2 Kgs. 23:8a + 9 lessens somewhat but
does not eliminate the conflict with Deut. 18:6–8:[51]

> And if a Levite comes from one of your towns out of all Israel where
> he resides—and he may come according to the desire of his heart—
> to the place which Yahweh will choose, and if he ministers in the

---

[48] For recent discussion cf. P. S. Ash, "Solomon's? District? List," *JSOT* 67 (1995)
67–86, and V. Fritz, "Die Verwaltungsgebiete Salomos nach 1 Kön. 4,7–19,"
Meilenstein: Festgabe für Herbert Donner (ed. by M. Görg; Ägypten und Altes Testament
30; Wiesbaden: Harrassowitz, 1995) 19–26. According to N. Naaman, "that the
data in the text is pre-Dtr is . . . common knowledge" ("Sources and Composition
in the History of Solomon," *The Age of Solomon: Scholarship at the Turn of the Millennium*
[ed. by L. K. Handy; SHCANE 11; Leiden/New York/Köln: Brill, 1997] 60 n. 6).
See also the following note.

[49] See further H. M. Niemann, "The Socio-Political Shadow Cast by the Biblical
Solomon," *The Age of Solomon: Scholarship at the Turn of the Millennium* (ed. by L. K.
Handy; SHCANE 11; Leiden/New York/Köln: Brill, 1997) 279–83 (quotation from
p. 283).

[50] See now R. W. Klein, "Reflections on Historiography in the Account of
Jehoshaphat," *Pomegranates and Golden Bells: Studies in Biblical, Jewish, and Near Eastern
Ritual, Law, and Literature in Honor of Jacob Milgrom* (ed. by D. O. Wright et al.; Winona
Lake: Eisenbrauns, 1995) 643–57 (with earlier literature).

[51] For the translation (beginning with the apodosis at v. 8) cf., e.g., S. R. Driver,
A Critical and Exegetical Commentary on the Book of Deuteronomy (ICC; New York/
Edinburgh: Scribners/Clark, 1885) 217; Mayes, *Deuteronomy*, 274–5; McConville,
Law and Theology, 145–7; R. K. Duke, "The Portion of the Levite: Another Reading
of Deuteronomy 18:6–8," *JBL* 106 (1987) 196; Nelson, "Role of the Priesthood,"
141 n. 28.

name of Yahweh his god like his brother-Levites who stand to minister there before Yahweh, they shall have equal portions to eat besides what he receives from the sale of his patrimony.

Like 23:8a + 9, this passage deals with a single class of cultic personnel, some stationed at the central sanctuary and some residing elsewhere.[52] The non-residents are authorized to serve at the central sanctuary with the same functions and perquisites as their resident brethren. The nature of that service is not specified in Deut. 18:6–8,[53] while 23:8a + 9 speaks only of sacrificial service. 23:8a + 9 may envision a permanent relocation of the non-resident personnel; Deut. 18:6–8 is less clear on this point, but a permanent relocation is not impossible.[54] The relocation in Deut. 18:6–8 is individual and clearly voluntary, however, while that in 23:8a + 9 is collective and compulsory and is accompanied by the service criterion of having eaten unleavened bread. Moreover, the persons relocated in 23:8a + 9 are already serving as priests in the "cities of Judah" before their move, but those relocated in Deut. 18:6–8 apparently are not.

Deut. 18:6–8 cannot be the legislative cause of the state of affairs

---

[52] The relevance of the so-called "Levitical cities" (Num. 35:108; Josh. 21:1–42; 1 Chron. 6:39–66) is unclear, not least because the dating of the institution reflected in the lists of cities (Josh. 21:13–19; 1 Chron. 6:54–60), N. Naaman argues that this portion of the larger list reflects historical reality in the reign of Josiah: see his *Borders and Districts in Biblical Historiography* (Jerusalem Biblical Studies 4; Jerusalem: Sinor, 1986) ch. 6, summarized in *idem*, "Hezekiah's Fortified Cities and the *lmlk* Stamps," 8, 10. For an 8th-century (Hezekian?) date for the entire list, based largely on archaeological considerations see R. G. Boling, "Levitical Cities: Archaeology and Texts," *Biblical and Related Studies Presented to Samuel Iwry* (ed. by A. Kort and S. Morschauser; Winona Lake: Eisenbrauns, 1985) 23–32. Other scholars consider them "creations from the postexilic period which sought to explain how the Levites fit into the early political, social, and theological structure of ancient Israel" (J. R. Spencer, in *ABD* [1992] 4.311, drawing on his *The Levitical Cities: A Study of the Role and Function of the Levites in the History of Ancient Israel* [unpublished dissertation, University of Chicago, 1980]).

[53] Some commentators (notably R. Abba, "Priests and Levites in Deuteronomy," *VT* 27 [1977] 265–6, and Duke, "Portion of the Levite," 199) maintain that ŠRT and ʿMD do not necessarily refer to priestly functions here, basing their skepticism on the non-priestly use of these verbs in a number of texts largely from "P," Chronicles, and Ezra. The use of these verbs elsewhere in Deuteronomy (17:21; 18:5; 21:5; cf. 10:8), however, strongly suggests that priestly functions are meant in 18:7. Nonetheless, priests did more than officiate at altars (cf. Deut. 33:8–11), making it impossible to say with complete certainty whether altar service is envisioned here.

[54] A. Cody infers from v. 8b (the meaning of which is obscure) that "the case envisioned is that of a Levite who wishes to establish himself permanently at the central sanctuary after having disposed of his affairs in the city of his origin" (*A History of Old Testament Priesthood* [Analecta Biblica 35; Rome: Pontifical Biblical Institute, 1969] 128).

envisioned in 2 Kgs. 23:8a + 9. If these two passages are, in fact, speaking of the same class of personnel,[55] one could imagine the state of affairs described in 23:8a + 9 as a modification of that leg-islated by Deut. 18:6–8: only those bamoth-priests who had also served at the Temple under the provisions of Deut. 18:6–8 were granted altar privileges there under the provisions of 23:8a + 9. If so, and if 23:8a + 9 reports an actual Josianic initiative, one could see Deut. 18:6–8 as a response to the conditions which obtained in Judah after the bamoth were "removed" by Hezekiah in the course of his anti-Assyrian rebellion (18:4) and before they were "rebuilt" by Manasseh (21:3) as much as a half-century later, a period dis-rupted by Hezekiah's reorganization of his realm and by the exi-gencies and devastation of war and rife with dispossessed priests, widows and orphans, and displaced persons of various sorts from both Judah and the north. But a similar situation obtained follow-ing the Babylonian triumph in the first quarter of the sixth century, severely disrupting the arrangements established under Josiah:[56] the Levites dispossessed by the fall of Judah and the Exile and then resettled in the hinterland (cf. 1 Chron. 5:27–6:32; Ezra 2:40–58) were allowed to participate in the Jerusalem cultus, but their "min-istrations" did not necessarily include altar service.

9.C. The Solomonic Bamoth on the Mount of Olives[57]

2 Kgs. 23:13 reports Josiah's actions on the Mount of Olives:

> wĕʾet-habbāmôt ʾăšer ʿal-pĕnê yĕrûšālaim ʾăšer mîmîn lĕhar-hammašḥît ʾăšer bānâ šĕlōmōh melek-yiśrāʾēl lĕʿaštōret šiqquṣ ṣîdōnîm wĕlikĕmôš šiqquṣ mōʾāb ûlĕmilkôm tōʿābat bĕnê-ʿammôn ṭimmēʾ hammelek;

and the bamoth east [or: in the vicinity][58] of Jerusalem south of the "Mount of the Destroyer," which Solomon the king of Israel built for

---

[55] Cf., e.g., Lohfink, "Cult Reform of Josiah," 474 n. 37.

[56] Rather than imagining the Jerusalem priesthood in 2 Kgs. 23:8a + 9 over-riding Deut. 18:6–8, Lohfink thinks "it is more likely . . . that this passage was not yet in the law at this time, and now expresses a further-reaching claim of the one-time rural Levites" ("Distributions of Functions," 346 [= *Great Themes from the Old Testament*, 67–8]).

[57] For a more comprehensive treatment of this material see W. B. Barrick, "Loving Too Well: The Negative Portrayal of Solomon and the Composition of the Kings History" *Estudios Bíblicos* (forthcoming).

[58] See J. F. Drinkard, "'al pĕnê as 'East of'," *JBL* 98 (1979) 285–6.

the Sidonian abomination Ashtoreth and for the Moabite abomination
Kemosh and for the Ammonite abhorrence Milkom the king defiled.

This passage is anticipated by 1 Kgs. 11:5–8:

> For Solomon walked after the Sidonian deity Ashtoreth and after the
> Ammonite abomination Milkom; and Solomon did evil in the eyes of
> Yahweh and did not wholly follow Yahweh as David his father had
> done. Then Solomon built a bamah for the Moabite abomination
> Kemosh on the mountain east [or: in the vicinity] of Jerusalem, and
> for the Ammonite abomination Molek; and so he did for all his for-
> eign wives, and he would burn (incense?)[59] and make sacrifices to their
> gods (LXX[L];[60] or: who would burn [incense?] and make sacrifices to
> their gods [MT]).

The charge of personal apostasy is recapitulated by Yahweh in
Ahijah's oracular exposition of his torn garment to Jerusalem (11:33):

> [Yahweh will tear the kingdom asunder] because he has [i.e., Solomon,
> with the Versions; or: they have, with MT] has forsaken me and has
> "bowed" to the Sidonian deity Ashtoreth and to the Ammonite deity
> Milkom, and has not walked in my ways doing right in my eyes like
> David his father did.

Both the singular and the plural readings are defensible, but in the
KH-2 context proposed below the singular is preferable[61] (as commentators generally agree):[62] Solomon built these bamoth for his own
worship of these foreign deities (cf. LXX[L] 11:8b).

These passages, read synchronically, are customarily assumed to
convey historically reliable information: Josiah did, in fact, "defile"
the bamoth which were, in fact, built by Solomon somewhere on

---

[59] See Chapter 3 n. 45 above.

[60] See below (especially n. 108).

[61] In 9:6–9 a plural referent also occurs unexpectedly: this is a demonstrably secondary passage which reinterprets Solomon's portended failure to "walk before me
as David your father walked *bĕtām lēbāb* and with uprightness, doing all that I have
commanded you" (vv. 4–5) in terms of the people having "gone and served other
gods and 'bowed' to them"; as a result of their apostasy "Israel" will go into exile
and the Temple will be destroyed, clear allusions to the historical realities of 587/6
(cf. Jer. 19:7–9) and thus indicative of a post-"Josianic" date of composition: see in
particular Knoppers, *Two Nations under God 1*, especially 109–10 (finding three stages
of composition for 9:1–9: vv. 1–2 ["Josianic" (his Dtr[1])], vv. 4–5, and vv. 6–9 [both
"from the exile or later"]).

[62] Cf. Knoppers, *Two Nations Under God 1*, 186–8 and ns. B-C, H. The plural is
favored by, e.g., Noth, *Könige 1*, 243; Nelson, *Double Redaction*, 113; Campbell, *Of
Prophets and Kings*, 29 and n. 18.

the Mount of Olives—*hammašḥît*, "the destroyer," usually considered a pun or corruption of *hammišḥâ*, "the anointing" (cf. Targ.), but in keeping with the mountain's close association with death and thus probably authentic for the period[63]—and dedicated to various foreign deities worshipped by his foreign wives. It is reasonable to suppose that Solomon would have taken steps to satisfy the religious needs of at least his principle foreign wives, along with their retainers and the merchants who followed in their wake.[64] Ahab's "house of Baal," built for his Sidonian-born queen Jezebel (1 Kgs. 16:32; cf. 18:19 and 21:26), would have served such a function as probably did the "house of Baal" in Jerusalem, destroyed at the downfall of her kinswoman Athaliah (2 Kgs. 10:18–27):[65] cultic "embassies" established by the state to further its diplomatic and commercial interests and patronized primarily (if not exclusively, unless promoted by an evangelical royal sponsor) by aliens residing in or otherwise closely associated with the capital (cf. the Catholic chapels maintained at state expense as part of the official households of the foreign

---

[63] No convincing explanation has been advanced for why a benign and rather obvious designation would have been replaced with a malevolent and comparatively obscure one; "anointing," not otherwise associated with this mountain, seems a very roundabout way to make a connection with "olives." Since the purported "pun"/"corruption" is consistent with the mountain's mortuary associations (see 1 Kgs. 2:37; cf. also Ex. 12:13, 33; 2 Sam. 24:16[1 Chron. 21:1]), tangibly documented by the numerous tombs cut into its western slope (see Chapter 3.A above), there is no reason why it should not be authentic. *har hazzêtîm*, "Mount of Olives" (Zech. 14:4) would be a later horticulturally-based substitute for the original; cf. the informal descriptor used in 2 Sam. 15:30, and note the absence of any nomenclature at all in Ezek. 11:23. Whether the original nomenclature derived from the tombs, or the practice of burying there during the monarchic period arose from an earlier tradition reflected in the nomenclature, the location implies some connection between the Solomonic installations and the funereal aspects of the site and its pre-Solomonic religious associations (cf. the report in 2 Sam. 15:30a, 32a, that it was customary to "'bow' to God/deities [*lē'lōhîm*]" at its summit, although this could be an anachronistic allusion to later practice); cf. the case for the god Nabu (Nergal) advanced by Curtis, "Investigation of the Mount of Olives," 137–77.

[64] See Chapter 7 n. 16 above. A location opposite the Temple, on the "dark" side of the Kidron (see below), would have had symbolic value for the regime's international "public relations," on which cf. C. Meyers, "The Israelite Empire: In Defense of King Solomon," *The Bible and its Traditions* (ed. by M. P. O'Connor and D. N. Freedman; Michigan Quarterly Review 22/3; Ann Arbor: University of Michigan, 1983) 420–2.

[65] Note Y. Yadin's suggestion that both "houses of Baal" were not actually built in the capital cities ("The 'House of Baal' of Ahab and Jezebel in Samaria and that of Athalia in Judah," *Archaeology in the Levant: Essays for Kathleen Kenyon* [ed. by P. R. Moorey and P. J. Parr; Warminster: Aris & Phillips, 1978] 127–35); cf. now J. A. Emerton, "The House of Baal in 1 Kgs. xvi 32," *VT* 47 (1997) 293–300.

queens of the Stuart kings).[66] The appeal of this historical reconstruction (now reinforced by "an Egyptian [commercial] enclave with
its own sanctuary" at IAII Ashkelon)[67] is undeniable, and its wide
acceptance is understandable: "It is a historical fact," asserts S. J.
De Vries, "that Solomon built, or allowed to be built, pagan shrines
near Jerusalem. . . . This was as much a part of his deliberate policy as his multiple marriages."[68] This conclusion is overly credulous,
however, for the reconstruction is beset by a number of serious historical, literary, and textual problems.

Dismantling the Historical Fact

There is, first of all, the very practical question of how these installations managed to survive intact the c. 300 years between their construction by Solomon and their desecration by Josiah. Continuity of
cultic loci is a truism in the ancient Near East, and not least of all
in ancient Palestine, but so too is the constant need to rebuild, ren-
ovate, and restore cultic and other installations to which years of
use, the impermanence of materials and workmanship, the effects of
nature, and socio-political circumstances have not been kind.[69]

---

[66] See, e.g., Robinson, *History of Israel*, 258; Bright, *History of Israel* 245, 252;
Ahlström, *Royal Administration*, 18, 62; Lowery, *Reforming Kings*, 106–8. The foreign
"embassy" analogy (used by Lowery, *Reforming Kings*, 107 *et passim*; cf., e.g., Robinson,
History of Israel, 258) is helpful, but the religious dimension, central for the biblical
phenomena, is normally a very minor factor in the modern embassy. A more precise analogy would be the French and Spanish embassies in Stuart London and
their extensions in the form of the private Catholic chapels maintained at state
expense as part of the official households of the foreign queens of Charles I (the
French Henrietta Maria), Charles II (the Portuguese Catherine of Braganza), and
James II (the Italian Maria of Modena). The influence of these ladies on the religious policies and personal beliefs of their husbands varied in fact but loomed large
in the rhetoric of Protestant extremists. The same can be said of two of Charles
II's chief mistresses (cf. Solomon's concubines): the English Barbara Duchess of
Cleveland and the French Louise Duchess of Portsmouth, both Catholics. Charles
II was unabashedly a ladies man, and the comparison with Solomon was not lost
on the Protestant propagandists of the time. See A. Fraser, *Royal Charles: Charles II
and the Restoration* (New York: Knopf, 1979). The fact that Catholicism was officially
illegal in Stuart England makes the analogy with ancient Judah (especially as refracted
through the Bible's theological prism) particularly useful.

[67] See Stager, "Ashkelon and the Archaeology of Destruction," 68*–9*.

[68] De Vries, *I Kings*, 143–4.

[69] See the germane discussions in *The Architecture of Ancient Israel: From the Prehistoric
to the Persian Periods* (ed. by A. Kempinski and R. Reich; Jerusalem: Israel Exploration
Society, 1992): especially R. Reich, "Building Materials and Architectural Elements
in Ancient Israel," 1–16, and E. Netzer, "Massive Structures: Processes in Construction
and Deterioration," 17–27; cf. also R. Reich, "Palaces and Residences in the Iron

Solomon's Temple, a contemporary structure of comparable function, is an apt example (cf., e.g., 2 Kgs. 12:1–17[2 Chron. 24:4–14]);[70] if built of comparable material (but cf. below), Solomon's bamoth, unprotected by the city wall, would have been more vulnerable to the ministrations of besiegers and despoilers, beginning already in Rehoboam's reign (1 Kgs. 14:25–28). It is especially difficult to imagine how they escaped the attention of Sennacherib's troops who, he claims, surrounded Jerusalem with earthworks, penning Hezekiah inside "like a bird in a cage."[71] That Josiah's reform-minded predecessors, most notably Hezekiah, also left them alone is another puzzlement.[72] Also to be considered is the severe earthquake of c. 750 (cf. Isa. 2:6–22; 5:14–17; Amos 1:1; Zech. 14:4–5), the effects of which may have been as devastating in and around Jerusalem as at nearby Gezer.[73] Another question concerns the patrons of these

---

Age," 202–22, and Z. Herzog, "Administrative Structures in the Iron Age," 223–30. For a maximalist inventory of archaeologically-known Solomonic structures see W. G. Dever, "Monumental Art and Architecture in Ancient Israel in the Period of the United Monarchy," *Recent Archaeological Discoveries and Biblical Research* (Samuel and Althea Stroum Lectures in Jewish Studies 6; Seattle/London: University of Washington, 1990) 85–117 (= a revised version of "Monumental Architecture in Ancient Israel in the Period of the United Monarchy," *Studies in the Period of David and Solomon and Other Essays* [ed. by T. Ishida; Winona Lake: Eisenbrauns, 1982] 269–306).

[70] See the brief discussion by C. L. Meyers, "The Elusive Temple," *BA* 45 (1982) 33–41.

[71] *ANET*, 287–8, possibly supported by Mic. 4:14; but cf. 2 Kgs. 19:32(Isa. 37:33). Although the Assyrian army probably encamped on the Northwest Hill overlooking the city (see D. Ussishkin, "The 'Camp of the Assyrians' in Jerusalem," *IEJ* 29 [1979] 127–42), in the quadrant of the city's circuit opposite the Mount of Olives, troops reconnoitering the neighborhood or foraging for foodstuffs and water surely would have reached this location.

[72] Lowery supposes from this silence that "Hezekiah's centralization reform did not include an attack on embassy row" (*Reforming Kings*, 207).

[73] For archaeological evidence of the earthquake at Gezer see W. G. Dever, "A Case-Study of Biblical Archaeology: The Earthquake of ca. 760 BCE," *E-I* 23 (1992) 27*–35*. According to Yeivin ("Divided Monarchy," 168–9): "Because of [this earthquake] the southern part of the Mount of Olives collapsed into the valley of Kidron, covering the spring of En-rogel. . . . There is little doubt that not only were the surroundings of Jerusalem damaged but that the houses in Jerusalem itself collapsed and probably part of the Temple." Similarly, e.g., B. Mazar, *The Mountain of the Lord* (Garden City; Doubleday, 1975) 157–8. This sounds like an exposition of Josephus's account of the earthquake which occasioned Uzziah's leprosy (*Ant.* 9.222–27), and this account itself may be a midrashic conflation of Amos 1:1, Zech. 14:5, and 2 Chron. 26:16–21, instead of independent testimony; D. N. Freedman and A. Welch claim that the account is "unsupported archaeologically" ("Amos's Earthquake and Israelite Prophecy," *Scripture and Other Artifacts: Essays on the Bible and Archaeology in Honor of Philip J. King* [ed. by M. D. Coogan *et al.*; Louisville: Westminster John Knox, 1994] 189).

installations in the intervening centuries: it might be imagined that some of the offspring of Solomon's foreign wives (e.g., Rehoboam [1 Kgs. 14:21b]) continued to adhere to the deities of their mothers, that other diplomatic marriages with devotees of these deities ensued, that alien merchants continued to patronize these installations, and/or that a stable Judahite foreign policy would have required their retention and upkeep[74]—contrivances all, carrying little conviction. In short, the proposition that cultic installations, built by Solomon on or about the Mount of Olives as religious expressions of his foreign policy, would have continued in use down to the reign of Josiah is impossible to accept without fabricating a set of hypothetical circumstances to be even faintly plausible. The synchronic continuity of Solomon's bamoth, like that of his Temple,[75] serves more of an ideological function in the KH and cannot be assumed to be simple factual reportage.

2 Kgs. 23:13 does not actually speak of diplomatic marriages nor of Solomon's women: that is a synchronic, readerly hypothesis drawn from 1 Kgs. 11:1–11 which seemingly supplies the historical background for this episode.[76] 1 Kings 11 paints a somber picture of the aged Solomon seduced into idolatry by his gargantuan foreign harem whose religious needs he provided for in these bamoth (vv. 7–8). These allegations are routinely granted considerable credibility by scholars and others interested in the "historical Solomon." Thus, e.g.,

---

[74] Of Manasseh's international diplomacy Rainey speculates ("Manasseh, King of Judah," 151): "These new political/economic ties were expressed in terms of the foreign cults established in Jerusalem. Many of the shrines to the various deities were doubtless associated with the embassies/consulates established by the diplomatic missions that came to Jerusalem (cf. during Solomon's reign 1 Ki. 11:4–8; and for the location of the many shrines in Manasseh's day, cf. 2 Ki. 23:13–14)." There is no actual evidence for any of this, and Rainey's inference from 23:13–14 (which surely would have mentioned any such structures for which Manasseh was responsible had they been there) seems especially specious. For other examples cf., e.g., Lowery, *Reforming Kings*, 107–8.

[75] Cf. J. Van Seters, "Solomon's Temple: Fact and Ideology in Biblical and Near Eastern Historiography," *CBQ* 59 (1997) especially 55–7, and *idem*, "The Chronicler's Account of Solomon's Temple-Building: A Continuity Theme," *The Chronicler as Historian* (ed. by M. P. Graham *et al.*; JSOTSup 238; Sheffield: Sheffield Academic, 1997) 283–300. See also the programmatic essay on this topic by P. R. Ackroyd, "The Temple Vessels: A Continuity Theme," *Studies in the Religious Tradition of the Old Testament* (London: SCM, 1987) 46–60 and accompanying notes (= *VTSup* 23 [1972] 166–81).

[76] Cf. S. Lasine, "The King of Desire: Indeterminacy, Audience, and the Solomon Narrative," *Semeia* 71 (1996) 103–5.

D. N. Freedman, while allowing that so many women "might dis-
tract the most pious of men," speaks of the "heartbreaking para-
dox . . . that the king most eloquently devoted to the worship of
Yahweh was equally devoted to honoring other gods";[77] B. W.
Anderson, more charitably, faults Solomon for "an excessive broad-
mindedness, most evident with respect to his harem,"[78] while Noth
resorts to the cliché of "the decadent successor" who squanders his
inheritance.[79] For De Vries:[80] "If Solomon was not quite so poorly
motivated as Dtr supposes, a level-headed evaluation based on sober
criticism will mark him down as more a menace than a benefactor
to authentic biblical faith." These modern assessments (more in the
nature of value-judgments, probably revealing more about the eval-
uators than about Solomon)[81] minimize the fact that Solomon's religious malfeasance is an obvious literary construct designed to explain
the awkward, unevadable fact of the schism: Yahweh authorized the
secession of the north as a punishment for Solomon's sin(s) (1 Kgs.
11:9–13, 29–39). This is pure theology which ignores the messier
social, political, economic, cultural, and personality factors which
together were certainly the effective cause of the schism. Theological
explanations of complex historical events cannot be accepted on face
value because they usually skew the facts in the service of a higher,
meta-historical agenda.[82] Since Solomon's religious misconduct is not
independently mentioned elsewhere in the biblical record (Neh. 13:26

---

[77] D. N. Freedman, "The Age of David and Solomon," *The Age of the Monarchies:
Political History* (ed. by A. Malamat; World History of the Jewish People 4:1; Jerusalem:
Massada, 1979) 123. According to R. Flint (in *Dictionary of the Bible* [ed. by J. Hastings;
Edinburgh: Clark, 1902] 4.568), Solomon's "mode of life had left him prematurely
worn out in both body and mind, so as to be . . . in a senile condition and hardly
responsible for his actions."

[78] B. W. Anderson, *Understanding the Old Testament* (3rd edn.; Englewood Cliffs:
Prentice-Hall, 1975) 196.

[79] Noth, *History of Israel*, 216.

[80] De Vries, *I Kings*, 143–4.

[81] These assessments essentially equate the "Solomon" they find in the narrative
with the "Solomon" of history, itself a dubious leap of faith. For the complexities
of "reading" the Solomon narrative see Lasine, "King of Desire," 85–118, and *idem*,
"Solomon and the Wizard of Oz: Power and Invisibility in a Verbal Palace," *The
Age of Solomon: Scholarship at the Turn of the Millennium* (ed. by L. K. Handy; SHCANE
11; Leiden/New York/Köln: Brill, 1997) 375–91.

[82] Numerous examples could be cited to illustrate this point, but one must suffice:
the attribution by Esarhaddon's scribes of the destruction of Babylon to Marduk's
anger over the Babylonians' misconduct, including religious misconduct, with no
mention of the involvement of the Assyrian army (which was, in fact, considerable)
or of the social, economic, political, and purely personal factors which had fueled

is plainly derivative), there is no *a priori* warrant for giving the accusation any benefit of the doubt.[83] As a literary construct for polemical purposes, the negative picture of Solomon may well be a complete
fabrication with little or no foundation in fact. Moreover, the pericope is suspicious on purely literary grounds: if the fairly glittering
representation of Solomon's reign in 1 Kgs. 9:26–10:29 is meant to
be even slightly critical of Solomon, as many recent commentators
contend,[84] that criticism is so understated as to be practicably inaudible,

---

Sennacherib's profoundly anti-Babylonian foreign policy; what is all the more remarkable is that this exercise in "revisionist" theological historiography took place only
a decade after the event and apparently for a primarily Babylonian (not Assyrian)
readership: see J. A. Brinkman, "Through a Glass Darkly: Esarhaddon's Retrospects
on the Downfall of Babylon," *Studies in Literature from the Ancient Near East by Members
of the American Oriental Society Dedicated to Samuel Noah Kramer* (ed. by J. M. Sasson;
American Oriental Series 65; New Haven: American Oriental Society, 1984) 35–42
(= *JAOS* 103 [1983] 35–42).

[83] For post-biblical Jewish tradition and speculation see S. J. D. Cohen, "From
the Bible to the Talmud: The Prohibition of Intermarriage," *HAR* 7 (1983) 23–39,
and especially *idem*, "Solomon and the Daughter of Pharaoh: Intermarriage, Conversion,
and the Impurity of Women," *JANES* 16–17 (1984–1985) 23–37, and the literature
cited there (especially p. 24 n. 3); L. S. Schearing, "A Wealth of Women: Looking
Behind, Within, and Beyond Solomon's Story," and S. R. Shimoff, "The Hellenization
of Solomon in Rabbinic Texts," *The Age of Solomon: Scholarship at the Turn of the
Millennium* (ed. by L. K. Handy; SHCANE 11; Leiden/New York/Köln: Brill, 1997)
428–56, and 457–69, respectively. For the treatment of Solomon by Josephus see
also L. H. Feldman, "Josephus as an Apologist to the Greco-Roman World: His
Portrait of Solomon," *Aspects of Religious Propaganda in Judaism and Early Christianity*
(ed. by E. Schluser-Fiorenza; Notre Dame, IN: University of Notre Dame, 1976)
69–98, *idem*, "Josephus' Portrait of Solomon," *HUCA* 66 (1982) 103–67 (abbreviated
as "Josephus' View of Solomon," *The Age of Solomon: Scholarship at the Turn of the
Millennium* [ed. by L. K. Handy; SHCANE 11; Leiden/New York/Köln: Brill, 1997]
348–74), and D. C. Duling, "The Eleazar Miracle and Solomon's Magical Wisdom
in Flavius Josephus's *Antiquitates Judaicae* 8.42–49," *HTR* 78 (1985) especially 12–23.

[84] Including K. I. Parker, "Repetition as a Structuring Device in 1 Kings 1–11,"
JSOT 42 (1988) 19–27, and *idem*, "Solomon the Philosopher King? The Nexus of
Law and Wisdom in 1 Kings 1–11," *JSOT* 53 (1992) 75–91; L. Eslinger, *Into the
Hands of the Living God* (Bible and Literature Series 24; JSOTSup 84; Sheffield:
Almond, 1989) ch. 5; M. Brettler, "The Structure of 1 Kings 1–11," *JSOT* 49
(1991) 87–97; A. Frisch, "Structure and its Significance: The Narrative of Solomon's
Reign (1 Kings 1–12.24)," *JSOT* 51 (1991) 3–14; J. T. Walsh, "Symmetry and the
Sin of Solomon," *Shofar* 12 (1993) 11–27, and *idem*, "The Characterization of Solomon
in First Kings 1–5," *CBQ* 57 (1995) 471–93; E. G. Newing, "Rhetorical Art of the
Deuteronomist: Lampooning Solomon in First Kings," *Old Testament Essays* 7 (1994)
247–60; M. A. Sweeney, "The Critique of Solomon in the Josianic Edition of the
Deuteronomistic History," *JBL* 114 (1995) 607–22; P. A. Viviano, "Glory Lost: The
Reign of Solomon in the Deuteronomistic History," *The Age of Solomon: Scholarship
at the Turn of the Millennium* (ed. by L. K. Handy; SHCANE 11; Leiden/New York/
Köln: Brill, 1997) 336–47; D. S. Williams, "Once Again: The Structure of the
Narrative of Solomon's Reign," *JSOT* 86 (1999) 49–66.

in sharp and clumsy contrast to the neon-like obtrusiveness of the criticism in chapter 11; it is strange indeed that the same narrator who daubs the tarnish on Solomon's reign so artfully now feels compelled to sketch his downfall in this artless, ham-fisted fashion "to prevent any misunderstanding about the great King Solomon."[85] Clearly, the literary and compositional aspects of this material must be sifted carefully before jumping to historical conclusions about the "historical Solomon."

The relevant textual evidence also is problematic (cf. LXX).[86] 1 Kgs. 11:7 (MT), unlike 2 Kgs. 23:13, reports that Solomon built only one, possibly two, bamah installation(s) dedicated to only two deities at a less precisely identified location near Jerusalem. 11:8 implies that he built bamoth at this location for the deities worshipped by *each* of his foreign wives, or that he built a single bamah as a sort of pantheon for the worship of all these deities. Only three foreign deities are mentioned (Edomite, Egyptian, and "Hittite" deities [cf. 11:1] are conspicuously absent) in connection with Solomon's bamoth (1 Kgs. 11:7; 2 Kgs. 23:13) and his own apostasy (1 Kgs. 11:5, 33), but the references are inconsistent:

1 Kgs. 11:5 (lacking in LXX)	1 Kgs. 11:7
ʿaštōret ʾĕlōhê ṣîdōnîm	——
——	kĕmôš šiqquṣ môʾāb
milkôm šiqquṣ ʿammônîm	mōlek šiqquṣ bĕnê ʿammôn
	[LXX adds: Astartē bdelugmati Sidōniōn]

1 Kgs. 11:33	1 Kgs. 23:13
ʿaštōret šiqquṣ ṣîdonîm	ʿaštōret šiqquṣ ṣîdōnîm
kĕmôš ʾĕlōhê môʾāb	kĕmôš šiqquṣ môʾāb
milkôm ʾĕlōhê bĕnê-ʿammôn	milkôm tôʿăbat bĕnê-ʿammôn

These lists seem to be compositionally related in some fashion, but the nature of that relationship is not at all clear. Considerable exegetical and text-critical ingenuity has been expended (beginning already with the Versions) attempting to harmonize very similar but fundamen-

---

[85] Eslinger, *Into the Hands of the Living God*, 154.

[86] For recent discussions of the textual evidence, including earlier scholarly literature, see Knoppers, *Two Nations Under God 1*, 140–3 (with a restored *Urtext*, the point of departure for my own below), and Eynikel, *Reform of King Josiah*, especially 260–8. Cf. also the classic treatments by Burney, *Notes*, 152–7, Montgomery, *Kings*, 231–6, and Gray, *I–II Kings*, 271–80. See further below.

tally incompatible representations of a putative historical reality about which no other information exists.

Toward a New Historical Fact

2 Kgs. 23:13 reverberates intertextually with both the building notice in 1 Kgs. 11:7–8a and Ahijah's recapitulation in 11:33. The list of deities in 23:13 (which does not identify the worshippers) is virtually congruent with the one in 11:33 (which concerns Solomon [with the Versions] or the people [with MT]), but markedly different from the one in 11:7–8a (which identifies the worshippers as Solomon's wives [MT] or Solomon himself [LXX^L]) which foreshadows it synchronically. Viewed diachronically, this state of affairs suggests that the 11:33 || 23:13 couplet is primary, both verses belonging to the same compositional stratum—presumably the "Josianic" KH-2—which is either earlier or later than the stratum containing 11:7 and 11:5.

1 Kgs. 11:1–11 is an artless jumble of material, much simplified in the LXX, and no doubt reflecting a complicated compositional and textual history. It is impossible to believe that either version is the handiwork of a single author-compiler or redactor, "deuteronomistic" or otherwise:

A. *nāšîm* in vv. 1, 3b, 4, and 8 could mean either "wives" or "women." In v. 3a, however, *nāšîm* must mean "wives," glossed as *śārôt* ("princesses," or the like), and differentiated from "concubines" (*pilagšîm*); *nāšîm* elsewhere in the pericope must mean "women" for consistency, unless we suppose that his concubines did not theologically seduce him but his wives did. If the seductresses are meant to be specifically his wives, however, mention of other women in v. 3a needlessly confuses the issue.

B. MT v. 1a characterizes Solomon's "wives/women" with two uncoordinated qualifiers, *nākĕrîyôt* and *rabôt*. The LXX differentiates the two concepts in its ordering of this material: the pericope begins with *kai ho basileus Salōmōn en philogunēs*, probably representing *wĕhammelek šĕlōmōh 'āhab nāšîm rabôt* of MT v.1aα,[87] followed by MT v. 3; this is followed by a second equivalent of MT v. 1a which speaks only to the foreign-ness of Solomon's women (*kai elabe gunaikas allotrias, kai tēn thugatera pharaō*), followed

---

[87] *Philogunēs*, like Eng. "womanizer," implies more than a few women.

by v. 2. Both the list of nations (v. 1b) and the quoted scripture (v. 2a) speak to the foreign-ness of the women, while v. 3 speaks to their number.

C. The reference to Pharaoh's daughter (v. 1aβ: *wĕ'et-bat-parʿōh*) usually is seen as a late gloss because it sits ungrammatically at the head of the uncoordinated list of nations in v. 1b to which it is assumed to belong,[88] but it follows quite naturally after the reference to Solomon's other amours, reminding the reader of her introduction in 3:1b.[89] Significantly, this is the only reference to Pharaoh's daughter that occupies exactly the same place in the MT and LXX versions.

D. The MT and the LXX contain slightly different lists of foreign women whom Solomon "loved," in addition to Pharaoh's daughter.[90] The original list included at least "Moabites" (#1), "Ammonites" (#2), "Edomites" (#3b), and "Hittites" (#5) which appear in the same position in both series; the MT adds "Sidonians" (#4, an intertextual inference from 5:15–27?), the LXX adds "Arameans" (#3a, a dittograph of "Edomites" [#3b]?) and "Amorites" (#6), and it is impossible to determine whether any of these are also original. There is no obvious model for any permutation of these items; the closest is Ezra 9:1–2 (with 4–5 matches), a list of "the peoples of the lands" with whom the people and religious leaders of Yehud had wrongfully intermarried:[91] Canaanites (possibly understood to include Sidonians [cf.

---

[88] E.g., Burney, *Notes*, 154; Montgomery, *Kings*, 231, 245 ("syntactically impossible"); Gray, *I–II Kings*, 272 n. d.; Jones, *1–2 Kings*, 233; S. J. D. Cohen, "Solomon and the Daughter of Pharaoh: Intermarriage, Conversion, and the Impurity of Women," *JANES* 16–17 (1984–1985) 26; Auld, "Solomon at Gibeon," 6*; Knoppers, *Two Nations Under God 1*, 141 n. D.

[89] Well put by Jobing ("Value of Solomon's Age," 478 [= "'Forced Labor'," 64]): "Pharaoh's daughter functions in chaps. 3–10 to establish that the cause of Solomon's eventual fall is already there when he is in his glory; simply waiting for the turn to the negative, when she will again be the very first person mentioned (11:1)." Cf. also Eslinger, *Into the Hands of the Living God*, 129–30; Sweeney, "Critique of Solomon," 613–7.

[90] For Notes D and E cf. in particular G. N. Knoppers, "Sex, Religion, and Politics: The Deuteronomist on Intermarriage," *HAR* 14 (1994) 121–41, and *idem*, "Solomon's Fall and Deuteronomy," especially 394–409.

[91] Deut. 23:4 prohibits "Ammonites and Moabites" (cf. 1 Kgs. 11:7) from entering the assembly, while v. 8 speaks more positively of "Edomites" and "Egyptians" in the same connection, a typological distinction not recognized in our lists. Neh. 13:23 speaks of "Jews who had married women of Ashdod, Ammon, and Moab." "Moabites and Ammonites," together with men from Edom, figure in 2 Chronicles 20: for these nationalities in the context of post-Exilic concerns see P. R. Davies,

Gen. 10:15]), Hittites, Perizzites, Jebusites, Ammonites, Moabites, Egyptians, and Amorites,[92] including five of the seven indigenous nations of Deut. 7:1–5 (cf. Ex. 34:11–16; 1 Kgs. 9:20) with whom the Israelites are not to intermarry and of which only "Hittites" and "Amorites" also occur in our lists.

E. The scriptural citation (v. 2a) also has no obvious model. It distantly resembles Deut. 7:3, but most closely approximates Josh. 23:11–12, a portion of Joshua's exhortation which deals with sexual intercourse (*B'*, as here) and intermarriage with the "nations left here among you" (cf. v. 11). Particularly striking is the fact that the citation is identified as Yahweh's words, from which it can be inferred that the original source had already achieved an authoritative scriptural status and thus may antedate the citation by some considerable time.

F. V. 3a is the stuff of legend and folklore, not of daybooks or court histories—700 wives and 300 concubines would have constituted two-fifths the estimated population of Jerusalem (the "City of David") at this time![93] *śārôt* in v. 3a and all of v. 3b are not in the LXX version.

"Defending the Boundaries of Israel in the Second Temple Period: 2 Chronicles 20 and the 'Salvation Army'," *Priests, Prophets and Scribes: Essays on the Formation and Heritage of Second Temple Judaism in Honour of Joseph Blenkinsopp* (ed. E. Ulrich *et al.*; JSOTSup 149; Sheffield: JSOT, 1992) 43–54.

[92] For discussion of this material see the commentaries and T. Ishida, "The Structure and Historical Implications of the Lists of Pre-Israelite Nations," *Bib* 60 (1979) 461–90. M. Fishbane sees the "Ammonites" and "Moabites" as a "tendentious addition" in both Ezra 9:1 and Neh. 13:23 (*Biblical Interpretation in Ancient Israel* [Oxford: Clarendon, 1985] 124 n. 52).

[93] Y. Shiloh, "The Population of Iron Age Palestine in the Light of a Sample Analysis of Urban Plans, Areas, and Population Density," *BASOR* 239 (1980) 30. Nonetheless, according to N. H. Snaith, "there is no need to doubt the accuracy of these numbers" ("The First and Second Books of Kings: Introduction and Exegesis," *IB* [1954] 3.102); cf. Gray, *I–II Kings*, 274. On the "sixty queens and eighty concubines" mentioned in Song 6:8 see M. H. Pope, *Song of Songs* (AB 7C; Garden City: Doubleday, 1977) 567–9; cf. Schearing, "Wealth of Women," 446–7 and n. 61. By contrast, Rehoboam is credited with eighteen wives and sixty concubines (2 Chron. 1:21), Abijah with fourteen wives (2 Chron. 13:21), and David with only seven wives (1 Chron. 3:1–9) and a similarly modest number of concubines (2 Sam. 15:16). If the numbers for Rehoboam and Abijah are artificial, reflecting the Chronicler's ideological understanding of royal family-size, the gargantuan size of Solomon's harem in Kings is all the more suspicious. On Rehoboam's Ammonite mother see now A. Malamat, "Naamah, the Ammonite Princess, King Solomon's Wife," *RB* 106 (1999) 35–40, pointing out that Solomon's regnal years indicate that the marriage was arranged by David and thus was not a Solomonic initiative.

G. The LXX version of 11:4aβ–8 orders the material very differently
   from the MT: 4b→4aβ→7→5a→8→6. MT v. 5 (two deities worshipped by Solomon) and MT v. 7 (two deities for which Solomon
   built a bamah) are merged to form a single triad of deities as in
   11:33 and 2 Kgs. 23:13, but in an aberrant word-order: Kemosh-
   "Milkom,"[94]-Astoreth, rather than Astoreth-Kemosh-Milkom.

H. The formal evaluation of Solomon (v. 6) more naturally comes
   at the end of the unit in the LXX, but this is at odds with its
   typical KH placement as "a preface to particular offenses."[95] The
   MT sequence recalls the evaluation of Manasseh (2 Kgs. 21:2a +
   3a) and the pseudo-evaluation of Rehoboam (1 Kgs. 14:22a + 23)
   where the specific offense is building bamoth; both of these passages are post-"Hezekian," and the latter almost certainly post-
   "Josianic."[96]

I. V. 8a presupposes v. 7 and supplies the antecedent for *le'lohêhen*
   in v. 8b. MT v. 8b reports, "they [Solomon's foreign wives]
   maqṭîrôt ûmēzabbeḥôt le'lohêhen," the Hiphil of *QṬR* pointing to a
   post-"Josianic" origin;[97] the LXX[L] version, however, has masc. sing.
   verbs which make Solomon himself the idolatrous worshipper as
   foreshadowed by 3:3b (probably KH-4).[98]

The MT and the LXX versions of this pericope evolved differently
from a common ancestor which can be tentatively reconstructed:

> **¹And King Solomon loved many** *foreign* **wives/women as well**
> **as Pharaoh's daughter**: *Moabites, Ammonites, Edomites,* < ~~omit w/LXX:~~
> ~~Sidonians,~~> *Hittites,* < + w/LXX: *Amorites* ' ²*from the peoples concerning*
> *whom Yahweh said to the children of Israel, "May you not penetrate them, nor*
> *they penetrate you, for surely they will turn away your heart after their gods"; to*
> *these Solomon clung in love.* ³He had 700 wives—*princesses*—and 300 con-
> cubies; <~~omit w/LXX: and his women turned away his heart.~~> ⁴**And**
> **when Solomon was old his wives/women turned away his**

---

[94] Molek was not an Ammonite deity: there is universal agreement that MT's
lmlk is a scribal error for *lmlkm* (with LXX[L] and Pesh.): see Day, *Molech*, 32, 74,
and Knoppers, *Two Nations Under God 1*, 141, 142–3 n. O.

[95] Cf. Knoppers, *Two Nations Under God 1*, 142 n. L (citing Deut. 7:4; 9:7ff.; Josh.
23:16; Judg. 2:19–20; 3:7–8; 10:6–7).

[96] For traces of an earlier actual evaluation of Rehoboam see 2 Chron. 12:13–14
and 3 Reg. 14:22–23. Cf. also the LXX "supplement" and the discussion by C. S.
Shaw, "The Sins of Rehoboam: The Purpose of 3 Kingdoms 12:4A–Z," *JSOT* 73
(1997) 55–64.

[97] With, e.g., Campbell, *Of Prophets and Kings*, 87 n. 51 ("post-dtr").

[98] This attribution is advocated in "Loving Too Well" (forthcoming).

**heart after other gods; and his heart was not wholly true with
his god Yahweh as was the heart of his father David.** <~~omit
w/LXX: ⁵And Solomon went after the Sidonian deity Ashtoreth and
the Ammonite abomination Milcom~~.> {⁶And Solomon did what was
evil in the eyes of Yahweh, and did not wholly follow Yahweh as his
father David had done.} *⁷Then Solomon built a bamah for the Moabite abomination Kemosh, and for the Ammonite abomination "Milcom,"* < + w/LXX:
and for the Sidonian abomination Ashtoreth ' *on the mountain east of [or: in the
vicinity of]*⁹⁹ *Jerusalem;* *⁸and he did so for all his foreign wives/women, burning
incense and sacrificing to their gods.*

In the earliest version of Solomon's seduction (in bold) the issue is
the number of seductresses, consistent with Deut. 17:17a's admoni-
tion that a king should "not multiply wives for himself, lest his heart
turn away,"[100] but using NṬH rather than SWR to describe their
impact on his "heart."[101] Commentators who detect critical elements
in the preceding presentation of Solomon's reign[102] find the rationale of that criticism also in the "Law of the King," and its presentation understated as here with the criticism softened by having
Solomon in his dotage at the time (recalling the example of David
[1 Kgs. 1:1–4]). If the reference to Pharaoh's daughter is original,
11:1a should belong to the same compositional stratum as 3:1b–2,
as 3:3a which inaugurates the *'HB* motif and which is probably
"Josianic" KH-2 or later,[103] and as the *inclusio* with 9:24a which is

---

[99] See n. 58 above.

[100] For discussion of the "Law of the King" see the commentaries and, e.g.,
F. Garcia Lopez, "Le Roi d'Israel: Dt 17:14–20," *Das Deuteronomium: Entstehung,
Gestalt und Botschaft* (ed. by N. Lohfink; BETL 68; Leuven: University, 1985) 277–97;
Brettler, "Structure of 1 Kings 1–11," 92–4; G. N. Knoppers, "The Deuteronomist
and the Deuteronomic Law of the King: A Reexamination of a Relationship," *ZAW*
108 (1996) 329–46. The pericope probably has a pre-deuteronomic core, arising
perhaps among critics of Hezekiah (cf. Isa. 2:6–9).

[101] *NṬH* used in this metaphorical way cannot be dubbed "deuteronomic phraseology" (so Weinfeld, *Deuteronomy and the Deuteronomic School*, 321) without qualification.
It occurs nowhere in Deuteronomy (cf. Deut. 16:19; 24:17, 19 [all in Hiphil]; 4:34;
5:15; 7:19; 11:2; 26:8 [all in Qal]) and is practically unique in 1 Kgs. 11:2, 3, 4
(all in Hiphil), 9 (in Qal); the closest parallels are Josh. 24:23 and 1 Kgs. 8:58, both
arguably "deuteronomistic" passages, and also Ps. 119:36, 112, and 141:4 and Prov.
2:2, and 21:1 which are not. *SWR*, used in Deut. 17:17 and frequently (e.g., 4:9;
9:12, 16; 11:16, 28; 17:20; 28:14; 31:29; 1 Kgs. 15:5; etc.) clearly is the "deutero-
nom(ist)ic" idiom. This same qualification applies to the "deuteronomic" identification of *bāmâ/bāmôt* in the sense of "cult place(s)" (*ibid.*, 323, 326) which is not found
in Deuteronomy 12 (the most relevant pericope to find it) or elsewhere in that
corpus.

[102] See the references cited in n. 84 above.

[103] As advocated in "Loving Too Well" (forthcoming).

no earlier than KH-2.[104] It is reasonable to suppose that all of these are the handiwork of the "Josianic" KH-2 author-compiler. This *Urtext* was revised at least once and substantially, shifting the focus to the foreign-ness of Solomon's wives. Stylistically, the new material (in italics) was added appositionally, as if an alternative version or pesher-like exposition is being appended to the original. The triad of deities preserved in LXX v.7 is an inverted quotation of the normative list in v. 33 and 2 Kgs. 23:13[105] and thus KH-3 or later,[106] the verse "correcting" the *Urtext* by taking note of the creation of the bamoth attacked by Josiah, and later redistributed in MT to create v. 5 as a doublet of sorts.[107] V. 8b, if the LXX[L] reading is accepted,[108] would close an *inclusio* with 3:3b—also KH-3 or later[109]—darkening Solomon's entire reign with the shadow of idolatry; in terms of narrative continuity, the bamoth built by Solomon in 11:7 (|| 23:13) are those at which he himself worshipped according to 3:3b. V. 3a is a parenthetical interpolation like 9:16; although it is compatible with the proposed original of v. 1a (but cf. Note A above), it probably was added subsequently as an amplification of it.[110] V. 6 may have been added to v. 4aβ by means of a *Wiederaufnahme*

---

[104] *Ibid.*

[105] For the stylistic device see Beentjes, "Inverted Quotations in the Bible," 506–23, and Peckham, "Writing and Editing," especially 366–71.

[106] The relatively rare *'āz* + Imperfect construction used in 11:7aα, suggests an interpolation only redactionally related to its immediate context: see I. Rabinowitz, "*'āz* Followed by Imperfect Verb-Forms in Preterite Contexts: A Redactional Device in Biblical Hebrew," *VT* 34 (1984) 53–62.

[107] The locational notice in v. 7aβ (*bāhār 'ăšer 'al-pĕnê yĕrûšālāim*) is missing from the LXX and is usually considered a secondary harmonization with 2 Kgs. 23:13: so, e.g., Burney, *Notes*, 154; Montgomery, *Kings*, 232; Gray, *I–II Kings*, 273 n. b, 279; Jones, *1–2 Kings*, 236; De Vries, *I Kings*, 142 n. b, 143; Campbell, *Of Prophets and Kings*, 87 n. 51; Knoppers, *Two Nations Under God 1*, 142 n. N. In my opinion, the original addition contained both the triad of deities and the locational notice, and was imperfectly preserved in both the MT (by breaking up the triad) and the LXX (by omitting the locational notice).

[108] See Knoppers, *Two Nations Under God 1*, 141, 143 n. R. Few modern commentators adopt this reading, but Knoppers points out that the other ancient readings can be best explained as attempts to absolve Solomon from this extremely defaming example of idolatry (cf. the Chronicler's Solomon); cf. also Burney, *Notes*, 154–5. For a revocalization of MT yielding references to cultic equipment see M. Cohen, "*maqṭîrôt ûmĕzabbĕḥôt lĕ'lōhêhen* (1 Rois xi 8b)," *VT* 41 (1991) 332–41.

[109] As advocated in "Loving Too Well" (forthcoming).

[110] If not an actual *Wiederaufnahme*, *wayyattû nāšāyw 'et-libbô* in v. 3b certainly resonates with *nāšāyw hiṭṭû 'et-lĕbābô* in v. 4a. V. 3b is not found in the LXX, however, and may be spurious: cf. Knoppers, *Two Nations Under God 1*, 141 n. A.

(... *kĕdāwid ʾābîw* in both) before or concurrently with the addition of vv. 7–8; use of the evaluative *hārāʿ* points to a definitely post-"Hezekian," probably post-"Josianic" origin. If vv. 3 and/or 6 represent an intermediate stage (post-"Josianic" KH-3),[111] the refocusing of the pericope and the addition of 3:3 would have occurred at a later stage (KH-4), closer in time to the post-Exilic mixed-marriage controversy reported in Ezra 9–10 and Neh. 13:23–30a.

1 Kgs 11:7–8 is thus a imperfect, secondary, midrashic attempt to place the datum reported in 2 Kgs. 23:13 in an historical context: "it was in the course of [*ʾāz*] the turning of his heart by his foreign wives that Solomon built a bamah...." By this analysis, 23:13 originally had no counterpart in 1 Kings 11. Indeed, there is no reason to expect it to have been otherwise: "the horses which the kings of Judah had dedicated to the sun" at the entrance to the Temple (23:11), the altars "which the kings of Judah had made" on its roof (v. 12a), and the komer-priests "whom the kings of Judah had ordained to burn offerings in the bamoth in the cities of Judah and around Jerusalem" (v. 5a) are introduced to the reader with no informational forewarning of any kind (so also Ahaz's "dial" [20:9–11]). These notices, like v. 13,[112] presumably also refer to phenomena which actually existed in the Josianic era and were affected by his religious pogrom even though the author-compilers of the KH did not see fit to mention them earlier. In the case of Solomon's bamoth, this oversight was corrected secondarily and imperfectly by the insertion of 11:7–8.[113]

If this compositional analysis approximates reality, the only likely historical datum in this material is the claim in 2 Kgs. 23:13 that Josiah "defiled" one or more cultic installations[114] on the Mount of

---

[111] If 11:3 is KH-3, the fact that the Chronicler's account contains no echo of this verse would support the contention that his *Vorlage* was the "Josianic" KH-2 edition.

[112] *Pace* Gleis who considers 23:13 to be "historisch völlig unglaubwürdig" (*Bamah*, 111 and n. 595).

[113] The same impulse that prompted the secondary identification of "Ahaz's upper-chamber" in 23:12a (see p. 76 and n. 43 above).

[114] The common assumption from 2 Kgs. 23:13 is that three "bamoth" (*bāmôt*), one for each deity listed, were "defiled," even though 1 Kgs. 11:7aα claims only one "bamah" (*bāmâ*). Whatever the compositional origin of 11:7aα, it is hard to account for this discrepancy: if 11:7aα is secondary and dependent on 23:13, it must be the handiwork of an incredibly inattentive and careless redactor; if it antedates 23:13, the pl. there must be questioned. The LXX of 23:13 presupposes *hbyt* ("the house") rather than MT's *hbmwt* ("the bamoth"), a unique reading customar-

Olives which were reputedly constructed by Solomon. The factuality of the Solomonic attribution is suspect for the reasons cited above. It is probably legendary (cf. the attribution of Nehushtan to Moses [18:4b]), more in the nature of a folkloristic etiology than a remembered fact, and as such perhaps derives from the reign of Hezekiah. The antiquarian interest in Solomon by "the men of Hezekiah" (Prov. 25:1) surely was not limited to his legendary wisdom.[115] This interest would have been linked to the political agenda of that regime and its apologists, both before and after the disaster of 701; the internationalism which brought power and prosperity to Solomon's legendary Israel would have been seen as an historical precedent and validating paradigm for Hezekiah's policies and pretensions on the international scene (cf. 2 Kgs. 20:12–19; 2 Chron. 32:27–29).[116]

---

ily ignored or dismissed as a scribal mistake (*hupsēlon* in 1 Kgs. 11:7 rules out a deliberate harmonization). It is not impossible that the translator's *Vorlage* actually read *hbmh* of which *hbyt* might be considered a somewhat easier corruption. The evidence, such as it is, raises the possibility that Solomon was credited with having built a *single* bamah-installation for the worship of several foreign deities, and that Josiah "defiled" that installation. As a "house" for multiple deities, Solomon's bamah would have mirrored his Temple in Josiah's day functionally (cf. 23:4) and perhaps to some extent even architecturally: standing opposite each other on supernaturally-charged mountains, separated by the Wadi Kidron with its tombs and other necromantic associations, they would certainly have been seen as rival cultic "houses" by Josiah and other adherents of a "reformed" state-sponsored Yahwism.

[115] Few would disagree with J. L. Crenshaw's assessment (*Old Testament Wisdom: An Introduction* [Atlanta: John Knox, 1981] 94; cf. pp. 45, 48): "There is no reason for the tradition to arise associating Hezekiah with wisdom unless a historical basis for such thinking existed, although legends do seem to cling to this king (Isaiah 36–39) just as they do to Solomon, whom Hezekiah sought to resemble." That the reference is the fictive product of intertextual exegesis (cf. the "historical" superscriptions of certain psalms) is well argued by M. Carasik, "Who Were the 'Men of Hezekiah' (Proverbs xxv 1)?" *VT* 44 (1994) 289–300, but I am not convinced.

[116] See Chapter 7.A above. The Chronicler casts Hezekiah positively as a second Solomon: see 2 Chron. 30:26 and cf. 32:23 with 9:13–16, 22–24; see further, in addition to the commentaries, Halpern, "Sacred History and Ideology," 50–2, M. A. Throntveit, "Hezekiah in the Books of Chronicles," *Society of Biblical Literature 1988 Seminar Papers* (SBLSP 27; ed. by D. L. Lull; Atlanta: Scholars, 1988) 302–11, and *idem*, "The Idealization of Solomon as the Glorification of God in the Chronicler's Royal Speeches and Royal Prayers," *The Age of Solomon: Scholarship at the Turn of the Millennium* (ed. by L. K. Handy; SHCANE 11; Leiden/New York/Köln: Brill, 1997) 411–27. The comparison in Kings is more equivocal: e.g., Hezekiah's hospitality toward the visiting envoys of Merodach-baladan (2 Kgs. 20:13) echoes Solomon's treatment of the Queen of Sheba (1 Kgs. 10:1–13), but is construed negatively by Isaiah's commentary (vv. 14–19), at least some of which is secondary (vv. 17–19, perhaps KH-3: cf., e.g., Gray, *I–II Kings*, 702; Jones, *1–2 Kings*, 584, 590; Cogan-Tadmor, *II Kings*, 262–3): for discussion see C. T. Begg, "2 Kings 20:12–19 as an Element of the Deuteronomistic History," *CBQ* 48 (1986) 27–38, and for historical

Hezekiah's various construction projects and administrative initiatives (e.g., those implied by the *lmlk*-stamped jars) have Solomonic ana-logues.[117] It is conceivable that the "Solomonic" bamah-installation(s) came into existence or was(were) revitalized at this time.

The claim that one of Solomon's wives was the daughter of Pharaoh (1 Kgs. 3:1b; 9:16; 9:24; 11:1) also suits a Hezekian context and, in a different arrangement reflecting well on Solomon (cf. LXX, except-ing 11:1), probably belongs to the KH-1 stratum of material.[118] That a "Hezekian" work would capitalize on a tradition associating Solomon with Egypt to his benefit can be inferred from Egypt's likely role in Hezekiah's maneuverings on the international scene (cf., e.g., Isa. 20; 31:1-7; 31:1-3),[119] as well as the strong cultural interest in things Egyptian among some Judahite elites during this period[120]—not least four unique cube-shaped tombs at Silwan (#3, 28, 34, 35), cut out from the bedrock on three or four sides, each with an Egyptian-style cornice along the upper edge of the facade, a gabled ceiling, and in some cases (unquestionably #3, the so-called "Tomb of Pharaoh's Daughter") a pyramid-shaped roof. These tombs are dated to the late 8th century on palaeographic grounds (the Shebna inscription from tomb #35), and the earliest of the simpler and more numer-ous Silwan tombs with flat ceilings probably are contemporary.[121] The unknown individual buried in Tomb #3 certainly was a person of consequence in Hezekiah's court, a colleague of the majordomo Shebna, another of Hezekiah's "new men" perhaps even of Egyptian ancestry.

The locational notice for Solomon's bamah/oth in 2 Kgs. 23:13 could equally describe the location of the Silwan cemetery which Josiah also attacked, suggesting that the cultic installation(s) may have

---

analogues see *idem*, "Hezekiah's Display (2 Kgs. 20,12–19)," *BN* 38–39 (1987) 14–8. The historical context of this episode is the inter-national political situation of the late 8th century. For a recent overview of the period see Ahlström, *History of Ancient Palestine*, 692–716.

[117] See Chapter 7 n. 21 above.

[118] As argued in my "Loving Too Well" (forthcoming).

[119] For Egypt's international machinations during this period see, e.g., Bright, *History*, 280–1, 284–6; Miller-Hayes, *History of Ancient Judah and Israel*, 352–3, 358–63; Ahlström, *History of Ancient Palestine*, 692–6.

[120] E.g., Hezekiah's seal which bears a 2-winged beetle pushing a ball of dung symbolizing the rising sun, familiar from Egypt and Phoenicia and consistent with the iconography of the contemporary *lmlk* sealings: see Chapter 7 (p. 161 and n. 83) above.

[121] Ussishkin, *Village of Silwan*, 43–63, 281–2, 320–32. Cf. also Chapter 7.B above.

been related to the tombs in some way. It is possible, for example, that the installation(s) too was/were carved out of the mountain (thereby accounting for its/their physical survival since Solomon's day?) rather than erected on top of it.[122] The earliest extant rock-cut structures in the Silwan necropolis are several Phoenician-like tombs with gabled ceilings, many unfinished, plausibly dating from the mid-9th century before the anti-Phoenician purge engineered by Jehoiada stopped construction.[123] Some euhemeristic explanation(s) of these tombs (more "politically correct" than their historical connection to Athaliah) surely had arisen by Hezekiah's era for Shebna and his colleagues to construct their tombs nearby: perhaps they were imagined to have been part of the "house" Solomon allegedly built for Pharaoh's daughter, and/or the bamoth he allegedly built for three foreign deities;[124] perhaps several of these and/or the foreign-looking monolithic tombs had by Josiah's day become associated with cultic practices to which the reformers objected;[125] finally, although the earliest extant Silwan structures may be no earlier than the mid-9th century, it is possible that a few structures now obliterated by later quarrying could not have been cut out of the slope further north as early as Solomon's reign when foreign (notably Phoenician) architectural style was in vogue in the new governmental citadel on the other side of the Wadi Kidron.

---

[122] 2 Kgs. 23:13, so precise in identifying the mountain, is silent on the relationship of Solomon's installation(s) to the mountain, but *bāhār* in 11:7a (literally "in the mountain"; so too the location of the cemetery in 23:16) points in this direction; so does Isaiah's reference to Shebna's tomb *bassela*ʿ (literally "in the rock" [Isa. 22:16b]) which well describes the monolithic "Tomb of the Royal Steward" (#35).

[123] See Ussishkin, *Village of Silwan*, 43–63, 281–2, 320–32.

[124] It was once supposed (e.g., by F. de Saulcy in 1854) that the "Tomb of Pharaoh's Daughter" (#3) was a small temple in Egyptian style erected by Solomon for his Egyptian wife, and G. Perrot and C. Chipiez (in 1890) supposed it was actually "one of the cult places established by Solomon [which later] was demolished and it was decided to hew out a tomb" (*apud* Ussishkin, *Village of Silwan*, 4, 45, also noting Vincent's report [1912] that some Jerusalem Christians in his day called the tomb "Madhbah Bint Farʿun," "Altar of Pharaoh's Daughter" [p. 43 n. 3]).

[125] Analogous to Kenyon's "Cave 1," halfway down the slope of the south-eastern hill in Jerusalem, above the Gihon spring (see Chapter 5 n. 47 above). It appears to have been a tomb "recycled" for some other function which came to an end with the erection of the new inner city-wall and adjacent street c. 700. Although its new function is disputed, it possibly served as the "shop" for an intermediary of some sort, "where [poorer] people came to make offerings to enhance fertility, or to have their fortunes told" (Steine, "Two Popular Cult Sites," 25; cf. Prag, "Summary of the Reports," in Eshel-Prag, *Excavations by K. M. Kenyon in Jerusalem 1961–1967*, 4, 209–16).

In any event, the proximity of the Kidron tombs supports the sup-position that "filling their places with human bones" in v. 14b refers to the means by which Solomon's bamah/oth was/were "defiled."[126] The grammatical antecedent of *mĕqômām* in 23:14b is not the fem. *bāmôt* (much less the sing. **bāmâ*) in v. 13, but the masc. *šiqquṣ* (used twice) and by association the fem. *tô'ăbâ*: as Josiah's purification of the Temple focused on the cultic paraphernalia of the deities housed there, his "defilement" of Solomon's bamah/oth focused on the deities who resided there, undoubtedly in the form of their cult-images whose "places" (cf. the cult niche containing three stelae in the Arad temple)[127] were filled with bones. The bones used in the "defiling" of the bamoth in "the cities of Judah" (v. 8a) may have replaced the cult objects there. And like Solomon's Temple, his bamah/oth too had an altar which also was "defiled" by contact with human bones which in this instance were burned as well (v. 16a). 2 Chron. 34:4–5 suggests that the Chronicler may have thought that the altar was below the bamah, somewhere in the Kidron/Hinnom complex, and this could well be historically correct, the ideological function of an altar as a nexus with "the other world" facilitating the devel-opment of the Gehenna tradition.[128]

9.D. THE TOPHET IN THE BEN-HINNOM VALLEY

The "tophet" in the Ben-Hinnom Valley also was "defiled" (v. 10), but this verse is probably secondary to the "original" reform report (see Chapter 5.E above) and there is no indication of the manner of "defilement" envisioned by the author-compiler responsible for this notice. Jer. 7:32 envisions burying in Tophet, while v. 33 (in the manner of a neo-Assyrian treaty curse) promises that the unburied or disinterred "corpses of this people will be food for the birds of the air and for the beasts of the field" (cf. 19:6–9). Both passages

---

[126] So, e.g., Miller-Hayes, *History of Ancient Israel and Judah*, 398: "Also defiled were the high places (altar shrines) on the mountain east of Jerusalem ('Mount of Olives'). . . . Their pillars were broken, the Asherahs were cut down, and the site strewn with human bones, rendering them unclean."

[127] See the works cited in Chapter 8 n. 21 and this chapter nn. 13–17 above. Cf. the LB temple at Hazor, on which see G. W. Ahlström, "Heaven on Earth— At Hazor and Arad," *Religious Syncretism in Antiquity* (ed. by B. A. Pearson; Missoula: Scholars, 1975) 67–83.

[128] See Chapter 3 n. 26 above.

imagine that human corpses will be used, in different ways, to impede the normal cultic activity conducted there—a rhetorical "defilement," consistent with the methodology used by Josiah to "defile" the bamoth in "the cities of Judah" and on the Mount of Olives in the "original" reform report—which provides an intertextual explanation of the "defilement" of the tophet in 23:10. This intertextual connection may belie a compositional one insofar as 23:10 may be, in fact, a doublet of 23:16a.

CHAPTER TEN

SOME HISTORICAL ASPECTS OF JOSIAH'S REFORM (IV): THE MAN AND THE MONUMENT

Two issues arising from the preceding analyses of 1 Kings 13 and 2 Kgs. 23:4–20, although beyond the primary concerns of the present work, nonetheless call for comment.

10.A. THE MAN BEHIND THE MAN-OF-GOD

History does know of a Judahite prophet, who disclaimed to be called such, who visited Bethel and there made oracular pronouncement against its sanctuary and priesthood in the reign of a king named "Jeroboam." The similarities between what is known about Amos of Tekoa from the book bearing his name and what is reported about the anonymous Judahite man-of-god in 1 Kings 13 are striking, but the differences (as most commentators are also quick to point out) would seem to preclude more than a tangential relationship between the two figures.[1] The analyses presented above have found the most damaging biographical discrepancies—identification of the king as Jeroboam b. Nebat, his direct personal encounter with the man-of-god, the destruction of the altar while the man-of-god is present, the episode with the old prophet from Bethel and its aftermath—to be literary creations with no claim to factuality. The burning of bones rings true (cf. Amos 2:1; 6:10), but many other similarities in content are also fictional—destruction of the altar (cf. 3:14; 9:1a), slaughter of the Bethel priesthood (cf. 7:17; 8:3; 9:1b), the destruction of the bamoth-houses and their altars (cf. 2:8a, 14a; 7:9), a lion as an agent of personal destruction (cf. 3:4, 8, 12; 5:19), theological wordplay with the verb *ŠWB* (cf. 4:6–11).[2] But the book of Amos is no

---

[1] Cf. Lemke, "Way of Obedience," 315–6; McKenzie, *Trouble with Kings*, 55–6. For a more sympathetic appraisal see J. L. Crenshaw, *Prophetic Conflict: Its Effect upon Israelite Religion* (BZAW 124; Berlin/New York: de Gruyter, 1971) 39–49 (especially 41–2).

[2] Cf. further C. Levin, "Amos und Jeroboam I," *VT* 45 (1995) 307–17.

more a compositional unity than are 1 Kings 13 and 1 Kgs. 23:4–20:
it is the product of an analogous creative process whereby material
directly attributable to Amos himself was augmented over time by
"remembered deeds and sayings of the prophet," transmitted sepa-
rately, and by material with no connection to the historical Amos
at all.[3] The biographical narrative, the only account of Amos's visit
to Bethel (7:10–17),[4] is obviously one such augmentation, and it need
not stand closer to the historical realities of that visit than 2 Kgs.
23:4–20 *in toto* does to the historical realities of Josiah's reform. The
historical Amos stands behind the Amos of 7:10–17, and in the same
way but at greater distance he probably stands behind the man-of-
god of 1 Kgs. 13:1–32 and 2 Kgs. 23:16–18,[5] but he is not identical with either.

One example must suffice to illustrate the relationship between
Amos and 1 Kgs. 13:1–10. The Amos tradition knows of an earthquake which seriously damaged the Bethel sanctuary. Amos 9:1a,
which undoubtedly derives directly from Amos himself, envisions
Yahweh "standing upon the altar" directing the "shattering" and
"shaking" of structural components of the sanctuary (cf. 7:13b) in
what seems certainly to be earthquake imagery.[6] It is reasonable to
suppose that he also foresaw the altar being damaged in the same
fashion; the Amos corpus only records the prediction that "the horns
of the altar will be cut off and fall to the ground" (3:14b), juxtaposed with the "smiting" of the royal residences (v. 15a; cf. 6:11) as
the capitals of the sanctuary are "smitten" in 9:1a. A compiler of
the corpus associates Amos's career with an earthquake in the reigns
of Jeroboam II of (North-)Israel and Uzziah of Judah (1:1). That
this was an exceptionally destructive earthquake is evident in the

---

[3] See, e.g., Wolff, *Joel and Amos*, 106–13 (quotation from p. 108).

[4] See the pertinent discussions by P. R. Ackroyd, "A Judgment Narrative between
Kings and Chronicles? An Approach to Amos 7:9–17," *Canon and Authority: Essays
in Old Testament Religion and Theology* (ed. by G. W. Coats and B. O. Long: Philadelphia:
Fortress, 1977) 71–87, and H. G. M. Williamson, "The Prophet and the Plumb-
Line: A Redaction-Critical Study of Amos vii," *OTS* 26 (1990) 101–21 (especially
pp. 119–21); cf. now J. K. Hoffmeier, "Once Again the 'Plumb Line' Vision of
Amos 7.7–9: An Interpretive Clue from Egypt?" *Boundaries of the Ancient Near Eastern
World: A Tribute to Cyrus H. Gordon* (ed. by M. Lubetski *et al.*; JSOTSup 273; Sheffield:
Sheffield Academic, 1998) 304–19.

[5] Cf. G. W. Ahlström, "King Josiah and the *DWD* of Amos vi.10," *JSS* 26 (1981)
7–9 and especially n. 5.

[6] *Pace* J. Ouellete, "The Shaking of the Thresholds in Amos 9:1," *HUCA* 43
(1977) 23–7.

archaeological record;[7] it may well have seriously damaged the Bethel sanctuary, including its altar, and just conceivably might have occurred while a ritual was in progress. 1 Kgs. 13:3 + 5 imagines that altar to have been split apart by some extraordinary means, such as an earthquake, during the reign of a king "Jeroboam" as predicted by a visiting Judahite man-of-god. These verses preserve not the actual words of the historical Amos, but his "remembered deeds and sayings" echoing 3:4b and 9:1a but not otherwise documented in the Amos corpus.

The vitality of the Amos tradition may be further demonstrated by Zech. 14:1–5. This late eschatological prophecy envisions a catastrophic earthquake from which the people of Judah will flee "as you fled from the earthquake in the days of Uzziah" (v. 5b), an obvious allusion to both Amos 1:1 and 9:1b–4. The image of Yahweh standing upon the mountain which splits in two beneath him (v. 4) recalls his stance atop the Bethel altar directing the destruction of the sanctuary in Amos 9:1a, but it duplicates exactly the impossible scene of Jeroboam standing upon that altar while it breaks apart under his feet in 1 Kgs. 13:1–7. The mountain in question is the Mount of Olives. Given the numerous examples of earthquake imagery in a theophanic context which might as well have been used in this passage (cf. Mic. 1:2–9 and especially Amos 4:13),[8] this instance of inner-biblical exegesis triangulates Amos, the Judahite man-of-god, and the Mount of Olives—a combination based either on a biblical representation of Josiah's reform in which 2 Kgs. 23:16–20 was not preceded by v. 15, or on the dim recollection that Amos as the Judahite man-of-god had been buried in Jerusalem near the Mount of Olives.[9]

---

[7] See Chapter 9 n. 73 above.

[8] Cf. recently C. L. Meyers and E. M. Meyers, *Zechariah 9–14* (AB 25C; New York: Doubleday, 1993) 415–29, 495–8 (especially pp. 419–21). Meyers-Meyers minimize the direct allusion to Ezek. 11:23 and overlook the indirect allusion to 1 Kgs. 13:1–7.

[9] A recollection perhaps reinforced by the survival of the "monument." This probably should be viewed as a Jerusalem folk-tradition comparable to the one spanning some 700 years and which proves to be historically credible, discussed by Ussishkin, "'Camp of the Assyrians' in Jerusalem," 137–42.

10.B. Who Was Buried in Amos's Tomb?

If 2 Kgs. 23:18b is to be believed, the tomb of the man-of-god also contained the remains of a prophet who had come to Jerusalem from the region of Samaria. There is nothing implausible about this assertion. The immense increase in the size of Jerusalem and in the number of settlements in marginal areas in Judah in the century between Hezekiah and Josiah was due, at least in part, to the settling of refugees from the north;[10] these newcomers undoubtedly brought with them traditions and probably documents of various sorts, and possibly even the remains of some deceased worthies (cf. Gen. 50:25 and Ex. 13:19; Josh. 24:32). It is not at all inconceivable, therefore, for a northern prophet, coming to Judah alive or dead,[11] to have been buried in Jerusalem during this period. Nor is it impossible to imagine circumstances under which a northern prophet could have been buried in Jerusalem even earlier. If a Judahite visitor to Bethel, critical of the northern regime and of the religious and social conditions it sanctioned, could be deported for foretelling the horrors of exile, it is not beyond belief that a (North-)Israelite prophet, equally outspoken in his criticisms and no doubt equally objectionable to the authorities, might have fled across the border to escape imprisonment or death (cf. Jer. 26:20–23).

Hosea b. Beeri naturally comes to mind in this connection. His compatibility with the "deuteronom(ist)ic" movement is such that his absence in the Kings History is especially conspicuous and not easily explained.[12] The manifest points of contact between Hosea and both Deuteronomy and Jeremiah have usually been attributed to "a current of northern thought flowing down to Judah, following the fall of Samaria."[13] That current may have begun by Hosea himself

---

[10] See Chapter 7.A (especially pp. 146–8 and accompanying notes) above.

[11] Note that Eshmunazar (pp. 178–9 above) is fearful that his casket or his bones be moved to a tomb elsewhere, not that they be destroyed.

[12] Cf. C. Begg, "The Non-Mention of Amos, Hosea and Micah in the Deuteronomistic History," *BN* 32 (1986) 41–53 (with earlier literature).

[13] Weinfeld, *Deuteronomy and the Deuteronomic School*, 366; see further *idem*, "The Emergence of the Deuteronomic Movement: The Historical Antecedents," *Das Deuteronomium: Entstehung, Gestalt und Botschaft* (ed. by N. Lohfink; BETL 68; Leuven: University, 1985) 76–98, and *idem*, *Deuteronomy 1–11*, especially 44–57. For Hosean affinity with Deuteronomy see F. R. McCurley, "The Home of Deuteronomy Revisited: A Methodological Analysis of the Northern Theory," *A Light unto my Path:*

who could have taken up residence in Jerusalem (explaining the survival of his preaching in a distinctly Judahite corpus), been buried there, and, together with his sepulchral colleague Amos, was commemorated by a funerary monument which Josiah took pains to preserve.

Old Testament Studies in Honor of Jacob M. Myers (Gettysburg Theological Studies 4; Philadelphia: Temple University, 1974) 295–317; Weinfeld, *Deuteronomy and the Deuteronomic School*, Appendix B; Tigay, *Deuteronomy*, xxiii–xxiv.

BIBLIOGRAPHY

Abba, R. "Priests and Levites in Deuteronomy," *VT* 27 (1977) 257–267.

Albertz, R. *A History of Israelite Religion in the Old Testament Period 1* (trans. by J. Bowden; OTL; Louisville: Westminster/John Knox, 1994).

Abu Assaf, A. *Der Tempel von ʿAin Dara* (Damaszener Forschungen 3; Mainz am Rhein: Zabern, 1990).

Ackerman, S. "'And the Women Knead Dough': The Worship of the Queen of Heaven in Sixth-Century Judah," *Gender and Difference in Ancient Israel* (ed. by P. L. Day; Philadelphia: Fortress, 1989) 109–124.

——. "Child Sacrifice: Returning God's Gift—Barren Women Give Birth to Exceptional Children," *BRev* 9/3 (1993) 20–28, 56.

——. *Under Every Green Tree: Popular Religion in Sixth-Century Judah* (HSM 46; Atlanta: Scholars, 1992).

Ackroyd, P. R. *I–II Chronicles, Ezra, Nehemiah* (London: SCM, 1973).

——. "A Judgment Narrative between Kings and Chronicles? An Approach to Amos 7:9–17," *Canon and Authority: Essays in Old Testament Religion and Theology* (ed. by G. W. Coats and B. O. Long: Philadelphia: Fortress, 1977) 71–87.

——. "A Subject People: Judah under Persian Rule," *The Chronicler and his Age* (JSOTSup 101; Sheffield: JSOT, 1991) 188–238.

——. "The Temple Vessels: A Continuity Theme," *Studies in the Religious Tradition of the Old Testament* (London: SCM, 1987) 46–60 and accompanying notes (= *VTSup* 23 [1972] 166–181).

Aejmelaeus, A. "Function and Interpretation of *kî* in Biblical Hebrew," *JBL* 105 (1986) 193–209.

Aharoni, Y. "Excavations at Tel Beer-Sheba," *BA* 35 (1972) 111–127.

——. "Excavations at Tel Beer-Sheba: Preliminary Report of the Fourth Season, 1972," *TA* 1 (1974) 32–42.

——. "The Horned Altar at Beer-sheba," *BA* 37 (1974) 2–6.

Ahlström, G. W. "Heaven on Earth—At Hazor and Arad," *Religious Syncretism in Antiquity* (ed. by B. A. Pearson; Missoula: Scholars, 1975) 67–83.

——. *The History of Ancient Palestine from the Palaeolithic Period to Alexander's Conquest* (ed. by D. V. Edelman; JSOTSup 146; Sheffield: JSOT, 1993).

——. "King Josiah and the *DWD* of Amos vi.10," *JSS* 26 (1981) 7–9.

——. *Royal Administration and National Religion in Ancient Palestine* (SHANE 1; Leiden: Brill, 1982).

Albright, W. F., "The Site of Bethel and its Identification," *The Excavation of Bethel (1934–1960)* (ed. by J. L. Kelso; AASOR 39; Cambridge, MA; ASOR, 1968) 1–3.

——. "The High Place in Ancient Palestine," *VTSup* 4 (1957) 242–258.

Allen, L. C. "More Cuckoos in the Textual Nest: At 2 Kings xxiii.5; Jeremiah xvii.3, 4; Micah iii.3; vi.16 (LXX); 2 Chronicles xx.25 (LXX)," *JTS* 24 (1973) 69–74.

Alter, R. "Introduction to the Old Testament," *The Literary Guide to the Bible* (ed. by R. Alter and F. Kermode; Cambridge: Belknap/Harvard University, 1987) 11–35.

——. "A Literary Approach to the Bible," *Commentary* (December, 1975) 70–77.

Anbar, M. "La 'Reprise'," *VT* 38 (1988) 385–398.

Anderson, B. W. *Understanding the Old Testament* (3rd edn.; Englewood Cliffs: Prentice-Hall, 1975).

Andersen, F. I., and Freedman, D. N. *Amos* (AB 24A; New York: Doubleday, 1989).

———. *Hosea* (AB 24; Garden City: Doubleday, 1980).

Ap-Thomas, D. R. "Jerusalem," *Archaeology and Old Testament Study* (ed. by D. W. Thomas; Oxford: Clarendon, 1967) 276–295.

Ash, P. S. "Solomon's? District? List," *JSOT* 67 (1995) 67–86.

Ashe, G. *Avalonian Quest* (London: Methuen, 1982).

———. *The Discovery of King Arthur* (Garden City: Doubleday, 1985).

Auld, A. G. "The Deuteronomists and the Former Prophets, or What Makes the Former Prophets Deuteronomistic?" *Those Elusive Deuteronomists: The Phenomenon of Pan-Deuteronomism* (ed. by L. S. Schearing and S. L. McKenzie; JSOTSup 268; Sheffield: Sheffield Academic, 1999) 116–126.

———. *Kings without Privilege: David and Moses in the Story of the Bible's Kings* (Edinburgh: Clark, 1994).

———. "Prophets through the Looking Glass: Between Writings and Moses," *JSOT* 27 (1983) 3–23.

———. "Reading Joshua after Kings," *Words Remembered, Texts Renewed: Essays in Honour of John F. A. Sawyer* (ed. by J. Davies *et al.*; JSOTSup195; Sheffield: Sheffield Academic, 1995) 167–181.

———. "Salomo und die Deuteronomisten: Eine Zukunftvision?" *TZ* 48 (1992) 343–355.

———. "Solomon at Gibeon: History Glimpsed," *E-I* 24 (1993) 1*–7*.

———. "What Was the Main Source of the Books of Chronicles?" *The Chronicler as Author: Studies in Text and Texture* (ed. by M. P. Graham and S. L. McKenzie; JSOTSup 263; Sheffield: Sheffield Academic, 1999) 91–99.

Austel, H. J. *Prepositional and Non-Prepositional Complements with Verbs of Motion in Biblical Hebrew* (unpublished dissertation, University of California at Los Angeles, 1969).

Avalos, H., in *ABD* (1992) 5.1090.

Avigad, N. "Baruch the Scribe and Jerahmeel the King's Son," *IEJ* 28 (1978) 52–56.

———. "The Epitaph of a Royal Steward from Siloam Village," *IEJ* 3 (1953) 137–152.

———. "The Governor of the City," *IEJ* 26 (1976) 178–182.

———. "The 'Governor of the City' Bulla," *Ancient Jerusalem Revealed* (ed. by H. Geva; Jerusalem/Washington DC: Israel Exploration Society/Biblical Archaeological Society, 1994) 138–140.

Bagatti, B., and Milik, J. T. *Gli Scavi del "Dominus Flevit"* (Jerusalem: Franciscan, 1958).

Bailey, K. E., and Holladay, W. L. "The 'Young Camel' and the 'Wild Ass' in Jer. II 23–25," *VT* 18 (1969) 256–260.

Bailey, L. R. "Gehenna: The Topography of Hell," *BA* 49 (1986) 187–191.

Barkay, G. "A Bowl with the Hebrew Inscription *QDŠ*," *IEJ* 40 (1990) 124–129.

———. "Excavations at Ketef Hinnom in Jerusalem," *Ancient Jerusalem Revealed* (ed. by H. Geva; Jerusalem/Washington DC: Israel Exploration Society/Biblical Archaeological Society, 1994) 85–106.

———. "'Your Poor Brother': A Note on an Inscribed Bowl from Beth Shemesh," *IEJ* 41 (1991) 239–241.

———. "The Iron Age II–III," *The Archaeology of Ancient Israel* (ed. by A. Ben-Tor; trans. by R. Greenberg; New Haven/London: Yale University/Open University of Israel, 1992) 302–373.

———. "A Second 'Governor of the City' Bulla," *Ancient Jerusalem Revealed* (ed. by H. Geva) 141–144.

——— and Kloner, A. "Jerusalem Tombs from the Days of the First Temple," *BARev* 12/2 (1986) 22–39.

———, Kloner, A., and Mazar, A. "The Northern Necropolis of Jerusalem during the First Temple Period," *Ancient Jerusalem Revealed* (ed. by H. Geva; Jerusalem/Washington DC: Israel Exploration Society/Biblical Archaeological Society, 1994) 119–127.

——— and Vaughn, A. G. "*lmlk* and Official Seal Impressions from Tel Lachish," *TA* 23 (1996) 61–74.

———. "New Readings of Hezekian Official Seal Impressions," *BASOR* 304 (1996) 29–54.

Barnes, W. H. "Non-Synoptic Chronological References in the Books of Chronicles," *The Chronicler as Historian* (ed. by M. P. Graham *et al.*; JSOTSup 238; Sheffield: Sheffield Academic, 1997) 106–131.

Barnhart, C. L., *et al.* (eds.), *The Barnhart Dictionary of New English since 1963* (Bronxville/New York/San Francisco/London: Barnhart/Harper & Row, 1973).

Barrick, W. B., in *ABD* (1992) 3.196–200.

———, in *JBL* 118 (1999) 532–534.

———. "The Bamoth of Moab," *MAARAV* 7 (1991) 69–78.

———. "Burning Bones at Bethel: A Closer Look at 2 Kings 23:6a," *SJOT* 14/1 (2000) 3–15.

———. "Dynastic Politics, Priestly Succession, and Josiah's Eighth Year," *ZAW* 112 (2000) 564–582.

———. "The Funerary Character of 'High-Places' in Ancient Palestine: A Reassessment," *VT* 25 (1975) 565–595.

———. "Genealogical Notes on the 'House of David' and the 'House of Zadok'," *JSOT* (forthcoming).

———. "Loving Too Well: The Negative Portrayal of Solomon and the Composition of the Kings History," *Estudios Bíblicos* (forthcoming).

———. "On the 'Removal of the "High-Places"' in 1–2 Kings," *Bib* 55 (1974) 57–59.

———. "On the Meaning of *bêt-hab/bāmôt* and *bātê-habbāmôt* and the Composition of the of the Kings History," *JBL* 115 (1996) 621–642.

———. "What Do We Really Know about 'High Places'?" *SEÅ* 45 (1980) 50–57.

Barthélemy, D. *Critique textuelle de l'Ancien Testament 1* (OBO 50/1; Fribourg/Gottingen: Universitaires/Vandenhoeck & Ruprecht, 1982).

Becking, B. "From Apostasy to Destruction: A Josianic View on the Fall of Samaria (2 Kings 17,21–23)," *Deuteronomy and Deuteronomic Literature: Festschrift C. H. W. Brekelmans* (ed. by M. Vervenne and J. Lust; BETL 133; Leuven: University, 1997) 279–297.

Beentjes, P. C. "Inverted Quotations in the Bible: A Neglected Stylistic Pattern," *Bib* 63 (1982) 506–523.

Begg, C. T. "A Bible Mystery: The Absence of Jeremiah in the Deuteronomistic History," *IBS* 7 (1985) 139–164.

———. "The Destruction of the Calf (Ex. 32,20/Deut. 9,21)," *Das Deuteronomium: Entstehung, Gestalt und Botschaft* (ed. by N. Lohfink; BETL 68; Leuven: University, 1985) 208–251.

———. "The Destruction of the Golden Calf Revisited (Exod. 32,20/Deut. 9,21)," *Deuteronomy and Deuteronomic Literature: Festschrift C. H. W. Brekelmans* (ed. by M. Vervenne and J. Lust; BETL 133; Leuven: University, 1997) 469–479.

———. "Hezekiah's Display (2 Kgs. 20,12–19)," *BN* 38–39 (1987) 14–18.

———. "The Non-Mention of Amos, Hosea and Micah in the Deuteronomistic History," *BN* 32 (1986) 41–53.

———. "2 Kings 20:12–19 as an Element of the Deuteronomistic History," *CBQ* 48 (1986) 27–38.

Beit Arieh, I. "The Edomites in Cisjordan," *You Shall Not Abhor an Edomite for He Is your Brother: Edom and Seir in History and Tradition* (ed. by D. V. Edelman; Archaeology and Biblical Studies 3; Atlanta: Scholars, 1995) 33–40.

Ben-Dov, M. "A Fragmentary First Temple Period Hebrew Inscription from the Ophel," *Ancient Jerusalem Revealed* (ed. by H. Geva; Jerusalem/Washington DC: Israel Exploration Society/Biblical Archaeological Society, 1994) 73–75.

Ben Zvi, E. "The Account of the Reign of Manasseh in II Reg 21,1–18 and the Redactional History of the Book of Kings," *ZAW* 103 (1991) 355–373.
——. "The Chronicler as Historian; Building Texts," *The Chronicler as Historian* (ed. by M. P. Graham *et al.*; JSOTSup 238; Sheffield: Sheffield Academic, 1997) 132–149.
——. *A Historical-Critical Study of the Book of Zephaniah* (BZAW 198; New York/Berlin: de Gruyter, 1991).
——. "Isaiah 1,4–9, Isaiah, and the Events of 701 BCE in Judah," *SJOT* 5/1 (1991) 95–111.
——. "Prelude to a Reconstruction of the *Historical* Manassic Judah," *BN* 81 (1996) 31–44.
——. "A Sense of Proportion: An Aspect of the Theology of the Chronicler," *SJOT* 9/1 (1995) 37–51.
Benzinger, I. *Der Bücher der Könige* (KHCAT 9; Tübingen: Mohr, 1899).
Berlejung, A. "Washing the Mouth: The Consecration of Divine Images in Mesopotamia," *The Image and the Book: Iconic Cults, Aniconism, and the Rise of Book Religion in Israel and the Ancient Near East* (ed. by K. van der Toorn; CBET 21; Leuven: Peeters, 1997) 45–72.
Berlin, A. "A Search for a New Biblical Hermeneutics: Preliminary Observations," *The Study of the Ancient Near East in the Twenty-First Century: The William Foxwell Albright Centennial Conference* (ed. by J. S. Cooper and G. N. Schwartz; Winona Lake: Eisenbrauns, 1996) 195–207.
——. *Zephaniah* (AB 25A; New York: Doubleday, 1994).
Berlinerblau, J. "Preliminary of the Sociological Study of Israelite 'Official Religion'," *Ki Baruch Hu: Ancient Near Eastern, Biblical, and Judaic Studies in Honor of Baruch A. Levine* (ed. by R. Chazan *et al.*; Winona Lake: Eisenbrauns, 1999) 153–169.
Berridge, J. M., in *ABD* (1992) 3.664–666.
Berry, G. R. "The Code Found in the Temple," *JBL* 39 (1920) 44–51.
Bestwick, S. "Valley of Hinnom," *PEFQSt* (1881) 102–104.
Beyse, K.-M., in *TDOT* (1980) 4.473–477.
Bieńkowski, P. A. "Some Remarks on the Practice of Cremation in the Levant," *Levant* 14 (1982) 80–89.
Biran, A., in *ABD* (1992) 2.12–17.
——. *Biblical Dan* (Jerusalem: Israel Exploration Society, 1994).
——. "Sacred Spaces: Of Standing Stones, High Places and Cult Objects at Tel Dan," *BARev* 24/5 (1998) 38–45, 70.
——. "Tel Dan," *IEJ* 19 (1969) 121–123, 239–241.
——. "Tel Dan," *BA* 37 (1974) 26–51.
——. "Tel Dan: Biblical Texts and Archaeological Data," *Scripture and Other Artifacts: Essays on the Bible and Archaeology in Honor of Philip J. King* (ed. by M. D. Coogan *et al.*; Louisville: Westminster John Knox, 1994) 1–17.
Birch, W. F. "The Valley of Hinnom and Zion," *PEFQSt* (1882) 55–58.
Bird, P. A. "The End of the Male Cult Prostitute: A Literary-Historical and Sociological Analysis of Hebrew *qādēš-qĕdēšîm*," *Congress Volume, Cambridge 1995* (ed. by J. A. Emerton, VTSup 66; Leiden/New York/Köln: Brill, 1997) 64–75.
Blenkinsopp, J. "Deuteronomy and the Politics of Post-Mortem Existence," *VT* 45 (1995) 1–16.
——. "The Judaean Priesthood during the Neo-Babylonian and Achaemenid Periods: A Hypothetical Reconstruction," *CBQ* 60 (1998) 25–43.
——. *Sage, Priest, Prophet: Religious and Intellectual Leadership in Ancient Israel* (Library of Ancient Israel; Louisville: Westminster John Knox, 1995).
Bloch-Smith, E. "Cult of the Dead in Judah: Interpreting the Material Remains," *JBL* 111 (1992) 213–224.

——. *Judahite Burial Practices and Beliefs about the Dead* (JSOTSup 123/ASOR Monograph 7; Sheffield: JSOT, 1992).

Blomquist, T. H. *Gates and Gods: Cults in the City Gates of Iron Age Palestine—An Investigation of the Archaeological and Biblical Sources* (CBOT 46; Stockholm: Almqvist & Wiksell International, 1999).

Bodi, D. "Les *gillûlîm* chez Ézéchiel et dans l'Ancien Testament, et les différentes pratiques cultuelles associées à ce terme," *RB* 100 (1993) 481–510.

Boling, R. G. "Levitical Cities: Archaeology and Texts," *Biblical and Related Studies Presented to Samuel Iwry* (ed. by A. Kort and S. Morschauser; Winona Lake: Eisenbrauns, 1985) 23–32.

Borowski, O. "Hezekiah's Reforms and the Revolt against Assyria," *BA* 58 (1995) 148–155.

Bosman, H. L. "Redefined Prophecy as Deuteronomic Alternative to Divination in Deut. 18:9–22," *Acta Theologia* 16 (1996) 1–23.

Botterweck, G. J., in *TDOT* (revised, 1977) 1.374–388.

Bourke, S. "Excavations in the Iron Age Extra-Mural Quarter on the South-East Hill of Jerusalem: Review Article," *PEQ* 124 (1992) 59–62.

Brandes, M. "Destruction et Mutilation de Statues en Mésopotamie," *Akkadica* 16 (1980) 28–41.

Braun, R. L. "Martin Noth and the Chronicler's History," *History of Israel's Tradition: The Heritage of Martin Noth* (ed. by S. L. McKenzie and M. P. Graham; JSOTSup 182; Sheffield: Sheffield Academic, 1994) 63–80.

——. "Solomon, the Chosen Temple Builder: The Significance of 1 Chronicles 22, 28, and 29 for the Theology of Chronicles," *JBL* 95 (1976) 581–590.

——. "Solomonic Apologetic in Chronicles," *JBL* 92 (1973) 503–516.

Brettler, M. Z. "2 Kings 24:13–14 as History," *CBQ* 53 (1991) 547–551.

——. *The Creation of History in Ancient Israel* (London/New York: Routledge, 1995).

——. "Ideology, History, and Theology in 2 Kings xvii 7–23," *VT* 39 (1989) 268–282.

——. "The Structure of 1 Kings 1–11," *JSOT* 49 (1991) 87–97.

Bright, J. *A History of Israel* (Philadelphia: Westminster, 1959 [1st edn.], 1972 [2nd edn.], 1981 [3rd edn.]).

——. *Jeremiah* (AB 21; Garden City: Doubleday, 1965).

Brinkman, J. A. "Babylonia under the Assyrian Empire," *Power and Propaganda: A Symposium on Ancient Empires* (ed. by M. T. Larsen; Mesopotamia 7; Copenhagen: Akademisk, 1979) 223–250.

——. "Through a Glass Darkly: Esarhaddon's Retrospects on the Downfall of Babylon," *Studies in Literature from the Ancient Near East by Members of the American Oriental Society Dedicated to Samuel Noah Kramer* (ed. by J. M. Sasson; American Oriental Series 65; New Haven: American Oriental Society, 1984) 35–42 (= *JAOS* 103 [1983] 35–42).

Brokelmann, C. *Hebräische Syntax* (Neukirchen: Erziehungsvereins, 1956).

Brodsky, H., in *ABD* (1992) 1.710–712.

Broshi, M. "The Expansion of Jerusalem in the Reigns of Hezekiah and Manasseh," *IEJ* 24 (1974) 21–26.

—— and Finkelstein, I. "The Population of Palestine in Iron Age II," *BASOR* 287 (1992) 47–60.

—— and Gibson, S. "Excavations along the Western and Southern Walls of the Old City of Jerusalem," *Ancient Jerusalem Revealed* (ed. by H. Geva; Jerusalem/Washington DC: Israel Exploration Society/Biblical Archaeological Society, 1994) 147–150.

Brown, S. *Late Carthaginian Child Sacrifice and Sacrificial Monuments in their Mediterranean Context* (JSOT/ASOR Monograph 3; Sheffield: JSOT, 1991).

Burney, C. F. *Notes on the Hebrew Text of the Books of Kings* (Oxford: Clarendon, 1903).

Cahill, J. M. "Rosette Stamp Seal Impressions from Ancient Judah," *IEJ* 45 (1995) 230–252.

Campbell, A. F. *Of Prophets and Kings: A Late Ninth-Century Document (1 Samuel 1–2 Kings 10)* (CBQM 17; Washington DC: Catholic Biblical Association of America, 1986).

Carasik, M. "Who Were the 'Men of Hezekiah' (Proverbs xxv 1)?" *VT* 44 (1994) 289–300.

Carnes, M. C., ed., *Past Imperfect: History according to the Movies* (New York: Holt, 1995).

Carroll, R. P. *Jeremiah: A Commentary* (OTL; Philadelphia: Westminster, 1986).

——. "Synchronistic Deconstructions of Jeremiah: Diachrony to the Rescue?" *Synchronic or Diachronic? A Debate on Method in Old Testament Exegesis* (ed. by J. C. de Moor; OTS 34; Leiden: Brill, 1995) 39–51.

——. "Razed Temple and Shattered Vessels: Continuities and Discontinuities in the Discourses of Exile in the Hebrew Bible. An Appreciation of the Work of Peter R. Ackroyd on the Occasion of his Eightieth Birthday," *JSOT* 75 (1997) 93–107.

Catron, J. E. "Temple and *bāmāh*: Some Considerations," *The Pitcher is Broken: Memorial Essays for Gösta W. Ahlström* (ed. by S. W. Holloway and L. K. Handy; JSOTSup 190; Sheffield: Sheffield Academic, 1995) 150–165.

Cazelles, H. "*Ḥammānim-ḥamon/ḥumun* et l'Expansion phenicienne," *"Où demeures-tu?" (Jn 1,38): La Maison depuis le Monde Biblique—En Hommage au Professeur Guy Couturier à l'Occasion de ses soixante-cinq Ans* (ed. by J.-C. Petit; Quebec: Fides, 1994) 99–107.

——. "La Vie de Jérémie dans son Contexte National et International," *Le Livre de Jérémie: Le Prophète et son Milieu, les Oracles et leur Transmission* (ed. by P.-M. Bogaert; BETL 54; Leuven: University, 1981) 21–39.

Chaney, M. L. "Debt Easement in Israelite History and Tradition," *The Bible and the Politics of Exegesis: Essays in Honor of Norman K. Gottwald on his Sixty-Fifth Birthday* (ed. by D. Jobling *et al.*; Cleveland: Pilgrim, 1991) 127–139.

Christensen, D. L. "Zephaniah 2:4–15: A Theological Basis for Josiah's Program of Political Expansion," *CBQ* 46 (1984) 669–682.

Claburn, W. E. "The Fiscal Basis of Josiah's Reform," *JBL* 92 (1973) 11–22.

Classen, W. T. "Speaker-Oriented Functions of *kî* in Biblical Hebrew," *JNSL* 11 (1983) 29–46.

Clements, R. E., in *TWAT* (1990) 7.10–18.

——. "The Deuteronomic Law of Centralisation and the Catastrophe of 587 BCE," *After the Exile: Essays in Honour of Rex Mason* (ed. by J. Barton and D. J. Reimer; Macon: Mercer University, 1996) 5–25.

Clines, D. J. A., and Exum, J. C. "The New Literary Criticism," *The New Literary Criticism and the Hebrew Bible* (ed. by J. C. Exum and D. J. A. Clines; JSOTSup 143; Sheffield/Valley Forge: JSOT/Trinity, 1993) 11–25.

Clymer, L. "Cromwell's Head and Milton's Hair: Corpse Theory in Spectacular Bodies of the Interregnum," *Eighteenth Century: Theory and Interpretation* 40 (1999) 91–112.

Cody, A. *A History of Old Testament Priesthood* (Analecta Biblica 35; Rome: Pontifical Biblical Institute, 1969).

Cogan, M. "The Chronicler's Use of Chronology as Illuminated by Neo-Assyrian Royal Inscriptions," *Empirical Models for Biblical Criticism* (ed. by J. H. Tigay; Philadelphia: University of Pennsylvania, 1985) 198–203.

——. "For We, like You, Worship your God: Three Biblical Portrayals of Samaritan Origins," *VT* 38 (1988) 286–292.

——. *Imperialism and Religion: Assyria, Judah and Israel in the Eighth and Seventh Centuries BCE* (SBLM 19; Missoula: Scholars, 1974).

——. "Israel in Exile: The View of the Josianic Historian," *JBL* 97 (1978) 40–44.

——. "Judah under Assyrian Hegemony: A Re-Examination of Imperialism and Religion," *JBL* 112 (1993) 403–414.

——. "A Note on Disinterment in Jeremiah," *Gratz College Anniversary Volume on the Occasion of the Seventy-fifth Anniversary of the Founding of the College 1895–1970* (ed. by I. D. Passow and S. T. Lachs; Philadelphia: Gratz College, 1971) 29–34.

——. "The Road to En-Dor," *Pomegranates and Golden Bells: Studies in Biblical, Jewish, and Near Eastern Ritual, Law, and Literature in Honor of Jacob Milgrom* (ed. by D. P. Wright *et al.*; Winona Lake: Eisenbrauns, 1995) 319–326.

—— and Tadmor, H. *II Kings* (AB 11; Garden City: Doubleday, 1988).

——. "Gyges and Ashurbanipal: A Study in Literary Transmission," *Or* 46 (1977) 65–85.

Coggins, R. J. *The First and Second Books of the Chronicles* (CBC; Cambridge: Cambridge University, 1976).

——. "What Does 'Deuteronomistic' Mean?" *Those Elusive Deuteronomists: The Phenomenon of Pan-Deuteronomism* (ed. by L. S. Schearing and S. L. McKenzie; JSOTSup 268; Sheffield: Sheffield Academic, 1999) 22–35 (= *Words Remembered, Texts Renewed: Essays in Honour of John F. A. Sawyer* [ed. by J. Davies *et al.*; JSOTSup 195; Sheffield: Sheffield Academic, 1995] 135–148).

Cohen, M. "*maqṭîrôt ûmĕzabbĕḥôt lĕʾlōhêhen* (1 Rois xi 8b)," *VT* 41 (1991) 332–341.

Cohen, R. and Yisrael, Y. "Smashing the Idols: Piecing together an Edomite Shrine in Judah," *BARev* 22/4 (1996) 41–51, 65.

Cohen, S. J. D. "From the Bible to the Talmud: The Prohibition of Intermarriage," *HAR* 7 (1983) 23–39.

——. "Solomon and the Daughter of Pharaoh: Intermarriage, Conversion, and the Impurity of Women," *JANES* 16–17 (1984–1985) 23–37.

Cohn, E. W. "The History of Jerusalem's Benjaminite Gate: A Case of Interrupted Continuity?" *PEQ* 118 (1986) 138–143.

Cohn, R. L. "Literary Technique in the Jeroboam Narrative," *ZAW* 97 (1985) 23–35.

Conheeney, J. and Pipe, A. "Notes on Some Cremated one from Tyrian Cinerary Urns (AUB Rescue Action 'Tyre 1991')," in Seeden, "*Tophet* in Tyre?" 83–5.

Conroy, C. "Reflections on the Exegetical Task: Apropos of Recent Studies on 2 Kgs. 22–23," *Pentateuchal and Deuteronomistic Studies* (ed. by C. Brekelmans and J. Lust; BETL 94; Leuven: University, 1990) 255–268.

Craigie, P. C. *Jeremiah 1–25* (with P. H. Kelley and J. F. Drinkard, Jr.; WBC 26; Waco: Word, 1991).

Crenshaw, J. L. *Old Testament Wisdom: An Introduction* (Atlanta: John Knox, 1981).

——. *Prophetic Conflict: Its Effect upon Israelite Religion* (BZAW 124; Berlin/New York: de Gruyter, 1971).

Cripps, R. S. *A Critical and Exegetical Commentary on the Book of Amos* (2nd edn.; London: SPCK, 1955 [originally 1929]).

Croatta, J. S., and Soggin, J. A. "Die Bedeutung von *šdmwt* im Alten Testament," *ZAW* 64 (1962) 44–50.

Cross, F. M. "A Bulla of Hezekiah, King of Judah," *Realia Dei: Essays in Archaeology and Biblical Interpretation in Honor of Edward F. Campbell, Jr., at his Retirement* (ed. by P. H. Williams, Jr., and T. Hiebert; Scholars Press Homage Series 23; Atlanta: Scholars, 1999) 62–6.

——. *Canaanite Myth and Hebrew Epic: Essays in the History of the Religion of Israel* (Cambridge: Harvard University, 1973) (= "The Structure of the Deuteronomistic History," *Perspectives on Jewish Learning* [ed. by J. M. Rosenthal; Chicago: Spertus College of Judaica, 1967] 3.9–24).

——. "King Hezekiah's Seal Bears Phoenician Imagery," *BARev* 25/2 (1999) 42–45, 60.

——. "A Phoenician Inscription from Idalion: Some Old and New Texts Relating to Child Sacrifice," *Scripture and Other Artifacts: Essays on the Bible and Archaeology in*

Honor of Philip J. King (ed. by M. D. Coogan *et al.*; Louisville: Westminster John Knox, 1994) 93–107.

—— and Freedman, D. N. "Josiah's Revolt against Assyria," *JNES* 12 (1953) 56–58.

Crossan, J. D., in *ABD* (1992) 5.146–147.

——. *In Parables: The Challenge of the Historical Jesus* (New York: Harper & Row, 1973).

Cryer, F. H. *Divination in Ancient Israel and its Near Eastern Environment* (JSOTSup 142; Sheffield: JSOT, 1994).

Curtis, E. L., and Madsen, A. A. *A Critical and Exegetical Commentary on the Books of Chronicles* (ICC; New York/Edinburgh: Scribner's/Edinburgh, 1910).

Curtis, J. B. "Astral Worship and the Date of Deuteronomy," *PEGLMBS* 14 (1994) 87–93.

——. "An Investigation of the Mount of Olives in the Judaeo-Christian Tradition," *HUCA* 28 (1957) 137–177.

Daniels, R. V. *Year of the Heroic Guerrilla: World Revolution and Counterrevolution in 1968* (New York: Basic Books, 1989).

Davies, P. R. "Defending the Boundaries of Israel in the Second Temple Period: 2 Chronicles 20 and the 'Salvation Army'," *Priests, Prophets and Scribes: Essays on the Formation and Heritage of Second Temple Judaism in Honour of Joseph Blenkinsopp* (ed. E. Ulrich *et al.*; JSOTSup 149; Sheffield: JSOT, 1992) 43–54.

Day, J. *Molech: A God of Human Sacrifice in the Old Testament* (University of Cambridge Oriental Publication 41; Cambridge: Cambridge University, 1989).

Dearman, J. A. "The Son of Tabeel (Isaiah 7.6)," *Prophets and Paradigms: Essays in Honor of Gene M. Tucker* (ed. by S. B. Reid; JSOTSup 229; Sheffield: JSOT Academic, 1991) 33–47.

——. "The Tophet in Jerusalem: Archaeology and Cultural Profile," *JNSL* 22 (1996) 59–71.

—— and Mattingly, G. L., in *ABD* (1992) 4.708–709.

Delcor, M. "Le culte de la 'Reine du Ciel' selon Jer 7,18; 44,17–19, 25, et ses survivances: Aspects de la religion populaire féminine aux alentours de l'Exil en Juda et dans les communautés juives d'Egypte, *Environnement et Tradition de l'Ancien Testament* (AOAT 228; Kevelaer/Neukirchen-Vluyn: Butzon & Bercker/Neukirchener, 1990) 138–159 (= *AOAT* 211 [1982] 101–122).

——. "Les cultes étrangers en Israël au moment de la réforme de Josias d'après 2R 23: Étude de religions sémitiques comparées," *Environnement et Tradition de l'Ancien Testament* (AOAT 228; Kevelaer/Neukirchen-Vluyn: Butzon & Bercker/Neukirchener, 1990) 105–137 (= *AOAT* 212 [1981] 91–123).

——. "Réflexions sur la Pâque du temps de Josias d'aprés 2 Rois 23, 21–23," *Environnement et Tradition de l'Ancien Testament* (AOAT 228; Kevelaer/Neukirchen-Vluyn: Butzon & Bercker/Neukirchener, 1990) 90–104 (= *Hénoch* 4 [1982] 205–219).

Delitzsch, F. *Die Lese- und Schreibfehler im Alten Testament* (Berlin: Vereinigung Wissenschaftlicher, 1920).

Deller, K., in *Or* 34 (1965) 382–386.

Derchain, P. "Les plus ancien Témoignages de Sacrifices d'Enfants chez les Sémites occidentaux," *VT* 20 (1970) 351–355.

Deutsch, R. "First Impression: What We Learn from King Ahaz's Seal," *BARev* 24/3 (1998) 54–56, 62.

—— and Heltzer, M. *Forty New Ancient West Semitic Inscriptions* (Tel Aviv/Jaffa; Archaeological Center, 1994).

——. *Windows to the Past* (Tel Aviv-Jaffa: Archaeological Center, 1997).

Dever, W. G., in *ABD* (1992) 1.651–652.

——. "Archaeological Methods and Results: A Review of Two Recent Publications," *Or* 40 (1971) 459–471.

——. "A Case-Study of Biblical Archaeology: The Earthquake of ca. 760 BCE," *E-I* 23 (1992) 27*–35*.
——. "Monumental Art and Architecture in Ancient Israel in the Period of the United Monarchy," *Recent Archaeological Discoveries and Biblical Research* (Samuel and Althea Stroum Lectures in Jewish Studies 6; Seattle/London: University of Washington, 1990) 85–117 (= a revised version of "Monumental Architecture in Ancient Israel in the Period of the United Monarchy," *Studies in the Period of David and Solomon and Other Essays* [ed. by T. Ishida; Winona Lake: Eisenbrauns, 1982] 269–306).
——. *Recent Archaeological Discoveries and Biblical Research* (Seattle/London: University of Washington, 1990).
——. "The Silence of the Text: An Archaeological Commentary on 2 Kings 23," *Scripture and Other Artifacts: Essays on the Bible and Archaeology in Honor of Philip J. King* (ed. by M. D. Coogan *et al.*; Louisville: Westminster John Knox, 1994) 143–168.
——. "Social Structure in Palestine in the Iron II Period on the Eve of Destruction," *The Archaeology of Society in the Holy Land* (ed. by T. E. Levy; New York: Facts on File, 1995) 417–431.
——. "What Did the Biblical Writers Know, and When Did They Know It?" *Hesed ve-Emet: Studies in Honor of Ernest S. Frerichs* (ed. by J. Magness and S. Gitin; Brown Judaic Studies 320; Atlanta: Scholars, 1998) 241–257.
De Vries, S. J. *I Kings* (WBC 12; Waco: Word, 1985).
——. *1 and 2 Chronicles* (FOTL 11; Grand Rapids, Eerdmans, 1989).
Diebner, B., and Nauerth, C. "Die Inventio des *spr htwrh* in 2 Kön 22: Struktur, Intention und Funktion von Auffindungslegenden," *Dielheimer Blätter zum Alten Testament* 18 (1984) 95–118.
Dietrich, W. "Josia und das Gesetzbuch (2 Reg xxii)," *VT* 27 (1977) 13–35.
——. *Prophetie und Geschichte: Eine redaktionsgeschichtliche Untersuchung zum deuteronomistischen Geschichtswerk* (FRLANT 108; Göttingen: Vandenhoeck & Ruprecht, 1972).
Dillard, R. B. "The Chronicler's Solomon," *WTJ* 43 (1980) 289–300.
——. "The Literary Structure of the Chronicler's Solomon Narrative," *JSOT* 30 (1984) 85–93.
——. *2 Chronicles* (WBC 15; Waco: Word, 1987).
——. "Reward and Punishment in Chronicles: The Theology of Immediate Retribution," *WTJ* 46 (1984) 164–172.
Dion, P. E. "Deuteronomy 13: The Suppression of Alien Religious Propaganda in Israel during the Late Monarchical Era," *Law and Ideology in Monarchic Israel* (ed. by B. Halpern and D. W. Hobson; JSOTSup 124; Sheffield: JSOT, 1991) 147–216.
Donohue, V. A. "A Gesture of Submission," *Studies in Pharaonic Religion and Society in Honour of J. Gwyn Griffiths* (ed. by A. Lloyd; London: Egypt Exploration Society, 1992) 82–114.
Dougherty, R. P. "Cuneiform Parallels to Solomon's Provisioning System," *AASOR* 5 (1923–1924) 23–65.
Douglas, M. *Purity and Danger: An Analysis of Concepts of Population and Taboo* (2nd edn.; London: Routledge & Kegan Paul, 1969).
Dozeman, T. B. "The Way of the Man of God from Judah: True and False Prophecy in the Pre-Deuteronomic Legend of 1 Kings 13," *CBQ* 44 (1982) 379–393.
Drijvers, H. J. W. "Aramaic *ḤMNʾ* and Hebrew *ḤMN*: Their Meaning and Root," *JSS* 33 (1988) 165–180.
Drinkard, J. F. "'*al pĕnê* as 'East of'," *JBL* 98 (1979) 285–286.
——. "The Literary Genre of the Mesha Inscription," *Studies in the Mesha Inscription and Moab* (ed. by A. Dearman; Archaeology and Biblical Studies 2; Atlanta: Scholars, 1989) 131–154.
Driver, S. R. *The Book of the Prophet Jeremiah* (London: Hodder & Stoughton, 1906).

——. *A Critical and Exegetical Commentary on the Book of Deuteronomy* (ICC; New York/ Edinburgh: Scribners/Clark, 1885).

Duhm, B. *Das Buch Jeremiah* (KHCAT 11; Leipzig/Tübingen: Mohr, 1901).

Duke, R. K. "The Portion of the Levite: Another Reading of Deuteronomy 18:6–8," *JBL* 106 (1987) 193–201.

——. "Punishment or Restoration? Another Look at the Levites of Ezekiel 44.6–16," *JSOT* 40 (1988) 61–81.

Duling, D. C. "The Eleazar Miracle and Solomon's Magical Wisdom in Flavius Josephus's *Antiquitates Judaicae* 8.42–49," *HTR* 78 (1985) 1–25.

Dutcher-Wells, P. "The Social Location of the Deuteronomists: A Sociological Study of Factional Politics in Late Pre-Exilic Judah," *JSOT* 52 (1991) 77–94.

Ebach, J., and Rüterswörden, U. "Unterweltbeschwörung im Alten Testament: Untersuchhungen zur Begriffs- und Religionsgeschichte des *'ob*," *UF* 9 (1977) 57–70, 12 (1980) 205–220.

Edelman, D. V. "Biblical Molek Reconsidered," *JAOS* 107 (1987) 727–731.

——. "Huldah the Prophet—of Yahweh or Asherah?" *A Feminist Companion to Samuel and Kings* (ed. by A. Brenner; Feminist Companion to the Bible 5; Sheffield: Sheffield Academic 1994) 231–250.

——. *King Saul and the Historiography of Judah* (JSOTSup 121; Sheffield: JSOT, 1991).

——. "The Meaning of *qiṭṭēr*," *VT* 35 (1985) 395–404.

Ehrlich, C. S. "Coalition Politics in Eighth Century BCE Palestine: The Philistines and the Syro-ephraimite War," *ZDPV* 107 (1991) 48–58.

Eissfeldt, O. *Molk als Opferbegriff im Punischen und Hebraischen und das Ende des Gottes Moloch* (Beitrage zur Religionsgeschichte des Altertums 3; Halle: Niemeyer, 1935).

Eitam, D. "Royal Industry in Ancient Israel during the Iron Age Period," *The Town as Regional Economic Centre in the Ancient Near East: Proceedings of the Tenth International Economic History Congress, Leuven, August 1990* (ed. by E. Aerts; Studies in Social and Economic History 20; Leuven: Leuven University, 1990) 56–65.

Elat, M. "The Impact of Tribute and Booty on Countries and People within the Assyrian Empire," *AfO* 9 (1982) 244–251.

——. "The Monarchy and the Development of Trade in Ancient Israel," *State and Temple Economy in the Ancient Near East: Proceedings of the International Conference organized by the Katholieke Universiteit Leuven from the 10th to the 14th of April 1978* (ed. by E. Lipinski; Orientalia Lovaniensia Analecta 6; Leuven: Department Orientalistiek, 1979) 2.526–546.

Elayi, J. "Name of Deuteronomy's Author Found on Seal Ring," *BARev* 13/5 (1987) 54–56.

Elitzur, Y. "Rumah in Judah," *IEJ* 44 (1994) 123–128.

Emerton, J. A. "The Biblical High Place in the Light of Recent Study," *PEQ* 129 (1997) 116–132.

——. "The High Places of the Gates in 2 Kings xxiii 8," *VT* 44 (1994) 455–467.

——. "The House of Baal in 1 Kgs. xvi 32," *VT* 47 (1997) 293–300.

Endres, J. C., *et al.*, eds. *Chronicles and its Synoptic Parallels in Samuel, Kings, and Related Biblical Texts* (Collegeville, MN: Liturgical, 1998).

Ephal, I. "'The Samarian(s)' in the Assyrian Sources," *"Ah Assyria . . .": Studies in Assyrian History and Ancient Near Eastern Historiography Presented to Hayim Tadmor* (ed. by M. Cogan and I. Ephal; ScrHier 33; Jerusalem: Magnes, 1991) 36–45.

Eshel, H. "A *lmlk* Stamp from Beth-El," *IEJ* 39 (1989) 60–62.

Eshel, I., and Prag, K., eds., *Excavations by K. M. Kenyon in Jerusalem 1961–1967, 4: The Iron Age Cave Deposits on the South-east Hill and Isolated Burials and Cemeteries Elsewhere* (British Academy Monographs in Archaeology 6; Oxford: Oxford University, 1995).

Eslinger, L. *Into the Hands of the Living God* (Bible and Literature Series 24; JSOTSup 84; Sheffield: Almond, 1989).

——. "Josiah and the Torah Book: Comparison of 2 Kgs 22:1–23:28 and 2 Chr. 34:1–35:19," *HAR* 10 (1985) 37–62.

Etz, D. V. "The Genealogical Relationships of Jehoram and Ahaziah, and of Ahaz and Hezekiah, Kings of Judah," *JSOT* 71 (1996) 39–53.

Eynikel, E. "The Portrait of Manasseh and the Deuteronomistic History," *Deuteronomy and Deuteronomic Literature: Festschrift C. H. W. Brekelmans* (ed. by M. Vervenne and J. Lust; BETL 133; Leuven: University, 1997) 233–261.

——. "Prophecy and Fulfillment in the Deuteronomistic History: 1 Kgs. 13; 2 Kgs. 16–18," *Pentateuchal and Deuteronomistic Studies: Papers Read at the XIIIth IOSOT Congress* (ed. by C. Brekelmans and J. Lust; BETL 94; Leuven: University, 1990) 227–237.

——. *The Reform of King Josiah & the Composition of the Deuteronomistic History* (OTS 33; Leiden/New York/Köln: Brill, 1996).

Fales, F. M. "Kilamuwa and the Foreign Kings: Propaganda vs. Power," *Welt des Orients* 10 (1979) 6–22.

Feldman, L. H. "Josephus as an Apologist to the Greco-Roman World: His Portrait of Solomon," *Aspects of Religious Propaganda in Judaism and Early Christianity* (ed. by E. Schluser-Fiorenza; Notre Dame, IN: University of Notre Dame, 1976) 69–98.

——. "Josephus' Portrait of Solomon," *HUCA* 66 (1982) 103–167 (abbreviated as "Josephus' View of Solomon," *The Age of Solomon: Scholarship at the Turn of the Millennium* [ed. by L. K. Handy; SHCANE 11; Leiden/New York/Köln: Brill, 1997] 348–374).

——. "Prophets and Prophecy in Josephus," *JTS* 41 (1990) 386–422 (= *Society of Biblical Literature 1988 Seminar Papers* [ed. by D. J. Lull; SBLSP 27; Atlanta: Scholars, 1988] 424–441).

Finkel, I. L. "Necromancy in Ancient Mesopotamia," *AfO* 29–30 (1983–1984) 2–17.

Finkelstein, I. "The Archaeology of the Days of Manasseh," *Scripture and Other Artifacts: Essays on the Bible and Archaeology in Honor of Philip J. King* (ed. by M. D. Coogan et al.; Louisville: Westminster John Knox, 1994) 169–187.

—— and Silberman, N. A. *The Bible Unearthed: Archaeology's New Vision of Ancient Israel and the Origin of its Sacred Texts* (New York/London/Toronto/Sydney/Singapore: Free, 2001).

Fishbane, M. *Biblical Interpretation in Ancient Israel* (Oxford: Clarendon, 1985).

Fleishman, J. "The Age of Legal Maturity in Biblical Law," *JANES* 21 (1992) 35–48.

Fleming, D. "The Biblical Tradition of Anointing Priests," *JBL* 117 (1998) 401–414.

——. *The Installation of Baal's High Priestess at Emar* (HSS; Atlanta: Scholars, 1992).

Flint, R., in *Dictionary of the Bible* (ed. by J. Hastings; Edinburgh: Clark, 1902) 4.559–569.

Fox, N. "Royal Officials and Court Families: A New Look at *yldym* (*yĕlādîm*) in 1 Kings 12," *BA* 59 (1996) 225–232.

Franken, H. J. "Cave I at Jerusalem—An Interpretation," *Trade, Contact, and the Movement of Peoples in the Eastern Mediterranean: Studies in Honour of J. Basil Hennessy* (ed. by S. Bourke and J.-P. Descœudres; Mediterranean Archaeology Supplement 3; Sydney: Mediarch, 1995) 233–240.

—— and Steiner, M. L. *Excavations by K. M. Kenyon in Jerusalem 1961–1967, 2: The Iron Age Extra-Mural Quarter on the South-East Hill* (British Academy Monographs in Archaeology 2; Oxford: Oxford University, 1990).

Fraser, A. *Cromwell: The Lord Protector* (New York: Knopf, 1974).

——. *Royal Charles: Charles II and the Restoration* (New York: Knopf, 1979).

Freedman, D. N. "The Age of David and Solomon," *The Age of the Monarchies: Political History* (ed. by A. Malamat; World History of the Jewish People 4:1; Jerusalem: Massada, 1979) 101–125, 327–329.

—— and Welch, A. "Amos's Earthquake and Israelite Prophecy," *Scripture and Other Artifacts: Essays on the Bible and Archaeology in Honor of Philip J. King* (ed. by M. D. Coogan et al.; Louisville: Westminster John Knox, 1994) 188–198.

Frevel, C. "Vom Schreiben Gottes: Literarkritik Komposition und Auslegung von 2 Kön 17,34–40," *Bib* 72 (1991) 23–48.

Friedman, R. E. "The Deuteronomistic School," *Fortunate the Eyes that See: Essays in Honor of David Noel Freedman in Celebration of his Seventieth Birthday* (ed. by A. B. Beck et al.; Grand Rapids/Cambridge, UK: Eerdmans, 1995) 70–80.

——. *The Exile and Biblical Narrative* (HSM 22; Chico: Scholars, 1981).

——. "From Egypt to Egypt: Dtr¹ and Dtr²," *Traditions in Transformation: Turning Points in Biblical Faith* (ed. by B. Halpern and J. D. Levenson; Winona Lake: Eisenbrauns, 1981) 167–192.

Frisch, A. "Structure and its Significance: The Narrative of Solomon's Reign (1 Kings 1–12.24)," *JSOT* 51 (1991) 3–14.

Fritz, V. "The Meaning of the Word *ḤAMMĀN/ḤMNʾ*," *Folia Orientalia* 21 (1980) 103–115 (= "Die Bedeutung des Wortes *hamman/hmnʾ*," *Wort und Wirklichkeit* [ed. by B. Benzing et al.; Meisenheim am Glan: Hain, 1976] 1.41–50, slightly revised as "Die Bedeutung von *hammān* im Hebraischen und vom *hmnʾ* in dem palmyreni-schen Inschriften," *BN* 15 [1981] 9–20).

Fritz, V. "Die Verwaltungsgebiete Salomos nach 1 Kön. 4,7–19," *Meilenstein: Festgabe für Herbert Donner* (ed. by M. Görg; Ägypten und Altes Testament 30; Wiesbaden: Harrassowitz, 1995) 19–26.

Fry, E. "Cities, Towns and Villages in the Old Testament," *BT* 30 (1979) 434–438.

Frymer-Kensky, T. "Pollution, Purification, and Purgation in Biblical Israel," *The Word of the Lord Shall Go Forth: Essays in Honor of David Noel Freedman in Celebration of his Sixtieth Birthday* (ed. by C. L. Meyers and M. O'Connor; Winona Lake: Eisenbrauns, 1983) 399–414.

Fuller, L. E. *The Historical and Religious Significance of the Reign of Manasseh* (Leipzig: Drugulin, 1912).

Gadegaard, N. H. "On the So-Called Burnt Offering Altar in the Old Testament," *PEQ* 110 (1978) 35–45.

Galil, G. "Gebaʿ-Ephraim and the Northern Boundary of Judah in the Days of Josiah," *RB* 100 (1993) 358–367.

Gane, R. "The Role of Assyria in the Ancient Near East during the Reign of Manasseh," *AUSS* 35 (1997) 21–32.

Garcia Lopez, L. F. "Le Roi d'Israel: Dt 17:14–20," *Das Deuteronomium: Entstehung, Gestalt und Botschaft* (ed. by N. Lohfink; BETL 68; Leuven: University, 1985) 277–297.

Geva, H. "The Western Boundary of Jerusalem at the End of the Monarchy," *IEJ* 29 (1979) 84–91.

Gevaryahu, H. "Isaiah and Hezekiah: Prophet and King," *Dor le-Dor* 16 (1987–1988) 78–85.

Giancarlo, T. "La Locuzione *mĕboʾ bêt-JHWH* (2 Re 23,11aβ) nelle Versioni antiche," *RivB* (1997) 387–407.

Gianto, A. "Some Notes on the Mulk Inscription from Nebi Yunis (RES 367)," *Bib* 68 (1987) 397–401.

Gibson, J. C. L. "Coordination by Vav in Biblical Hebrew," *Words Remembered, Texts Renewed: Essays in Honour of John F. A. Sawyer* (ed. by J. Davies et al.; JSOTSup 195; Sheffield: Sheffield Academic, 1995) 272–279.

——. *Textbook of Syrian Semitic Inscriptions I: Hebrew and Moabite Inscriptions* (Oxford: Clarendon, 1971).

——. *Textbook of Syrian Semitic Inscriptions II: Aramaic Inscriptions* (Oxford: Clarendon, 1975).

Gieselmann, B. "Die sogenannten josianische Reform in der gegenwärtigen Forschung," *ZAW* 106 (1994) 223–242.

Gitay, Y. "Isaiah and the Syro-Ephraimite War," *The Book of Isaiah/Le Livre d'Isaïe: Les Oracles et leurs Reflectures Unité et Complexité de l'Ouvrage* (ed. by J. Vermeylen; BETL 81; Leuven: University, 1989) 217–230.

Gitin, S. "Incense Altars from Ekron, Israel and Judah: Context and Typology," *E-I* 20 (1989) 52*–67*.

——. "The Neo-Assyrian Empire and its Western Periphery: The Levant, with a Focus on Philistine Ekron" *Assyria 1995: Proceedings of the 10th Anniversary Symposium of the Neo-Assyrian Text Corpus Project, Helsinki, September 7–11, 1995* (ed. by S. Parpola and R. M. Whiting; Helsinki: Neo-Assyrian Text Corpus Project at the University of Helsinki, 1997) 77–103.

——. "New Incense Altars from Ekron: Context, Typology and Function," *E-I* 23 (1992) 43*–49*.

——. "Tel Miqne-Ekron: A Type-Site for the Inner Coastal Plain in the Iron Age II Period," *Recent Excavations in Israel: Studies in Iron Age Archaeology* (ed. by S. Gitin and W. G. Dever; AASOR 49; Winona Lake: Eisenbrauns, 1989) 23–58.

——. "Tel-Miqne-Ekron in the 7th Century BCE: The Impact of Economic Innovation and Foreign Cultural Influences on a Neo-Assyrian Vassal City-State," *Recent Excavations in Israel: A View to the West* (ed. by S. Gitin; Archaeological Institute of America Colloquia and Conference Papers 1; Dubuque, IA: Kendall/Hunt, 1995) 61–79.

——. "Urban Growth and Decline at Ekron in the Iron II Period," *BA* 50 (1987) 206–222.

——, Dothan, T., and Naveh, J. "A Royal Dedicatory Inscription from Ekron," *IEJ* 47 (1997) 1–16.

Glatt-Gilad, D. A. "The Role of Huldah's Prophecy in the Chronicler's Portrayal of Josiah's Reform," *Bib* 77 (1996) 16–31.

Gleis, M. *Die Bamah* (BZAW 251; Berlin/New York: de Gruyter, 1997).

Golani A., and Sass, B. "Three Seventh-Century BCE Hoards of Silver Jewelry from Tel Miqne-Ekron," *BASOR* 311 (1998) 57–81.

Goldberg, J. "Two Assyrian Campaigns against Hezekiah and Later Eighth Century Biblical Chronology," *Bib* 80 (1999) 360–390.

Gonçalves, F. J. "Isaie, Jérémie et la Politique internationale de Juda," *Bib* 76 (1998) 282–299.

Görg, M. "Die Priestertitel *kmr* und *khn*," *BN* 39 (1985) 7–14.

——. "*Topaet* (Tofet): 'Die (Stätte) des Feuergottes'?" *BN* 43 (1988) 12–13.

Grabbe, L. L. *Priests, Prophets, Diviners, Sages: A Socio-Historical Study of Religious Specialists in Ancient Israel* (Valley Forge, PA: Trinity International, 1995).

Gras, M., Rouillard, P., and Teixidor, J. "The Phoenicians and Death," *Berytus* 39 (1991) 127–176.

Gray, J. *II Kings: A Commentary* (2nd ed.; OTL; Philadelphia: Westminster, 1970).

Greenfield, J. C. "Scripture and Inscription: The Literary and Rhetorical Element in Some Early Phoenician Inscriptions," *Near Eastern Studies in Honor of W. F. Albright* (ed. by H. Goedicke; Baltimore: Johns Hopkins University, 1971) 253–268.

Gruber, M. I., in *DDD* (1995) 655–8.

Gubel, E. "The Iconography of Inscribed Phoenician Glyptic," *Studies in the Iconography of Northwest Semitic Inscribed Seals* (ed. by B. Sass and C. Uehlinger; Fribourg/Göttingen: University/Vandenhoeck & Ruprecht, 1992) 101–129.

Guthe, H. "Das Passahfest nach Dtn. 16," *Abhandlungen zur semitischen Religionskunde und Sprachwissenschaft Wolf Wilhelm Grafen von Baudissin . . . überreicht . . .* (ed. by W. Frankenberg and F. Küchler; BZAW 33; Giessen: Töpelmann, 1918) 217–232.

Haak, R. D. *Habakkuk* (VTSup 44; Leiden/New York/København/Köln: Brill, 1992).

——. "Zephaniah's Oracles against the Nations" (unpublished paper presented to the Chicago Society of Biblical Research, 2 February 1992).

Hallo, W. W. "Disturbing the Dead," *"minhah le-nahum": Biblical and Other Studies*

Presented to Nahum M. Sarna in Honour of his 70th Birthday (ed. by M. Brettler and M. Fishbane; JSOTSup 154: Sheffield: JSOT, 1993) 183–192.

——. "Royal Ancestor Worship in the Biblical World," *Sha'arei Talmon: Studies in the Bible, Qumran, and the Ancient Near East presented to Shemaryahu Talmon* (ed. by M. Fishbane *et al.*; Winona Lake: Eisenbrauns, 1992) 381–401.

Halpern, B. "The Baal (and the Asherah) in Seventh-Century Judah: Yhwh's Retainers Retired," *Konsequente Traditionsgeschichte; Festschrift für Klaus Baltzer zum 65. Geburtstag* (ed. by R. Bartelmus *et al.*; OBO 126; Freiburg/Göttingen: Universitäts/Vandenhoeck & Ruprecht, 1993) 115–154.

——. "The Centralization Formula in Deuteronomy," *VT* 31 (1981) 20–38.

——. "Eli's Death and the Israelite Gate: A Philological-Architectural Correlation," *E-I* 26 (1999) 52*–63*.

——. "Erasing History: The Minimalist Assault on Ancient Israel," *BRev* 10/6 (1995) 26–35, 47.

——. "'The Excremental Vision': The Doomed Priests of Doom in Isaiah 28," *HAR* 10 (1986) 109–121.

——. *The First Historians: The Hebrew Bible and History* (San Francisco: Harper & Row, 1988).

——. "Jerusalem and the Lineages in the Seventh Century BCE: Kinship and the Rise of Individual Moral Liability," *Law and Ideology in Monarchic Israel* (ed. by B. Halpern and D. W. Hobson; JSOTSup 124; Sheffield: JSOT, 1991) 11–107.

——. "Sacred History and Ideology: Chronicles' Thematic Structure—Indications of an Earlier Source," *The Creation of Sacred Literature: Composition and Redaction of the Biblical Text* (ed. by R. E. Friedman; University of California Publications, Near Eastern Studies 22; Berkeley/Los Angeles/London: University of California, 1981) 35–54.

——. "Sybil, or the Two Nations? Archaism, Kinship, Alienation, and the Elite Redefinition of Traditional Culture in Judah in the 8th–7th Centuries BCE," *The Study of the Ancient Near East in the Twenty-First Century: The William Foxwell Albright Centennial Conference* (ed. by J. S. Cooper and G. N. Schwartz; Winona Lake: Eisenbrauns, 1996) 320–338.

——. "Why Manasseh Is Blamed for the Babylonian Exile: The Evolution of a Biblical Tradition," *VT* 48 (1998) 473–514.

—— and Vanderhooft, D. S. "The Editions of Kings in the 7th–6th Centuries BCE," *HUCA* 62 (1991) 179–244.

Hammershaimb, E. *The Book of Amos: A Commentary* (trans. by J. Sturdy; New York: Schocken, 1970).

Handy, L. K. *Among the Host of Heaven: The Syro-Palestinian Pantheon As Bureaucracy* (Winona Lake: Eisenbrauns, 1994).

——. "Calling the Kings to Reform: Josiah, Esarhaddon, Nabonidus" (unpublished paper presented at the annual meeting of the Society of Biblical Literature in Chicago, 22 November 1988).

——. "Hezekiah's Unlikely Reform," *ZAW* 100 (1988) 111–115.

——. "Historical Probability and the Narrative of Josiah's Reform in 2 Kings," *The Pitcher Was Broken: Memorial Essays for Gösta W. Ahlström* (ed. by S. W. Holloway and L. K. Handy; JSOTSup 190; Sheffield: Sheffield Academic, 1995) 252–275.

——. "Josiah after the Chronicler," *PEGLMWBS* 14 (1994) 95–103.

——. "The Role of Huldah in Josiah's Cult Reform," *ZAW* 106 (1994) 40–52.

Haran, M. *Temples and Temple Service in Ancient Israel: An Inquiry into the Character of Cult Phenomena and the Historical Setting of the Priestly School* (Oxford: Oxford University, 1978).

Hartley, J. E. and Dwyer, T. "An Investigation into the Location of the Law on Offerings to Molek in the Book of Leviticus," *"Go to the Land I Will Show You":*

Studies in Honor of Dwight W. Young (ed. by J. E. Coleson and V. H. Matthews; Winona Lake: Eisenbrauns, 1996) 81–93.

Haupt, P. "Hinnom and Kidron," *JBL* 38 (1919) 45–48.

Hayes J. H., and Kuan, J. K. "The Final Years of Samaria (730–720 BC)," *Bib* 72 (1991) 153–181.

Healey, J. P., in *ABD* (1992) 1.168–169.

Heard, W. J., in *ABD* (1992) 5.13–15.

Heaton, E. W. *The Hebrew Kingdoms* (The New Clarendon Bible; London: Oxford University, 1968).

Heider, G. C., in *ABD* (1992) 4.895–898.

——, in *DDD* (1995) 1090–1097.

——. *The Cult of Molek: A Reassessment* (JSOTSup 43; Sheffield: JSOT, 1985).

Heltzer, M. "Some Questions Concerning the Economic Policy of Josiah, King of Judah," *IEJ* 50 (2000) 105–108.

Hendel, R. "The Date of the Siloam Inscription: A Rejoinder to Rogerson and Davies," *BA* 59 (1996) 233–237.

Hennessy, J. B. "Excavation of a Late Bronze Age Temple at Amman," *PEQ* 98 (1966) 155–162.

——. "Preliminary Report on the Excavations at the Damascus Gate, 1961–1964," *Levant* 2 (1960) 22–27.

——. "Thirteenth Century BC Temple of Human Sacrifice at Amman," *Phoenicia and Its Neighbors* (ed. by E. Lipinski and E. Grubel; Studia Phoenicia 3; Leuven: Peeters, 1985) 85–104.

Hermann, S. *A History of Israel in Old Testament Times* (2nd edn.; trans. by J. Bowden; Philadelphia: Fortress, 1981).

Herr, B. "Der wahre bezeugt seine Botschaft mit dem Tod: Ein Versuch zu 1 Kön 13," *BZ* 41 (1997) 69–78.

Herr, L. G. "Stratigraphy," *The Amman Airport Excavations, 1976* (ed. by L. G. Herr; ASOR 48; Winona Lake: Eisenbrauns, 1983) 11–31.

Herzog, Z. "Administrative Structures in the Iron Age," *The Architecture of Ancient Israel: From the Prehistoric to the Persian Periods* (ed. by A. Kempinski and R. Reich; Jerusalem: Israel Exploration Society, 1992) 223–230.

——. "The Stratigraphy of Israelite Arad: A Rejoinder," *BASOR* 267 (1987) 77–79.

——, Aharoni, M., and Rainey A. F. "Arad: An Ancient Israelite Fortress with a Temple to Yahweh," *BARev* 13/2 (1987) 16–35.

——, Rainey, A. F., and Moshkovitz, S. "The Stratigraphy at Beer-sheba and the Location of the Sanctuary," *BASOR* 225 (1977) 49–58.

——, Aharoni, M., Rainey, A. F., and Moshkovitz, S. "The Israelite Fortress at Arad," *BASOR* 254 (1984) 1–34.

Higginbotham, C. R. "Elite Emulation and Egyptian Governance in Ramesside Canaan," *TA* 23 (1996) 154–169.

——. "The Egyptianizing of Canaan," *BARev* 24/3 (1998) 36–43.

Hillers, D. R. "Dust: Some Aspects of Old Testament Imagery," *Love & Death in the Ancient Near East: Essays in Honor of Marvin H. Pope* (ed. by J. H. Marks and R. M. Good; Guilford, CT: Four Quarters, 1987) 105–109.

——. "Palmyrene Aramaic Inscriptions and the Old Testament, especially Amos 2:8," *Zeitschrift für Althebräistik* 8 (1995) 55–62.

——. *Treaty-Curse and the Old Testament Prophets* (Biblica et Orientalia 16; Rome: Pontifical Biblical Institute, 1964).

Hobbs, T. R., in *ABD* (1992) 5.1172–1173.

——. *2 Kings* (WBC 13; Waco: Word, 1985).

——. "The 'Fortresses of Rehoboam': Another Look," *Uncovering Ancient Stones: Essays in Memory of H. Neil Richardson* (ed. by L. M. Hopfe; Winona Lake: Eisenbrauns, 1994) 41–64.

Hoffman, Y. "The Deuteronomist and the Exile," *Pomegranates and Golden Bells: Studies in Biblical, Jewish, and Near Eastern Ritual, Law, and Literature in Honor of Jacob Milgrom* (ed. by D. P. Wright *et al.*; Winona Lake: Eisenbrauns, 1995) 659–675.

Hoffmann, G. "Kleinigkeiten," *ZAW* 2 (1882) 175.

Hoffmann, H.-D. *Reform und Reformen: Untersuchungen zu einem Grundthema der deuteronomistischen Geschichtsschreibung* (ATANT 66; Zurich: Theologische, 1980).

Hoffmeier, J. K. "Further Evidence for Infant Sacrifice in the Ancient Near East," *BARev* 13/2 (1987) 60–61.

——. "Once Again the 'Plumb Line' Vision of Amos 7.7–9: An Interpretive Clue from Egypt?" *Boundaries of the Ancient Near Eastern World: A Tribute to Cyrus H. Gordon* (ed. by M. Lubetski *et al.*; JSOTSup 273; Sheffield: Sheffield Academic, 1998) 304–319.

Hoffner, H. A., in *TDOT* (revised, 1977) 1.130–134.

——. "Second Millennium Antecedents to the Hebrew *'ôb*," *JBL* 86 (1967) 385–401.

Hoftijzer, J. "Holistic or Compositional Approach? Linguistic Remarks to the Problem," *Synchronic or Diachronic? A Debate on Method in Old Testament Exegesis* (ed. by J. C. de Moor; OTS 34; Leiden: Brill, 1995) 98–114.

Høgenhaven, J. "Prophecy and Propaganda: Aspects of Political and Religious Reasoning in Israel and the Ancient Near East," *SJOT* 3/1 (1989) 125–141.

——. "The Prophet Isaiah and Judaean Foreign Policy under Ahaz and Hezekiah," *JNES* 49 (1990) 351–354.

Holland, T. A. "A Study of Palestinian Iron Age Baked Clay Figurines, with Special Reference to Jerusalem: Cave I," in Eshel-Prag, *Excavations by K. M. Kenyon in Jerusalem 1961–1967*, 4, 159–189 (= *Levant* 9 [1977] 121–155).

Holladay, Jr., J. S. "The Kingdoms of Israel and Judah: Political and Economic Centralization in the Iron IIA–B (ca. 1000–750 BCE)," *The Archaeology of Society in the Holy Land* (ed. by T. E. Levy; New York: Facts on File, 1995) 368–398.

——. "Religion in Israel and Judah under the Monarchy: An Explicitly Archaeological Approach," *Ancient Israelite Religion: Essays in Honor of Frank Moore Cross* (ed. by P. D. Miller *et al.*; Philadelphia: Fortress, 1987) 249–299.

Holladay, W. L. "A Coherent Chronology of Jeremiah's Early Career," *Le Livre de Jérémie: Le Prophète et son Milieu, les Oracles et leur Transmission* (ed. by P.-M. Bogaert; BETL 54; Leuven: Leuven University 1981) 58–73.

——. "A Fresh Look at 'Source B' and 'Source C' in Jeremiah," *VT* 25 (1975) 409–412.

——. *Jeremiah 1* (Hermeneia; Philadelphia: Fortress, 1986).

——. *Jeremiah 2* (Hermeneia; Minneapolis: Fortress Augsburg, 1989).

——. *The Root "Subh" in the Old Testament* (Leiden: Brill, 1958).

——. "'On Every High Hill and Under Every Green Tree'," *VT* 11 (1961) 170–176.

Hollenstein, H. "Literarkritische Erwägungen zum Bericht über die Reformmassnahmen Josias 2 Kön. xxiii 4ff.," *VT* 27 (1977) 321–336.

Holloway S. W., in *ABD* (1992) 4.70–73.

Hooker, E. M. "The Significance of Numa's Religious Reform," *Numen* 10 (1963) 87–132.

Hoppe, L. J. "Jerusalem in the Deuteronomistic History," *Das Deuteronomium: Entstehung, Gestalt, und Botschaft* (ed. by N. Lohfink; BETL 68; Leuven: University, 1985) 107–110.

Horowitz, W. "The Reverse of the Neo-Assyrian Planisphere CT 33,11," *Die Rolle der Astronomie in den Kulturen Mesopotamiens: Beiträge zum 3. Grazer Morgenländischen Symposiun (23.–27. September 1991)* (ed. by H. D. Galter; Grazer Morgenländische Studien 3; Graz: n. pb., 1993) 149–159.

Houtman, C., in *DDD* (1995) 1278–1283.

Hunt, R. C. "The Role of Bureaucracy in the Provisioning of Cities: A Framework for Analysis of the Ancient Near East," *The Organization of Power: Aspects of Bureaucracy in the Ancient Near East* (2nd edn.; ed. by McG. Gibson and R. D. Biggs; Studies in Ancient Civilization 46; Chicago: Oriental Institute, 1991) 141–168.

Hyatt, J. P. "The Beginning of Jeremiah's Prophecy" *ZAW* 78 (1966) 204–214.

———. "The Book of Jeremiah: Introduction and Exegesis," *IB* (1956) 5.794–1141.

Isbell, C. D. "2 Kings 22:3–23:24 and Jeremiah 36: A Stylistic Comparison," *JSOT* 8 (1978) 33–45.

Iserson, K. V. *Death to Dust: What Happens to Dead Bodies?* (Tucson: Galen, 1994).

Ishida, T. "The Structure and Historical Implications of the Lists of Pre-Israelite Nations," *Bib* 60 (1979) 461–490.

Irvine, S. A. *Isaiah, Ahaz, and the Syro-Ephraimitic Crisis* (SBLDS 123; Atlanta: Scholars, 1990).

Irwin, W. A. "The Attitude of Isaiah in the Crisis of 701," *JR* 16 (1936) 406–418.

Irwin, W. H. "The Smooth Stones of the Wadi? Isaiah 57,6," *CBQ* 29 (1967) 31–40.

Jackson, K. P. "The Language of the Mesha Inscription," *Studies in the Mesha Inscription and Moab* (ed. by A. Dearman; Archaeology and Biblical Studies 2; Atlanta: Scholars, 1989) 96–129.

——— and Dearman, J. A. "The Text of the Mesha Inscription," *Studies in the Mesha Inscription and Moab* (ed. by A. Dearman; Archaeology and Biblical Studies 2; Atlanta: Scholars, 1989) 93–95.

Jacobsen, T. "The Graven Image," *Ancient Israelite Religion: Essays in Honor of Frank Moore Cross* (ed. by P. D. Miller *et al.*; Philadelphia: Fortress, 1987) 15–32.

Janowski, B., in *DDD* (1995) 1381–1384.

Japhet, S. *I–II Chronicles: A Commentary* (OTL; Louisville: Westminster John Knox, 1993).

———. "From the King's Sanctuary to the Chosen City," *Jerusalem: Its Sanctity and Centrality to Judaism, Christianity, and Islam* (ed. by L. I. Levine; New York: Continuum, 1999) 3–15 [= *Judaism*, 46 (1997) 129–141]).

———. *The Ideology of the Book of Chronicles and its Place in Biblical Thought* (2nd edn.; trans. by A. Barber; Beiträge zur Erforschung des Alten Testaments und des Antiken Judentums 9; New York/Frankfort am Main/Berlin/Bern/Paris/Wein: Lang, 1997).

———. "The Temple in the Restoration Period: Reality and Ideology," *Union Seminary Quarterly Review* 44 (1991) 195–251.

Jenni, E. "Zwei Jahrzehnte Forschung über Josua bis Könige," *TR* 27 (1961) 1–32, 97–140.

Jensen, J., in *ABD* (1992) 3.392–395.

Jepsen, A. "Die Reform des Josia," *Festschrift Friedrich Baumgärtel zum 70. Geburtstag 14. Januar 1958* (ed. by L. Rost; EF A/10; Erlangen: Universitatsbibliothek Erlangen, 1959) 97–108.

Jones, D. "The Cessation of Sacrifice after the Destruction of the Temple in 586 BC," *JTS* 14 (1963) 12–31.

Jones, G. H. *1–2 Kings* (NCB; Grand Rapids/London: Eerdmans/Marshall, Morgan & Scott, 1984).

Joosten, J. "Biblical Hebrew *wĕqāṭal* and Syriac *hwā qāṭel* Expressing Repetition in the Past," *ZAH* 5 (1992) 1–14.

Kang, S.-M. "The Authentic Sermon of Jeremiah in Jeremiah 7:1–20," *Texts, Temples, and Traditions: A Tribute to Menahem Haran* (ed. by M. V. Fox *et al.*; Winona Lake: Eisenbrauns, 1996) 147–162.

Kapelrud, A. S. *The Message of the Prophet Zephaniah: Morphology and Ideas* (Oslo: Universitets, 1975).

Keel, O., and Uehlinger, C. *Gods, Goddesses, and Images of God in Ancient Israel* (trans. by T. H. Trapp; Minneapolis: Augsburg Fortress, 1998).

——. "Jahwe und die Sonnengottheit von Jerusalem," *Ein Gott allein? JHWH-Verehrung und biblischer Monotheismus im Kontext der israelitischen und altorientalischen Religionsgeschichte: 13. Kolloquium der Schweizerischen Akademieder Geistes- und Sozialwissenschaften 1993* (ed. by W. Dietrich and M. A. Klopfenstein; Freiburg: Universitäts, 1994) 269–306.

Kelso, J. L., in *IDB* [1962] 1.391–393.

——, in *The Excavation of Bethel (1934–1960)* (ed. by J. L. Kelso; AASOR 39; Cambridge, MA; ASOR, 1968).

Kempinski, A. "From Death to Resurrection: The Early Evidence," *BARev* 21/5 (1995) 56–65, 82.

Kenyon, K. M. "Excavations in Jerusalem, 1963," *PEQ* 99 (1964) 7–18.

——. "Israelite Jerusalem," *Near Eastern Archaeology in the Twentieth Century: Essays in Honor of Nelson Glueck* (ed. by J. A. Sanders; Garden City: Doubleday, 1970) 232–253.

——. *Jerusalem: Excavating 3000 Years of History* (London: Thames & Hudson, 1967).

van Keulen, P. S. F. *Manasseh through the Eyes of the Deuteronomists: The Manasseh Account [2 Kings 2:1:1–18] and the Final Chapters of the Deuteronomistic History* (OTS 38; Leiden/New York/Köln: Brill, 1996).

——. "The Meaning of the Phrase *wn'spt 'l-qbrtyk bšlwm* in 2 Kings xxii 20," *VT* 46 (1996) 256–260.

King, P. J. "The Eighth, the Greatest of Centuries?" *JBL* 108 (1989) 3–15.

——. *Jeremiah: An Archaeological Companion* (Louisville: Westminster/John Knox, 1993).

Kitchen, K. A. "Ancient Orient, 'Deuteronomism,' and the Old Testament," *New Perspectives on the Old Testament* (ed. by J. B. Payne; Evangelical Theological Society Supplementary Volume 3; Waco/London: Word, 1970) 1–24.

Kletter, R. "Pots and Politics: Material Remains of Late Iron Age Judah in Relation to its Political Borders," *BASOR* 314 (1999) 19–54.

Klein, R. W., in *ABD* (1992) 1.992–1002.

——. "Reflections on Historiography in the Account of Jehoshaphat," *Pomegranates and Golden Bells: Studies in Biblical, Jewish, and Near Eastern Ritual, Law, and Literature in honor of Jacob Milgrom* (ed. by D. O. Wright *et al.*; Winona Lake: Eisenbrauns, 1995) 643–57.

——. *Textual Criticism of the Old Testament: The Septuagint after Qumran* (Guides to Biblical Scholarship; Philadelphia: Fortress, 1974).

Kleinig, J. W. "Recent Research in Chronicles," *CR:BS* 2 (1994) 43–76.

Kloner, A., and Davis, D. "A Burial Cave of the Late First Temple Period on the Slope of Mount Zion," *Ancient Jerusalem Revealed* (ed. by H. Geva; Jerusalem/Washington DC: Israel Exploration Society/Biblical Archaeological Society, 1994) 107–110.

Klopfenstein, M. A. "I Könige 13," *"Parresia": Karl Barth zum 80. Geburtstag* (ed. by E. Busch *et al.*; Zurich: EVZ, 1966) 639–672.

Knauf, E. A., in *ZDPV* 104 (1988) 174–176.

——. "From History to Interpretation," *The Fabric of History: Text, Artifact and Israel's Past* (ed. by D. V. Edelman; JSOTSup 127; Sheffield: JSOT, 1991) 26–64.

——. "L'Historiographie deutéronomiste' (DtrG) Existe-t-elle?" *Israël Construit son Histoire: L'historiographie deutéronomiste à la lumière des recherches récentes* (ed. by A. de Pury, T. Römer, and J.-D. Macchi; Le Monde de la Bible 34; Geneva: Labor et Fides, 1996) 409–418.

Knoppers, G. N. "The Deuteronomist and the Deuteronomic Law of the King: A Reexamination of a Relationship," *ZAW* 108 (1996) 329–346.

——. "History and Historiography: The Royal Reforms," *The Chronicler as Historian* (ed. by M. P. Graham *et al.*; JSOTSup 238; Sheffield: Sheffield Academic, 1997) 178–203.

——. "Sex, Religion, and Politics: The Deuteronomist on Intermarriage," *HAR* 14 (1994) 121–141.

——. "Solomon's Fall and Deuteronomy," *The Age of Solomon: Scholarship at the Turn of the Millennium* (ed. by L. K. Handy; SHCANE 11; Leiden/New York/Köln: Brill, 1997) 392–410.

——. *Two Nations Under God, The Deuteronomistic History of Solomon and the Dual Monarchies 1: The Reign of Solomon and the Rise of Jeroboam* (HSM 52; Atlanta: Scholars, 1993).

——. *Two Nations Under God, The Deuteronomistic History of Solomon and the Dual Monarchies 2: The Reign of Jeroboam, the Fall of Israel, and the Reign of Josiah* (HSM 53; Atlanta: Scholars, 1994).

Koch, K. "Gefüge und Herkunft des Berichts über die Kultreformen des Königs Josia: Zugleich ein beitrag zur Bestimmung hebräischer 'Tempora'," *Alttestamentlicher Glaube und Biblischer Theologie: Festschrift für Horst Dietrich Preuss zum 65. Geburtstag* (ed. by J. Hausmann and H.-J. Zobel; Stuttgart/Berlin/Köln: Kohlhammer, 1992) 80–92.

Kuemmerlin-McLean, J. K., in *ABD* (1992) 4.468–469.

Kuhl, C. "Die 'Wiederaufnahme': Eine literarkritisches Prinzip?" *ZAW* 64 (1952) 1–11.

Laato, A. *Josiah and David Redivivus: The Historical Josiah and the Messianic Expectations of Exilic and Postexilic Times* (CBOT 33; Stockholm: Almqvist & Wiksell, 1992).

——. "The Royal Covenant Theology in Judah," *"Lasset uns Brücken bauen . . .": Collected Communications to the XVth Congress of the International Organization for the Study of the Old Testament, Cambridge 1995* (ed. by K.-D. Schunck and M. Augustin; Beiträge zur Erforschung des Alten Testaments und des Antiken Judentums 42; Frankfort am Main/Berlin/New York/Wien: Peter Lang, 1998) 93–100.

——. "Second Samuel 7 and Ancient Near Eastern Royal Ideology," *CBQ* 59 (1997) 244–269.

Lapp, P. W. "The Pottery of Palestine in the Persian Period," *Archäologie und Altes Testament: Festschrift für Kurt Galling* (ed. by A. Kuschke and E. Kutsch; Tübingen: Mohr, 1970) 179–197.

Lasine, S. "The King of Desire: Indeterminacy, Audience, and the Solomon Narrative," *Semeia* 71 (1996) 85–118.

——. "Manasseh as Villain and Scapegoat," *The New Literary Criticism and the Hebrew Bible* (ed. by J. C. Exum and D. J. A. Clines; JSOTSup 143; Sheffield/Valley Forge: JSOT/Trinity, 1993) 163–183.

——. "Solomon and the Wizard of Oz: Power and Invisibility in a Verbal Palace," *The Age of Solomon: Scholarship at the Turn of the Millennium* (ed. by L. K. Handy; SHCANE 11; Leiden/New York/Köln: Brill, 1997) 375–391.

Layton, S. C. "The Steward in Ancient Israel: A Study of Hebrew (*ʾăšer*) *ʿal-habbayit* in its Near Eastern Setting," *JBL* 109 (1990) 633–649.

Lehmann, M. R. "A New Interpretation of the Term *šdmwt*," *VT* 3 (1953) 361–371.

Lemaire, A. "Coupe astrale inscrite et astronomie araméenne," *Michael: Historical, Epigraphical and Biblical Studies in Honor of Prof. Michael Heltzer* (ed. by Y. Avishuir and R. Deutsch; Tel Aviv-Jaffa: Archaeological Center, 1999) 195–211.

——. "The Tel Dan Stela as a Piece of Royal Historiography," *JSOT* 81 (1998) 3–14.

——. "Vers l'Histoire de la Redaction des Livres des Rois," *ZAW* 98 (1986) 221–236.

Lemke, W. F. "The Synoptic Problem in the Chronicler's History," *HTR* 58 (1968) 349–363.

——. "The Way of Obedience: 1 Kings 13 and the Structure of the Deuteronomistic History," *Magnalia Dei/The Mighty Acts of God: Essays on the Bible and Archaeology in Memory of G. Ernest Wright* (ed. by F. M. Cross *et al.*; Garden City: Doubleday, 1976) 301–326.

Leslie, E. A. *Jeremiah* (New York: Abingdon, 1954).

Levenson, J. R. "From Temple to Synagogue: 1 Kings 8," *Traditions in Transformation* (ed. by B. Halpern and J. D. Levenson; Winona Lake: Eisenbrauns, 1981) 143–166.

——. "Who Inserted the Book of the Torah?" *HTR* 68 (1975) 203–233.

Levin, C. "Joschija im deuteronomistischen Geschichtswerk," *ZAW* 96 (1984) 351–371.

Levine, B. A. "The Epilogue to the Holiness Code: A Priestly Statement on the Destiny of Israel," *Judaic Perspectives on Ancient Israel* (ed. by J. Neusner *et al.*; Philadelphia: Fortress, 1987) 9–34.

——. *Leviticus* (JPSTC 3; Philadelphia/New York/Jerusalem: Jewish Publication Society, 1989).

Lewis, T. J. *Cults of the Dead in Ancient Israel and Ugarit* (HSM 39; Atlanta: Scholars, 1989).

——. "Death Cult Imagery in Isaiah 57," *HAR* 11 (1987) 267–284.

Lipschits, O. "The History of the Benjamin Region under Babylonian Rule," *TA* 26 (1999) 155–90.

Little, R. M. "Human Bone Fragment Analysis," *The Amman Airport Excavations, 1976* (ed. by L. G. Herr; AASOR 48; Winona Lake: ASOR, 1983) 47–55.

Liverani, M. "L'Histoire de Joas," *VT* (1974) 452–453.

Lohfink, N., in *IDBSup* (1976) 229–232.

——. "Die Bundesurkunde des Königs Josias," *Bib* (1963) 261–288, 461–498.

——. "The Cult Reform of Josiah of Judah: 2 Kings 23:22–23 as a Source for the History of Israelite Religion," *Ancient Israelite Religion: Essays in Honor of Frank Moore Cross* (ed. by P. D. Miller *et al.*; Philadelphia: Fortress, 1987) 459–475.

——. "Deutéronome et Pentateuque: État de la Recherche," *Le Pentateuque: Débats et Recherches—XIVᵉ Congrès de l'ACFEB, Angers (1991)* (ed. by P. Haudebert; Lectio Divina 151; Paris: Cerf, 1992) 35–64.

——. "Distribution of the Functions of Power: The Laws Concerning Public Offices in Deuteronomy 16:18–18:22," *A Song of Power and the Power of Song: Essays on the Book of Deuteronomy* (ed. by D. L. Christensen; Sources for Biblical and Theological Study 3; Winona Lake: Eisenbrauns, 1993) 336–352 (= *Great Themes from the Old Testament* [trans. by R. Walls; Chicago: Franciscan Herald, 1981] 55–75).

——. "Die Gattung 'Historischen Kurzgeschichte' in den letzten Jahren von Juda und in der Zeit des Babylonischen Exils," *ZAW* 93 (1978) 319–347.

——. "Der junge Jeremia als Propagandist und Poet: Zum Grundstock von Jer 30–31," *Le Livre du Jérémie: Le Prophète et son Milieu; Les Oracles et leurs Transmission* (ed. by P.-M. Bogaert; BETL 54; Leuven: University, 1981) 351–368.

——. "Recent Discussion on 2 Kings 22–23: The State of the Question," *A Song of Power and the Power of Song: Essays on the Book of Deuteronomy* (trans. by L. M. Maloney; ed. by D. L. Christensen; Sources for Biblical and Theological Study 3; Winona Lake: Eisenbrauns, 1993) 36–61 (= *Das Deuteronomium: Entstehung, Gestalt und Botschaft* [ed. by N. Lohfink; BETL 68; Leuven: Leuven University, 1985] 24–48).

——. "Was There a Deuteronomistic Movement?" *Those Elusive Deuteronomists: The Phenomenon of Pan-Deuteronomism* (ed. by L. S. Schearing and S. L. McKenzie; JSOTSup 268; Sheffield: Sheffield Academic, 1999) 36–66 (= *Jeremia und die "deuteronomistische Bewegung"* [ed. by W. Gross; BBB 98; Weinheim: Beltz Athenäum, 1995] 313–382).

Long, B. O. *1 Kings, with an Introduction to Historical Literature* (FOTL 9; Grand Rapids: Eerdmans, 1984).

——. *2 Kings* (FOTL 10; Grand Rapids: Eerdmans, 1991).

——. "Framing Repetitions in Biblical Historiography," *JBL* 106 (1987) 385–399.

Lowery, R. H. *The Reforming Kings: Cults and Society in First Temple Judah* (JSOTSup 120; Sheffield: JSOT, 1991).

Luckenbill, D. D. *The Annals of Sennacherib* (OIP 2; Chicago: University of Chicago, 1924).

Lundbom, J. R., in *ABD* (1992) 3.706–721.

——. *Jeremiah 1–20* (AB 21A; New York: Doubleday, 1999).

——. "The Lawbook of the Josianic Reform," *CBQ* 38 (1976) 293–302.
Lust, J. "On Wizards and Prophets," *VTSup* 26 (1974) 133–142.

Malamat, A. "The Historical Background of the Assassination of Amon, King of Judah," *IEJ* 3 (1953) 26–29.
——. "Naamah, the Ammonite Princess, King Solomon's Wife," *RB* 106 (1999) 35–40.
Malul, M. "Some Measures of Population Control in the Ancient Near East," *Michael: Historical, Epigraphical and Biblical Studies in Honor of Prof. Michael Heltzer* (ed. by Y. Avishuir and R. Deutsch; Tel Aviv-Jaffa: Archaeological Center, 1999) 221–236.
Manor, D. W., and Herion, G. A., in *ABD* (1992) 1.331–336.
Mare, W. H., in *ABD* (1992) 4.37–38.
Margalit, B. "Studies in NW Semitic Inscriptions," *UF* 26 (1994) 271–315.
——. "Why Mesha of Moab Sacrificed his Oldest Son," *BARev* 12/6 (1986) 62–63, 76.
Margalith, O. "The Political Background of Zerubbabel's Mission and the Samaritan Schism," *VT* 41 (1991) 312–323.
——. "Religious Life in Jerusalem on the Eve of the Fall of the First Temple," *Fucus: A Semitic/Afrasian Gathering in Remembrance of Albert Ehrman* (ed. by Y. L. Arbeitman; Amsterdam Studies in the Theory and History of Linguistic Science 4.58; Philadelphia/Amsterdam: John Benjamins, 1988) 335–352.
Mayes, A. D. H. *Deuteronomy* (NCB; Grand Rapids/London: Eerdmans/Marshall, Morgan & Scott, 1979).
——. "King and Covenant: A Study of 2 Kings Chs. 22–23," *Hermathena* 125 (1978) 34–46 (= an abbreviated version of *Deuteronomy*, 96–98).
——. *The Story of Israel between Settlement and Exile: A Redactional Study of the Deuteronomistic History* (London: SCM, 1983).
Mazar, A. *Archaeology of the Land of the Bible 10,000–586 BCE* (ABRL; New York: Doubleday, 1990).
——. "Iron Age Burial Caves North of the Damascus Gate," *IEJ* 26 (1976) 1–8.
——. "Temples of the Middle and Late Bronze Ages and the Iron Age," *The Architecture of Ancient Israel from the Prehistoric to the Persian Periods* (ed. by A. Kempinski and R. Reich; Jerusalem: Israel Exploration Society, 1992) 184–186.
—— and Netzer. E. "On the Israelite Fortress at Arad, *BASOR* 263 (1986) 87–91.
Mazar, B. *The Mountain of the Lord* (Garden City; Doubleday, 1975).
McCarter, P. K. "The Bulla of Nathan-Melech, the Servant of the King," *Realia Dei: Essays in Archaeology and Biblical Interpretation in Honor of Edward F. Campbell, Jr., at his Retirement* (ed. by P. H. Williams, Jr., and T. Hiebert; Scholars Press Homage Series 23; Atlanta: Scholars, 1999) 142–153.
——. *I Samuel* (AB 8; Garden City: Doubleday, 1980).
McClellan, T. L. "Towns to Fortresses: The Transformation of Urban Life from the 8th to 7th Century BC," *Society of Biblical Literature Seminar Papers 1978* (ed. by P. J. Achtemeier; Missoula: Scholars, 1978) 277–286.
McConville, J. G. "1 Kings viii 46–53 and the Deuteronomic Hope," *VT* 42 (1992) 67–79.
——. *Law and Theology in Deuteronomy* (JSOTSup 33; Sheffield: JSOT, 1984).
——. "Narrative and Meaning in the Books of Kings," *Bib* 70 (1989) 50–73.
——. "Priests and Levites in Ezekiel: A Crux in the Interpretation of Israel's History," *TynBul* 34 (1983) 4–9.
McCurley, F. R. "The Home of Deuteronomy Revisited: A Methodological Analysis of the Northern Theory," *A Light unto my Path: Old Testament Studies in Honor of Jacob M. Myers* (Gettysburg Theological Studies 4; Philadelphia: Temple University, 1974) 295–317.

McKane, W. *A Critical and Exegetical Commentary on Jeremiah 1* (ICC; Edinburgh: Clark, 1986).

———. *A Critical and Exegetical Commentary on Jeremiah 2* (ICC; Edinburgh: Clark, 1996.)

———. "Jeremiah II 23–25: Observations on the Versions and History of Exegesis," *OTS* 17 (1972) 73–88.

McKay, J. *Religion in Judah under the Assyrians* (SBT 2nd Series 26; Naperville: Allenson, 1973).

McKenzie, J. L. *Second Isaiah* (AB 20; Garden City: Doubleday, 1968).

McKenzie, S. L., in *ABD* (1992) 2.160–168.

———. "The Book of Kings in the Deuteronomistic History," *History of Israel's Tradition: The Heritage of Martin Noth* (ed. by S. L. McKenzie and M. P. Graham; JSOTSup 182; Sheffield: Sheffield Academic, 1994) 281–307.

———. "The Chronicler as Redactor," *The Chronicler as Author: Studies in Text and Texture* (ed. by M. P. Graham and S. L. McKenzie; JSOTSup 263; Sheffield: Sheffield Academic, 1999) 70–90.

———. *The Chronicler's Use of the Deuteronomistic History* (HSM 33; Atlanta: Scholars 1984).

———. "Mizpah of Benjamin and the Date of the Deuteronomistic History," *"Lasset uns Brücken bauen . . .": Collected Communications of the XVth Congress of the International Organization for the Study of the Old Testament, Cambridge 1995* (ed. by K.-D. Schunck and M. Augustin; Beiträge zur Erforschung des Alten Testaments und des Antiken Judentums 42; Frankfurt am Main/Berlin/Bern/New York/Paris/Wein: Lang, 1998) 149–155.

———. "Postscript: The Laws of Physics and Pan-Deuteronomism," *Those Elusive Deuteronomists: The Phenomenon of Pan-Deuteronomism* (ed. by L. S. Schearing and S. L. McKenzie; JSOTSup 268; Sheffield: Sheffield Academic, 1999) 262–271.

———. *The Trouble with Kings: The Composition of the Book of Kings in the Deuteronomistic History* (VTSup 42; Leiden: Brill, 1991).

McWilliams, J. C. *The 1960s Cultural Revolution* (Guides to Historic Events of the Twentieth Century (London/Westport, Conn.: Greenwood, 2000).

Mead, J. K. "Kings and Prophets, Donkeys and Lions: Dramatic Shape and Deuteronomistic Rhetoric in 1 Kings xiii," *VT* 49 (1999) 191–205.

Mead, M. *Culture and Commitment: A Study of the Generation Gap* (Garden City: Natural History/Doubleday, 1970).

Mesnard, H. "Les Constellations du Livre de Job," *Revue belge de philologie et d'histoire* 30 (1952) 135–146.

Mettinger, T. N. D. *The Dethronement of Sabaoth: Studies in the Shem and Kabod Theologies* (CBOT 18; Lund: Gleerup, 1982).

———. "The Name and the Glory: The Zion-Sabaoth Theology and its Exilic Successors," *JNSL* 24 (1998) 1–24.

———. *Solomonic State Officials: A Study of the Civil Government Officials of the Israelite Monarchy* (CBOT 5, Lund: Gleerup, 1971).

———. "YHWH SABAOTH—The Heavenly King on the Cherub Throne," *Studies in the Period of David and Solomon and Other Essays* (ed. by T. Ishida; Winona Lake: Eisenbrauns, 1982) 109–138.

Meyer, R. "Auffallender Erzählungsstil in einem angeblichen Auszug aus der 'Chronik der Könige von Juda'," *Festschrift für Friedrich Baumgartel zum 70. Geburtstag, 14 Januar 1958 Gewidmet* (ed. by L. Rost; ErF A/10; Erlangen: Universitatsbibliothek Erlangen, 1959) 119–123.

Meyers, C. L., in *ABD* (1992) 4.141–143.

———. "The Elusive Temple," *BA* 45 (1982) 33–41.

———. "The Israelite Empire: In Defense of King Solomon," *The Bible and its Traditions* (ed. by M. P. O'Connor and D. N. Freedman; Michigan Quarterly Review 22/3; Ann Arbor: University of Michigan, 1983) 412–428.

——— and Meyers, E. M. *Zechariah 9–14* (AB 25C; New York: Doubleday, 1993).

Milgrom, J. "The Date of Jeremiah, Chapter 2," *JNES* 14 (1955) 65–69.

———. "Korah's Rebellion: A Study in Redaction," *De la Tôrah au Messie: Mélange Henri Cazelles* (ed. by M. Carrez *et al.*; Paris: Desclée, 1981) 135–146.

———. *Leviticus 1–16* (AB 3; New York: Doubleday, 1991).

———. *Numbers* (JPSTC 4; New York/Philadelphia: Jewish Publication Society, 1990).

———. "The Rationale for Biblical Impurity," *JANES* 22 (1993) 107–111.

———. "The Rebellion of Korah, Numbers 16–18: A Study in Tradition History," *Society of Biblical Literature 1988 Seminar Papers* (ed. by D. J. Lull; SBLSP 27; Atlanta: Scholars 1988) 570–573.

Miller, J. M., in *ABD* (1992) 4.882–893.

———. "The Moabite Stone as a Memorial Stele," *PEQ* 106 (1974) 9–18.

——— and Hayes, J. H. *A History of Ancient Judah and Israel* (Philadelphia: Westminster, 1986).

Minette de Tillesse, C. "Joiaqim, Repoussoir de 'Pieux' Josias: Parallélismes entre II Reg 22 et Jer 36," *ZAW* 105 (1993) 355–359.

Moenikes, A. "Zur Redaktionsgeschichte des sogenannten Deuteronomistischen Geschichtswerk," *ZAW* 104 (1992) 333–348.

Montgomery, J. A. "Archival Data in the Book of Kings," *JBL* 53 (1934) 46–52.

———. *A Critical and Exegetical Commentary on the Books of Kings* (ed. by H. S. Gehman; ICC; Edinburgh: Clark, 1951).

———. "The Holy City and Gehenna," *JBL* 27 (1908) 24–47.

Moscati, S. "Non è un Tofet a Tiro," *Rivista di Studi Fenici* 21 (1993) 147–152.

——— and Ribichini, S. *Il Sacrificio dei Bambini: Un Aggiornamento* (Problelmi Attuli di Scienzae di Cultura 266; Rome: Accademia Nazionale de Lincei, 1991).

Muilenburg, J. "The Linguistic and Rhetorical Usages of the Particle *kî* in the Old Testament," *Hearing and Speaking the Word: Selections from the Work of James Muilenburg* (ed. by T. F. Best; Chico: Scholars, 1984) 208–233 (= *HUCA* 32 [1961] 135–160).

Mullen, E. T., in *ABD* (1992) 3.301–304.

Myers, J. M. *II Chronicles* (AB 13; Garden City: Doubleday, 1965).

Naaman, N. "Beth-aven, Bethel and Early Israelite Sanctuaries," *ZDPV* 103 (1987) 13–21.

———. *Borders and Districts in Biblical Historiography* (Jerusalem Biblical Studies 4; Jerusalem: Sinor, 1986).

———. "The Debated Historicity of Hezekiah's Reform," *ZAW* 107 (1995) 105–117.

———. "The Dedicated Treasures Buildings within the House of YHWH where Women Weave Coverings for Asherah (2 Kings 23:7)," *BN* 83 (1996) 17–18.

———. "Hezekiah and the Kings of Assyria," *TA* 21 (1994) 235–254.

———. "The Kingdom of Judah under Josiah," *TA* 18 (1991) 3–71.

———. "Royal Inscriptions and the Histories of Joash and Ahaz, Kings of Judah," *VT* 48 (1998) 337–344.

———. "Sennacherib's Campaign to Judah and the Date of the *lmlk* Stamps," *VT* 29 (1979) 61–86.

———. "Sources and Composition in the History of Solomon," *The Age of Solomon: Scholarship at the Turn of the Millennium* (ed. by L. K. Handy; SHCANE 11; Leiden/New York/Köln: Brill, 1997) 57–80.

Nakhai, B. A. "What's a Bamah? How Sacred Space Functioned in Ancient Israel," *BARev* 20/3 (1994) 18–29, 77–78.

Nakanose, S. *Josiah's Passover* (Bible and Liberation Series; Maryknoll, NY: Orbis, 1993).

Naveh, J. "A Fragment of an Ancient Hebrew Inscription from the Ophel," *IEJ* 32 (1988) 195–198.

Niemann, H. M. "The Socio-Political Shadow Cast by the Biblical Solomon," *The Age of Solomon: Scholarship at the Turn of the Millennium* (ed. by L. K. Handy; SHCANE 11; Leiden/New York/Köln: Brill, 1997) 279–283.

Nelson, R. D. *The Double Redaction of the Deuteronomistic History* (JSOTSup 18; Sheffield: JSOT, 1981).

——. "*Realpolitik* in Judah (687–609 BCE)," *Scripture in Context II: More Essays on the Comparative Method* (ed. by W. W. Hallo *et al.*; Winona Lake: Eisenbrauns, 1983) 177–189.

——. "The Role of the Priesthood in the Deuteronomistic History," *VTSup* 43 (1991) 132–147.

Netzer, E. "Massive Structures: Processes in Construction and Deterioration," *The Architecture of Ancient Israel: From the Prehistoric to the Persian Periods* (ed. by A. Kempinski and R. Reich; Jerusalem: Israel Exploration Society, 1992) 17–27.

Newing, E. G. "Rhetorical Art of the Deuteronomist: Lampooning Solomon in First Kings," *Old Testament Essays* 7 (1994) 247–260.

Nicholson, E. W. *The Book of the Prophet Jeremiah*, 1 (CBC; Cambridge: Cambridge University, 1973).

Niehr, H., in *DDD* (1995) 811–814.

——. "JHWH in der Rolle des Baalšamem," *Ein Gott allein? JHWH-Verehrung und biblischer Monotheismus im Kontext der israelitischen und altorientalischen Religionsgeschichte: 13. Kolloquium der Schweizerischen Akademieder Geistes- und Sozialwissenschaften 1993* (ed. by W. Dietrich and M. A. Klopfenstein; Freiburg: Universitäts, 1994) 307–326.

——. "Die Reform des Joschija: Methodische, historische und religionsgeschichtliche Aspekte," *Jeremia und die "deuteronomistische Bewegung"* (ed. by W. Gross; BBB 98; Weinheim: Beltz Athenäum, 1995) 33–55.

——. "Religio-Historical Aspects of the 'Early Post-Exilic' Period," *The Crisis of Israelite Religion: Transformation of Religious Tradition in Exilic and Post-Exilic Times* (ed. by B. Becking and M. C. A. Korpel; OTS 42; Leiden/Boston/Köln: Brill, 1999) 228–244.

Norin, S. "The Age of Siloam Inscription and Hezekiah's Tunnel," *VT* 48 (1998) 37–48.

North, C. R. "The Essence of Idolatry," *Von Ugarit nach Qumran: Festschrift O. Eissfeldt* (2nd edn.; ed. by J. Hempel and L. Rost; BZAW 77; Berlin: Töpelmann, 1961) 151–160.

Nötscher, F. Das Buch Jeremias (HSAT 7.2; Bonn: Hanstein, 1934).

Noth, M. *The History of Israel* (2nd edn.; trans. by P. R. Ackroyd; New York: Harper & Row, 1960).

——. *Könige 1* (BKAT 9/1; Neukirchen-Vluyn: Neukirchener, 1968).

——. *Überlieferungsgeschtliche Studien*, 1 (Tübingen: Niemeyer, 1943; 2nd edn., 1957; 3rd edn., 1967), later translated into English as *The Deuteronomistic History* (trans. by J. Doull *et al.*; JSOTSup 15; Sheffield: JSOT, 1981), and *The Chronicler's History* (trans. by H. G. M. Williamson; JSOTSup 50; Sheffield: JSOT, 1987).

O'Brien, M. A. "The Book of Deuteronomy," *CR:BS* 3 (1995) 95–128.

O'Connell, K. G. "The List of Seven Peoples in Canaan: A Fresh Analysis," *The Answers Lie Below: Essays in Honor of Lawrence Edmund Toombs* (ed. by H. O. Thompson; Lanham/New York/London: University Press of America, 1984) 221–241.

Oded B. "II Kings 17: Between History and Polemic," *Jewish History* 2 (1987) 37–50.

——. "Judah and the Exile," *Israelite and Judaean History* (ed. by J. H. Hayes and J. M. Miller; OTL; Philadelphia: Westminster, 1977) 436–488.

Oestreicher, T. *Das deuteronomische Grundsetz* (BFCT 47. 4; Gütersloh: Bertelsmann, 1923).

Ogden, G. S. "The Northern Extent of Josiah's Reforms," *Australian Biblical Research* 26 (1978) 26–34.

del Olmo Lete, G. "La 'capilla' o 'templete' (ḥmn) del Culto ugaritico," *Aula Orientalis* 2 (1984) 277–280.

Olmstead, A. T. *History of Palestine and Syria to the Macedonian Conquest* (New York/London: Scribner's Sons, 1939).

Omanson, R. L. "Translating *Bamoth*," *BT* 46 (1995) 309–320.

Otto, E. "The Pre-Exilic Deuteronomy as a Revision of the Covenant Code," *Kontinuum und Proprium: Studien zur Sozial- und Rechtsgeschichte des Alten Orients und des Alten Testaments* (Orientalia Biblica et Christiana 8; Wiesbaden: Harrowitz, 1996) 112–122.

Overholt, T. W. "Some Reflections on the Date of Jeremiah's Call," *CBQ* 33 (1971) 165–184.

Ouellete, J. "The Shaking of the Thresholds in Amos 9:1," *HUCA* 43 (1977) 23–27.

Pardee, D. G. *Handbook of Ancient Hebrew Letters: A Study Edition* (Sources of Biblical Literature 15; Chico: Scholars, 1982).

——. "The Judicial Plea from Mesad Hashavyahu (Yavneh-Yam): A New Philological Study," *MAARAV* 1 (1978) 33–66.

——. "*Marziḥu, Kispu*, and the Ugaritic Funerary Cult: A Minimalist View," *Ugarit, Religion and Culture (Proceedings of the International Colloquium on Ugarit, Religion and Culture; Edinburgh, July 1994): Essays Presented in Honour of Professor John C. L. Gibson* (ed. by N. Wyatt *et al.*; UBL 12; Münster: Ugarit, 1996) 273–287.

——. "RS 1.005 and the Identification of the *GTRM*," *Ritual and Sacrifice in the Ancient Near East: Proceedings of the International Conference Organized by the Katholieke Universiteit Leuven from the 17th to the 20th of April 1991* (ed. by J. Quaegebeur; OLA 55; Leuven: Peeters, 1993) 303–317.

Parker, K. I. "Repetition as a Structuring Device in 1 Kings 1–11," *JSOT* 42 (1988) 19–27.

——. "Solomon the Philosopher King? The Nexus of Law and Wisdom in 1 Kings 1–11," *JSOT* 53 (1992) 75–91.

Parker, S. B. "Did the Authors of the Books of Kings Make Use of Royal Inscriptions?" *VT* 50 (2000) 357–378.

——. *Stories in Scripture and Inscriptions: Comparative Studies on Narratives in Northwest Semitic Inscriptions and the Hebrew Bible* (New York/Oxford: Oxford University, 1997).

Parpola, S., and Watanabe, K. *Neo-Assyrian Treaties and Loyalty Oaths* (SAA 2; Helsinki: University of Helsinki, 1988).

Paul, M. J. "Hilkiah and the Law (2 Kings 22) in the 17th and 18th Centuries: Some Influences on W. M. L. de Wette," *Das Deuteronomium: Entstehung, Gestalt und Botschaft* (ed. by N. Lohfink; BETL 68; Leuven: Leuven University, 1985) 9–12.

Paul, S. M. *Amos* (Hermeneia; Minneapolis: Augsburg Fortress, 1991).

Peake, A. S. *Jeremiah and Lamentations*, 1 (New-Century Bible 16; New York: Frowde, [1910]).

Peckham, B. "Phoenicia and the Religion of Israel: The Epigraphic Evidence," *Ancient Israelite Religion: Essays in Honor of Frank Moore Cross* (ed. by P. D. Miller *et al.*; Philadelphia: Fortress, 1987) 79–99.

——. "Writing and Editing," *Fortunate the Eyes that See: Essays in Honor of David Noel Freedman in Celebration of his Seventieth Birthday* (ed. by A. B. Beck *et al.*; Grand Rapids/Cambridge, UK: Eerdmans, 1995) 364–383.

Person, R. F. "II Kings 24.18–25, 30 and Jeremiah 52: A Text-Critical Case Study in the Redaction History of the Deuteronomistic History," *ZAW* 105 (1993) 174–205.

——. *Second Zechariah and the Deuteronomic School* (JSOTSup 167; Sheffield: JSOT, 1993).

Petty, R. J. *Asherah: Goddess of Israel* (American University Studies 7.74; New York/Bern/Frankfort am Main/Paris: Peter Lang, 1990).

Pfeiffer, R. H. "Three Assyriological Footnotes to the Old Testament," *JBL* 47 (1928) 184–187.

Phillips, A. *Deuteronomy* (CBC; Cambridge: Cambridge University, 1973).

Pixley, G. V. "Micah: A Revolutionary," *The Bible and the Politics of Exegesis: Essays in Honor of Norman K. Gottwald on His Sixty-Fifth Birthday* (ed. by D. Jobling *et al.*; Cleveland: Pilgrim, 1991) 53–60.

Pope, M. H. "The Cult of the Dead at Ugarit," *Probative Pontificating in Ugaritic and Biblical Literature: Collected Essays* (ed. by M. S. Smith; UBL 10; Münster: Ugarit, 1994) 225–250 (= *Ugarit in Retrospect: Fifty Years of Ugarit and Ugaritic* [ed. by G. D. Young; Winona Lake: Eisenbrauns, 1981] 159–179).

———. "Notes on the Rephaim Texts from Ugarit," *Probative Pontificating in Ugaritic and Biblical Literature* (ed. by M. S. Smith; UBL 10; Münster: Ugarit, 1994) 185–224 (= *Essays on the Ancient Near East in Memory of Jacob Joel Finkelstein* [ed. by M. Ellis; Memoirs of the Connecticut Academy of Arts and Sciences 19; Hamden, CT: Archon, 1977] 163–182).

———. *Song of Songs* (AB 7C; Garden City: Doubleday, 1977).

Porten, B., in *ABD* (1992) 2.445–455.

Postgate, J. N. "The Land of Assur and the Yoke of Assur," *World Archaeology* 23 (1992) 247–263.

Prag, K. "Summary of the Reports on Caves I, II and III and Deposit IV," in Eshel-Prag, *Excavations by K. M. Kenyon in Jerusalem 1961–1967, 4,* 209–216.

Preuss, H. D., in *TDOT* (1978) 3.1–5.

Priest, J. "Huldah's Oracle," *VT* 30 (1980) 366–368.

Provan, I. W. *1–2 Kings* (NIBC; Peabody, MA/Carlisle, Cumb.: Hendrickson/Paternoster, 1995).

———. *Hezekiah and the Books of Kings: A Contribution to the Debate about the Composition of the Deuteronomistic History* (BZAW 72; Berlin/New York: de Gruyter, 1988).

Rabinowitz, I. "'*āz* Followed by Imperfect Verb-Forms in Preterite Contexts: A Redactional Device in Biblical Hebrew," *VT* 34 (1984) 53–62.

von Rad, G. "The Deuteronomic Theology of History in I and II Kings," *The Problem of the Hexateuch and Other Essays* (trans. by E. W. T. Dicken; New York: Harper & Row, 1966) 205–221 (= *Deuteronomium-Studien* [FRLANT 40; Göttingen: Vandenhoeck & Ruprecht, 1947] 52–64).

Rahmani, E. Y. "Ancient Jerusalem's Funerary Customs and Tombs: Part Two," *BA* 44 (1981) 229–235.

Rainey A. F. "The Biblical Shephelah of Judah," *BASOR* 251 (1983) 1–22.

———. "Dust and Ashes," *TA* 1 (1974) 77–83.

———. "Hezekiah's Reform and the Altars at Beer-sheba and Arad," *Scripture and Other Artifacts: Essays on the Bible and Archaeology in Honor of Philip J. King* (ed. by M. D. Coogan *et al.*; Louisville: Westminster John Knox, 1994) 333–354.

———. "Manasseh, King of Judah, in the Whirlpool of the Seventh Century BCE," *"kinatlùtu ša dārâti": Raphael Kutscher Memorial Volume* (ed. by A. F. Rainey; Tel Aviv Occasional Publications 1; Tel Aviv: Tel Aviv University, 1993) 147–164.

———. "No Bama at Beer-Sheva," *BARev* 3/3 (1977) 18–21, 56.

Redford, D. B., in *ABD* (1992) 1.135–137.

———. *Akhenaten: The Heretic King* (Princeton: Princeton University, 1984).

———. "Studies in Relations between Palestine and Egypt during the First Millennium BC: The Taxation System of Solomon," *Studies on the Ancient Palestinian World Presented to Professor F. V. Winnett* (ed. by J. W. Wevers and D. B. Redford; Toronto Semitic Texts and Studies 2; Toronto: University of Toronto, 1972) 141–156.

Reich, R. "The Ancient Burial Ground in the Mamilla Neighborhood, Jerusalem," *Ancient Jerusalem Revealed* (ed. by H. Geva; Jerusalem/Washington DC: Israel Exploration Society/Biblical Archaeological Society, 1994) 119–127.

———. "Building Materials and Architectural Elements in Ancient Israel,", *The*

Architecture of Ancient Israel: From the Prehistoric to the Persian Periods (ed. by A. Kempinski and R. Reich; Jerusalem: Israel Exploration Society, 1992) 1–16.

——. "Palaces and Residences in the Iron Age," *The Architecture of Ancient Israel: From the Prehistoric to the Persian Periods* (ed. by A. Kempinski and R. Reich; Jerusalem: Israel Exploration Society, 1992) 202–222.

—— and Brandi, B. "Gezer under Assyrian Rule," *PEQ* 117 (1985) 41–54.

—— and Shukron, E. "Jerusalem, Mamilla," *Excavations and Surveys in Israel* 14 (1994) 93–94.

Reiner, E. *Astral Magic in Babylonia* (Transactions of the American Philosophical Society 85/4; Philadelphia: American Philosophical Society, 1995).

Reis, P. T. "Vindicating God: Another Look at 1 Kings xiii," *VT* 44 (1994) 376–386.

Reisner, G. A., *et al.*, *Harvard Excavations at Samaria: 1908–1910* (Cambridge: Harvard University, 1924).

Ribichini, S. "Tofet e Necropoli II," *Rivista di Studi Fenici* 34.1 (1996) 77–83.

Risdon, D. L. "A Study of the Cranial and other Human Remains from Palestine Excavated at Tell Duweir (Lachish) by the Wellcome-Marston Archaeological Research Expedition," *Biometrika* 31 (1939) 99–166.

Reuter, E. *Kultzentralisation: Zur Entstehung und Theologie von Dtn 12* (Athenäums Theolische Monografien, Theologie; BBB 87; Frankfort am Main: Hain, 1993).

Roberts, J. J. M. *Nahum, Habakkuk, and Zephaniah: A Commentary* (OTL; Louisville: Westminster John Knox, 1991).

Robinson, J. *The Second Book of Kings* (CBC; Cambridge: Cambridge University, 1976).

Robinson, T. H. *A History of Israel* (Oxford: Clarendon, 1932).

Rochberg-Halton, F. *Babylonian Horoscopes* (Transactions of the American Philosophical Society 88/1; Philadelphia: American Philosophical Society, 1998).

Rofé, A. "Classes of the Prophetical Stories: Didactic Legenda and Parable," *Studies on Prophecy* (VTSup 26; Leiden: Brill, 1974) 143–164.

——. *The Prophetical Stories: The Narratives about the Prophets in the Hebrew Bible* (Jerusalem: Magnes, 1988).

Rogerson, J., and Davies, P. R. "Was the Siloam Tunnel Built by Hezekiah?" *BA* 59 (1996) 138–149.

Römer, T. C. "The Book of Deuteronomy," *The History of Israel's Tradition: The Heritage of Martin Noth* (ed. by S. L. McKenzie and M. P. Graham; JSOTSup 182; Sheffield: Sheffield Academic, 1994) 178–212.

——. "Transformations in Deuteronomistic and Biblical Historiography: On 'Book-Finding' and other Literary Strategies," *ZAW* 109 (1997) 1–11.

—— and de Pury, A. "L'historiographie deutéronomiste (HD): Histoire de la recherche et enjeux du débat," *Israël Construit son Histoire: L'historiographie deutéronomiste à la lumière des recherches récentes* (ed. by A. de Pury, T. Römer, and J.-D. Macchi; Le Monde de la Bible 34; Geneva: Labor et Fides, 1996) 9–120.

Rooaert, A. "A Neo-Assyrian Statue from Til Barsib," *Iraq* 58 (1996) 79–87.

Rose, M. "Bemerkungen zum historischen Fundament des Josia-Bildes in II Reg 22f.," *ZAW* 89 (1977) 50–63.

Rösel, H. N. *Von Josua bis Jojachin: Untersuchen zu den deuteronomistischen Geschichtsbüchern des Alten Testaments* (VTSup 75; Leiden/Boston/Köln: Brill, 1999).

Rowley, H. H. "The Early Prophecies of Jeremiah and their Setting," *Men of God: Studies in Old Testament History and Prophecy* (London: Nelson, 1963) 133–168 (= *BJRL* 45 [1962–1963] 198–234).

——. "Hezekiah's Reform and Rebellion," *Men of God: Studies in Old Testament History and Prophecy* (London: Nelson, 1963) 98–132 (= *BJRL* 44 [1961–1962] 395–461).

Rudolph, R. *Jeremia* (HAT 12; Tübingen: Mohr, 1947).

Rye, O. S. *Pottery Technology: Principles and Reconstruction* (Manuals on Archaeology 4; Washington, DC: Taraxacum, 1981).

Sabottka, L. *Zephanja: Versuch einer Neuuersetzung mit philologischem Kommentar* (Biblica et Orientalia 25; Rome: Biblical Institute, 1972).

Sader, H. "Phoenician Stelae from Tyre," *Berytus* 39 (1991) 101–126.

——. "Phoenician Stele from Tyre (continued)," *Studi epigraphici e linguistici* 9 (1992) 53–79.

Sakellarakis, Y. and Sapouna-Sakellaraki, E. "Drama of Death in a Minoan Temple," *National Geographic* 159/2 (1981) 205–222.

Šanda, A. *Die Bücher der Könige*, 2 vols. (EHAT; Münster: Aschendorff, 1911–1912).

Sass, B. "The Pre-Exilic Hebrew Seals: Iconism vs. Aniconism," *Studies in the Iconography of Northwest Semitic Inscribed Seals* (ed. by B. Sass and C. Uehlinger; Fribourg/Göttingen: University/Vandenhoeck & Ruprecht, 1992) 194–256.

Sasson, J. M. "Letter to the Editor," *BARev* 13/2 (1987) 12, 60.

Savran, G. "1 and 2 Kings," *The Literary Guide to the Bible* (ed. by R. Alter and F. Kermode; Cambridge: Belknap/Harvard University, 1987) 146–164.

Schearing, L. S. "A Wealth of Women: Looking Behind, Within, and Beyond Solomon's Story," *The Age of Solomon: Scholarship at the Turn of the Millennium* (ed. by L. K. Handy; SHCANE 11; Leiden/New York/Köln: Brill, 1997) 428–456.

Schein, S. "Between Mount Moriah and the Holy Sepulchre: The Changing Traditions of the Temple Mount in the Central Middle Ages," *Traditio* 40 (1984) 175–195.

Schmid, K. "Manasse und der Untergang Judas: 'Golaorientierte' Theologie in den Königsbüchern?" *Bib* 78 (1997) 87–99.

Schmidt, B. B. *Israel's Beneficent Dead: Ancestor Cult and Necromancy in Ancient Israelite Religion and Tradition* (2nd edn.; Winona Lake: Eisenbrauns, 1996).

Schniedewind, W. M. "The Chronicler as an Interpreter of Scripture," *The Chronicler as Author: Studies in Text and Texture* (ed. by M. P. Graham and S. L. McKenzie; JSOTSup 263; Sheffield: Sheffield Academic, 1999) 158–180.

——. "History and Interpretation: The Religion of Ahab and Manasseh in the Book of Kings," *CBQ* 55 (1993) 649–661.

——. "The Problem with Kings: Recent Study of the Deuteronomistic History," *RelStRev* 22 (1996) 22–27.

——. "The Source Citations of Manasseh: King Manasseh in History and Homily," *VT* 41 (1991) 450–461.

——. "Tel Dan Stela: New Light on Aramaic and Jehu's Revolt," *BASOR* 302 (1996) 75–90.

Schoors, A. "The Particle *kî*," *OTS* 21 (1981) 240–276.

Schwartz, J. "Jubilees, Bethel and the Temple of Jacob," *HUCA* 56 (1985) 63–85.

Scott, L. "Pottery," *A History of Technology* (ed. by C. Singer *et al.*; New York/London: Oxford University, 1965) 1.376–412.

Scott, R. B. Y. "The Book of Isaiah, Chapters 1–39: Introduction and Exegesis," *IB* (1956) 5.165–381.

Scurlock, J. "Ghosts in the Ancient Near East: Weak or Powerful?" *HUCA* 68 (1997) 77–96.

Seeden, H. "A Tophet in Tyre?" *Berytus* 39 (1991) 39–87.

Seeligmann, I. "Indications of Editorial Alteration," *VT* 11 (1961) 201–221.

Segal, J. B. *The Hebrew Passover from the Earliest Times to AD 70* (London Oriental Series 12; London: Oxford University, 1963).

Shanks, H. "The Biblical Minimalists," *BRev* 13/3 (1997) 32–9, 50–2.

——. "Everything You Ever Knew about Jerusalem Is Wrong (Well, Almost)," *BARev* 25/6 (1999) 20–29.

[——]. "Yadin Answers Beer-Sheva Excavator: Reply to Rainey's 'No Bama at Beer-Sheva'," *BARev* 3/4 (1977) 3–4.

——. "Yigael Yadin Finds a Bama at Beer-Sheva," *BARev* 3/1 (1977) 3–12.

[——]. "Who—or What—Was Molech?" *BARev* 22/4 (1996) 13.

Shaw, C. S. "The Sins of Rehoboam: The Purpose of 3 Kingdoms 12:4A–Z," *JSOT* 73 (1997) 55–64.

Shiloh, Y. "Iron Age Sanctuaries and Cult Elements in Palestine," *Symposia Celebrating the Seventy-Fifth Anniversary of the Founding of the American Schools of Oriental Research* (ed. by F. M. Cross; Cambridge: ASOR, 1979) 147–157.

——. "Judah and Jerusalem in the Eighth-Sixth Centuries BCE," *Recent Excavations in Israel: Studies in Iron Age Archaeology* (ed. by S. Gitin and W. G. Dever; AASOR 49; Winona Lake: Eisenbrauns, 1989) 97–105.

——. "The Material Culture of Judah and Jerusalem in Iron Age II: Origins and Influences," *The Land of Israel: Cross-Roads of Civilizations* (ed. by E. Lipiński; Orientalia Loveniensia Analecta 19; Leuven: Peeters, 1985) 113–146.

——. "The Population of Iron Age Palestine in the Light of a Sample Analysis of Urban Plans, Areas, and Population Density," *BASOR* 239 (1980) 25–35.

Shimoff, S. R. "The Hellenization of Solomon in Rabbinic Texts," *The Age of Solomon: Scholarship at the Turn of the Millennium* (ed. by L. K. Handy; SHCANE 11; Leiden/New York/Köln: Brill, 1997) 457–469.

Simon, U. "I Kings 13: A Prophetic Sign—Denial and Persistence," *HUCA* 47 (1976) 81–117.

Sinclair, L. A. "Bethel Pottery of the Sixth Century B.C.," *The Excavation of Bethel (1934–1960)* (ed. by J. L. Kelso; AASOR 39; Cambridge, MA; ASOR, 1968) 70–76.

Singer-Avitz, L. "Beersheba—A Gateway Community in Southern Arabian Long-Distance Trade in the Eighth Century BCE," *TA* 26 (1999) 3–74.

Sivan, S D. *Grammatical Analysis and Glossary of the Northwest Semitic Vocables in Akkadian Texts of the 15th–13th Century BC* (AOAT 214; Kevelaer/Neukirchen-Vluyn: Butzon & Bercker/Neukirchener, 1984).

Skinner, J. *I–II Kings* (New-Century Bible 7; New York: Frowde, [1893]).

——. *The Book of Ezekiel* (Expositor's Bible; New York/Cincinnati: Eaton & Mains/Jennings & Graham, n.d.).

——. *Prophecy and Religion: Studies in the Life of Jeremiah* (Cambridge: Cambridge University, 1926).

Smelik, K. A. D. "King Mesha's Inscription: Between History and Fiction," in *idem, Converting the Past: Studies in Ancient Israelite and Moabite Historiography* (OTS 28; Leiden/New York/Köln: Brill, 1992) 59–92.

——. "The Literary Structure of King Mesha's Inscription," *JSOT* 46 (1990) 21–30.

——. "Moloch, Molekh or Molk-Sacrifice?" *SJOT* 9/1 (1995) 133–142.

——. "The Portrayal of King Manasseh: A Literary Analysis of II Kings xxi and II Chronicles xiii," *Converting the Past: Studies in Ancient Israelite and Moabite Historiography* (OTS 28; Leiden: Brill, 1992) 129–189.

Smend, R. "Das Gesetz und die Völker: Ein Beitrag zur deuteronomistischen Redaktionsgeschichte," *Probleme biblischer Theologie: Gerhard von Rad zum 70. Geburtstag* (ed. by H. W. Wolff; Munich: Kaiser, 1971) 494–509.

——. *Die Entstehung des Alten Testaments* (Theologische Wissenschaft 1; Stuttgart: Kohlhammer, 1978).

Smith, M. S. *The Early History of God: Yahweh and the other Deities in Ancient Israel* (San Francisco: Harper & Row, 1990).

—— and Bloch-Smith, E. "Death and Afterlife at Ugarit and Ancient Israel," *JAOS* 108 (1988) 277–284.

Smith, M. "A Note on Burning Babies," *JAOS* 95 (1975) 477–479.

——. *Palestinian Parties and Politics that Shaped the Old Testament* (ACLS Lectures on the History of Religions 9; New York/London: Columbia University, 1971).

——. "Pseudepigraphy in the Israelite Literary Tradition," *Studies in the Cult of Yahweh* (ed. by S. J. D. Cohen; Religions in the Greco-Roman World 130/1; Leiden/New York/Köln, 1996) 1.55–72 (= *Entretiens sur l'Antiquité classique, XVIII: Pseudepigrapha I*,18 [1972] 191–215).

Smyth, F. "Quand Josias fait son oeuvre ou le Roi bien enterré: Une Lecture synchronique de 2 R 22,1–23,28," *Israël Construit son Histoire: L'historiographie deutéronomiste à la lumière des recherches récentes* (ed. by A. de Pury, T. Römer, and J.-D. Macchi; Le Monde de la Bible 34; Geneva: Labor et Fides, 1996) 325–339.

Snaith, N. H. "The Cult of Molech," *VT* 16 (1966) 123–124.

——. "The First and Second Books of Kings: Introduction and Exegesis," *IB* (1954) 3.3–338.

——. *Leviticus and Numbers* (London: Nelson, 1967).

——. "The Meaning of *śĕ'îrîm*," *VT* 25 (1975) 115–118.

Soggin, J. A. *A History of Ancient Israel* (trans. by J. Bowden; Philadelphia: Westminster, 1984).

——. "Jacob in Shechem and in Bethel (Genesis 35:1–7)," *"Sha'arei Talmon": Studies in the Bible, Qumran, and the Ancient Near East Presented to Shemaryahu Talmon* (ed. by M. Fishbane and E. Tov; Winona Lake: Eisenbrauns, 1992) 195–197.

——. "'Your Conduct in the Valley': A Note on Jeremiah 2,23a," *Old Testament and Oriental Studies* (Biblica at Orientalia 29; Rome: Biblical Institute, 1975) 78–83 (= *RSO* 36 [1961] 207–211).

Spalinger, A. J. "A Canaanite Ritual Found in Egyptian Military Reliefs," *Journal of the Society for the Study of Egyptian Antiquities* 8 (1978) 47–60.

——. "The Concept of the Monarchy during the Saite Epoch—An Essay of Synthesis," *Or* 47 (1978) 12–36.

——. "Psammetichus, King of Egypt: I," *JARCE* 13 (1976) 133–147.

——. "Psammetichus, King of Egypt: II," *JARCE* 15 (1978) 49–57.

Spencer, J. R., in *ABD* (1992) 4.310–311.

——. *Levitical Cities: A Study of the Role and Function of the Levites in the History of Ancient Israel* (unpublished dissertation, University of Chicago, 1980).

Speyer, W. "Bücherfunde in der Glaubenswerbung der Antike. Mit einem Ausblick auf Mittelalter und Neuzeit," *Hypomnemata* 24 (1970) 125–128.

Spieckermann, H. *Juda unter Assur in der Sargonidenzeit* (FRLANT 129; Göttingen: Vandenhoeck & Ruprecht, 1982).

Spronk, K. *Beatific Afterlife in Ancient Israel and in the Ancient Near East* (AOAT 219; Kevelaer/Neukirchen-Vluyn: Butzon & Bercker/Neukirchener, 1986).

Stade, B. and Schwally, F. *The Books of Kings* (trans. by R. E. Brünnow and P. Haupt; SBOT 9; Baltimore/Leipzig: Johns Hopkins University, 1904).

Stager, L. E. "The Archaeology of the Family in Ancient Israel," *BASOR* 260 (1985) 1–36.

——. "The Archaeology of the East Slope of Jerusalem and the Terraces of the Kidron," *JNES* 41 (1982) 111–121.

——. "Ashkelon and the Archaeology of Destruction; Kislev 604 BCE," *I-E* 25 (1996) 61*–74*.

——. "The Rite of Child Sacrifice at Carthage," *New Light on Ancient Carthage* (ed. by J. G. Pedley; Ann Arbor: University of Michigan, 1980) 1–11.

——. "A View from the Tophet," *Phönizier im Westen* (ed. by H. G. Niemeyer; Madrider Beiträge 8; Mainz: von Zabern, 1982) 155–166.

—— and Wolff, S. R. "Child Sacrifice at Carthage—Religious Rite or Population Control?" *BARev* 10/1 (1984) 30–51.

——. "Production and Commerce in Temple Courtyards: An Olive Press in the Sacred Precinct at Tel Dan," *BASOR* 243 (1981) 95–102.

Steinberg, N. "The Deuteronomic Law Code and the Politics of State Centralization," *The Bible and the Politics of Exegesis: Essays in Honor of Norman K. Gottwald on His Sixty-Fifth Birthday* (ed. by D. Jobling *et al.*; Cleveland: Pilgrim, 1991) 161–170.

Steine, M. "Two Popular Cult Sites of Ancient Palestine: Cave 1 in Jerusalem and E 207 in Samaria," *SJOT* 11/1 (1997) 16–28.

Stern, E. "Limestone Incense Altars," in Y. Aharoni *et al.*, *Beer-Sheba I: Excavations at Beer-Sheba, 1969–1971 Seasons* (Institute of Archaeology Publications 2; Tel Aviv: Tel Aviv University Institute of Archaeology, 1973) 52–53.

——. *The Material Culture of the Land of the Bible in the Persian Period, 538–332 BC* (Jerusalem/Warminster: Israel Exploration Society/Aris & Phillips, 1982).

——. "Religion in Palestine in the Assyrian and Persian Periods," *The Crisis of Israelite Religion: Transformation of Religious Tradition in Exilic and Post-Exilic Times* (ed. by B. Becking and M. C. A. Korpel; OTS 42; Leiden/Boston/Köln: Brill, 1999) 245–255.

Stoebe, H. J. *Das erste Buch Samuelis* (KAT 8:1; Gütersloh: Mohn, 1973).

Stohlmann, S. "The Judaean Exile after 701 BCE," *Scripture in Context II: More Essays on the Comparative Method* (ed. by W. W. Hallo *et al.*; Winona Lake: Eisenbrauns, 1983) 147–175.

Stolz, F. "Der Streit um die Wirklichkeit in der Sudreichsprophetie des 8. Jahrhunderts," *Wort und Dienst* 12 (1973) 9–30.

Sweeney, M. A. "The Critique of Solomon in the Josianic Edition of the Deuteronomistic History," *JBL* 114 (1995) 607–622.

——. "A Form Critical Reassessment of the Book of Zephaniah," *CBQ* 53 (1991) 388–408.

——. "Jesse's New Shoot in Isaiah 11: A Josianic Reading of the Prophet Isaiah," *A Gift of God in Due Season: Essays on Scripture and Community in Honor of James A. Sanders* (ed. by R. D. Weis and D. M. Carr; JSOTSup 225; Sheffield: Sheffield Academic, 1996) 103–118.

——. "Jeremiah 30–31 and King Josiah's Program of National Restoration and Religious Reform," *ZAW* 108 (1996) 569–583.

——. "Sargon's Threat against Jerusalem and Isaiah 10, 27–32," *Bib* 75 (1994) 457–470.

Suzuki, Y. "Deuteronomic Reformation in View of the Centralization of the Administration of Justice," *Annual of the Japanese Biblical Institute* 13 (1987) 22–58.

Tadmor, H., and Cogan, M. "Ahaz and Tiglath-pileser in the Book of Kings: Historiographical Considerations," *Bib* 60 (1979) 491–508.

Talstra, E. "De Hervorming van Josia, of de Kunst van den Beeldenstormen," *Gereformeerd Theologisch Tijdschrift* 88 (1988) 143–161.

Talmon, S. "The New Hebrew Letter from the Seventh Century BCE in Historical Perspective," *King, Cult and Calendar in Ancient Israel: Collected Studies* (Jerusalem: Magnes, 1986) 79–88 (= *BASOR* 177 [1965] 29–38).

——. "Polemics and Apology in Biblical Historiography—2 Kings 17:24–41," *Literary Studies in the Hebrew Bible: Form and Content—Collected Studies* (Leiden/Jerusalem: Brill/Magnes, 1993) 134–159 (= a somewhat different version in *The Creation of Sacred Literature: Composition and Redaction in the Biblical Text* [ed. by R. E. Friedman; University of California Publications, Near Eastern Studies 22; Berkeley/Los Angeles/London: University of California, 1981] 57–68).

——. "The Presentation of Synchroneity and Simultaneity in Biblical Narrative," *Literary Studies in the Hebrew Bible: Form and Content—Collected Studies* (Leiden/Jerusalem: Brill/Magnes, 1993) 112–133 (= *Studies in Hebrew Narrative Art throughout the Ages* [ed. by J. Heinemann and S. Werses; ScrHier 27; Jerusalem: Magnes, 1978] 9–26).

Talshir, Z. "The Three Deaths of Josiah and the Strata of Biblical Historiography (2 Kings xxiii 29–30; 2 Chronicles xxxv 20–5; 1 Esdras I 23–31)." *VT* 46 (1996) 213–236.

Tarler, D., and Cahill, J. M., in *ABD* (1992) 2.64–65.

Tatum, L. "King Manasseh and the Royal Fortress at Horvat Usa," *BA* 54 (1991) 136–145.

Taylor, J. G. *Yahweh and the Sun: Biblical and Archaeological Evidence for Sun Worship in Ancient Israel* (JSOTSup 111; Sheffield: JSOT, 1993).

——. "A Response to Steve A. Wiggins, 'Yahweh: The God of the Sun?'" *JSOT* 71 (1996) 107–119.

——. "Was Yahweh Worshipped as the Sun?" *BARev* 20/3 (1994) 52–61, 90–91.

Thompson, J. A. *The Book of Jeremiah* (NICOT; Grand Rapids: Eerdmans, 1980).

Throntveit, M. A. "Hezekiah in the Books of Chronicles," *Society of Biblical Literature 1988 Seminar Papers* (SBLSP 27; ed. by D. L. Lull; Atlanta: Scholars, 1988) 302–311.

——. "The Idealization of Solomon as the Glorification of God in the Chronicler's Royal Speeches and Royal Prayers," *The Age of Solomon: Scholarship at the Turn of the Millennium* (ed. by L. K. Handy; SHCANE 11; Leiden/New York/Köln: Brill, 1997) 411–427.

——. *When Kings Speak: Royal Speech and Royal Prayer in Chronicles* (SBLD 93; Atlanta: Scholars, 1987).

Tigay, J. H. *Deuteronomy* (JPSTC 5; Philadelphia/Jerusalem: Jewish Publication Society, 1996).

Todd, E. W. "The Reforms of Hezekiah and Josiah," *SJT* 9 (1965) 288–293.

Toloni, G. "Una Strage di Sacerdoti? Dalla Storiografia alla Storia in 2 Re 23,4b–5," *Estudios Biblicos* 56 (1998) 41–60.

Tomes, R. "The Reason for the Syro-Ephraimite War," *JSOT* 59 (1993) 55–71.

van der Toorn, K. "Echoes of Judaean Necromancy in Isaiah 28,7–22," *ZAW* 100 (1988) 199–217.

——. *Family Religion in Babylonia, Syria and Israel: Continuity and Change in the Forms of Religious Life* (Studies in the History and Culture of the Ancient Near East 7; Leiden/New York/Köln: Brill, 1996).

——. "The Iconic Book: Analogies between the Babylonian Cult of Images and the Veneration of the Torah," *The Image and the Book: Iconic Cults, Aniconism, and the Rise of Book Religion in Israel and the Ancient Near East* (ed. by K. van der Toorn; Contributions to Biblical Exegesis & Theology 21; Leuven: Peeters, 1997) 229–248.

Trebolle-Barerra, J. "Redaction, Recension, and Midrash in the Books of Kings," *BIOSCS* 15 (1982) 12–35.

Turner, V. "Dead and the Dead in the Pilgrimage Process," *Religious Encounters with Death* (ed. by F. Reynolds and E. Waugh; University Park: Pennsylvania State University, 1977) 24–39.

Tushingham, A. D. "The Western Hill under the Monarchy," *ZDPV* 95 (1979) 39–55.

Twain, Mark (Clemens, S. L.) *The Innocents Abroad* (in *The Complete Travel Books of Mark Twain* [ed. by C. Neider; Garden City: Doubleday, 1966 (originally published in 1869)]).

Uehlinger, C. "Gab es eine joschijanische Kultreform? Plädoyer für ein begründetes Minimum," *Jeremia und die "deuteronomistische Bewegung"* (ed. by W. Gross; BBB 98; Weinheim: Beltz Athenäum, 1995) 57–89.

Ussishkin, D. *The Conquest of Lachish by Sennacherib* (Tel Aviv University Publications of the Institute of Archaeology 6; Tel Aviv: Tel Aviv University, 1982).

——. "The Date of the Judaean Shrine at Arad," *IEJ* 38 (1988) 142–157.

——. "The Necropolis from the Time of the Kingdom of Judah at Silwan, Jerusalem," *BA* 33 (1970) 34–46.

——. "A Recently Discovered Tomb in Siloam," *Jerusalem Revealed: Archaeology in the Holy City 1968–1974* (ed. by Y. Yadin, Jerusalem: Israel Exploration Society, 1975) 62–65.

——. *The Village of Silwan: The Necropolis from the Period of the Judean Kingdom* (trans. by I. Pommerantz; Jerusalem: Israel Exploration Society/Yad Izhak Ben-Zvi, 1993).

Van Leewen, C. "Die Partikel *'im*," *OTS* 18 (1973) 15–48.

Van Seters, J. "The Chronicler's Account of Solomon's Temple-Building: A Continuity

Theme," *The Chronicler as Historian* (ed. by M. P. Graham *et al.*; JSOTSup 238; Sheffield: Sheffield Academic, 1997) 283–300.

——. "The Deuteronomistic History: Can It Avoid Death by Redaction?" *The Future of the "Deuteronomistic History"* (ed. by T. Römer; BETL 147; Leuven: University, 2000) 213–222.

——. "Divine Encounter at Bethel (Gen 28,10–22) in Recent Literay-Critical Study of Genesis," *ZAW* 110 (1998) 503–513.

——. *In Search of History* (New Haven: Yale, 1983).

——. "The Law on Child Sacrifice in Exod. 22,30–31," *ETL* 74 (1998) 364–372.

——. "On Reading the Story of the Man of God from Judah in 1 Kings 13," *The Labour of Reading: Desire, Alienation, and Biblical Interpretation* (ed. by F. C. Black *et al.*; SBL Semeia Studies 36; Atlanta: Scholars, 1999) 225–234.

——. "Solomon's Temple: Fact and Ideology in Biblical and Near Eastern Historiography," *CBQ* 59 (1997) 45–57.

Van Winkle, D. W. "1 Kings xii 25–xiii 34: Jeroboam's Cultic Innovations and the Man of God from Judah," *VT* 46 (1996) 101–114.

——. "I Kings xiii: True and False Prophecy," *VT* 39 (1989) 31–43.

Vaughan, P. H. *The Meaning of "bāmâ" in the Old Testament: A Study of Etymological, Textual, and Archaeological Evidence* (SOTSM 3; Cambridge: Cambridge University, 1974).

Vaughn, A. G. *Theology, History, and Archaeology in the Chronicler's Account of Hezekiah* (Archaeology and Biblical Studies 4; Atlanta: Scholars, 1999).

de Vaux, R. *Ancient Israel: Its Life and Institutions* (trans. by J. McHugh, New York: McGraw-Hill, 1961).

Vermes, G. "Leviticus 18:21 in Ancient Jewish Bible Exegesis," *Studies in Aggadah, Targum and Jewish Liturgy in Memory of Joseph Heinemann* (ed. by J. J. Petuchowski and E. Fleischer; Jerusalem: Magnes/Hebrew Union College, 1981) 108–124.

Viviano, P. A. "2 Kings 17: A Rhetorical and Form-Critical Analysis," *CBQ* 49 (1987) 548–559.

——. "Glory Lost: The Reign of Solomon in the Deuteronomistic History," *The Age of Solomon: Scholarship at the Turn of the Millennium* (ed. by L. K. Handy; SHCANE 11; Leiden/New York/Köln: Brill, 1997) 336–347.

Vriezen, K. J. H. "Cakes and Figurines: Related Women's Cultic Offerings in Ancient Israel," *On Reading Prophetic Texts: Gender-Specific and Related Studies in Memory of Fokkelien van Dijk-Hemmes* (ed. by B. Becking and M. Dijkstra; Leiden/New York/Köln: Brill, 1996) 251–263.

van der Waerden, B. L. "History of the Zodiac," *AfO* 16 (1952) 216–230.

Walker, C., and Dick, M. B. "The Induction of the Cult Image in Ancient Mesopotamia: The Mesopotamian *mis pî* Ritual," *Born in Heaven, Make on Earth: The Making of the Cult Image in the Ancient Near East* (ed. by M. B. Dick; Winona Lake: Eisenbrauns, 1999) 55–121.

Waltke, B. K., and O'Connor, M. *An Introduction to Biblical Hebrew Syntax* (Winona Lake: Eisenbrauns, 1990).

Walsh, J. T. "The Characterization of Solomon in First Kings 1–5," *CBQ* 57 (1995) 471–493.

——. "The Contexts of 1 Kings xiii," *VT* 39 (1989) 355–370.

——. "Symmetry and the Sin of Solomon," *Shofar* 12 (1993) 11–27.

Washburn, D. L. "Perspective and Purpose: Understanding the Josiah Story," *Trinity Journal* 12 (1991) 59–78.

Watson, D. F., in *ABD* (1992) 2.926–928.

——, in *ABD* (1992) 3.202–203.

Watson, W. G. E. *Classical Hebrew Poetry: A Guide to Its Techniques* (JSOTSup 26; Sheffield: JSOT, 1984).

Weidner, E. "Weise Pferde im Alten Orient," *BiOr* 9 (1952) 157–159.

Weinberg, S. S. "A Moabite Shrine Group," *Muse* 12 (1978) 30–48.

Weinfeld, M., in *ABD* (1992) 2.168–183.

——. "Burning Babies in Ancient Israel," *UF* 10 (1978) 411–413.

——. "Cult Centralisation in the Light of a Neo-Babylonian Analogy," *JNES* 23 (1964) 202–212.

——. *Deuteronomy 1–11* (AB 5; New York: Doubleday, 1991).

——. *Deuteronomy and the Deuteronomic School* (Oxford: Clarendon, 1972).

——. "The Emergence of the Deuteronomic Movement: The Historical Antecedents," *Das Deuteronomium: Entstehung, Gestalt und Botschaft* (ed. by N. Lohfink; BETL 68; Leuven: University, 1985) 76–98.

——. "The Worship of Molech and of the Queen of Heaven and its Background," *UF* 4 (1972) 133–154.

Weippert, H. "Die 'deuteronomistischen' Beurteilungen der Könige von Israel und Juda und das Problem der Redaktion der Königsbucher," *Bib* 53 (1972) 301–339.

——. "Das deuteronomistische Geschichtswerk: Sein Zeil und Ende in der neueren Forschung," *TR* 50 (1988) 213–249.

Westermann, C. *Die Geschichtsbücher des Alten Testaments: Gab es ein deuteronomistisches Geschichtswerk?* (TBü 87; Gütershoh: Kaiser, 1994).

Wevers, J. W. "Principles of Interpretation Guiding the Fourth Translation of the Book of the Kingdoms (3 Kgs. 22:1–4 Kgs. 25:30)," *CBQ* 14 (1952) 40–56.

Whitley, C. F. "The Date of Jeremiah's Call," *VT* 14 (1964) 467–483.

Whitney, J. T. "'Bamoth' in the Old Testament," *TynBul* 30 (1979) 125–147.

Wiggins, S. A. "Yahweh: The God of the Sun?," *JSOT* 71 (1996) 89–106.

Wilcoxen, J. A. "The Political Background of Jeremiah's Temple Sermon," *Scripture in History and Theology: Essays in Honor of J. C. Rylaarsdam* (ed. by A. L. Merrill and T. W. Overholt; Pittsburgh Theological Monograph 17; Pittsburgh: Pickwick, 1977) 151–166.

Williams, D. S. "Once Again: The Structure of the Narrative of Solomon's Reign," *JSOT* 86 (1999) 49–66.

Williamson, H. G. M., in *VT* 37 (1987) 112–114.

——. "The Composition of Ezra i–iv," *JTS* 34 (1983) 1–30.

——. "The Death of Josiah and the Continuing Development of the Deuteronomistic History," *VT* 32 (1982) 242–247.

——. *1–2 Chronicles* (NCBC; Grand Rapids/London: Eerdmans/Marshall, Morgan & Scott, 1982).

——. "Isaiah xi 11–16 and the Redaction of Isaiah i–xii," *VTSup* 61 (1995) 343–357.

——. *Israel in the Books of Chronicles* (Cambridge: Cambridge University, 1977).

——. "The Prophet and the Plumb-Line: A Redaction-Critical Study of Amos vii," *OTS* 26 (1990) 101–121.

——. "Reliving the Death of Josiah: A Reply to C. T. Begg," *VT* 37 (1987) 9–15.

Willis, J. T. "Historical Issues in Isaiah 22,15–25," *Bib* 74 (1993) 60–70.

——. "Textual and Linguistic Issues in Isaiah 22,15–25," *ZAW* 105 (1993) 377–399.

Wilson, R. R. "Poetry and Prose in the Book of Jeremiah," *Kī Baruch Hu: Ancient Near Eastern, Biblical, and Judaic Studies in Honor of Baruch A. Levine* (ed. by R. Chazan et al.; Winona Lake, IN: Eisenbrauns, 1999) 412–427.

——. "Who Was the Deuteronomist? (Who Was Not the Deuteronomist?): Reflections on Pan-Deuteronomism" *Those Elusive Deuteronomists: The Phenomenon of Pan-Deuteronomism* (ed. by L. S. Schearing and S. L. McKenzie; JSOTSup 268; Sheffield: Sheffield Academic, 1999) 67–82.

Wiseman, D. J. *1–2 Kings: Introduction and Commentary* (TOTC 9; Downers Grove/Leicester: Inter-Varsity, 1993).

Wolff, H. W. *Hosea* (trans. by G. Stansell; ed. by P. D. Hanson; Hermeneia; Philadelphia: Fortress, 1974).

——. *Joel and Amos* (trans. by W. Janzen *et al.*; ed. by S. D. McBride; Hermeneia; Philadelphia: Fortress, 1977).

——. *Micah* (trans. By G. Stansell; CC; Minneapolis: Augsburg, 1990).

Wolff, S. R. "Archaeology in Israel," *AJA* 98 (1994) 481–520.

Wood, B. G., in *ABD* (1992) 4.38–39.

Wright, D. P., in *ABD* (1992) 6.729–741.

——. *The Disposal of Impurity: Elimination Rites in the Bible and in Hittite and Mesopotamian Literatures* (SBLDS 101; Atlanta: Scholars, 1987).

——. "Purification from Corpse-Contamination in Numbers xxxi 19–24," *VT* 35 (1985) 213–223.

——. "The Spectrum of Priestly Impurity," *Priesthood and Cult in Ancient Israel* (ed. by G. A. Anderson and S. M. Olyan; JSOTSup 125; Sheffield: JSOT, 1991) 150–181.

Wright, J. W. "The Fight for Peace: Narrative and History in the Battle Accounts in Chronicles," *The Chronicler as Historian* (ed. by M. P. Graham *et al.*; JSOTSup 238; Sheffield: Sheffield Academic, 1997) 150–177.

Würthwein, E. "Die Erzählung vom Gottesmann aus Juda in Bethel: Zur Komposition von 1 Kön 13," *Wort und Geschichte: Festschrift für Karl Elliger zum 70. Geburtstag* (ed. by H. Gese and H.-P. Ruger; AOAT 18; Neukirchen-Vluyn: Neukirchener, 1973) 181–189.

——. "Die josianische Reform und das Deuteronomium," *ZTK* 73 (1976) 395–423.

Wyatt, N. "The Old Testament Historiography of the Exilic Period," *Studia Theologica* 33 (1979) 45–67.

Yadin, Y. "Beer-Sheba: The High Place Destroyed by King Josiah," *BASOR* 222 (1976) 5–17.

——. "The 'House of Baal' of Ahab and Jezebel in Samaria and that of Athalia in Judah," *Archaeology in the Levant: Essays for Kathleen Kenyon* (ed. by P. R. Moorey and P. J. Parr; Warminster: Aris & Phillips, 1978) 127–135.

Yeivin, S. "The Divided Kingdom: Rehoboam-Ahaz/Jeroboam-Pekah," *The Age of the Monarchies: Political History* (ed. by A. Malamat; World History of the Jewish People 4:1; Jerusalem: Massada, 1979) 126–179.

——. "The Sepulchres of the Kings of the House of David," *JNES* 7 (1948) 30–45.

Yezerski, I. "Burial-Cave Distribution and the Borders of the Kingdom of Judah toward the End of the Iron Age," *TA* 26 (1999) 253–270.

Younger, Jr., K. L. "Sargon's Campaign against Jerusalem—A Further Note," *Bib* 77 (1996) 108–110.

Zatelli, I. "Astrology and the Worship of the Stars in the Bible," *ZAW* 103 (1991) 86–100.

Zevit, Z. "Deuteronomistic Historiography in 1 Kings 12–2 Kings 17 and the Reinvestiture of the Israelian Cult," *JSOT* 32 (1985) 57–73.

Zimboni, O. "The Iron Age Pottery of Tel Eton and its Relation to the Lachish, Tell Beit Mirsim and Arad Assemblages," *TA* 12 (1985) 63–90.

Zimmerli, W. *Ezekiel 1* (trans. by R. E. Clements; ed. by F. M. Cross *et al.*; Hermeneia; Philadelphia: Fortress, 1979).

Zorn, J. R. "An Inner and Outer Gate Complex at Tell en-Nasbeh," *BASOR* 307 (1997) 53–66.

Zwickel, W. "I Sam 31, 12f. und der Quadratbau auf dem Flughafengelände bei Amman," *ZAW* 105 (1993) 165–174.

——. "Die Wirtschaftsreform des Hiskia und die Sozialkritik der Propheten des 8. Jahrhunderts," *EvT* 59 (1999) 356–377.

INDEX OF TERMS

BIBLICAL INDEX

OLD TESTAMENT

New Testament

Matt.

2:12   54

Apocrypha/Pseudepigrapha

1 Maccabees

1:20–28   174n.6
1:24b   174n.6
4:36–52   174n.6

Tobit

3:11   163n.90
12:19   54

Jubilees

31–32   45n.59